Interfacing Thought

Interfacing Thought

Cognitive Aspects of Human-Computer Interaction

edited by John M. Carroll

A Bradford Book
The MIT Press
Cambridge, Massachusetts
London, England

Second printing, 1988

This book was set in Palatino by Asco Trade Typesetting Ltd., Hong Kong, and printed and bound by Halliday Lithograph in the United States of America.

Library of Congress Cataloging-in-Publication Data

Interfacing thought.
"A Bradford book."
Includes bibliographies and index.
1. Interactive computer systems. 2. Human engineering. I. Carroll, John M., 1950–.
QA76.9.I58I59 1987 004'.01'9 86-20974
ISBN 0-262-03125-6

Contents

Contributors

John R. Anderson
Department of Psychology
Carnegie-Mellon University
Pittsburgh, PA

Philip J. Barnard
MRC Applied Psychology Unit
Cambridge, UK

John B. Black
Teachers College
Columbia University
New York, NY

John M. Carroll
IBM Research
Yorktown Heights, NY

Mitchell DeRidder
Department of Psychology
University of Texas
Austin, TX

Donald J. Foss
Department of Psychology
University of Texas
Austin, TX

Dana S. Kay
Computer Science Department
Yale University
New Haven, CT

Thomas K. Landauer
Bell Communication Research
Morristown, NJ

Clayton H. Lewis
Computer Science Department
University of Colorado
Boulder, CO

Jean McKendree
Department of Psychology
Carnegie-Mellon University
Pittsburgh, PA

Thomas W. Malone
Sloan School of Management
Massachusetts Institute of Technology
Cambridge, MA

Richard E. Mayer
Department of Psychology
University of California
Santa Barbara, CA

Donald A. Norman
Institute for Cognitive Studies
University of California
San Diego, CA

Judith Reitman Olson
Graduate School of Business Administration
University of Michigan
Ann Arbor, MI

Peter G. Polson
CLIPR
University of Colorado
Boulder, CO

Phyllis Reisner
IBM Almaden Research Center
San Jose, CA

Mary Beth Rosson
IBM Research
Yorktown Heights, NY

Elliot M. Soloway
Computer Science Department
Yale University
New Haven, CT

John Whiteside
Digital Equipment Corporation
Nashua, NH

Dennis Wixon
Digital Equipment Corporation
Nashua, NH

Preface

John M. Carroll

One of the most active new research areas in cognitive science is that of human-computer interaction. This work concerns itself with the design of "user interfaces," that is, computers as experienced and manipulated by human users. Its principal goal is to provide an understanding of how human motivation, action, and experience place constraints on the usability of computer equipment. The area has grown prodigiously in the last several years.

Computers Are Culturally Pervasive One obvious reason for this growth is that computers are playing increasingly prominent and direct roles in the conduct of human affairs. The emergence of the microcomputer has brought computer presence into our living rooms, kitchens, and game rooms—to say nothing of our workplaces. Computer systems are no longer remote, enormous, and unknown gargantuans to which decks of cards are submitted through intermediaries. They are diverse; they are personal; they talk to us on the phone; they are in our cars. They are an important part of life to a rapidly increasing number of people. All this has made computer problems into important problems.

In the 1930s social scientists concerned themselves with the effects of the automobile on people's lives. In the 1950s and '60s, attention was directed at the effects of television. Computers promise to have a cultural impact at least as great as these.

Computers Can Be Problematic for People The human implications of human-computer interaction include many novel learning and skill-adjustment problems. Indeed, the pervasiveness of computing devices in daily life can be as much a frightening and difficult obstacle as it can be an exciting and empowering development. People often experience serious and frustrating difficulties when they attempt to use computers. Tasks they formerly could accomplish now must be relearned; competent secretaries, accountants, and lawyers are—at least temporarily—returned to varying levels of incompetence until they can master "the system." People often see their difficulties with computers as arbitrarily imposed hurdles that exclude them from participation in activities.

These learning and skill-performance problems are now clearly acknowledged in the industry. Where once new computer systems were developed to store and retrieve more information faster, they are now hawked as "easy to use." Where once the spotlight was on the hardware internals of computers, it has largely shifted to the user interface, to the computer as it is experienced and manipulated by the person using it. This reflects an awareness of the problems people experience, but it is all too often wishful thinking; labeling a computer "easy to use" does not make it easy to use. Clearly these are questions in cognitive science: What are the bases of learning and skill problems? How can these problems be eased?

Integrating Basic Cognitive Theory and Application The chapters in this volume provide an interim report on the project of establishing an applied science of human-computer interaction grounded in the framework of cognitive science. They also explore the intriguing, complementary prospect that applied research in human-computer interaction can contribute in a variety of ways to the development of cognitive science itself. For example, Tom Landauer, in his chapter, observes that basic cognitive psychology has been chronically impeded by the lack of an applied discipline through which to determine the boundary conditions and completeness of its concepts and descriptions. One example he discusses is applying laboratory results on decision time and motor selection to the practical task of designing computer menu structures for ease of use.

Don Norman makes the point that an applied science of human-computer interaction turns out to need all of basic cognitive science and more besides. When we come to basic cognitive theory for principles that can be applied to problems in human-computer interaction, we often find far less than we need: What makes things easier to learn? Which designs accord with natural inclinations of human skill and which do not? It seems like basic cognitive science ought to inform us on these matters, but quite often the basic science that exists is paradigm bound to simple, artificial tasks and cannot be usefully scaled up. Landauer's review of research on names for computer commands also makes this point.

In basic cognitive science it is possible to study an area like word recognition as if human language behavior and experience really occurred word by word, but for an applied endeavor such an unrealistic idealization is unacceptable; it is too obvious that the real situation is more complicated. To make an adequate analysis, we need to take multiple disciplinary perspectives—psychology, linguistics, anthropology, sociology, and computer science—*simultaneously*. As Norman suggests, human-computer interaction, as applied cognitive science, begins to appear as a superset of basic cognitive science!

Developing Cognitive Theory Even within the conventionally recognized scope of cognitive science, theoretical work on human-computer interaction is extending theory. Don Foss and Mitch DeRidder address the metatheoretical problem of choosing between alternative user interface designs as an example of the general problem of choosing between alternative cognitive theories. An interface design after all is a codification of a theory about what will be easy for people to learn and to use. They propose that selection criteria for choosing between alternatives be based on measured transfer of learning; the ease of transition between knowledge states in learning an interface would determine the adequacy of that interface design (and of the cognitive theory it codifies).

Peter Polson's approach to the analysis of transfer of learning is to develop an articulate cognitive description of what is learned (represented as a set of "productions") and then to test specific empirical predictions under the assumption that a production once learned is automatically available in later learning. This formalizes the everyday experience that prior knowledge has an impact on future learning efforts, sometimes facilitating learning and sometimes interfering with learning. Traditional efforts to understand this important phenomenon were often directed at simple and artificial domains (the old standby of nonsense word lists). Polson's work demonstrates how a cognitive description of transfer can be applied to the learning of commands in a computer application, and indeed how such a theory might predict the cognitive consequences of user interface designs before those designs are ever implemented.

The management of limited resources in human performance is another traditional area of theoretical concern in cognitive science. Phil Barnard's chapter argues that cognitive science is in need of a more integrated theory of knowledge representation and information processing—one that focuses more attention on the coordinated control of sequences of behavior in relation to complex and dynamic environments, one that is less paradigm bound with respect to empirical data. Barnard outlines a distributed architecture for cognitive processes called "interacting cognitive subsystems" and applies it to the description of learning computer dialog structures (like menus and command languages). Like Foss and DeRidder and like Polson, Barnard makes the point that current limitations in cognitive theory make the application of theory piecemeal and heuristic. The approach in these three chapters is to develop the general theory base by taking the domain of human-computer interaction as exemplary.

Building Theoretical Perspectives from Established Research Areas Crosscutting the perspective of general cognitive theory is the complementary perspective of particular task domains. One of the important themes in recent cognitive science research is that particular task domains have their own distinctive structures. According to this view, general studies of, say, problem solving need to be augmented by studies of particular domains within which problem solving takes place (a well-known example is the domain of chess). The chapters by Clayton Lewis and by John Black, Dana Kay, and Elliot Soloway examine problems in human-computer interaction using prior cognitive research in other domains as a sort of sounding board. Lewis examines the similarities and the differences between learning mathematics and learning to use a computer application; Black, Kay, and Soloway examine those between reading and understanding a story and understanding computer text editors and programs.

This work is important in that it can help place aspects of the human-computer interaction domain within a larger space of task domains studied in cognitive science. It can help to identify that which is general across various domains and that which is particular to given domains. The principles brought to light in any given investigation have boundary conditions, but these will remain unknown until the principles are studied in a variety of situations. General human strategic biases and the particulars of the computer situation—the tasks, the goals, the available methods, the likely confusions—all interact powerfully and richly in determining how people construe their current situation, what they choose to do, and how they try to do it.

Broadening the Scope of Current Cognitive Science Analyses Several of the chapters in this volume undertake projects extending the scope of current cognitive science research. Tom Malone introduces the concept of "organizational interface" to refer to situations in which groups of people interact by means of computers (e.g., electronic mail applications). The point of organizational interfaces is that people do not perform routine tasks and solve problems by themselves. Traditional examinations of human performance—and of performance with computer systems in particular—has ignored organizational factors. Malone develops the organizational interface concept to suggest ways in which computer systems can be designed to facilitate group problem solving, and conversely to anticipate likely changes in how groups of people will solve problems in the future using computer systems.

Judy Olson extends current analytical techniques by assimilating global task analysis to current cognitive techniques for modeling lower-level aspects of planning. Many theorists have proposed schemes for analyzing human performance in terms of representations of tasks and of human information processing operations. For example, the transfer of learning work discussed by Polson and by Foss and DeRidder models human-computer interaction by representing how a computer application works with respect to how human cognitive capabilities and limitations are engaged. Typically, this work focuses on fairly low levels of task planning and execution (e.g., how to delete a line in an electronic document). Olson incorporates global task analysis, a consideration of tasks at the level of workplace organization, into this framework.

Another example of broadening the scope of current cognitive science analysis is the explicit role that motivation plays in the chapters by Malone and by myself and Mary Beth Rosson. Cognitive tasks like learning and problem solving are frequently analyzed in purely cognitive terms, that is, in terms of information transactions. However, it is clear from everyday experience, and all too salient to researchers in human learning and problem solving, that motivation may play at least as prepotent a role as any purely cognitive factor. A motivated learner often cannot be stopped—even by rather poorly designed user interface facilities. And a poorly motivated learner often cannot be helped. Bringing the consideration of such factors into the science of human-computer interaction from the first broadens the conventional outlook of cognitive science.

Making Ecological Tests of Cognitive Theories Human-computer interaction provides cognitive science with a good test bed for examining the ability of cognitive theories to apply in a complex, real domain. Jean McKendree and John Anderson take this approach in their study of learning to program in Lisp. The programming task is a complex example for applying and developing Anderson's ACT* theory of human cognitive skill. McKendree and Anderson find that speedup in programming tasks consists of two components, general strengthening of previously learned skill components and situation-specific new learning, which consists of organizing new skill components and combining frequently exercised skill components. McKendree and Anderson describe a mathematical model for their learning data, stressing that at a sufficiently fine grain of skill and knowledge analysis, simple and general mechanisms provide a very close fit.

Richard Mayer discusses a series of studies of learning to program in BASIC. Mayer examines the contrasts and relationships between conceptual and syntactic knowledge in the programming domain. He analyzes specific domain-relevant conceptions in terms of their impact on learning and their trainability. This work illustrates how a cognitive approach to learning can provide instructional designs for real training domains.

Guiding the Introduction of New Technology One of the exciting properties of the human-computer interaction domain is its rapid change. As technologies evolve, and as the cultural context vis-à-vis computing evolves in consequence, new research questions are raised, addressed, refined, altered, and finally superseded—as the technological and cultural givens again change. While this is not the sort of field one would enter to study endless parametric variations on some particular laboratory phenomenon, it also is not the sort of field that could ever become static! Because of all this it also represents a rather unusual opportunity for cognitive science: the opportunity to *change* future technology by producing an understanding of contemporary technology—and thereby perhaps to affect the future directly and constructively.

Here lies an important contrast between the direction and ambition of current research on human-computer interaction and earlier studies of the human impact of technological developments (the automobile and television). In these former cases, social scientists were merely observers and analysts. In the case of computer technology, this role is still available, and there are many descriptions of how computers are affecting contemporary life. But there is also a new role to play: Computer technology is more accessible, and more flexible; it is developing faster and with greater diversity. Cognitive scientists can observe and analyze these developments, but they can also participate in and indeed direct these developments.

Yet this may be more even than an opportunity; it is almost a call to arms. For, as stated above, it seems likely that computing technology will have a very great and continuing impact on our world. The problems that arise will be resolved in some way whether or not cognitive scientists provide the methodological and conceptual leverage to address them—there were user interfaces long before there were appreciable numbers of cognitive scientists trying to determine how to enhance usability!

It is of course too early to tell how significant and sustained may be the impact of cognitive science on applied work in human-computer interaction, or what reciprocal effect this applied work might have on cognitive science. Nevertheless, we should not mistake the opportunity and the challenge that this confluence of interests embodies. Mature science provides real empirical leverage in application, and serious applied work is systematically grounded in science. A gauntlet has been thrown.

This book grew out of a symposium, "The Computer: Tool and Topic," that I organized for the 1983 annual meeting of the Society for Computers in Psychology. John Anderson, Tom Landauer, Clayton Lewis, and Don Norman participated as speakers, and several of the other authors in this volume participated with questions from the floor.

Phyllis Reisner and John Whiteside helped to review the chapters, providing technical and editorial feedback that greatly improved them. Phyllis and John also agreed to contribute discussion chapters to facilitate further the kind of technical dialog that is often difficult to achieve in an edited book, but that seems especially important in a new research area.

Finally, I am grateful to my colleagues at the User Interface Institute for keeping me on track in a multitude of ways, and to the IBM Corporation for providing support for this project in the form of my time.

Interfacing Thought

1 Relations between Cognitive Psychology and Computer System Design

Thomas K. Landauer

Cognitive psychology is more intimately related to the design of computers than to that of traditional machines, such as automobiles and home appliances. There are several reasons. First, the new information technology is so flexible that functions change with bewildering frequency. It is ever less feasible to count on the existence of experienced operators. Unlike typewriters and automobiles, it seems unlikely that information machines of the future will stay the same long enough for public school training to prepare people for lifelong careers based on their use. Thus easy learning or self-evident operations are critical. Second, and equally important, the tasks for which computers are the tools are generally ones in which the human's thought processes themselves are being aided. The maturation of computer applications is taking us ever farther in this direction. The first jobs for computers involved routine information tasks like bookkeeping, in which mechanical procedures once done by humans could simply be assumed by machines. Computers increasingly are used to support dynamic interactive tasks, like text editing and financial simulation, in which the user's mind is an important and lively component of the total system. Designing tools for this kind of activity is an intimately cognitive-psychological activity. Its accomplishment can no longer be viewed as that of first designing a machine to do something, then designing the controls by which the operator guides the machine.

Although the need for greater consideration of users has been recognized for some time now, the response so far, by and large, has been shallow. In attempting to provide greater "user friendliness," designers and programmers have indeed paid more attention to the usability of their systems, and in doing so have exploited the much expanded power of the systems with which they work. For example, they often use the larger memories now available to store larger programs that are supposed to better support usability. But this has been done without much basis other than individual designer intuition and common sense. Undeniably, common sense, combined with some vigorous trial and error, has already done much to improve systems. Just as undeniably, however, there is much farther to go than we have come. People still complain bitterly about the difficulty of learning to use even text editors and spread sheets, which are among the most thoroughly evolved interactive devices. And there are as yet only a few cognitive tools available that offer totally new ways of accomplishing mental tasks—symbolic math languages are one example—although one would think that the capabilities of computation would open the way for hosts.

Psychologists have become increasingly involved in the design of new computer systems and in research and theory aimed at understanding the human component of the problem. For example, before divestiture, Bell Laboratories alone employed around 200 psychologists in work related to computer system development. Many times that number are employed by other software and hardware companies the world over, so psychology apparently has something to sell. Indeed, talking to applied psychologists and managers in such settings usually elicits tales of success. But tales of dissatisfaction and frustration are also common. It would not be altogether unfair to characterize the situation as follows. Although psychologists have brought to development efforts a dedicated professional interest in user problems, and have successfully acted as intelligent advocates of the interest of users, they have not brought an impressive tool kit of design methods or principles, nor have they effectively brought to bear a relevant body of scientific knowledge or theory.

In addition to helping to build better systems, one would also hope that the interaction of cognitive psychology with design would help to advance the science of mind. Many computer systems are created to interact with, aid, or replace mental processes. Surely the problems encountered in trying to make them do so ought to feed new and interesting psychological research. Computer technology should provide better opportunity for applied research that can contribute to the science of mind than anything we have had in the past. It offers an arena in which potential understanding of human mental powers and limitations can be tested.

The iterative interplay between the invention of new methods to support cognitive activities and the analysis of their successes and failures is a very exciting prospect. In my view, cognitive psychology has suffered from the lack of an applied discipline in which the completeness of its accounts could be measured, or from which a sorting of phenomena into those important for actual human function from those of merely scholastic interest could be made. Physics and chemistry have had engineering, physiology and biology have had medicine to play this role. But cognitive psychology has had only limited associations with artifact invention, primarily because the most interesting aspects of human cognition are complex information processes for which, until recently, the means for constructing useful new tools were lacking. We now have the opportunity, but we have not done much with it yet.

What I am concerned with here is the development of a more fruitful interconnection between the science of cognitive psychology and the science, art, and engineering of computer systems. What follows is a brief analysis and survey of the ways in which cognitive psychology has and can interact with computer system design. It offers some examples of work already accomplished, but only as illustrations. No new substantive contribution to the field is reported here. The analysis I propose is quite simple and straightforward. I suggest four principle ways in which cognitive psychology can interact with computer system invention and design.

1. We may apply existing knowledge and theory directly to design problems.

2. We may apply our armamentarium of psychological ideas and theoretical machinery to the creation of new models, analyses, and engineering tools.

3. We may apply our well-developed methods of empirical research and data analysis to the evaluation of designs, design alternatives, and design principles.

4. We can use problems encountered in design to inform and guide our research into the fundamentals of mental life

Each of these relations is discussed in somewhat more detail, with, in each case, a few notable current issues being given particular attention.

1 Application of Existing Knowledge and Principles

One potential way to relate cognitive psychology to system design is to search for existing knowledge and theory that bears on recognized design problems. One problem that seemed ripe for this approach was the assignment of names to commands. Many interactive systems require the user to enter one or more characters as a cue for the system to perform one or another operation; these are known as commands. For example, s/hte/the might be the command needed to change "hte" to "the" in a line, where "s" is the abbreviated name of a "substitute" command. The character string "name" can be assigned at random as long as it can be a unique code for the system to interpret (the necessity of uniqueness can sometimes be relaxed if interactive disambiguation is feasible). In many applications people appeared to have difficulty in learning to enter the right strings to effect the correct operations, or at least that was one way to describe their struggles and confusions with new systems. Various people—users, critics and even programmers (see Norman, 1981)—blamed the difficulty of learning new systems on poor selection of command names. Because the learning of the names of commands appeared to be extremely similar to the classic laboratory paradigm of paired-associate memorization, psychologists interested in the matter thought they had found a perfect opportunity to apply things they knew. Paired-associate learning is a very well-developed area, with a rich literature of findings and phenomena and a goodly number of reasonably accurate, if somewhat restricted, theories.

The most directly applicable findings seemed to be a constellation of results showing that almost any kind of prior knowledge of the stimulus or response member of a pair in which the learner was to learn to associate the response to the stimulus, or any prior degree of association between the two, caused more rapid learning (as, for example, reviewed in Goss and Nadine, 1965, Postman, 1971, or Underwood and Schultz, 1960). To summarize roughly what the laboratory findings seem to say regarding the command name learning situation, they suggest that the response terms, the "names," should be "highly available." Availability means that (1) the names should be regularly spelled, well-known words that the user will not have to learn as words or as spellings, and that are common in the use of language to which they are accustomed, and thus easy for users to think of; (2) they should be words or obvious abbreviations of words that are related in meaning to the topic of learning, that is, to the category or meanings of other names in the set being learned; (3) yet they should be discriminable from other names in the set as much as is needed so that no two responses will be improperly confused with each other; and (4) if feasible, the words that are to be responses, that is, the names, should already have some "natural" association with the stimuli, that is, with the mental or environmental conditions in which they are appropriate.

Attempts to apply this set of principles to the selection of command names, and more especially the research aimed at demonstrating an advantage of so doing, are instructive in a number of ways. The earliest reported experiments (e.g., Black and Sebrechts, 1981) used a typical laboratory paper-and-pencil version of a paired-associate task, except that they substituted some representation of the nature of the computer operation for the stimulus and the name of the command for the response. They studied text editing operations that were described either in a phrase or by before-and-after examples of the effect of the commands. In some versions the "responses" were intuitively assigned names, those that some existing system uses. In other conditions, names were chosen by asking college students to suggest terms that they thought would be appropriate for the operations. As expected, superior learning occurred for paired-associate lists when presumably more discriminable and highly associated names were the responses.

At about the same time, Landauer, Galotti, and Hartwell (1983) performed an experiment in which they taught the first half-dozen commands of an actual text editor to typing students, with different kinds of names given to the commands for different groups. One set of names, "add," "omit," and "change," was chosen in an elaborate procedure of eliciting, from other typing students, the verbs that they would use to describe the operations of editing that those commands are designed to effect, in a setting in which they imagined themselves to be instructing another typist. For a second group the commands, "append," "delete," and "substitute" were the words chosen by the editor's original programmers, and in a third group the commands were named with randomly chosen unrelated words, "allege," "cipher," and "deliberate." There was a slight, but far from significant, advantage to either natural names or the programmer's names over the unrelated words, but no appreciable mean difference between the more natural and the programmer selected command names.

Barnard et al. (1982) also failed to demonstrate overall performance time effects for command name choice in an interactive text manipulation context, and Scapin (1981), in a paper-and-pencil study, found less common names easier to learn.

Subsequently, Grudin and Barnard (1984), determined, one might infer, to exonerate experimental psychology, conducted another experiment. Adult subjects learned 12 commands for a system that had many of the characteristics of a text editor, but was designed to have pairs of commands that were similar in function except for the objects to which they applied, e.g., whether the command put a word at the end of a sentence or at the beginning. In this somewhat simplified and artificial interactive setting there was a significant advantage for experimenter-chosen "specific" over unrelated words.

I do not propose to resolve the apparent conflicts between these various experiments here (but see Landauer and Galotti, 1984). Rather, I want to use them to illustrate two simple points. First, it is possible for some very well-established phenomena that have robust effects in abstracted laboratory tasks to have very different levels of influence when embedded in more complex tasks. The system taught by Landauer et al. was difficult to learn; beginners made many mistakes in applying command names and were confused and frustrated. Indeed they manifested just those difficulties that had led many critics (Ledgard et al., 1980; Black and Sebrechts, 1981; Norman, 1981; Carroll, 1982) to propose the use of more "natural" names for commands. Nevertheless, simply using "natural" names had no appreciable benefit, and much more extreme and contrived contrasts proved necessary to demonstrate naming effects. Apparently something else makes the learning of text editors difficult. Even though it is demonstrably easier to learn names with appropriate prior characteristics (e.g., Black and Sebrechts, 1981; Grudin and Barnard, 1984) in special circumstances, such factors do not appear to contribute much to the overall difficulty of learning the rudiments of interactive computing under ordinary conditions.

The point of applied research is to understand what matters in realistic contexts. In regard to naming, then, the proper conclusion from the work so far is not that an effect is there if you look for it in the right way, although this is true. The important lesson is that what really makes things difficult must be looked for elsewhere. A second point of interest also derives from these experiments. A different variable concerning the assignment of command names, the manner in which differences between names were "mapped" to operations requiring syntactic constructions following the name, appeared to make a very large difference in ease of learning. For example, in some versions of the experimental editor, removing a word within a line required the command construction "name /hte//", but removing a whole line did not require the slashes or the input of the incorrect text. Using the same command name for both, whether "substitute" or "delete," created marked confusion relative to using substitute for one case and delete for the other. This was equally true if the two names were the unrelated terms "cipher" and "deliberate." Nothing in the traditional verbal-learning literature corresponds well to these mapping differences, and previous psychological knowledge therefore affords little help (or hindrance.)

Somewhat more success has been achieved in a few other attempts to apply prior knowledge. (However, it must be admitted that for both of the examples to follow, insufficient replication and critical notice has yet been reported to justify much bragging.) One example is a recent attempt by

Landauer and Nachbar (1985) to apply some well-known laws governing decision and motor selection time to menu choice. In a typical menu-driven access to a large database, users are given a series of choice frames by use of which they guide an hierarchical tree search. For example, the first frame of a dictionary search interface might present the choices (1) apple—mother (2) motor—trouble (3) under—zebra. If the user chooses (1), the next screen would present a further subdivision into (1) apple—cap (2) car—keep (3) key—mother, and so forth.

The problem is this: Given that items are selected by indicating one of b alternatives in each of several successive hierarchically organized menus, and given that the total set can be meaningfully subdivided in many different ways, what menu structure is optimal? Two laws are potentially relevant.

1. Broader menus necessarily require a decision among more alternatives. Hick's law (Welford, 1980) states that mean response time in simple decision tasks is a linear function of the transmitted information, which, for equally likely alternatives, gives

$$rt = k' + c' \log_2 b, \tag{1}$$

where b is the number of alternatives, and k' and c' are constants.

2. Sometimes more alternatives per screen will require targets that are physically smaller and harder to select. Fitts's law (1954) states that mean movement time is a function of the log of distance (d) over width (w) of target: that is,

$$mt = k + c \log_2 (d/w). \tag{2}$$

In a touch-screen menu, for example, the user touches an appropriately indicated area on the screen, the target, to indicate a choice. The target's distance is nearly independent of the number of alternatives, but the width may decrease as the screen is divided into more regions. In Landauer and Nachbar's experiments the available screen height was equally divided among the choices, so the touch target width varied inversely with the number of alternatives. For this case, then,

$$mt = k'' + c'' \log_2 b.$$

If the decision and movement components are assumed to be accomplished in succession, their mean times will add, giving mean choice time, ct, for a menu of b items

$$
\begin{aligned}
ct &= dt + mt \\
&= k' + c' \log_2 b + k'' + c'' \log_2 b \qquad (3) \\
&= k + c \log_2 b.
\end{aligned}
$$

Data from experiments with 2–16 alphabetically and numerically arranged alternatives fit the predicted functions closely. This particular functional form has an important implication for the design of hierarchical menu schemes. The total search time from root to leaf in a symmetrical search tree is given by

$$
\begin{aligned}
T &= (\text{number of steps})(\text{mean time per step}) \\
&= \log_b N\,(\text{time per step}),
\end{aligned}
$$

where b is the branching factor, i.e., the number of alternatives at each step, and N is the number of terminal nodes. Substituting the mean time per step for human choice as given in equation (3) yields

$$T = \log_b N(k + c \log_2 b).$$

Note that the additive constant k now should include the system response time to change menus. On multiplying out,

$$
\begin{aligned}
T &= k \log_b N + c \log_b N \log_2 b \\
&= k \log_b N + c \log_2 N,
\end{aligned}
$$

we see that b, the number of alternatives, affects the total time only by determining the number of steps. Therefore, for situations in which equation (2) holds, search time will be minimized by using as broad menus as feasible within space and display constraints.

The empirical menu-use experiments confirmed this expectation; very narrow and deep menu sequences took as much as twice as long to traverse as very broad and shallow ones. The question of how far this analysis generalizes needs more research. In a second, unpublished, experiment, Nachbar and I used key-controlled cursor movement instead of pointing for target selection, and 4–64 alternatives, and got equally good fits. But the expected results for choice domains less well ordered than alphabetically or numerically arranged sets are still an open question. Variations in depth and breadth of menus for computer concepts and other semantic categories have produced less clear results (Miller, 1981; Snowberry, Parkinson, and Sisson, 1983; Tullis, 1985). One aspect of such studies is that the division of a natural set into more or fewer arbitrary partitions does not necessarily yield equally good categories for human recognition, or ones to which equally comprehensible names can be assigned. In other words, the "naturalness" of the categories needs to be considered, as well as the information processing time functions for equally good alternatives as described by equation (3).

Another unresolved issue is the effect of errors. In the cursor-selection experiment, total errors, as well as time, decreased with greater menu breadth, as they did in Tullis's (1985) study of semantic categories. However, in using touch screens with many alternatives, thus very small targets, total incorrect responses increased. Errors are likely to be more costly, on average, for deeper menus where larger error recovery paths are possible. Nevertheless, further studies are needed to define the effects for various modes of error correcting.

A final issue raised by these experiments was the relation between performance and preference. On questioning, participants did not like best the conditions that led to the fastest and most accurate searches. The relation between these outcomes has not frequently been considered in human information processing research, but is an important practical concern and poses an intriguing theoretical problem for cognitive psychology broadly construed.

Another example of applying principles is Card's application of Fitts's law to the comparison of pointing devices. (Card, English, and Burr, 1978; Card, Moran, and Newell, 1983). In this instance, the principle was used as a way of describing performance on a set of devices, mouse, joystick, and keys, that had been invented without recourse to any formal psychological knowledge. The result was an elegant and revealing analysis of reasons for the superiority of the mouse over the other devices in the task studied and the invention of a quick engineering test for proposed pointing methods. Card used the good fit to Fitts's law to argue that no pointing device would be likely to do much better than the mouse, since its constants, i.e., information transfer rates, were about as low as any previously observed in motor-control experiments. This is a valid and extremely useful conclusion, at least if properly restricted to the tasks on which it was based, and to the relatively passive devices so far developed for the purpose. What I wish, however, is that such analyses, instead of leading only to intelligent choice among existing alternatives, would be used to point the way to the invention of new methods. Card et al. show that a fundamental limit to the performance with today's pointers is the eye-hand control rates of the human operator. What they did not undertake was the application of their understanding of human pointing to the specification of a device that would improve the human performance, an aid rather than a mere transducer. Perhaps some of the human system's noise could be overcome, or some intelligence could be applied to infer the desired target more accurately. As I shall remark below, such challenges are of special interest to the application of psychology in this area.

I am at a loss to come up with any better examples of the application of prior knowledge or theory in this field, or even many more to equal them. I find this dismaying. Articles and books claiming to give guidance for designers do list a number of basic facts about perception, memory, and problem solving that are believed to be important to designers. Some, such as specifications for the size, contrast, and font of characters to be presented on a CRT screen or colors and physical properties of phosphors and flicker rates are well founded and of obvious relevance to some design tasks. But they do not thrill one as applications of cognitive psychology. The more cognitive variables discussed usually fail to make contact with the designer's job in an easily understood way, or at least in a way that has given rise to empirical demonstrations of value. For example, one of the most frequently cited principles is the fact that short-term memory can only be relied on to maintain around five chunks. Setting aside the practical difficulty of identifying "chunk," I doubt that knowledge of this principle has often influenced a design. I suppose a perverse designer or a diabolical experimenter could figure out a way to make an interface require working memory for 20 items, but I have yet to see this principle actually put to use in a convincing manner.

There may be several reasons for the lack of successful application of known principles. One is that not enough people really understand the principles or their basis. One example is a recent theoretical paper on the menu breadth problem discussed above. It assumed choice time linear with number of alternatives on the basis of Sternberg's findings for memory set scanning with a fixed number of alternative responses, a vaguely analogous but actually irrelevant principle. Probably there are too few people who understand both psychological principles and systems with sufficient depth. Perhaps this will change as more sophistication on both sides develops.

Another and more fundamental reason for limited application of principles is that the way in which cognition has been studied in the psychology laboratory has often promoted an interest in variables of only theoretical importance, ones that can reveal something about the workings of the mind—but not necessarily ones having large and robust effects. The factors that actually account for the difficulties encountered in real life are not necessarily objects of study. A great deal of experimental research in cognitive psychology has been concerned with hypothesis testing, where the existence of a qualitative result—that something has or has not a given effect—may decide a theoretical issue. This is quite a good strategy for advancing theory because it finesses a large number of difficult questions of measurement, scaling, and explicit modeling assumptions. However, it carries with it a greatly diminished interest in the true size of effects, so much so that it has become depressingly common for journal articles to report significance levels without giving data on the differences between means or distributions. Authors adopt a language in which there are said to be effects or no effects, as if the world exists in binary states. Although a great deal can be done to build theories and understand nature with this kind of black-and-white picture, it tends to leave us in a rather helpless position when it comes to choosing principles on which to found technology or understand peoples' behavior in its natural setting.

Another reason for the applicative poverty of cognitive psychology is that the theories we have pursued have led away from rather than toward attempts to describe in full the performance in any given task situation. Thus we have been, quite rightly, fascinated with analyzing the act of reading an isolated word so as to discover the processes and organization by which it is accomplished. This leads us into intricate and clever debates to resolve such questions as whether there is any stage at which individual letters are identified as such. A good deal of progress has been made in learning how to study and understand such hidden processes. However, while analysis has proceeded apace, the analog of chemical synthesis has been almost completely lacking. That is, we have not found out how much of what kind of process ability acquired in what way needs to be combined how with others in order to produce effective reading, or even word recognition. We have hardly begun looking for what factors have large effects and what small when in combination with what others. As a result, the intense and sophisticated work in this area has not yet contributed substantially to writing, calligraphy, typography, the teaching of reading, or the design of improved text presentation via computers.

Lest this sound too pessimistic, my view is that we have indeed learned a great deal about processes that will someday be of importance in the practical world, and perhaps especially in the potential world of computer aids. But we have not learned enough of the right things to make the knowledge productive for application. There are far too many holes, and too many uncertainties in what principles are relevant to what tasks. Nonetheless, it seems likely that we shall find the knowledge at hand useful as some of the building blocks we shall need. The fact that current knowledge is not sufficient on its own does not mean that it is useless—only that it will need supplementing and filling out to form the basis of a synthetic discipline.

2 Application of Theoretical Machinery

Cognitive psychology has developed a number of tools for thinking about mental processes that may be used to understand the tasks for which computer systems are designed, without there being any direct sharing of content. One example is the form of theory in which a complex human performance is modeled by a flow diagram or computer program that defines some set of component processes and the order in which they are accomplished. Starting with a view of skilled performance based on earlier cognitive theories (Miller, Galanter, and Pribraun, 1960; Newell and Simon, 1972) and deriving hypothesized subprocesses from observations and protocols of expert performance, Card, Moran, and Newell (1983) formulated on "engineering model" for predicting the temporal characteristics of interacting with a keyboard-driven system. The model makes little use of substantive principles from earlier discoveries in cognitive psychology. However, it has a very familiar form and style. For the stable performance of highly practiced operators of text editors, Card, Moran, and Newell obtained reasonably stable estimates of response time for subcomponents like the selection and execution of certain commands. Combining these according to the time-additive dictates of their flow model yielded predictions for total task performance times that were fairly good, i.e., within about 30% of observed times, for a certain range of tests.

It is less clear that the model has strong prescriptive properties, that it can tell the designer much about how to design a good system in the first place. For one thing, it can be argued that the model, as so far developed, underplays many of the important determinants of real performance with interesting systems—for example, aspects of learning, transfer, error generation, and nonoptimal selection of alternative methods by users (Olson and Nilsen, 1985). The model was developed to give predictions of the time that experts require for certain components of an overall system, given a detailed specification of the system design and some preliminary measurements. This is quite useful for comparing two or more versions that one might be considering, and for tuning a system under development. It is obviously a very significant step in an important direction.

It is certainly too much to expect all the problems to have been solved in one project. However, some of my goals for the field are exemplified by what is missing in this work. The engineering model approach seems aimed primarily at providing feedback evaluation for the design process, rather than fundamental knowledge useful as its foundation. Take the treatment of errors as an example. The main development in the Card, Moran, and Newell book deals with error-free performance. Errors are considered, but not what causes them or where to expect them, and only as another subcomponent of performance whose time costs can be estimated and modeled. That is, given a determination of how many errors of what kind will occur, the model can be extended to predict the time taken up by commission and correction of errors, as well as performance of correct sequences. But the data and theory are not brought to bear on what design features lead to what kinds of errors. In Card, Moran, and Newell's study of text editing, for example, my calculations from the published data show 35% of expert's time and over 80% of the variance in time to be attributable to errors.[1] This implies that analysis of the source of errors might lead to the design of much more effective editing aids.

The attitude seemingly implicit in the engineering model approach, and, I believe, too widely held in the human-factors world, is that invention and design are engineering acts in which scientific psychology has no part to play. The psychological analysis is used only to create a shortcut measure of usability, not to produce understanding and insight to guide the creative process. This is too modest, and dull, an aspiration.

A related application of a similar mode of theory is that of Polson and Kieras (1985). They used the machinery of a production system-based cognitive simulation program to model what a user must know in order to operate a system. They go on to assert that the difficulty of learning an operation will depend on the number of new productions needed to acquire the skill. From a scientific point of view there is something slightly circular in the method, because the choice of what and how many productions to use for a given of task is not rigorously specifiable. Nevertheless, in their hands, and potentially in that of people experienced in using their theoretical model, it is possible to make better than gross intuitive predictions about the relative difficulty of systems and of the amount of transfer between the learning of one and another.

Again the application of theoretical technique from cognitive psychology seems to have yielded the beginnings of an effective engineering tool. As in the case of Card, Moran, and Newell's keystroke models, what we might call the "mentalstroke" model offers more promise of description than of prescription. Eventually we would like cognitive psychological theory to tell programmers how to invent and design, but for the time being we should be delighted to have some methods that, even at a rather approximate level of precision, and even if they require a component of human judgment, are capable of helping us to evaluate one design versus another.

Another approach was illustrated first by some early—for this field—work of Phyllis Reisner (1981). In this the theory schema is borrowed primarily from linguistics rather than cognitive psychology as such. The idea is that action sequences in some kinds of interactive interfaces can be described by a grammatical structure in a manner similar to the description of linguistic utterances. Such descriptions can both expose inconsistencies in existing designs and offer a plausible basis for designing consistent rule-governed interactive methods. Her work, and others that have followed (e.g., Payne and Green, 1983) make is appear likely that systems susceptible to tidy grammatical descriptions will be easier to learn and use than those that are not. This seems a promising way to go, especially since one can imagine using grammars to *generate* important aspects of design. However, what grammatical descriptions will prove to be best in the sense that they give most leverage on the specification of humanly usable systems is still a very open question.

3 Application of Investigative and Analytic Methods

There are two very elementary but fundamental methodological facts that are taken for granted by all experimental psychologists, but astonishingly often fail to be appreciated by others. The first is that behavior is always quite variable between people and between occasions. The second is that it is feasible to obtain objective data on behavior. In system development environments, ignorance of these two truths all too often leads to an evaluation of new ideas or designs by the opinions of a handful of unrepresentative people. Psychologists with proper organizational support can make an extremely valuable contributions simply by insisting on observing sufficient numbers of representative users on a set of representative benchmark tasks, and taking some systematic measures of task time, errors, opinions, examples of error types, and both user and observer intuitions about sources of ease and difficulty. Designers are constantly surprised at the value of such observations. The reason they are so surprised is that the performance and reactions of real users are so various and so often different from their own (because a designer is also one of the set of variable reactors). What might be termed the "naive intuition fallacy," that everyone else will behave and react similarly to oneself, appears to be very widely and strongly endorsed. The only professionals whose training tends to disabuse them of this error are experimental psychologists who have the experience of running experiments with live human subjects and being repeatedly surprised by their behavior.

On the other hand, the training of most psychologists has featured hypothesis testing by factorial laboratory experiments in which the goal is to find some critical variable that will have an effect that confirms or disconfirms a theory. The application of psychological research in support of design is quite different. It often requires new ways of thinking and considerable ingenuity on the part of the scientist. For example, it is often desirable to evaluate the usability of a tool that does not yet exist and is going to be hard to build. Thus, Gould, Conti, and Hovanyecz (1983) found out how well a nonexistent speech recognition-based typewriter would satisfy by substituting a human for the missing electronic components. Other research aims at discovering the main variables or factors that will make performance easy or difficult. To do this requires a method that will reveal large mean effect sizes under realistic conditions.

To put this somewhat differently, what application needs most, at least at present and probably into the future as well, are exploratory research paradigms rather than hypothesis testing ones. Experimental psychology has not been particularly productive in evolving such paradigms. Nonetheless, many of the basic tools of our trade can be applied with considerable leverage. Here are a few examples. Several groups of investigators have studied the question of how abbreviations for things like command names should be formed (e.g., Ehrenreich and Porcu, 1982; Hirsch-Pasek, Nudelman and Schneider, 1982; Streeter, Ackroff, and Taylor, 1983; see Ehrenreich, 1985, for a review). The Streeter, Ackroff, and Taylor approach is a nice example of the exploratory paradigm. They first had representative users nominate abbreviations for a set of words like those that might be used as commands in a real system. They characterized and classified the kinds of abbreviations that people gave and discovered (as usual) that there was a lot of variability both between people and within a given individual in the apparent rules being used. Puzzled and prompted by these results, they went on to evaluate a number of possible schemes for assigning abbreviations, including (1) using for each command name the most popular abbreviation given by the subjects, (2) using a rule that captured the maximum number of abbreviations, and (3) using some other rule. What they found is that using any consistent rule for the whole word set is what is most important. Even abbreviations for words that would be spontaneously abbreviated otherwise by most people were learned more easily if they conformed to a common rule. (As a substantive matter it is worth noting that here naturalness—interpreted as the popularity of an individual abbreviation—was pitted against rule governedness and lost.)

A somewhat more extensive example of exploratory research in which variability in behavior figures prominently is the work on indexing by Furnas et al. (1983). In a variety of domains, ranging from editing command names to recipe databases, they studied the names users spontaneously chose for desired items. The data uniformly falsified the common intuition that there is one best or only a few good names for most objects. Instead there are almost always many names, no one of which is very dominant. Simulation models based on these data showed that giving every entry as many names as people spontaneously wished to look them up under, typically around 30, would increase first-try success from 15–20% to 75–85%, without unacceptable increases in ambiguity. Next, controlled experiments (Gomez and Lochbaum, 1984), in which a laboratory version of a recipe database was searched by homemakers, demonstrated that an actual interactive system with "rich aliasing" could achieve the predicted benefits.

Other research and analytic techniques have also been put to good use. For example, multidimensional scaling was employed by Tullis (1985) to produce an apparently very successful organization of a database for menu presentation and choice. Finally, Egan and Gomez (1985) have exploited a set of standard measurements of individual differences in cognitive abilities to analyze the difficulties posed to users by a text editor. In this case, exploration of the characteristics of the task was accomplished by exploring the characteristics of people who find it easy or difficult. They found, for example, that the older the learner, the harder it was to master text editing, and that most of the difficulty correlated with age involved the construction of abstract text locating commands. This in turn led to the discovery that so-called full screen editors are easier to use, and their difficulty much less dependent on the user's age, primarily because they allow a simpler mode of indicating the text to be modified.

There are, of course, many other examples. Only these few are mentioned to give a sense of the range of possibilities. The overall point is that with some ingenuity many of the classical techniques of cognitive psychological research can be turned into exploratory and analytic methods appropriate to investigating issues relevant to design. It may be worth repeating that, in this mode, little substantive psychological theory or knowledge is applied. Instead, and this is important, new phenomena are added to the purview of the field.

Before leaving this section, I would like to mention some technical difficulties in employing cognitive psychological methods in applied settings. Perhaps the most challenging problem is to achieve the proper degree of representativeness in the experimental situations chosen for study. We wish to understand real users performing real tasks. But how can we choose full-scale settings in a way that ensures generality? If we test a principle as it is embedded in one system—say, one powerful editor—what can we say with confidence about its effect in others? Usually very little. How shall we ever rise above this difficulty? The ideal way would be to study a sample of systems drawn representatively from all systems that exist or might exist. Clearly this is impossible, if only because there is no way to describe the universe from which to draw the sample. Another approach, represented in the work by Furnas et al. described above, is simply to study several tasks, but to choose them so that they differ from each other widely and in most of the ways that one can imagine would be relevant to the phenomena in question. For example, Furnas et al. studied spontaneous name selection for text editing operations, system commands, cooking recipe index terms, common knowledge lookup keys, and want ad categories. If they all yield results with the same implications, as in this case they all envinced great diversity, then a sort of informal Bayesian inference allows one to conclude that such results are to be expected in most other situations as well. (Prior: a phenomenon not due to fundamental and general causes has high probability of varying greatly over cases. Observation: phenomenon observed in many disparate situations. Conclusion: causes probably general.)

Discussing robustness and generality brings up the issue of the use of statistics. The proper use of statistics in the kind of research being described here is somewhat different from its use in theory testing. When the issue is whether there is or is not an effect of a particular kind, then a significance test with a conservative acceptance probability level is appropriate. But when we want to know about the importance of variables or factors, we really are interested primarily in estimates of mean effect size. We still want to take account of the fact that behavior is intrinsically variable and not fool ourselves into believing that a particular effect size is a true value when chance may have thrown it off. For this we want to put confidence intervals around effects sizes. Psychologists are too sophisticated at significance tests and too inexperienced with confidence intervals. This point is often made in textbooks and discussions of academic research, but is frequently ignored in practice. It is of much greater import for applied research.

Here is another aspect of statistics that needs more careful consideration. Consider the problem of comparing two features or two systems. If one obtains some benchmark behavioral measurement on the two, what sort of statistics are wanted? Suppose the decision is simply which is best, as in "Which font should I use?" Then a statistical test is irrelevant. One should just choose the one with the best mean effect. Now, obviously, if only a small number of subjects had been run and the data are highly variable, that judgment may be little better than a guess. But the only solution is to get more or better data if one wants higher confidence; a statistical test will not help a bit. On the other hand, putting confidence intervals on the data will help one know how good the bet is.

Put this another way. You are choosing between incorporating feature *a* and feature *b* and you have tested the system with both. You do a standard statistical test and get a significance level of .33 favoring *b*. The way to read this is that chances are 2 : 1 that (*b*) is at least a little better than (*a*). Clearly, if all other things were equal about the choice, you would choose (*b*) even though a .33 significance level is often described in the academic psychological literature as "absolutely no difference." In the applications field we should get used to using statistical methods to arrive at posterior odds ratios of this kind and using them in our decisions. If one has compared two systems and wants to tell others which is better, mean differences and confidence intervals, along with an odds ratio, would properly communicate the needed information from the study.

Of course, the choice between systems or between features is seldom one in which everything else is equal; usually there are differential costs to the various possible choices. The machinery for making wise decisions under combinations of uncertainties and costs is available, but this is not something into which we can delve here. Suffice it to say that neither a yes/no significance test alone nor a mean difference alone is useful. If one wants to make an informed decision, the information needed is the estimated mean effect size along with an odds ratio and/or confidence interval.

I shall mention one last matter. It is sometimes asserted that psychological research is not useful for system design because it is too unwieldy, expensive, and slow. Usually people making this statement have in mind an elaborate experiment in which all of the potential features in a system at each of their potentially interesting values or instantiations are compared. It would be rash to claim that such experiments would not be useful, but certainly most of the criticisms of them are true. What is really wrong with the assertion of inutility is its implicit assumption that this is the only way to do psychological research on system design. In fact, at this stage of maturity in the field, it may be among the worst ways to proceed. The main reason is that the choice of variables, factors, and levels is bound to be very poorly motivated. They would have to be chosen intuitively by designers or from the infinite number of possible values available, clearly a matter of endless thrashing in a muddy morass. We have seen, above, that there are many firmer research paths to follow.

4 Applied Research on Computer System Design as a Source of Problems and Theory for Cognitive Psychology

The human mind is an artifact of human culture. Although it is not constructed by the deliberate design of a team of people, nevertheless it is just one realization of an infinitely pliable system, programmed by culture, education, the knowledge base of the society, and the demands of the tasks and environments in which it finds itself. What phenomena of human cognitive processes to study is a very difficult scientific issue. Granted that the mind is an extraordinarily flexible, general-purpose device that might perform a vast variety of tasks each in a vast variety of ways, which does the scientist who wishes to study the "real" mind choose?

I believe that we want to study the human cognitive system doing those things that it now usually does or those things that it will be doing in the future, or just possibly those that it used to do in the past. There is no sense in which we can study cognition meaningfully divorced from the task contexts in which it finds itself in the world. I assert that the human mind is a construction on the capabilities of the brain and the culture in which it is embedded, and that in studying it we must be sure that we learn about the way it would behave in just those contexts. Otherwise we shall be doing merely scholastic play (although I do, of course, admit that scholastic play may sharpen our wits for more serious work). To draw the example almost to an absurd length, consider the human cognitive system to be a structure like a bridge, and therefore cognitive psychologists to be those who are interested in understanding the structure and function of bridges. We may, of course, take the bridge apart and use the girders to construct an oil derrick or box in its bottom and float it in the ocean as a barge. But we shall then be unlikely to gain direct insights into bridges. We might learn something relevant, but we would have to be very lucky to do so. The science of mind is, I assert, not the science of what the mind can do in a laboratory situation artificially rigged to make it relevant to one of our theories, but what it does in a situation naturally or artificially rigged by itself and its culture. (I hasten to repeat, the abstracted laboratory experiment is an essential tool, but it must answer questions raised by nature, and its answers must be tested against nature.)

Given this view, the only way to find out what the mind is like, and to stumble across questions that need to be understood more fully, is to study it in its natural habitat. Since the mind does not have any set natural habitat, we need to study it in the habitats in which it frequently finds or wishes to find itself. At the moment it seems to wish to find itself in constant interaction with computer systems, so this is where we must track it down.

An added advantage of choosing computer use as a "real" task for analysis is that it also offers attractive avenues for synthesis. Once having identified the problems and issues involved in this aspect of human mental life, having then, perhaps, taken them to the laboratory and understood them better, we should be able to test the sufficiency of our knowledge by trying to design computer systems that will function better. Computers have obvious advantages for trying to construct tools based on knowledge of cognitive functions because they have the information processing power to become involved in interactive tasks that include communications, information storage, inference, problem solving, and the like. The opportunity to try to build artifacts that interact with human cognition was extremely restricted before the advent of computer systems, but is much more open now. A concrete example might help to clarify this point. If we really understood the fundamentals of reading and its dominating, or rate-limiting factors, we might be able to build ways of presenting text that would materially increase the speed and accuracy of comprehension. The flexibility of computer systems ought to help us realize ideas of this kind and test them, thus giving us a rather new and powerful way to try out our theories.

One of the chief advantages of using applied cognitive tasks as a source of research problems is that the level of analysis, the kinds of components and processes, that become part of our theories will be dictated by what is important to human cognitive life, rather than by pretheoretical preferences for some style of explanation on the part of the scientist. An example is found in the work on indexing and information retrieval mentioned above. This started with no preconceptions of what kinds of theory or psychology might be relevant, and was forced to consider the distribution of word use in reference, and thus such matters as the difference between the distribution of word use within people and in populations, and so forth. This level of analysis was unlikely to have arisen from traditional cognitive psychology, but turns out to be the one needed to understand a very significant problem in human cognitive life. If one reacts to the work that resulted as not being relevant to cognitive theory, I think one must think very carefully about which is at fault. I believe it is just this kind of confrontation that is among the most worthwhile outcomes of the developing relationship between cognitive psychology and computer system design.

5 Summary

The dominant characteristic of work on human cognition in the context of computer design is that computer systems and the tasks and problems with which they help people are large and complex. The tasks tend to involve many detailed cognitive processes going on simultaneously and successively, and the designs of interactive procedures have an enormous number of details, any one of which may affect the interactive performance. This causes many problems. It means that previous research findings and theories are likely, at best, to be relevant to only a small portion of the total situation. It means that testing the effectiveness of one total system against that of others is likely to yield information of extremely limited generality. What one will have tested is "one mess against another." So many differences will exist between one system and another that the features or factors to blame or credit will be obscure. By the same token, some traditional methods, like factorial experiments, will not be very practical. There are too many features to examine, and the likelihood of interactions among effects not included in the experiments is too great.

It seems to me that mutually beneficial relations between cognitive psychology and system design can nevertheless occur. The essence of the investigative procedure I advocate is as follows. The investigator, applied psychologist, or system designer should set up a situation in which people doing a task that is, one hopes, to be aided by a computer system can be observed and recorded in some detail. From this the range of problems that are encountered and the things that people, novice or expert, can do well are noted. In the system design process, often the difficulties noticed will have obvious solutions and a fix can be made in the next iteration. This process of tuning a design by iterative user testing has been found extremely effective, for example, in the development of the Apple Lisa and Macintosh systems, which profited from very frequent user tests conducted by the applications software manager himself. Notice that features found at fault in such a process are identified in a context that is very realistic and includes most of the complexity under which the user will actually operate. Note also that traditional experimental design is neither terribly useful nor necessary for this process. One wants to observe and discover the kinds of difficulties being experienced; guessing ahead of time what factors to vary and control in an experiment might be hopeless. Moreover, the appropriate statistical test is "Which is the best bet?" rather than "Are we sure?" so while more data makes one surer, large effects observed with a handful of subjects are a sufficient screening method to help improve tuning. It really does not matter a great deal whether sometimes the tuning is done wrong because the observation was really a chance result, at least if the decision is not costly in programming time or system resources. In any event, the question of how much data should be collected and what level of certainty achieved can be weighed against anticipated costs and benefits.

This is fine for system development, but what it does it have to do with the science of human cognition? I maintain that the same process is well suited for generating the problems and serving as a testing ground for investigations of true scientific value in cognitive psychology. When particular problems are encountered repeatedly and found to be severe, in the context of a fully working (or partly working) system, but the fix or cure for the problems is not obvious to the designer, one has identified a prime candidate for deeper research. These problems suggest variables that are important to human performance and that need studying. Moreover, having subjected them to whatever study methods are needed for fuller understanding, the psychologist is in a position to test that new understanding by trying to design a system that overcomes the problem. And again the test will occur in just the right context, embedded in all of the complexity in which humans function.

Thus, it seems to me, a research cycle that starts and ends—or at least starts and periodically return to—full-scale system design problems is a very promising way to do and use cognitive psychology. By no means is it the only good way. Certainly the more traditional and academic pursuits of trying to understand obviously important cognitive processes like perception and reading will continue to be the mainstream of the field. Nevertheless I believe that the increasing interaction of cognitive psychology with the particular design problems of a cognitively rich and powerful device can be of great benefit to both.

Note

1. Card, Moran and Newell present variability data only in terms of the coefficient of variability, sd/mean (sd = standard deviation). Unfortunately, this index does not have additive properties, so one cannot use it directly to analyze or compare

component sources of variation. The estimate given here was made by a crude reconstruction of the underlying variances, assuming the times for error and error-free components to be uncorrelated.

References

Barnard, P., Hammond, N., Maclean, A., and Morton, J. (1982). Learning and remembering interactive commands in a text-editing task. *Behavior and Information Technology*, 1, 347–358.

Black, J. B., and Sebrechts, M. M. (1981). Facilitating human-computer communications. *Applied Psycholinguistics*, 2, 149–177.

Card, S. K., English, W. K., and Burr, B. J. (1978). Evaluation of mouse, rate-controlled isometric joystick, step keys, and text keys for text selection on a CRT. *Ergonomics*, 21, 601–613.

Card, S. K., Moran, T. P., and Newell, A. (1983). *The Psychology of Human-Computer Interaction*, Hillsdale, NJ, Lawrence Erlbaum.

Carroll, J. M. (1982). Learning, using and designing file-names and command paradigms. *Behavior and Information Technology*, 1, 327–346.

Egan, D. E., and Gomez, L. M. (1985). Assaying, isolating, and accommodating individual differences in learning a complex skill. In R. Dillon (Ed.), *Individual Differences in Cognition*, Vol. 2, New York, Academic Press.

Ehrenreich, S. L. (1985). Computer abbreviations: evidence and synthesis. *Human Factors*, 27, 143–155.

Ehrenreich, S. L., and Porcu, T. A. (1982). Abbreviations for automated systems: Teaching operators the rules. In A. Badre and B. Schneiderman (Eds.) *Directions in Human Computer Interaction*, Norwood, NJ, Ablex, pp. 111–135.

Fitts, P. M. (1954). The information capacity of the human motor system in controlling amplitude of movement. *Journal of Experimental Psychology*, 47, 381–391.

Furnas, G. W., Landauer, T. K., Gomez, L. M., and Dumais, S. T. (1983). Statistical semantics: Analysis of the potential performance of keyword information systems. *Bell System Technical Journal*, 62, 1753–1806. Also in J. C. Thomas and M. Schneider (Eds.), *Human Factors and Computer Systems*, Norwood, NJ, Ablex, 1983.

Gomez, L. M., and Lochbaum, C. C. (1984). People can retrieve more objects with enriched key-word vocabularies. But is there a human performance cost? *Proceedings of Interact 1984*, Amsterdam, Elsevier.

Goss, A. E., and Nadine, C. F. (1965). *Paired-Associate Learning. The Role of Meaningfulness, Similarity and Familiarization*, New York, Academic Press.

Gould, J. D., Conti, J., and Hovanyecz, T. (1983). Composing letters with a simulated listening typewriter. *Communications of the ACM*, 26, 295–308.

Grudin, J., and Barnard, P. (1984). The cognitive demands of learning and representing names for text editing. *Human Factors*, 26.

Hirsch-Pasek, K., Nudelman, S., and Schneider, M. L. (1982). An experimental evaluation of abbreviation schemes in limited lexicons. *Behavior and Information Technology*, 1, 359–369.

Landauer, T. K., and Galotti, K. A. (1984). What makes a difference when? Comments on Grudin and Barnard. *Human Factors*, 26, 423–429.

Landauer, T. K., and Nachbar, D. W. (1985). Selection from alphabetic and numeric menu trees using a touch screen: Breadth, depth and width. *CHI '85 Proceedings* (special issue of *SIGCHI*), New York, ACM.

Landauer, T. K., Galotti, K. A., and Hartwell, S. (1983). Natural command names and initial learning: A study of text-editing terms. *Communications of ACM*, 26, 495–503.

Ledgard, H., Whiteside, J. A., Singer, A., and Seymour, W. (1980). The natural language of interactive systems. *Communication of ACM*, 23, 110, 556–563.

Miller, D. P. (1981). The depth/breadth tradeoff in heirarchical computer menus. *Proceedings of the Human Factors Society*, pp. 296–300.

Miller, G. A. Galanter, E., and Pribram, K. H. (1960). *Plans and the Structure of Behavior*, New York, Holt, Rinehart and Winston.

Newell, A., and Simon, H. A. (1972). *Human Problem Solving*, Englewood Cliffs, NJ, Prentice-Hall.

Norman, D. A. (1981). The trouble with UNIX. *Datamation*, 27, 139–150.

Olson, J. R., and Nilsen, E. (1985). Analysis of the cognition involved in software interaction. Paper at 26th meeting, Psychonomic Society, Boston.

Payne, S. J., and Green, T. R. G. (1983). The user's perception of the interaction language: A two level model. In A. Janda (Ed.), *CHI '83 Conference Proceedings.*

Polson, P. G., and Kieras, D. E. (1985). A quantitative model of the learning and performance of text editing knowledge. In *CHI '85 Conference Proceedings* (special issue of *SIGCHI*), New York, ACM.

Postman, L. (1971). Transfer, interference and forgetting. In J. W. Kling and L. A. Riggs (Eds.), *Woodworth and Schlosberg's Experimental Psychology*, 3rd edition, New York, Hoft, Rinehart and Winston.

Reisner, P. (1981). Formal grammer and human factors design of an interactive software system. *IEEE Transactions on Software Engineering*, SE-7, 229–240.

Scapin, D. L. (1981). Computer commands in restricted natural language: Some aspects of memory of experience. *Human Factors, 23,* 365–375.

Snowberry, K., Parkinson, S. R., and Sisson, N. (1983). Computer display menus. *Ergonomics, 26,* 699–712.

Streeter, L. A., Ackroff, J. M., and Taylor, G. A. (1983). On abbreviating command names. *The Bell System Technical Journal, 62,* 1807–1828.

Tullis, T. S. (1985). Designing a menu-based interface to an operating system. *CHI '85 Proceedings* (special issue of *SIGCHI*), New York, ACM.

Underwood, B. J., and Schultz, R. W. (1960). *Meaningfulness and Verbal Learning,* Philadelphia, Lippincott.

Welford, A. T. (1980). Choice reaction time: Basic concepts. In A. T. Welford (Ed.), *Reaction Time,* New York, Academic.

2 Learning about Computers and Learning about Mathematics

Clayton H. Lewis

1 Cognitive Psychologists Are Studying Learning of Real-Life Skills, Including Elementary Mathematics and Computer Use

Over the last ten years students of learning have been carrying their ideas and methods out of the laboratory and examining learning of real-life skills. One area of study has been elementary mathematics, where investigators have uncovered much new information about how arithmetic and elementary algebra are learned. Another area recently attracting attention is computer use. Both university and industrial research groups are active in the effort to understand what happens when novices confront computers.

A comparison of findings can shed light on theory. Workers in both areas have a composite agenda. They wish to master the problems particular to the chosen domain, for immediate practical reasons, but they also wish to learn something general about how people learn that might produce insights of greater generality, that is, ideas about learning and problem solving with validity across domains. Accordingly, it is important to compare what has been learned in different domains to see how far common mechanisms and effects can be discerned. Finding differences instead of commonalities is important too. When they are unexpected they indicate the limitations of our understanding of the mechanisms involved, and when they are expected they confirm our ideas about what is happening within particular domains.

When computers are introduced as teaching aids the problems of the two domains are intertwined. Another reason to compare findings is that the two domains, until now quite separate, will be brought together as computers

---

The ideas in this chapter are based on work supported by IBM and the National Science Foundation. John Carroll and the members of the Watson Research Center Psychology Reading Group made valuable comments

are introduced into the algebra classroom. Students will be learning mathematics but also learning enough about the computerized teaching system to control it appropriately. One can anticipate that some of the problems and processes discovered in studies of learning to use computers will surface in the classroom in this situation.

In exploring these ideas I will be drawing largely on work that I and my collaborators have done (Mack, Lewis, and Carroll, 1983; Carry, Lewis, and Bernard, 1979; Lewis, 1980). Carry, Lewis, and Bernard (1979) present the findings from a study of equation-solving in elementary algebra in which thinking-aloud protocols were collected from college students with varying levels of skill. Mack, Lewis, and Carroll (1983) summarize findings from thinking-aloud studies of adults learning to use text-processing systems.

This restricted coverage will leave out a very important aspect of the interaction between computer use and mathematics, the possible conceptual overlap between the two domains. The work of the Logo community (e.g., Papert, 1980; Abelson and DiSessa, 1981), Eliot Soloway (Soloway, Lochhead, and Clements, 1982), and others suggests that the idea of procedure that is made explicit when students learn to program can be very useful in thinking about elementary mathematics. For example, Soloway, Lochhead, and Clements show that errors that are common when students are asked to write an equation describing the relationship between two quantities are much less common if the students are instead asked to write a program to calculate one quantity from the other. Lewis (1980) discusses the application of a semantics based on calculation to algebra problems that are difficult for students who are using a semantics based on symbol manipulation; the calculational semantics might well be easier to grasp if students were working in an environment in which they constructed and manipulated programs in addition to equations.

Unfortunately the studies of computer learning on which I draw here shed no real light on these possibilities. The learners are working with menu-based systems in which procedures are not made explicit and cannot be manipulated. Thus there appears to be little overlap of *concepts* between the computer and mathematical domains; accordingly the discussion will center on comparisons of the learning *processes*.

2 A Number of Common Themes Emerge from These Studies

Both elementary math and computer use are difficult. Many college students cannot solve even simple problems in algebra after years of instruction.

Text-processing learners achieve mastery on the job in much less time than that, but weeks of frustrating work may be required even for someone who is a skilled office worker and typist. Protocols from both domains show uncertainty and self-doubt accompanying the learners' efforts.

Poor feedback is a problem in both domains. Students of algebra receive little feedback on the correctness of their attempts. The feedback that is available is usually delayed and nonspecific, so that students have trouble identifying the particular steps in a solution that are in error. Text-processing learners are somewhat better off, in that more of their actions evoke some response from the computer, but the response is often difficult to interpret. For example, one system responds to commands with the prompt READY. This serves to signal an experienced user that the previous command has been successfully processed, but it gives the learner no information about what the effect of that command was. It says, in effect, "I have just done whatever it was you asked me to do," while the learner needs to know what the thing asked for really was. In both domains learners have difficulty improving their procedures using such impoverished information about their effects.

Both skills are influenced by positive and negative transfer. Equation solving requires students to carry over previously acquired knowledge of arithmetic. Much of the carry-over is positive (see, for example, the discussion of knowledge of fractional arithmetic in Larkin, 1978), while Davis (1983) argues that some is negative. For example, Matz (1980) attributes mistaken applications of factoring, as in statement I, to carrying over the idea from arithmetic that procedures are not restricted to particular numbers.

I Use of factoring in solving quadratic equations: (a) Correct: Given $(x - 1)(x - 2) = 0$, then $(x - 1) = 0$ or $(x - 2) = 0$. (b) Incorrect: Given $(x - 1)(x - 2) = 1$, then $(x - 1) = 1$ or $(x - 2) = 1$.

Similarly, using a text processor builds on typing skills for the entry of text, but some ideas about typewriters are violated by most text processors. For example, the CARRIAGE RETURN key functions as expected when new text is being entered, but causes a line to be split in most systems if it is pressed when the typing point is in the middle of existing text. One of the learner's tasks is to change his or her typing procedures as necessary to accommodate such differences, and many errors and confusions results.

Both skills require difficult discriminations. Patterns of errors in algebra suggest that learners group together distinct operations whose effect on expressions is generally similar. Thus in statement IIa the operations of dividing by a and subtracting a both give the effect of deleting a from both sides of an equation. Statement IIb shows an error that results if these two deletions are treated as the same operation. It appears that addition and multiplication, which add symbols to expressions, may also be grouped together. Statement IIIa shows two correct operations that involve counting the occurrences of a symbol and replacing them by one occurrence of the symbol qualified by the count. Statement IIIb shows two errors that result from failing to distinguish the detailed behavior of these similar operators.

II Deletion operations: (a) Correct: $x + a = b + a \rightarrow x = b$, $ax = ab \rightarrow x = b$ (correct when a is not zero). (b) Incorrect: $ax = b + a \rightarrow x = b$.

III Recombination operations: (a) Correct: $x + x + x \rightarrow 3x$, $xxx \rightarrow x^3$. (b) Incorrect: $p + p \rightarrow p^2$, $ax + bx + ab \rightarrow 2a + 2b + 2x$.

Text-processor learners are also expected to learn to discriminate operations whose visible effect is similar, and they too make errors as a result. Many systems offer several different ways to delete text, where the scope of the deletion may be determined differently for different operations. For example, one system has an operation that deletes a line of text completely, and another that deletes a line of text, leaving a blank line in its place. Learners have trouble mastering this distinction.

One system offers two ways of viewing text that extends beyond the limits of the display screen. When interacting with the text-editing portion of the system, one set of function keys controls this. When one is interacting with other portions of the system, a different key is used. Learners made many errors by pressing the wrong keys, indicating the difficulty of learning this distinction.

In both skills difficulties interact. Since the learners' ability to detect and analyze errors is limited, the effect of one error is often to cause others to occur. In algebra, if a student makes an arithmetic error in checking the solution to an equation, the effect may be to suggest that some correct operation carried out during the solution was really a mistake. Similarly, a text-processor learner may misinterpret the effects on an action because of an error in carrying out some other action. One learner concluded that many keys had no effect because he was trying them out at a time when by an earlier undetected error he had disabled the keyboard.

Learners have an impression of uncertainty in predictable domains. I have often been struck by comments that mathematics is "inconsistent," or that a computer's behavior is "unpredictable." Learners are often very unsure whether their ideas will prove correct or not at any given time. Both mathematics and computers are constructed to be consistent and predictable to a degree that exceeds anything else people are likely to experience, so what accounts for these contrary perceptions?

The problems described above suggest an answer. To see the consistency of mathematics or a computer, one must have the right analysis, one that makes all the necessary distinctions. One has to see the difference between deletions that result from dividing and deletions that come from subtraction. One has to see the difference between interacting with the editor in a system and interacting with some other part. On the way to acquiring these discriminations, a process lengthened by the impoverished feedback in both situations, an impression of consistency or predictability could result only from faith, and would be repeatedly contradicted by the experience of seeing one's evolving conceptions proved false by further experience.

3 There Are Divergences between the Learning Processes for the Two Skills

Against these similarities must be placed a number of diferences: Computer learning shows more looping, less backup, more problems in deciding on the relevance of information, and more abduction.

Computer learners may try the same thing repeatedly. There are many opportunities in learning elementary mathematics to construct procedures that if executed faithfully would loop forever. But learners seem to detect such difficulties and carry out a repair of the offending procedure that terminates the loop (see Van Lehn, 1983). While not common, long loops are occasionally observed in text-processor learners, who may execute essentially the same commands many times in succession.

Jack Carroll and Caroline Carrithers (personal communication) observed a learner trying the same incorrect operation 44 times consecutively. While the learner did vary the operation somewhat, sometimes intentionally and sometimes by error, all the attempts appeared to be intended to carry out a single operation that had worked the first time the learner tried it but then failed to work. The underlying problem was that when the operation, creating a document with a given name, was first carried out, it changed the state of the system in such a way that it could not be repeated, since creating a document with a name that had already been used was forbidden.

Computer learners have trouble selecting relevant information to attend to. Presentation of problems in mathematics is commonly restricted to the information necessary to solve the problem, though (rarely) word problems may include irrelevant facts. Equation solvers, for example, do not face the task of deciding which portions of the problem statement should be attended to and which ignored. In contrast, computing systems commonly display a wide variety of information, little of which is important for a particular task. A typical menu presents a mixture of requests for basic input that is always needed and requests for input relevant only to advanced and specialized tasks. Learners often have difficulty separating the two, and many errors and misconceptions result from attending to irrelevant information.

The vulnerability of computer learners to these relevance problems can be illustrated by a problem with a word-processor manual studied by Mack, Lewis, and Carroll (1983). It contained a small picture of the workstation to clarify the location of certain prompt information on the screen. The picture showed not just the screen but also other features of the front of the workstation, presumably to provide context. Barely visible in the picture was the power switch, which could just be seen to be in the OFF position. One learner saw this, and worried aloud whether this meant that he should have his workstation turned off for the current exercise. Fortunately he decided to proceed without turning his machine off.

Computer learners engage in abductive reasoning. Abduction (Peirce, 1958) is the reasoning process by which causes are inferred from their consequences. Thus if an event *A* is observed, and it is known that a circumstance *B* would explain *A*, then the truth of *B* may be hypothesized. Thinking-aloud protocols reveal that computer learners construct explanations of what they see as they work with the system (Lewis and Mack, 1982). There is no analogous process evident in protocols from equation solvers.

One computer learner (described in Lewis and Mack, 1982) misunderstood some instructions and found herself moving the cursor around on the screen of her word processor without actually entering any text. She concluded that she was creating a template by moving the cursor around the screen into which text would later be placed. Thus she dealt with the apparent oddity of the process she was seeing by making up a plausible story that could explain it.

By contrast, equation solvers seem quite lacking in curiosity about the rationale for the steps they perform. They seem to regard these symbolic operations as moves in a game like chess, whose rules are the way they are for no accessible reason.

What is behind these divergences? Are they accidental consequences of arbitrary differences between the way elementary math is taught and the way word-processor learners approach their task? It seems not. In the next section I argue that the contrasts are traceable to a single, essential difference between the learning situations.

4 The Learner Has to Learn What He or She Must Do in Either Domain, but the Computer Learner Must also Learn What the Computer Will Do

All of the divergences discussed above can be attributed to the presence of the computer. The mathematics learner works in a situation in which his or her actions in solving a problem have trivially predictable outcomes, in that writing something on a piece of paper has no interesting side effects. The writing appears, and that is that. In contrast, the computer learner's actions have effects mediated by the computer. Pressing a key may cause almost anything to happen, and often, even typically, the same key press will produce different effects at different times.

In this situation behavior that is irrational for the equation solver is rational for the text-processor learner. While it is clearly silly to suppose that writing down identical steps repeatedly can lead to any good outcome, it is quite reasonable to think that a command that did not work a moment ago might work now. In fact there are many cases in which this is true. Not only are there complex state and timing dependences in many systems, but at least one system is deliberately programmed in such a way that the nth repeated request for a certain action will be honored, while the first $n - 1$ requests are denied. Carroll and Carrithers's learner described above encountered the opposite case, in which an operation worked only the first time it was tried. Norman (1983) found that calculator users often pressed CLEAR repeatedly when starting a new problem; many calculators are designed so that repeated pressings really are needed if one wishes to clear the machine completely.

Because a computer, even a "dedicated" text-processing system, is normally designed to support a wide variety of tasks, the interface it presents to the learner usually contains information that is irrelevant to any given task. This poses the problem of information selection.

Abduction is the natural way to cope with controlling one's computer partner. Since one must be able to predict what it will do in response to one's own actions, one has to construct some sort of model (in a general sense) of the computer, including some way to identify the states it can be in and what the transitions among these states are. Because of the state dependence of its response to one's actions, no simpler notion will suffice.

The abductive behavior described by Lewis and Mack (1982) can be seen as building just such a model. The learner keeps track of what the computer is doing and why, that is, what changes of state are occurring and how they relate to the learner's actions, on the one hand, and the goal of the sequence of actions, on the other. This activity is not needed when solving an equation, because at least the immediate outcome of any action is clear.

Another effect of the computer on the learning system is to restrict the learner's freedom to correct sequences of actions. Working in one's head or on paper, one is free to go back to an earlier step and try another option, if one does not like the way things are going. Van Lehn (1983) discusses "backup repairs," in which learners who encounter an impasse in an arithmetic problem return to an earlier step in their solution and take another path.

The computer learner may wish to back up, but cannot do so unless the computer cooperates. Commonly the learner's actions have changed the state of the computer in a way that may not be easy to reverse. For example, an exercise in text processing may require the learner to create a new document, giving it a name, and then enter some text. If the learner makes mistakes in entering the text, and wishes to start the exercise over, the computer may very well not permit the steps that worked before to be repeated. This is because the operation of creating a document cannot be carried out if the document already exists, as it will on the second attempt.

At this level of analysis, then, the salient differences between the domains can be accounted for without any stress on the theories that might be developed within either one. This can be seen as good or bad, depending on whether one likes to think of our theories as being adequate or would prefer to see new ideas generated by extending them to new areas.

The reader must keep in mind that this discussion continues to ignore some deeper issues in the relationship between the domains, where the content of concepts about computing might interact with concepts about mathematics. Exploring these issues will require a more profound analysis that takes in what learners learn about computers, rather than concentrating, as here, on the characteristics of the learning process. It is interesting in this respect that work on mathematics learning has so far concentrated on ideas about what is learned and given less attention to the process, while work on learning about computers leans the other way. A more complete consideration of the relationships between the domains may await the redress of these imbalances.

5 This Burden of Dealing with the Computer as well as the Task Creates Challenges in Structuring Learning Environments Where Computers Are Used

On the practical side, these observations about the special problems of learning to deal with a computer should have impact on the design of computer aids to math pedagogy. They suggest that attention to the conceptual mathematical content of student interactions will not be sufficient for success, and that anticipating and counteracting the special problems of learning about the computer will also be essential. John Anderson has already remarked that user interface aids, such as spelling correction, have proved essential to the success of a sophisticated tutoring program in geometry (Anderson et al., 1984).

What design initiatives are likely to help? From a large literature (see, e.g., Mack, Lewis, and Carroll, 1983; Card, Moran, and Newell, 1983; Shneiderman, 1983; Carroll and Mack, 1984) two points may be selected. First, the complexity of the interface to be learned is decisive. As noted above, learner problems tend to compound, so that the difficulties to be associated with a collection of design features cannot be thought of as the sum of their separate difficulties, but more like a product. This puts (or should put) designers under extreme pressure to simplify, and to eliminate even seemingly trivial sources of confusion.

Second, it appears that learning to control a computer requires that learners be given some initiative; building an adequate model of an interface seems very difficult without the chance to experiment and explore. This brings with it a number of design requirements, including salience of the action repertoire at any point, clarity of feedback about the effects of learner actions, and the ability to recover from undesired effects of actions to pave the way for new attempts.

In addition to identifying the conceptual content they wish to convey, designers of instructional systems will need to understand and deal with these constraints.

References

Abelson, H., and DiSessa, A. (1981). *Turtle Geometry*, Cambridge MA, MIT Press.

Anderson, J. R., Boyle, F., Farrell, R., and Reiser, B. (1984). Cognitive principles in the design of computer tutors. Presented at IBM Institute on Software Human Factors, Davos, Switzerland, August 6–10.

Card, S. K., Moran, T. P., and Newell, A. (1983). *The Psychology of Human-Computer Interaction,* Hillsdale, NJ, Erlbaum.

Carroll, J. M., and Mack, R. L. (1984). Learning to use a word processor: By doing, by thinking, and by knowing. In J. Thomas and M. Schneider (Eds.), *Human Factors in Computing Systems,* Norwood, NJ, Ablex, pp. 13–52.

Carry, L. R., Lewis, C. H., and Bernard, J. E. (1979). Psychology of equation solving: An information processing study. Department of Curriculum and Instruction, University of Texas, Austin.

Davis, R. B. (1983). Complex mathematical cognition. In Herbert Ginsburg (Ed.), *The Development of Mathematical Thinking,* New York, Academic Press, pp. 253–290.

Larkin, K. M. (1978). An analysis of adult procedure synthesis in fraction problems. ICAI Report 14, Bolt Beranek and Newman, Cambridge, MA.

Lewis, C. H. (1980). Kinds of knowledge in algebra. Presented at American Educational Research Association Annual Meeting, Boston, 1980. (Available from ERIC.)

Lewis, C. H., and Mack, R. L. (1982). The role of abduction in learning to use a computer system. Research Report RC 9433, IBM Corporation, Yorktown Heights, NY.

Mack, R. L., Lewis, C. H., and Carroll, J. M. (1983). Learning to use word processors: Problems and prospects. *ACM Transactions on Office Information Systems,* 1, 254–271.

Matz, M. (1980). Towards a computational model of algebraic competence. *Journal of Mathematical Behavior,* 93–166.

Norman, D. A. (1983). Some observations on mental models. In Dedre Gentner and Albert Stevens (Eds.), *Mental Models,* Hillsdale, NJ, Erlbaum, pp. 7–14.

Papert, S. (1980) *Mindstorms,* New York, Basic Books.

Peirce, C. S. (1958). The logic of drawing history from ancient documents. In A. Burks (Ed.), *Collected Papers of Charles Sanders Peirce,* Cambridge, MA, Harvard University Press.

Shneiderman, B. (1983). Direct Manipulation: A step beyond programming languages. *Computer,* 57–69.

Soloway, E., Lochhead, J., and Clements, J. (1982). Does computer programming enhance problem solving ability? In Robert Seidel, Robert Anderson, and Beverly Hunter (Eds.), *The Goals of Computer Literacy in 1985,* New York, Academic Press, pp. 171–215.

Van Lehn, K. (1923). On the representation of procedures in repair theory. In H. Ginsburg (Ed.), *The Development of Mathematical Thinking,* New York, Academic Press, pp. 253–290.

3

Goal and Plan Knowledge Representations: From Stories to Text Editors and Programs

John B. Black, Dana S. Kay, and Elliot M. Soloway

Almost all of human behavior can be characterized in terms of goals and plans. In particular, most of what people do is devise plans of action and perform them in order to bring about some desired state of the world—that is, to accomplish a goal. Consequently, much of human knowledge about how to operate in the world is stored in memory in the form of plan and goal knowledge representations. The importance of goals and plans to human behavior is an important insight of modern cognitive psychology that was first pointed out by Miller, Galanter, and Pribram (1960). Curiously, there have been few studies of everyday human planning, but the goal-plan approach has been especially important and well-developed in the study of story understanding. More recently, goal and plan analyses have proven valuable in the study of human-computer interaction—both for interactive command language systems like text editors and for programming language systems. In this chapter, we show the value of using goal and plan knowledge representations to understand human behavior by examining the insights this approach has provided for the study of how people understand stories, how they learn and use computerized text editors, and how they program computers. We point out the parallel results in these three different domains and, perhaps more important, point out when there is a result in one domain that has not been investigated in one or two of the other domains. These areas of discrepancy seem like fruitful topics for future research.

1 Story Understanding

A crucial part of understanding or writing stories is using our knowledge of goals and plans to make inferences that link story statements into memory representations comprised of goals and plans (Schank and Abelson, 1977; Black, 1984; Black, Wilkes-Gibbs, and Gibbs, 1982). Evidence sup-

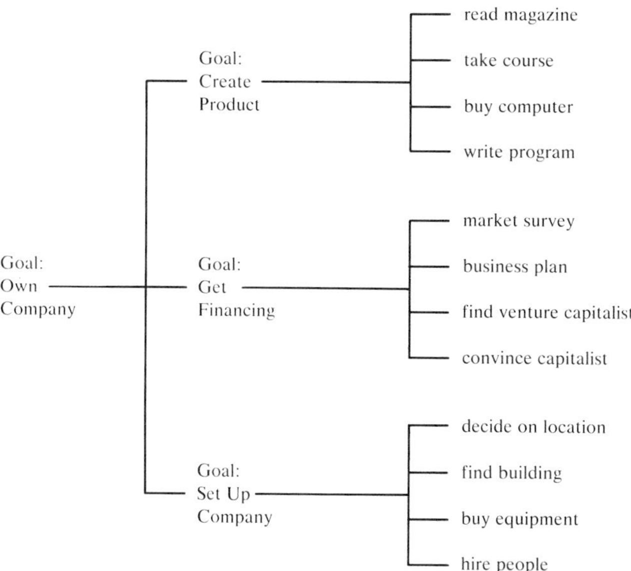

Figure 3.1
Goal-plan representation of a story.

porting this statement comes from results showing that readers store story information in memory using plan-based episode units and that when readers make goal-plan inferences linking story statement, the stories are more coherent and better remembered later. We shall examine these results, but first what does a goal-plan representation for a story look like?

Figure 3.1 gives a simplified goal-plan representation for the following example story:

Jim wanted to have a high-technology company of his own so he set out to start one. First he needed a product to sell, so he read the popular computer magazines, and took some courses in computer programming at a local college. He bought his own personal computer than spent many long nights writing a program he thought he could sell. Finally he completed the program, so now he needed financing to set up the company to sell the program and develop related programs. He conducted a marketing survey to determine the market for a program like his, then wrote a business plan for the company using the results from this survey. He researched venture capital companies and chose some to go see. After presenting his plan to several venture capitalists he found one that was willing to give him a substantial sum of money to start his business. Thus he was now ready to actually set up the company. He decided that Santa Clara County, California, was the best place for such a company since there were so many computer-related companies in that area. However, the area was very much in demand, so he had a hard time finding a suitable building for his company, but he finally did. He advertised in the computer trade magazines and newspapers for employees, then hired a number of good ones after interviewing the enormous number that applied. He bought the needed equipment at a discount and opened for business. Now Jim was happy because he had his own high-technology company.

In this story and in the goal-plan representation for it given in figure 3.1, the main story character has the overall goal of having his own company, but to accomplish that goal he must accomplish three subgoals, namely, creating a product to sell, getting financing for the company, and then actually setting up the company. Thus in the representation in figure 3.1, this top-level goal (to the left of the figure) is directly linked to these three subgoals. Each of the three subgoals in turn is linked to actions (rightmost in figure 3.1) that comprise plans for accomplishing them. For example, the main story character accomplishes the subgoal of creating the product by performing the actions of reading computer magazines, taking a programming course, buying a computer, and then writing a computer program. These goals together with their plan actions are the episodes of the story, so this example is a three-episode story.

If the information in stories is stored in memory in the form shown in figure 3.1, then there are a number of predictions that we can make and test in psychology experiments. Specifically, this representations shows the plan actions being stored in memory in somewhat independent memory units or chunks (the major subtrees or branches of the representation in figure 3.1), so one prediction is that the actions in different plans would be somewhat independent of one another in memory. Another kind of implication of this memory representation is that many goal-plan inferences will have to be made because the connections between the goals and the plan actions in the representation are not explicitly stated in the text. For example, the story text does not explicitly state that the story character bought a computer in order to create a product; the readers have to infer that connection using their own knowledge about the world. As we now describe, both of these kinds of predictions have been verified.

Black and Bower (1979) tested the independent memory unit prediction and found that goal-plan episodes showed independence in recall. In particular, they manipulated the length of episodes and found that the length of an episode affected the recall of the actions in that episode but not the recall of actions in other episodes. For example, one story used had an overall goal of trying to find a book on a university campus. The story consisted of two episodes: one episode described trying to find the book in the library, while the other described trying to find the book in the university bookstore. Black and Bower created a "short" version of each episode by including three actions in service of the goal (entering the library, looking in the card catalog, and finding the book location) and the outcome (the book was not there). They also created a "long" version of each episode by including five other actions (e.g., asking the librarian about the book). Adding the five actions in a given episode increased the recall of the original goal, outcome, and three actions for that episode, but had no effect on the statements in the other episode. Thus the goal-plan episodes showed independence in recall, and adding more statements so as to fill in the gaps between episode statements increased their recall.

Haberlandt (1980) found reading time evidence for episodes as independent memory units. In particular, when he measured the reading time for each statement in a story, he found that readers spent a relatively long time reading the beginnings and ends of episodes. This finding indicates that each time readers encounter a new episode, they spend time in the beginning activating the plan knowledge needed to understand the rest of the episode and at the end they pause to integrate and store the entire episode in memory. Thus Haberlandt's reading time results complement the memory results of Black and Bower in validating the hypothesis that goal-plan episodes are processing and memory units in story understanding.

The effects of goal-plan hierarchy on recall provide another kind of evidence that goal-plan episodes are basic building blocks in the memory representation of a story. Sometimes stories form a hierarchy of goals in which attempts to attain a goal evoke other goals that have to be attained first. In such cases, the episodes for the subordinate goals are embedded in the episode for the overall goal. For example, if we revised the "company" story given earlier so that the main character needed to get a college degree in computer science to create his product, then there would be a going-to-college episode embedded in and subordinate to the creating-the-product episode. Numerous investigators (e.g., Thorndyke, 1977; Black and Bower, 1980; Graesser, 1980) have found that the more subordinate such episodes are (i.e., the lower in the goal-plan hierarchy), the worse they are recalled. This finding is consistent with a memory retrieval process that starts at the top of the goal-plan hierarchy and works its way down. Thus the lower in the hierarchy an item is, the more likely that at least one connection will have been forgotten, so the more likely the item is to be irretrievable. Since goal-based episodes are the basic units of analysis in these hierarchies, these results also validate their value.

There have also been several studies that validate the inferencing predictions of goal-plan representations. Abbott and Black (1986) compared readers' recall of statements in a story that were connected either by repetition of several common concepts or by goal-plan inferences. The results showed that if one statement was recalled from a goal-plan set, then the other statements in the set were likely to be recalled, whereas the statement recall in the concept-repetition sets were basically independent. Abbott and Black also found that the time to recognize a statement as having been in the story was faster when it was preceded by another story statement from a goal-plan set, but that no speedup occurred when it was preceded by a statement from a concept-repetition set.

The harder it is for a reader to establish the goal-plan connections in a story, the longer it takes to read the story. Seifert, Robertson, and Black (1985) found that when they left a goal or plan statement to be inferred, the next statement in the story took longer to read then when the goal or plan statement was explicitly stated. For example, the last statement in

He wanted to be king.
He was tired of waiting.
He thought arsenic would work well.

took longer in this version than when the plan ("He decided to poison the king.") was explicitly stated (here it would be inserted as the next to last statement). However, even when such statements are omitted, readers later claim that they actually read them. This result is what we would expect if the readers were making these inferences during comprehension in order to construct a goal-plan memory representation of the story. Bower, Black, and Turner (1979) found similar false memory and reading time results, and in addition found that the readers tended to recall statements in the order called for by a plan rather than the order presented in the story. This result is what we would expect if the readers link the statements together into a plan unit in memory using their preexisting knowledge about plans, then use that plan representation to guide the memory retrieval.

If the plans we use to understand stories are much the same as the plans we use in everyday life, then it should be possible to learn plans by reading stories that we then use in other contexts. Gick and Holyoak (1980) tested this notion and found that there was little transfer to solving a problem even when a story using the plan needed to solve the problem was read immediately before the problem was tackled. For example, they gave their subjects the classic "radiation" problem frequently used in problem solving research. To solve this problem the subjects have to realize that they can break a lethal dosage radiation source into weaker sources, then focus the rays on a tumor so that they kill the tumor and not the good tissue surrounding it.

This is a fairly difficult problem to solve, so Gick and Holyoak gave the subjects a hint by having them read a story in which a king in one country invaded and conquered a castle in a neighboring country by breaking up his army into small groups who took different routes to the castle and seized the castle while avoiding the other army. Thus this story, like the radiation problem, involves a focusing plan. However, reading this story did not help the subjects solve the problem. With more research, however, Gick and Holyoak (1983) found that such transfer of plan knowledge does indeed take place, but that the subjects had to read two stories embodying the plan in different contexts before they used it to solve the problem. It seems that to abstract general, context-independent plans that we can use later, we need to be exposed to at least two specific examples of the plans. We shall return to this important transfer issue later in another context.

2 Using Interactive Command Languages

Most uses of computers now involve systems with interactive command languages (as opposed to programming languages). In fact, the most widely used systems are interactive command language systems for text editing, financial spreadsheets, and database retrieval. Most research on people learning and using command language systems has been with text editors, since editing text is a task that most people have experienced and know how to do. Goal-plan analysis has been applied to study expert use of text editors (e.g., Card, Moran, and Newell, 1980) and also to study how novices learn to use such systems and become expert with them (e.g., Kay and Black, 1985).

Figure 3.2 gives an example of a goal-plan analysis of changing one word into another with a hypothetical computerized text editor. In this example, the user is editing a text that contains the sentence:

In the situation, we should not go.

and wants to say "In this situation" instead of "In the situation." The cursor that serves as a pointer for the system is initially located at the beginning of this sentence (i.e., points to "I"), so first the user has the subgoal of moving the cursor to the right until it points at the space just after the "the." The plan to accomplish this goal involves the action of hitting the right arrow key six times to move the cursor to the right six places and thus to the desired location.

With the location subgoal attained, the user can move on to the subgoal of deleting the word "the." The plan for this involves hitting the backspace

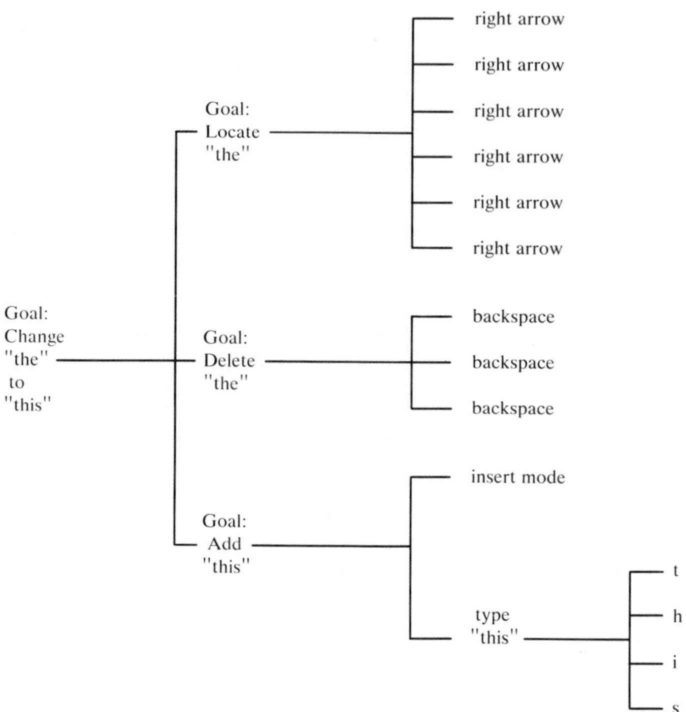

Figure 3.2
Goal-plan representation of a text editor interaction.

key three times, deleting one letter each time. Finally, the user is in a position to attain the subgoal of adding the word "this" in place of the deleted "the" by entering insert mode and typing the letters "t h i s."

One implication of such a representation of text editing interaction is that there should be pauses at the boundaries of these plans while the users evaluate what they have done and determine what the next relevant plan is (as there were pauses at episode boundaries when reading stories). Robertson and Black (1983, 1986) verified this prediction. For example, in the case given in figure 3.2, users would pause before the first right arrow while they planned their location move, and then the six right arrows would be pressed rapidly; but there would be another pause while they planned the delete, and then the backspaces would be pressed rapidly; and finally there would be a pause for planning the insert mode and another for remembering what word to type, but once the typing started the word would also be run off rapidly.

However, Robertson and Black found even more; they found that as the users become more experienced, some of these basic plans were combined into bigger ones, so some of the plan boundary pauses started to disappear, while others became more distinct. For example, in figure 3.2 the boundary between the locate and delete plans would disappear with experience, so that the whole sequence became a larger plan encompassing both locating and deleting. Thus a major component of learning a skill like how to use a computerized text editor involves combining elementary plans to make more complex ones. In fact, the interactive command language domain has turned out to be a good area in which to study how people come to acquire plans for accomplishing goals. Story understanding was not a good domain for that because most story understanding involves recognizing variations on already familiar plans rather than learning new plans.

Kay and Black (1985, 1986) have been able to trace out the plan acquisition process by having users at various levels of experience with text editing systems rate how similar pairs of system commands are. They found that the basis for such similarity judgments shifted dramatically from experience level to experience level and that this method could be used to map out the changes in knowledge representation that occur as users become experienced with a system. In particular, by combining their results with those of Robertson and Black and those of Sebrechts et al. (1983), Kay and Black concluded that learning to use a text editing system progressed through four phases. In the following, we explain each of these phases and describe the evidence supporting each.

2.1 Phase One: Preconceptions

Phase one represents the completely naive user who has had no experience using a text editor. At this stage of learning, users have preconceptions about the terminology to be used in text editing; users come to the text editing domain with a knowledge representation that may or may not correspond to the knowledge representations that will develop as text editing experience increases. Figure 3.3 presents an example of the type of knowledge structures that exist before any learning has taken place. In this structure, there are two actions (e.g., CENTER and BALANCE) that are related by prior knowledge (e.g., these are actions that make something even).

Evidence of this phase was found for the IBM Displaywriter text editor and the UCSD p-System text editor in the Sebrechts et al. study. In this study, naive subjects were given a six-hour training session in which they

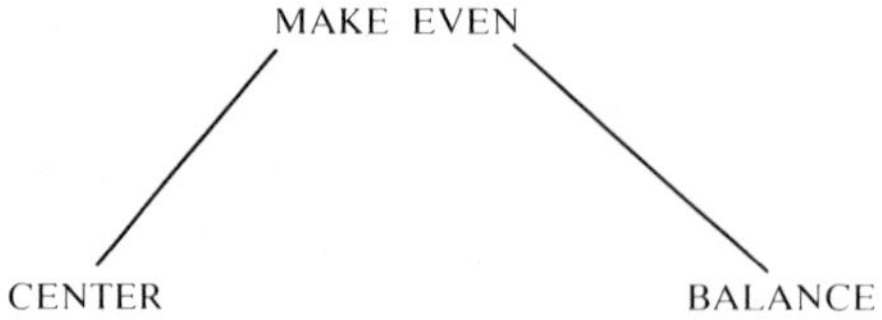

Figure 3.3
Learning phase one.

learned to use either the IBM Displaywriter or the UCSD p-System. Before and after training, the subjects were asked to rate the similarity of non-identical pairs of the commands used in each system. To analyze these ratings, Sebrechts et al. used three multivariate analysis techniques. From the results of a hierarchical clustering of the ratings before the training session, they found that initially the commands for both systems clustered based upon prior knowledge involving the command terms. For example, in the results of the clustering for the Displaywriter commands, CODE and MESSAGE, and CANCEL and DELETE were clustered together. CODE and MESSAGE are related in that one can use a code to convey a message. CANCEL and DELETE are related in that they both suggest the elimination of something. In both cases, the similarity of the command names reflects prior knowledge associations between the actions. Similar types of clusters were found in the UCSD system—e.g., FIND and GET, and HEADER and MARGIN.

Although there may be some correspondence between the prior knowledge representations of the commands and the text editing representations, in most situations, the two representations are quite different. Therefore, users in phase one of the learning process are confronted with the task of overcoming a bias toward interpreting the commands in terms of their prior knowledge associations. To accomplish this task and achieve any level of expertise, the previously existing knowledge representations must be reorganized to accommodate the acquisition of text editing knowledge.

2.2 Phase Two: Initial Learning

Initial text editing knowledge can be acquired from a manual, a class, self-teaching, or any combination of these. No matter what the learning method, the main goal that the user has is to overcome the prior knowledge bias that exists for the text editing commands. The accomplishment of this goal entails (1) learning the goals relevant to text editing and (2) learning the commands that can be used to accomplish these goals. The first part of the learning process takes place as soon as the user begins to edit and is exposed to various editing tasks. Knowledge of general goals allows for the generation of high-level goal structures that can be used to organize the editing commands. For example, if a user types the word "thee" instead of "the," then the goal or task that is instantiated is to erase the extra "e." However, before this goal can be accomplished, the user must learn the actual editing command(s) used. That is, the user must learn the functions of the commands and selectively choose the most appropriate command(s). To continue our example, a user might learn that the command BACKSPACE serves to get rid of unwanted text and decide to use BACKSPACE to remove the unwanted letter. At this time, the user learns that one of the possible goals to be found in text editing is to remove unwanted text and that one command accomplishing this goal is BACKSPACE. As a result of this learning, the user develops knowledge structures that link specific goals and commands. In the knowledge structures that exist at this phase, the goal is linked to the actions by OR links because one can use any one of the actions to accomplish the goal. For our example, the GOAL might be GET-RID-OF-TEXT and one action might be BACKSPACE. As more commands that get rid of text, such as DELETE and SPACE, are learned, they are added to the representation with OR links because the user knows that if you want to GET-RID-OF-TEXT, you can use BACKSPACE or DELETE or SPACE.

Kay and Black (1984, 1986) used a methodology similar to Sebrechts et al. but with a cross-sectional design. In this study, they examined the differences in the knowledge structures of novices and experts who naturally acquired text editing knowledge. They asked both types of users to rate the similarity of pairs of commands used in a local Yale University editor and analyzed these ratings using multivariate techniques. In the results of the hierarchical clustering for the novice users, commands were clustered based upon similarity of function in the editor. For example, INSERT, PUT, and REPLACE clustered together because all three commands are used to accomplish the goal of adding information. Therefore, all the commands are linked to the goal by OR links. That is, if one wants to add information, INSERT or PUT or REPLACE can be used. These results will later be contrasted with expert results in our discussion of phase three of the learning process.

It is important to note that although these users have acquired some text editing knowledge, the organization of this knowledge is based upon only the "result" of the commands and not the procedure that leads to this result. Because of this narrow focus, the users do not possess the knowl-

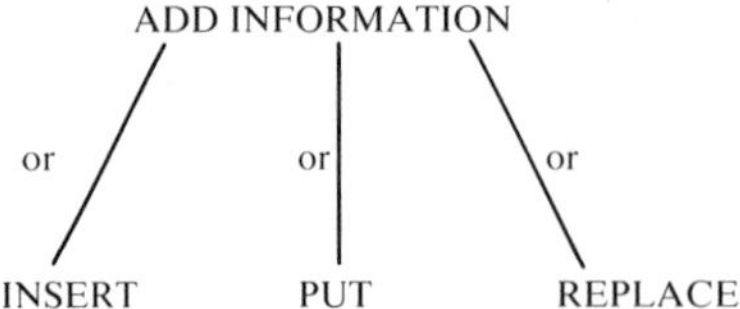

Figure 3.4
Learning phase two.

edge necessary to develop more complex structures, like plans. In particular, while the users know that PUT can be used to ADD INFORMATION, they do not readily know that PUT is merely the main action in a multi-action plan to accomplish this goal.

In addition to providing evidence for phase one, the results of the hierarchical clustering in Sebrechts et al. also illustrate the transition from phase one to phase two. After six hours of training, users no longer clustered commands by prior knowledge associations. The clusters changed to be based more on the function of the system. For example, DELETE, which was initially clustered with CANCEL, was clustered with BACKSPACE after training. In the Displaywriter system, either DELETE or BACKSPACE can be used to erase a piece of text.

Because novice users have not refined their knowledge of commands, several commands are often linked to a single goal by OR links. At this level of understanding, the user will employ any one of the actions linked to the goal to accomplish the goal. For example, in the knowledge structure presented in figure 3.4, PUT, INSERT, and REPLACE are conceptualized as similar because they all accomplish the goal of adding information to the text. With experience, the user will develop more complex representations of these commands and learn that although these commands all add information to the text, the added information comes from different sources. Evidence for this change in knowledge organization will be presented in phase three. For example, PUT uses information from the buffer and needs PICK or DELETE to put information into the buffer. However, INSERT needs only the information that is typed by the user.

Card, Moran, and Newell (1980) proposed the GOMS model to account for the text editing behavior of experts performing routine tasks. In this model, the expert knowledge representation consists of four components: goals, operators, methods, and selection rules. Goals are what the expert user is trying to accomplish (e.g., the word change in figure 3.2), operators are the actions the system allows to accomplish the goals (e.g., right arrow and backspace in figure 3.2), methods are the sequences of actions that will accomplish a goal (e.g., the repetition of three backspace operators accomplishes the goal of deleting "the" in figure 3.2), and selection rules are the conditions under which a given method is chosen to accomplish a given goal (e.g., users would probably only want to use the backspace method of deleting in figure 3.2 when the word to be deleted is short). Card, Moran, and Newell validated the GOMS model by showing that it could account for the sequence of operators experts use and the amount of time it takes them to accomplish routine tasks.

In terms of the GOMS model, the Kay and Black account of initial learning is that the goals and operators are acquired first. That is, novices are able to understand the general goals involved in text editing and the individual commands that are related to these goals. It is reasonable that the goal-action link would be the first link to be formed. During the initial learning of a system, the user is introduced to numerous command names and definitions with little reference made as to when each command should be used. If, instead of forming links between the commands and the goals that they accomplish, the first links to be formed were between commands, then the user would never know when to use each command and therefore would have to resort to a trial-and-error method of achieving a goal. Thus, the linking of the command to a goal provides the user with some aid in using the correct command in the correct situation.

Novices seem to conceptualize the commands merely by what goals they are relevant for accomplishing. Because at this level of specificity they have not yet acquired the procedures or plans that are associated with text editing, each text editing task becomes a problem solving task in which they must actively search through their representations of the commands and construct the sequence of commands necessary to accomplish the task.

2.3 Phase Three: Plan Development

Once the users have acquired the basic editing commands and goals, they learn that there are combinations of commands that are often used together to accomplish a goal. In phase three, users develop the ability to form plans by combining the actions that were organized separately in phase two. These plans correspond to the methods of the GOMS model. There are various ways that the transition from phase two to phase three takes place. For example, with the system that Kay and Black studied, users realize that there is inefficiency in repeating a command numerous times. To overcome this inefficiency they learn to use the ARGUMENT command, which automatically repeats another command for the number of times specified as the

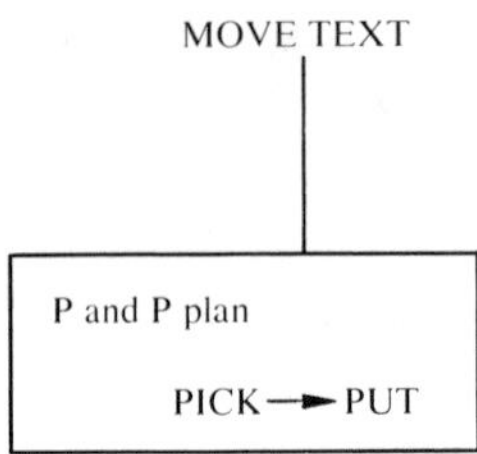

Figure 3.5
Learning phase three.

argument. Once they have this knowledge, users begin to notice that there are other commands that can be used together in a sequence. This realization leads to a reorganization of the knowledge representation to accommodate the command sequences or plans that are used to accomplish goals. This reorganization process entails modification of the goal-action links that were formed between the commands or actions that are used in a plan. At a higher level, links are formed between the goals and the plans that are used to achieve the goals.

Again both Kay and Black and Sebrechts et al. provide evidence for the development of phase three knowledge structures using the results of a hierarchical clustering analysis. As previously mentioned, the novice users organized commands as individual actions related to goals. On the other hand, expert users appear to use a more sequence-oriented organization. That is, the perceived similarity between the command pairs was based upon the use of the commands in a plan to accomplish the goal of moving a piece of text. For example, in the Kay and Black study, expert users clustered PICK and PUT together because these two commands are used together when a user wants to accomplish the goal of moving a piece of text. This example contrasts with the phase two knowledge representation example in which novice users clustered PUT with INSERT and REPLACE because each of the individual commands are used to accomplish the goal of adding information. These examples illustrate the change in the representation of the commands from goal-action links to goal-plan links. Figure 3.5 presents a graphic representation of the knowledge structure that underlies this result.

2.4 Phase Four: Increasing Expertise

Although the formation of simple plans results in some expertise in text editing, it is not until compound plans are formed that one can accomplish more advanced tasks. Phase four of the Kay and Black model accounts for this ability and represents the completion of the acquisition that results in knowledge representations similar to those proposed in the GOMS model of expert performance. In this phase, users (a) combine simple plans into more compound plans to accomplish major goals and (b) develop rules for selecting the best plan to achieve a given goal in a given situation. Once again, a reorganization of the knowledge results in the development of new links between the components of the representation. In this phase, we see a change from a one-to-one correspondence between goal and plan to a one-to-several correspondence: that is, in phase three each plan or sequence or actions is directly linked to a specific goal (e.g., move text), while in phase four there are multiple plans that can be linked to each goal. However, because there are multiple plans, the links that connect these plans must have selection rules that tell the users under what conditions to access the plan to accomplish the goal.

In the phase four knowledge structures, there are several plans that may be instantiated to achieve a given goal. To be sure that the correct plan is chosen from the set of applicable plans, the links that connect these plans to the goal are conditions or selection rules that must be met before a given plan is chosen. These conditions can be based on any distinguishing feature of the plans. Thus, at the highest level of expertise, goals are linked to plans using the conditions under which these plans are invoked, whereas goals were linked to simple plans in phase three and actions in phase two.

Robertson and Black (1983, 1986) present evidence for the evolution of compound plans. With increased experience, the time spent pausing between simple plans decreased, suggesting that users had combined the simple plans that they had learned to form compound plans. In addition, the decision time to initiate a compound plan (during which subjects chose what they thought was the most appropriate plan) decreased as the editing session progressed, suggesting the acquisition of selection rules that facilitate accessing the most appropriate plan. Figure 3.6 presents a concrete example of a phase four knowledge structure. In the editor Robertson and Black used, to change one word to another word there are three possible plans that may be invoked. The links connecting these three plans to the goal are conditions that must be met before the plans are selected. In the structure depicted, the conditions are based on the relationship between the lengths of the old word and of the new word.

In addition to providing evidence for the compound plans of phase four and indirect pause time evidence for selection rules, Robertson and Black

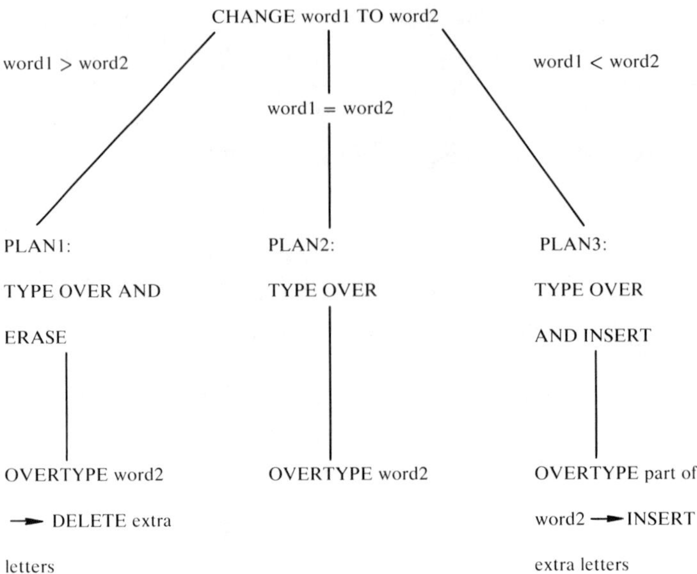

Figure 3.6
Learning phase four.

also found direct evidence for the development of selection rules. In the beginning of the training trials, when users had to change one word to another word, the majority of the users (approximately two-thirds) would DELETE the old word then INSERT the new word. However, as experience increased, these same users stopped using the DELETE-INSERT plan and began to OVERTYPE the old word with the new word. In this example, users appeared to develop a selection rule that can be stated as

IF you want to change one word to another
THEN use the OVERTYPE plan.

This type of selection rule organizes the plans according to the priority that they have in efficiently accomplishing the goal.

Thus, as we have seen, goal-plan analyses of text editing have provided both a valuable way to analyze behavior in text editing sessions and a framework within which to understand the changes in conceptualization that users go through as they become more expert with a system. One thing that has not been done for text editing, however, is to develop a systematic taxonomy of the kinds of text editing plans. Such a taxonomy has been developed for programming, which we shall discuss next.

3 Programming

Using an interactive command language system is like having a conversation with a computer: The user says something, then the computer says something, then the user says something else, then the computer responds, etc. Programming, on the other hand, is more like written communication between people: The user writes out a series of steps, and then gives them all at once to the computer. Thus there is even more similarity between programming and story understanding than there is between the use of interactive command language systems and story understanding. As with the other two domains, in recent years goal-plan analyses have yielded valuable insights into several aspects of programming.

Figure 3.7 gives an example of a goal-plan representation of a Pascal program that reads in and sums data until a stopping value of "99999" is reached, and then outputs the average of the data. The overall goal (to the left in the figure) is to report the average, and to accomplish this goal requires accomplishing two subgoals, namely: computing the average, then outputting the average. Computing the average in turn involves accomplishing three subgoals: computing the sum of the numbers in the data, counting the number of data items, and then dividing the sum by the count to yield the average. Computing the sum of the numbers uses what Soloway and his colleagues (Soloway et al. 1983; Ehrlich and Soloway, 1984) call the Running Total Loop Plan. This plan involves initializing a Total variable to zero, telling the user to enter a number, then reading that number and looping until the stopping value of "99999" is entered (the program statements to the right in figure 3.7 connected to the Running Total Loop Plan label). In the loop itself, the newly read number from the user is added to the Total variable, then the user is asked to input the next number, which is read, and the loop continues until the stopping value is inputted.

Similarly, counting the number of input items uses a Counter Loop Plan, which initializes a Count variable, and then loops like the Running Total Loop Plan, but incrementing the Count variable by 1 each time through the loop instead of adding a new value to a Total variable (figure 3.7). While conceptually separate, in practice the Counter Loop Plan and the Running Total Loop Plan can utilize many of the same program statements, and both plans can be executed with the same looping. Such combining of plans is very common in programming, but rare in stories and interactive command languages. This characteristic is part of what makes programming hard; the programmer must keep track of several plans at once, whereas typically in stories or interactive command languages the reader or user

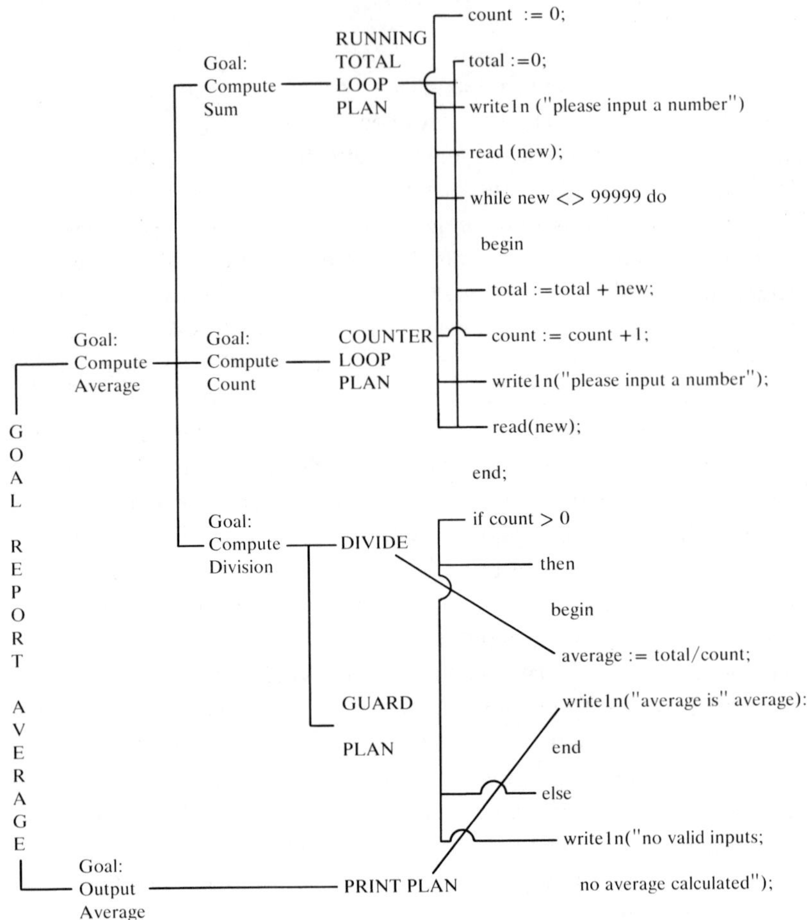

Figure 3.7
Goal-plan representation of a Pascal program.

need only track one plan at a time. In fact, it is interesting to speculate that the amount of such plan combination might be an important part of a goal-plan-based metric of program complexity.

Let us continue with the example in figure 3.7. After computing the total and count, the program needs to compute the division. This is not as straightforward as one might think (and novices usually do think), because first the program must check for a pathological case—namely, whether the count is zero (which would happen if the first input value were the stopping value "99999"). Thus to compute the division, the programmer first uses a Guard Plan to make sure the Count is greater than zero (and complains to the user if it is not); then, once that is assured, it can actually do the division. After this is accomplished the program can output the average.

Note that in the representation in figure 3.7, this Guard Plan is lower down in the goal-plan hierarchy (i.e., has more links between it and the overall goal) than the other plans are. Recall that in the story-understanding research, the level in a goal-plan hierarchy affected how well a story statement would be remembered. Thus we would also expect to find such an effect on the memory of statements in a program—e.g., the statements in the Guard Plan in our example would probably be less well remembered later. However, even more important, we would expect effects of goal-plan hierarchy on other aspects of programming performance. For example, it might have an effect on the likelihood of bugs and the ease with which the bugs could be detected. In fact, omitting Guard Plan statements from programs like our example is a very frequent bug (Spohrer, Soloway, and Pope, 1985). This is what we would expect from our hierarchy level analysis.

Soloway and his colleagues have also provided some empirical results verifying the validity of their goal-plan system. Just as skilled readers of stories can infer plan statements omitted from story texts (Seifert, Robertson, and Black, 1985), so skilled programmers can fill in omitted plan statements in programs. For example, in figure 3.7, when the Running Total Loop Plan is clearly indicated (as we have by naming a variable "Total"), the experienced programmer would have no trouble filling in the

```
total := total + new
```

statement if we put a blank line at that point in the program (Soloway and Ehrlich, 1984). Novice programmers, on the other hand, cannot do this as easily, because what makes them novices is that they have not mastered the programming plans as well as the experts.

Just as readers of stories reorder story statements so as to be in the order that plans claim they should be in (Bower, Black, and Turner, 1979), Soloway,

Bonar, and Ehrlich (1983) found that programmers show a tendency to put program statements in the order that their everyday plans indicate, even when that leads to bugs in their programs. In particular, Soloway, Bonar, and Ehrlich found the process/read loop construct in Pascal to be a major source of bugs because it mismatches the normal course of events in the real world; in the everyday world we get an object (read it), and then do something with it (process it), but in the Pascal loop world something is processed first and then read. Our example in figure 3.7 illustrates this: Within the loop a new value is added to the total, and then another new value is read—this is conceptually backward. Soloway, Bonar, and Ehrlich compared performance using this standard Pascal loop with performance using a new read/process loop as follows:

```
Read(New);
If New = 99999 then leave;
Sum := Sum + New;
Count := Count + 1;
```

(these statements replace the statements within the loop in figure 3.7). They found improved performance with this new read/process construct compared to the old process/read construct, even though the programmers in the study had much experience with the process/read construct and almost no experience with the read/process one. Thus, as the goal-plan approach predicts, when the design of programming languages mismatches normal human plans, that mismatch will be a source of bugs when the language is used.

We have just discussed a transfer of planning knowledge from the real world into the world of programming (negative transfer in this case), but we would also expect the transfer to go the other way; we would expect that goal-plan knowledge acquired in the context of programming would transfer to other domains. This is the goal-plan version of the general claim that learning to program will improve a person's mind (Papert, 1980). Unfortunately, the results of tests of this general claim have been mixed at best (e.g., Pea and Kurland, 1984). However, there is some evidence that the idea of interpreting symbolic expressions as plans rather than as descriptions does transfer from programming to algebra—at least sometimes and for some people (Ehrlich et al., 1985). In particular, after taking a programming course, college students were better at solving the following kind of problem:

> Write an equation to represent, There are six times as many students as professors at Columbia University.

After a programming course, students tend to get the right answer (6P = S, where S is the number of students and P the number of professors), but before the course they get it backward, P = 6S. One interpretation of why this happens is that the programmer students are viewing the equation as a plan for calculating the value of one variable given the other (e.g., calculating the number of professors when given the number of students), while the nonprogrammer students are directly translating words into symbols (i.e., "there are six students for every professor" becomes "6S = P"). Thus there is some evidence that a general planning orientation will transfer from programming to algebra, although again the evidence is mixed (Ehrlich et al., 1985).

This difficulty with finding transfer of knowledge between domains is reminiscent of the problems we described earlier that Gick and Holyoak (1980) had with getting plans to transfer from a story to solving a problem. Recall, however, that with further research Gick and Holyoak (1983) found that if they had their problem solvers read two stories that contained the plan needed to solve the problem, then there was transfer and the problem solvers did use the plan to solve the problem. Thus the readers only abstracted out the general form of the plan needed for transfer after they had experienced two specific versions of it. Of course, the transfer that Gick and Holyoak found occurred in ideal circumstances: reading the relevant stories immediately before solving the problem. In more realistic circumstances it might require more than two specific instances, but the general conclusion seem likely to be right—namely, to get general knowledge to transfer between domains we need to ensure that the learners experience the knowledge in more than one specific context in the initial domain so they can generalize the general knowledge from the specific cases (and make sure they realize they have seen more than one specific instance of the general knowledge). This is a conclusion that seems ripe for testing with transferring plans from programming to other domains.

Thus story-understanding research on transfer seems to offer advice for programming research on transfer, but that is not the only suggestion for programming research that emerges from research on stories and text editors. Recall that some of the main evidence for plans in story understanding is that the story statements that are in the same plan form a cohesive, independent unit in the memory representation of the story. Applying these research methods to programming plans, we would expect that remembering, understanding, or generating one program statement from a plan would help in remembering, understanding, or generating another program statement from the same plan more than it would a statement from another plan. Thus, for example, in the program in figure 3.7, does remembering that the program contains

total := 0

help a programmer remember it also contains

total := total + new

(both members of the loop plans) more than remembering that it contains

average := total/count

(which is in the separate division plan)? If such results obtain, then we would have stronger evidence for the psychological reality of the proposed system of programming plans.

Another suggestion for programming research comes from the study of text editing. Specifically, it would be informative to investigate whether the four learning phases that Kay and Black (1985, 1986) found with text editors also occurs when learning to program. For example, in the program in figure 3.7, inexperienced programmers might see

count := 0

and

total := 0

as going together because they are both initializations and

total := total + new

and

count := count + 1

as going together because they are alternative ways of computing; but with experience the programmers may come to see the statements in the same plan as going together—e.g.,

total := 0

going with

total := total + new

Regardless of whether the specific Kay and Black learning model also applies to programming, it would be valuable to conduct analogous studies that trace the development of the representation of programming knowledge with increasing experience in programming.

4 Conclusions

Analyzing human behavior in terms of goals and plans and characterizing the goal-plan knowledge behind that behavior has been an insightful approach to understanding human behavior in a number of areas. In this chapter, we have examined the use of goal-plan analysis in the study of people understanding stories, using a text editor and programming. We have also examined the fairly extensive amount of systematic, empirical research that has yielded results consistent with people using goal-plan knowledge representations in all these domains. For example, there is timing evidence that people process in terms of plan units both when understanding stories and when using text editors. For another example, there is evidence that people use the action order called for in everyday plans both when recalling stories and when writing programs.

Examining the goal-plan representations of various domains gives insight into both the commonalities in the domains and their distinguishing features. For example, comparing the goal-plan representations in figures 3.1, 3.2, and 3.7 shows a common pattern of having an overall goal broken down into subgoals until specific enough subgoals are found so that there are plans to accomplish them. Figures 3.1 and 3.2 (story understanding and text editing) are also similar in that their breakdown produces simple tree structures. Figure 3.7 (programming), on the other hand, looks more like a tangle of vines than a tree. This tangle results from the combination of plans that occurs in programming and that results in a given programming statement being related to more than one plan. This plan combination feature of programming is part of what makes writing and understanding programs harder than writing and understanding stories or using text editors.

Noting such similarities and differences across domains, however, also makes us wonder whether more similarity might be better in many cases. For example, why can't a program be more like a story? Stories are generally a pleasure to read and, with a little experience, a pleasure to write. Programs, on the other hand, are usually torture to read and write. Why this big difference? When writing a story, an author does not have to spell out every little detail because readers can (as we discussed earlier) use their goal-plan knowledge to fill in the details; all the author has to do is sketch enough of an outline to indicate to the reader what knowledge to activate.

Thus the author and the reader are freed from being bogged down in explicit details, so that they can soar through enjoyable flights of the imagination.

People reading programs can also infer missing steps if the relevant goals and plans have been indicated (as we discussed earlier); but, unfortunately, the computer system that has to execute the programs cannot make such inferences. Thus, unlike story writers, programmers are bogged down in nitty-gritty details, and that is why programming is such torture and a less efficient way to communicate. To escape this programming hell, we need computer systems that can read programs the way people read stories—that is, we need program interpreters and compilers that have the goal-plan knowledge necessary for making inferences so that programmers do not have to state everything explicitly.

Thus, as we have illustrated with this discussion, we think that in addition to helping understand human performance in a variety of areas, goal-plan representations can aid in the design of tools to aid performance in different areas. For example, noticing that understanding stories and programming both involve goals and plans, but also noticing the difference in how goals and plans are used in the two domains, gives us a basis for determining how to change the behavior in one domain (programming) to be more like behavior in the other (story understanding).

References

Abbott, V. A., and Black, J. B. (1986). Goal and plan representations of stories. In J. A. Galambos, R. P. Abelson, and J. B. Black (Eds.), *Knowledge Structures,* Hillsdale, NJ, Erlbaum.

Black, J. B. (1984). *Understanding and Remembering Stories,* San Francisco, Freeman.

Black, J. B., and Bower, G. H. (1979). Episodes as chunks in narrative memory. *Journal of Verbal Learning and Verbal Behavior,* 18, 309–318.

Black, J. B., and Bower, G. H. (1980). Story understanding as problem-solving. *Poetics,* 9, 223–250.

Black, J. B., Wilkes-Gibbs, D., and Gibbs, R. (1982). What writers need to know that they don't know they need to know. In M. Nystrand (Ed.), *What Writers Know,* New York, Academic Press.

Bower, G. H., Black, J. B., and Turner, T. J. (1979). Scripts in memory for text. *Cognitive Psychology,* 11, 177–220.

Card, S. K., Moran, T. P., and Newell, A. (1980). Computer text-editing: An information processing analysis of a routine cognitive skill. *Cognitive Psychology,* 12, 32–74.

Ehrlich, K., and Soloway, E. (1984). An empirical investigation of the tacit plan knowledge in programming. In J. C. Thomas and M. L. Schneider (Eds.), *Human Factors in Computing Systems*, Norwood, NJ, Ablex.

Ehrlich, K., Abbott, V., Salter, W., and Soloway, E. (1985). Issues and problems in studying transfer effects of programming. Unpublished manuscript, Department of Computer Science, Yale University, New Haven.

Gick, M. L., and Holyoak, K. J. (1980). Analogical problem solving. *Cognitive Psychology*, 12, 306–355.

Gick, M. L., and Holyoak, K. J. (1983). Schema induction and analogical transfer. *Cognitive Psychology*, 15, 1–38.

Graesser, A. C. (1980). *Prose Comprehension beyond the Word*, New York, Springer-Verlag.

Haberlandt, K. (1980). Story grammars and the reading time of story constituents. *Poetics*, 9, 99–116.

Kay, D. S., and Black, J. B. (1984). The changes in knowledge representations of computer systems with experience. *Proceedings of the Human Factors Society 28th Annual Meeting*, Santa Monica, Human Factors Society.

Kay, D. S., and Black, J. B. (1985). The evolution of knowledge representations with increasing expertise in using systems. *Proceedings of the Seventh Annual Meeting of the Cognitive Science Society*, Irvine, CA.

Kay, D. S., and Black, J. B. (1986). Knowledge transformations during the acquisition of computer expertise. CCT Report 86-2, New York, Teachers College, Columbia University.

Miller, G. A., Galanter, G., and Pribram, K. H. (1960). *Plans and the Structure of Behavior*, New York, Holt, Rinehart and Winston.

Papert, S. (1980). *Mindstorms*, New York, Basic Books.

Pea, R. D., and Kurland, D. M. (1984). Logo programming and the development of planning skills. Technical Report No. 6, Center for Children and Technology, Bank Street College of Education, New York.

Robertson, S. P., and Black, J. B. (1983). Planning in text editing behavior. In A. Janda (Ed.), *Human Factors in Computing Systems*, New York, North-Holland.

Robertson, S. P., and Black, J. B. (1986). Development of plan structures in computer text editing. Paper submitted for publication.

Schank, R. C., and Abelson R. P. (1977). *Scripts, Plans, Goals and Understanding*, Hillsdale, NJ, Erlbaum.

Sebrechts, M. M., Black, J. B., Galambos, J. A., Wagner, R. K., Deck, J. A., and Wikler, E. A. (1983). The effects of diagrams on learning to use a system. Learning and Using Systems Project Report 2, Yale University, New Haven.

Seifert, C. M., Robertson, S. P., and Black, J. B. (1985). Types of inferences generated during reading. *Journal of Memory and Language*, 24, 405–422.

Soloway, E., and Ehrlich, K. (1984). Empirical studies of programming knowledge. *IEEE Transactions on Software Engineering*, SE-10, 595–609.

Soloway, E., Bonar, J., and Ehrlich, K. (1983). Cognitive strategies and looping constructs: An empirical study. *Communications of the Association for Computing Machinery*, 26, 853–861.

Soloway, E., Ehrlich, K., Bonar, J., and Greenspan, J. (1983). What do novices know about programming? In B. Shneiderman and A. Badre (Eds.), *New Directions in Human-Computer Interaction*, Norwood, NJ, Ablex.

Spohrer, J. C., Soloway, E., and Pope, E. (1985). A goal/plan analysis of buggy Pascal programs. *Human Computer Interaction*, 1, 163–207.

Thorndyke, P. W. (1977). Cognitive structures in comprehension and memory of narrative discourse. *Cognitive Psychology*, 9, 77–110.

4 Cognitive Aspects of Learning and Using a Programming Language

Richard E. Mayer

This chapter is concerned with understanding how a user learns a new programming language. The premise of this chapter is that learning a programming language involves acquiring *syntactic* knowledge, such as specific details about valid vocabulary and code format; *semantic* (or conceptual) knowledge, such as concepts and structures that are language independent; and mappings between these two kinds of knowledge (Shneiderman and Mayer, 1979). In particular, this chapter focuses on the role of users' semantic (or conceptual) knowledge in successful learning of a programming language.

The chapter begins with introductory examples and definitions of conceptual knowledge relevant to BASIC. Then, findings are presented from four lines of cognitive research on human-computer interaction: identifying some conceptual prerequisites for learning BASIC, identifying some conceptual requirements for comprehending BASIC programs, diagnosing the conceptual knowledge acquired by beginning BASIC programmers, and providing explicit training of conceptual knowledge for beginning BASIC programmers. The chapter concludes by noting that any theory of how novices learn a programming language must include an understanding of the nature of users' conceptual knowledge.

This chapter was written while the author was on sabbatical leave at the Center for the Study of Reading, University of Illinois. Preparation of this report was supported in part by the National Science Foundation under grant MDR-8470248. Piraye Bayman conducted the research described in the sections titled "Do Novices Acquire Useful Models While Learning BASIC?" and "Can Students Be Taught to Acquire Useful Conceptual Knowledge?"; Jennifer Dyck conducted the research described in the sections titled "Is a User's Conceptual Knowledge Related to Learning BASIC?" and "Are Conceptual Features Similar for English and BASIC Statements?"; Bill Vilberg conducted one of the studies described in the section titled "Is a User's Conceptual Knowledge Related to Learning BASIC?"

1 Introduction

Consider the following procedure, called Program 1.

1. Put the first number shown below in Box-A.

2. Add the number 1 to the number shown in Box-A, and put this new number in Box-B.

3. Write down the number that is in Box-B.

If the first number shown below is 18, what is the output of this program? The answer, of course, is 19.

Program 1 can be translated into BASIC as follows, yielding Program 2.

```
10    INPUT A
20    LET B = A + 1
30    PRINT B
```

As you can see, the three statements in Program 1 correspond, respectively, to the three statements in Program 2.

Now, consider another procedure, called Program 3.

1. Put the number 4 in Box-A.

2. Put the number 5 in Box-B.

3. Add the numbers from Box-A and Box-B together, and put this new number in Box-C.

4. Write down the number that is in Box-C.

What is the output of this program? The answer, of course, is 9.

Again, Program 3 can be translated into BASIC, yielding Program 4, as follows:

```
10    LET A = 4
20    LET B = 5
30    LET C = A + B
40    PRINT C
```

The four statements in Program 3 correspond, respectively, to the four statements in Program 4.

In the above examples, Programs 1 and 3 are stated in English, and describe a series of actions (such as "putting" or "adding") concerning objects (such as numbers) at locations (such as "boxes"). Students in our research projects at Santa Barbara who had no prior experience with BASIC programming were able to answer correctly questions about Programs 1 and 3. Similarly, Programs 2 and 4, respectively, describe corresponding series of actions on objects at locations, but these programs are stated in BASIC. Students in our research projects at Santa Barbara who had no prior experience with BASIC programming were initially unable to answer correctly questions about Programs 2 and 4.

What is involved in learning BASIC? Shneiderman and Mayer (1979) have made a distinction between two kinds of knowledge required for learning a programming language—syntactic knowledge and semantic knowledge. Syntactic knowledge consists of specific details that are dependent on a programming language, including vocabulary and format rules. The vocabulary of the language involves the allowable letters, numbers, symbols, keywords, names, and character sets. For example, in BASIC, some of the keywords are "READ," "DATA," "INPUT," "PRINT," "LET," and so on. The format of the language involves rules for constructing lines of code, such as the rule that "READ" requires a line number to its left and variable name(s) to its right (separated by commas), and that there must be a corresponding "DATA" statement in the program. As can be seen, in these examples, syntactic knowledge is arbitrary, and hence may be difficult to learn.

In contrast, semantic knowledge[1] consists of general programming concepts that are independent of specific programming languages. Semantic knowledge consists of the underlying concepts and structures of programming, i.e., the internal elements that are referred to by the external lines of code. For example, the concepts underlying each line of BASIC code have been analyzed by Mayer (1979a, 1985) as consisting of actions (such as "putting," "erasing," "printing," "comparing," "adding," "assigning," etc.), objects (such as "numbers," "strings," "variables," "arrays," "pointers," "flags," "files," etc.), and locations (such as "memory spaces," "program lines," "output screen," etc.). These are some of the conceptual entities that may serve as the referents for BASIC code. In addition to these low-level notions concerning individual lines of code, semantic knowledge may include high-level notions concerning the structures underlying a program or program module. For example, semantic knowledge can include control structures involved in looping, iteration, or recursion and algorithm structures involved in fundamental tasks, such as sorting, alphabetizing, or matrix manipulations.

Mapping involves building connections between lines of code (i.e., external representations of syntax) and the corresponding concepts and structures (i.e., internal representations of semantics). For example, Shneiderman and Mayer (1979) point out that it may be easier for a person to learn a new syntactic representation for an existing semantic construct than to acquire a completely new set of semantic concepts. This is reflected in the observation that it is generally harder to learn a first language, such as BASIC or FORTRAN, than to learn a second one of these languages. Learning a first language requires building both syntactic and semantic knowledge as well as connections between them, while learning a second language involves learning only a new syntax that can be mapped onto already learned semantic constructs. However, if the second language is based on radically different conceptual knowledge—such as learning BASIC and LISP—learning may be as hard or more difficult.

The specific vocabulary and format rules are generally the main focus of instruction in a programming language. However, a premise of this chapter is that learners may attempt to understand the language by mapping it onto existing conceptions about actions, objects, locations, and programming structures. A related premise is that novices who are beginning to learn a programming language may come to the learning situation with "naive conceptions" of programming—with some concepts being useful and others unuseful. Similarly, there is evidence that science students often possess "naive conceptions" or "preconceptions" about science, such as having an "impetus" model of motion (Clement, 1982; McCloskey, 1983; McCloskey, Caramazza, and Green, 1980). One implication of the "naive conceptions" literature is that instructors should not assume that students come as "blank slates"; instead, instruction is needed that helps students replace their unuseful conceptions with useful ones.

The theme of this chapter, then, is that learning a programming language involves the acquisition and interrelating of useful syntactic knowledge and conceptual knowledge of the system. Another way of stating this hypothesis is to say that productive learning of a language such as BASIC depends partly on the user's underlying conceptions. We can call this the conceptual knowledge hypothesis, and we shall investigate this idea in the remainder of the chapter.

2 An Analysis of Conceptual Knowledge

The foregoing examples and definitions motivate the question, "What are the concepts underlying students' learning of a language such as BASIC?" A related question is, "How can we assess and describe a user's conceptual knowledge relevant to BASIC?" In order to better understand these questions, let us begin with a BASIC program:

```
10    INPUT A
20    LET B = A + 1
30    PRINT B
```

In the context of this program, our question becomes, "What does a user have to know in order to understand statements such as INPUT or LET or PRINT or to understand how the statements are related to one another in the above program?"

There have been several attempts to describe users' conceptual knowledge of computer programming languages (Bayman and Mayer, 1984; Card, Moran, and Newell, 1980; Carroll and Thomas, 1982; Du Boulay and O'Shea, 1981; Du Boulay, O'Shea, and Monk, 1981; Mayer, 1976, 1979a,b, 1981, 1985; Mayer and Bayman, 1981; Moran, 1981a,b; Norman, 1983; Young, 1981, 1983). This chapter will focus on what we have called "transactional analysis" (Mayer, 1979a, 1985) as a framework for describing a user's conceptual knowledge of BASIC.

The transactional analysis approach involves taking a BASIC statement, such as INPUT A or LET B + A + 1 or PRINT B, and trying to understand its microstructure and macrostructure. Microstructure refers to the conceptual parts or units that are referred to by the statement; macrostructure refers to the larger structure into which the statement fits within a program or program segment.

What is the microstructure of the statements in the above program? Each of the statements can be broken down into a list of transactions, with each transaction asserting some operation performed on some object in some location of the computer. For example, the transactions for INPUT A are stated in English below (with the Operation, Object, and Location given, respectively, in parentheses):

1. Write "?" on the output screen. (CREATE, Prompt, Screen)

2. Wait for a number to be entered from the keyboard, followed by depression of the RETURN key. (ALLOW, Command, Keyboard)

3. Write the entered number on the output screen next to "?" (CREATE, Number, Screen)

4. Find the number that was just entered. (FIND, Number, Screen)

5. Find the number currently in the memory space indicated in the INPUT statement. (FIND, Number, Memory)

6. Erase the number currently in that memory space. (DESTROY, Number, Memory)

7. Write the new number in that memory space. (CREATE, Number, Memory)

8. Go on to the next statement. (MOVE, Pointer, Program)

9. Do what the statement says. (ALLOW, Command, Program)

Similarly, the transactions for LET B = A + 1 are as follows:

1. Find the number in the formula. (FIND, Number, Program)

2. Put that number in the scratch pad. (CREATE, Number, Scratch Pad)

3. Find the number in the memory space indicated in the formula. (FIND, Number, Memory)

4. Put that number also in the scratch pad. (CREATE, Number, Scratch Pad)

5. Add the two numbers in the scratch pad together. (COMBINE, Number, Scratch Pad)

6. Find the number in the memory space indicated to the left of the equals. (FIND, Number, Memory)

7. Erase the number in that memory space. (DESTROY, Number, Memory)

8. Put the new sum from the scratch pad into this memory space. (CREATE, Number, Memory)

9. Go on to the next statement. (MOVE, Pointer, Program)

10. Do what the statement says. (ALLOW, Command, Program)

Finally, the transactions for PRINT B are

1. Find the number in the memory address indicated. (FIND, Number, Memory)

2. Write that number on the next available space on the output screen. (CREATE, Number, Screen)

3. Go on to the next statement. (MOVE, Pointer, Program)

4. Do what the statement says. (ALLOW, Command, Program)

As you can see, each transaction can be broken down into three elements: what operation takes place—such as FIND, CREATE, MOVE, etc.; where it takes place—such as memory space, program list, output screen, scratch pad, etc.; and what object is acted upon—such as number, command, pointer, etc.

An understanding of the microstructure of BASIC statements seems to be based on smaller elements, namely, transactions, and the locations, operations, and objects involved in transactions. In a previous set of studies, we have found that users' learning of BASIC is strongly influenced by making the locations of the computer more obvious (Mayer, 1975, 1976, 1981). For example, some of the key locations are:

input queue—a stack of numbers to be processed in sequence, with processed numbers being moved to the finish side of the queue,

output screen—a message pad that allows one piece of information per line,

keyboard—a typewriter used for giving commands from the user to the computer,

memory scoreboard—an array of erasable memory spaces with each being able to hold one number and each having an individual address name,

scratch pad—an erasable memory for making arithmetic computations,

wait-run light—a control panel that consists of a WAIT light when the computer is waiting for a command from the user and a RUN light when the computer is executing commands in a program, and

program list and pointer arrow—a list of commands to be carried out in sequence by the computer, with an arrow to keep track of the current command.

Subjects who are given training in how each of several key locations operate tend to be able to learn BASIC more effectively than students who are not given this pretraining (Mayer, 1975, 1976, 1981). It should also be pointed out that statements having the same keyword may actually consist of quite different lists of transactions; for example, the transactions for LET D = 0 are different from LET B = A + 1. In contrast, some statements can be grouped together because they all share the same underlying transactions; for example, LET C = 1 and LET D = 0 are based on the same underlying list of transactions. Thus, transactions may serve as the building blocks—or unit of analysis—for describing users' conceptual knowledge relevant to BASIC.

What is the macrostructure of the statements in the above program? Each statement is part of a three-line program that accomplishes a specific goal. Longer programs can often be decomposed into smaller units, which could be called "chunks," with each chunk accomplishing some specifiable goal. Thus, the macrostructure of the INPUT or LET or PRINT statements concerns the other statements that are in the same program or program chunk.

Does transactional analysis provide us with a useful analysis of users' conceptual knowledge of BASIC? The remainder of this chapter consists of four different attempts to use transactional analysis to study users' conceptual knowledge of BASIC. These sections provide some partial evidence that transactional analysis is a useful technique for describing users' conceptual knowledge of BASIC.

3 Is a User's Conceptual Knowledge Related to Learning BASIC?

Suppose that we asked some novices to learn elementary BASIC programming, including simple statements for INPUT, READ, DATA, LET, PRINT, GOTO, IF-GOTO, IF-THEN. We provide the novices with instructional materials (such as a textbook) and may even give hands-on access to a computer. After the training, we give the students a programming test to see how well they are able to use the information that has been taught. We find that some students perform very well on the programming test, whereas other students perform quite poorly.

Why do some students learn BASIC more effectively than others? According to the conceptual knowledge hypothesis, differences in learning may be due to differences in the prerequisite conceptions that users bring to the learning situation. In short, a user who has useful existing conceptions will learn better than a user who has unuseful conceptions. This is so because learning BASIC involves assimilating the new information about BASIC vocabulary and syntax to existing conceptions.

A straightforward way of measuring users' existing conceptions is to ask users to generate and comprehend programs that are stated in English, but that involve the same concepts as BASIC. For example, Jenny Dyck and I have designed a Procedure Comprehension Test (PCT) in which subjects answer questions such as the following:

1. Put 5 in Box-A.
2. Put 4 in Box-B.
3. Add the number in Box-A and the number in Box-B, put the result in Box-C.
4. Add the number in Box-A and the number in Box-C, put the result in Box-A.
5. Write down the numbers from Box-A, Box-B, Box-C.

What is the output of this program?

a. 5, 4, 9

b. 14, 4, 9

c. 14, 9, 9

d. 9, 4, 9

e. none of the above

Another fundamental aspect of writing BASIC programs involves being able to take a problem statement in English that involves random variables and translate that statement into another formal language. In order to tap this skill, we designed the Word Problem Translation Test (WPTT), which consisted of items such as the following:

A car rental service charges twenty dollars a day and fifteen cents a mile to rent a car. Find the expression for total cost C, in dollars, of renting a car for D days to travel M miles.

a. C = 20D + .15M

b. C = 15D + .20M

c. C = 20D + 15M

d. C = .15D + 20M

e. none of the above

In a series of four experiments, we gave students pretests (including the PCT and WPTT), we provided standard instructions in elementary BASIC, and we gave a programming posttest to determine how well students could generate and comprehend BASIC programs. Although the subject populations and methods of instruction varied, the results consistently showed a strong relationship between pretests, which measured program comprehension (such as the PCT) and problem translation (such as the WPTT), and the posttest, which measured learning BASIC. For example, the correlations between the PCT and the posttest were .39, .28, and .44 in studies 1–3, respectively; the correlations between the WPTT and the posttest were .28, .64, .55, and .61 for students 1–4, respectively. (Study 4 did not include the PCT.) All of the correlations except $r = .28$ are statistically significant at $p < .05$; subsequent regression analyses were able to account for more than 50% of the variance in posttest scores based on the pretest measures of users' existing conceptions. It should be pointed out that tests of general intellectual ability (including tests of logical ability, verbal ability, and spatial ability) were not as good predictors of success in learning BASIC as tests of specifically relevant conceptions like program comprehension (as measured by the PCT) and problem translation (as measured by the WPTT). These results are consistent with the idea that existing conceptual knowledge or intuitions (as measured by the tests of specific cognitive skills) are related to learning to write and comprehend BASIC programs.

4 Are Conceptual Features Similar for English and BASIC Statements?

What is involved in comprehending a BASIC statement such as INPUT A or LET A = B + 1 or PRINT C? According to the conceptual knowledge hypothesis, comprehending a statement involves encoding the transactions required for the statement (i.e., building the microstructure) and encoding the relations between the statement and each of the other relevant statements in the program (i.e., building the macrostructure). Thus, the time to comprehend a statement should depend on the number of transactions (T) required for that statement and the number of other statements in the program (C).

For example, the transactional analysis described in the section on "An Analysis of Conceptual Knowledge" revealed that PRINT A involves 4 transactions, INPUT A involves 9 transactions, and LET B = A + 1 involves 10 transactions. If a statement is embedded in a four-line program, then the number of other statements is 3; if a statement is embedded in a three-line program, then the number of other statements is 2.

In order to investigate users' comprehension of BASIC statements, Jenny Dyck and I conducted a study in our lab at Santa Barbara. Subjects who knew BASIC were presented with a series of problems such as

```
10    INPUT A
20    LET B = A + 1
30    PRINT B
```

The number for A is 5. What is the output?
(a) 10 (b) 5 (c) 6 (d) 1

The problems were presented on a computer terminal screen, and subjects responded by pressing the button corresponding to the correct answer. A subtraction technique was used to estimate the response time (RT) for each of eight types of statements. For example, to estimate the RT for the statement LET B = A + 1, the time for a short program such as,

```
10    INPUT A
20    PRINT A
```

was subtracted from the time for a longer program such as,

```
10      INPUT A
20      LET B = A + 1
30      PRINT B
```

An analysis of the results revealed that the RT for any particular type of BASIC statement was strongly related to the number of transactions (T) and number of other statements in the program (C) for that statement. For example, in the LET statement in the above program, T = 10 and C = 2. A stepwise regression analysis using RT (in seconds) as the criterion and T and C as predictors produced the following equation:

$$\text{BASIC RT} = (-1.23) + (0.18)T + (0.50)C$$

This equation was able to account for 74% of the variance in RTs on BASIC statements. Thus, microstructure and macrostructure variables, based on a transactional analysis of the underlying concepts, appear to be strongly related to users' comprehension processing of BASIC statements.

In order to determine whether the same conceptual variables could account as well for comprehension of English procedural statements, we conducted a corresponding study. The study and data analysis were identical to the one described above except that each BASIC statement was translated into a corresponding English statement. For example, INPUT A was translated as "Put the first number shown below in Box-A"; PRINT A was translated as "Write down the number that is in Box-A"; and LET B = A + 1 was translated as "Add the number 1 to the number from Box-A, and put this new number in Box-B." As with BASIC statements, the RTs to comprehend English statements were strongly related to microstructure and macrostructure variables. The stepwise regression equation predicting the RT for English statements was,

$$\text{English RT} = (-.20) + (0.16)T + (0.96)Q + (0.70)C$$

where T is the number of transactions, Q is a measure of the qualitative difficulty of the transactions (i.e., Q = 0 for standard transactions such as A = B + 1, Q = 1 for transactions in which a random variable assumed more than one value such as A = A + 1), and C is the number of other statements in the program. This equation was able to account for 88% of the variance in RTs, and is consistent with the idea that the same kinds of variables are related to comprehension of English statements as BASIC statements. However, it should also be noted that the Q variable (a measure of the quality of transactions) was not needed for BASIC (presumably because the equationlike notation of BASIC makes it easier to think of random variables) and BASIC response times were faster overall (presumably because of the more compact notation of BASIC).

In summary, while the notational differences between BASIC and English have some predictable relation to RT, there is also a consistent pattern in which RT for both BASIC and English depends on the same kinds of microstructure and macrostructure variables. For example, if we focus only on the relation between the number of transactions in a statement and the response time required to comprehend the statement, the correlation is .75 for BASIC and .68 for English with both correlations significant at $p < .05$. In addition, the pattern of response times on the eight statement types is remarkably similar for BASIC and English, yielding a correlation of .85 which is significant at $p < .05$. Again, these results are consistent with the idea that users' existing conceptions affect comprehension similarly for procedural statements that are given in BASIC and English.

5 Do Novices Acquire Useful Models While Learning BASIC?

Suppose that a group of novices has just completed a standard course in BASIC computer programming. They have worked at their own rates in reading textbook lessons and in having hands-on access to a computer. Furthermore, let us suppose that they have learned under a mastery system, in which a student must pass a test on the material in one lesson before being allowed to go on to the next lesson. In short, the students have mastered elementary BASIC programming, including the use of statements such as INPUT, READ, DATA, LET, PRINT, GOTO, IF-GOTO, IF-THEN.

In the course of learning BASIC, what kinds of conceptions have the novices acquired? Does hands-on access and self-paced instruction ensure that users will acquire useful conceptions? Does demonstration of mastery of the core material—such as being able to retain the material in the lessons—ensure that users acquire useful conceptions?

In order to answer these questions, Piraye Bayman and I conducted some studies in which students learned elementary BASIC programming under self-paced, mastery instructions. To ensure that students learned the material, students were required to pass mastery tests after each lesson. For example, a typical test item from one of the mastery tests was,

> Write a conditional GOTO statement such that the program control is transferred to line 10 if the value of variable A is less than 85.

Following mastery of the material—i.e., after students were able to pass tests covering the material—we tested the students concerning their conceptual knowledge of BASIC statements. In particular, we were interested in whether students possessed the appropriate transactions for each of several BASIC statements. One of the tests we designed, called the Procedure Specification Test (PST), presented a statement and asked the subject to list all the steps the computer would carry out to execute that statement. For example, the instructions for part of the test include the following:

Suppose the computer is executing a program and now it is on line 40:

40   LET A = B + 1

Can you list, in plain English, all of the steps that the computer has to carry out in order to execute this line? Think of the necessary actions of the computer for doing what is instructed in the statement. Express those actions in your own words as simple English sentences.
Your job, in this test, is to figure out the set of steps that the computer has to carry out for a given line of a program.
For example, think what the computer does step by step for the statement, 40 LET A = B + 1. Write the actions of the computer that you think of in your own words, on the following lines.
Use as many lines as you need.
The steps the computer carries out to execute 40 LET A = B + 1 are:

1. __________
2. __________
3. __________
4. __________
5. __________
6. __________
7. __________
8. __________

Make sure that you write only one action on each line.
Use plain English sentences.
Use as many lines as you need.

Subjects were asked to generate procedure specifications for several statements including LET A = B + 1, LET D = 0, INPUT A, and PRINT C.

A typical subject's protocol for LET A = B + 1 was as follows:

1. The computer reads the line.
2. The computer stores the equation A = B + 1 in memory.
3. The computer prints A on the screen.

As you can see, the subject has some misconceptions concerning the transactions underlying the LET statement. For example, the subject does not seem to understand the nature of memory spaces, i.e., that each space is labeled and contains one number.

In order to summarize the data, each subject's protocol for each statement was compared to the correct list of transactions. For example, the key correct transaction for LET A = B + 1 is "Assign the value of B + 1 to memory space A," and a typical incorrect transaction is "Write the equation in memory." If a subject correctly stated the key transaction and did not state any incorrect transactions, then the subject was given credit for having a correct conception of the statement. In one study, 27% of the subjects had a correct conception for LET B = A + 1, 43% for LET D = 0, 3% for INPUT A, and 33% for PRINT C. In another study, the corresponding percentages were, respectively, 63%, 74%, 26%, and 68%.

The foregoing results seem to show that users did not generally acquire correct conceptions for BASIC statements. In order to look more closely at users' misconceptions, we examined the most frequent incorrect transactions given for each statement. For LET A = B + 1, the most frequently given incorrect transactions were:

Store the equation in memory.

Write B + 1 in memory space A.

Print the value of A on the screen.

For LET D = 0, the most frequently given incorrect transactions were:

Store the equation in memory.

Print 0 on the screen.

For INPUT A, the most frequently given incorrect transactions were:

Store A in memory.

Print current value of A on the screen.

For PRINT C, the most frequently given incorrect transactions were:

Print the letter C on the screen.

Write the letter C in memory.

As you can see, subjects seem to have difficulty in understanding where the data come from (as in READ-DATA and INPUT statements) and where they are stored (as in READ-DATA, LET, and INPUT). Apparently, subjects do not understand the main locations of the computer, such as memory spaces, input queue, output screen, and so on. These results are presented in more detail in Bayman and Mayer (1983) and Bayman (1983).

6 Can Students Be Taught to Acquire Useful Conceptual Knowledge?

The foregoing section has shown that students who are given standard instruction in BASIC tend to acquire conceptual knowledge that is often incomplete or even incorrect. Most instruction in BASIC, including the standard instruction given to our subjects in the previously described studies, does not help the user to acquire useful underlying concepts concerning actions, objects, and locations. Instead, the instruction focuses on the syntax of the language.

Let us suppose that we were able to supplement standard instruction with some training in the transactions that underlie each statement. Would this conceptual training affect the quality of students' conceptual knowledge? Would conceptual training affect performance on programming tests that required creatively using the BASIC language? Is there a relationship between having correct conceptions and being able to solve programming problems?

In order to answer these questions, Piraye Bayman conducted an instructional study. Students learned BASIC using a standard textbook (Control Group) or using the same textbook but with added information about the transactions for each statement (Transactions Group). For example, an excerpt from the Control Group's textbook is:

Now assume that you type in:
LET A = 1 and press the RETURN key.
The value, 1, will be stored in variable A.

The corresponding excerpt from the Transactions Group's textbook is:

Now, assume that you type in:
LET A = 1 and press the RETURN key.

The steps the computer carries out are:

1. FIND the number stored in memory space A.
2. ERASE that number in memory space A.
3. WRITE the number, 1, in memory space A.
4. WAIT FOR the next statement to be entered from the keyboard.

As you can see, the Transaction Textbook includes lists of transactions for each statement, such as FIND, ERASE, WRITE, and WAIT FOR in the above example. In addition, the study included other versions of the Transaction Textbook, which presented the transactions in various formats including words and pictures.

After reading either the Control Textbook or one of the versions of the Transactions Textbook, subjects took tests to evaluate their conceptual knowledge—such as the Procedure Specification Test (PST) described in the previous section—and tests to evaluate their ability to solve programming problems—such as the Programming Test. The Programming Test included items that asked subjects to write programs, debug programs, and comprehend programs.

Previous studies (Mayer, 1975, 1981) indicated that the effects of conceptual training were strongest for low-ability students, presumably because high-ability students already possessed useful conceptual knowledge. Thus, in the present study, Bayman broke the Control and Transactions Groups into high-ability and low-ability subgroups on the basis of SAT-Quantitative scores.

First, the Procedure Specification Test was scored for each subject by determining the percentage of statements for which the subject reported a correct conception. For low-ability students, the Control subjects scored an average of 30% correct conceptions and the Transactions subjects scored an average of 53% correct conceptions; for high-ability, both the Control and the Transactions Groups averaged 67% correct conceptions. An analysis of variance conducted on these data revealed that the ability by treatment interaction (ATI) is statistically significant at $p < .05$, and is consistent with the assertion that conceptual training is effective for low-ability students but not for high-ability students. These results serve to validate the Transactions Textbook as an effective instructor of conceptual knowledge for students who would not normally acquire useful conceptual knowledge.

Second, the Programming Test was scored for each subject, yielding a score of percentage correct response. For low-ability subjects, the Control Group achieved 48%, compared to 58% for the Transactions Group; for high-ability subjects, corresponding scores were 74% for the Control Group and 65% for the Transactions Group. Again, an analysis of variance revealed that the ability by treatment interaction (ATI) is significant at $p < .05$, and is consistent with the idea that conceptual training increases the programming performance of the low-ability students but not the high-ability students. These results help to show that training in concepts about actions, objects, and location helps low-ability students to improve their ability to use BASIC creatively in solving problems.

Third, performance on the Procedure Specification Test and performance on the Programming Test correlated at $r = .56$ for all subjects. When the effects of general mathematical ability were partialed out, the correlation remained high at $r = .51$. These correlations are statistically significant at

$p < .01$, and are consistent with the idea that knowledge of correct conceptions is related to performance in solving programming problems.

In summary, the results of Bayman's study support the idea that direct instruction in underlying conceptions can be effective and that such training can enhance students' performance in solving programming problem. A more detailed report is available in Bayman (1983).

Conclusion

We began by suggesting that there is more to learning BASIC than learning the appropriate vocabulary (e.g., INPUT, LET, PRINT) and grammar (e.g., INPUT is followed by an address name, as in INPUT A). Learning BASIC also depends on the users' conceptions or intuition underlying BASIC, which we have called conceptual knowledge.

In the present chapter, we presented a framework, called "transactional analysis," for describing users' conceptual knowledge. Then, we examined four sets of empirical research studies that were motivated by transactional analysis. First, individual differences in novices' success in learning BASIC were strongly related to individual differences in novices' existing conceptions underlying BASIC. Second, time needed to comprehend procedural statements presented in BASIC and in English was strongly related to variables proposed by transactional analysis, i.e., to the number (and, sometimes, to the difficulty) of transactions and the number of other statements in the program. Third, novices who learned BASIC under standard instructional conditions tended to acquire conceptions that often consisted of incomplete or incorrect transactions. Finally, direct instruction in the transactions underlying each statement tended to improve the conceptual knowledge of poor students and to improve their ability to use BASIC to solve programming problems; in addition, the results showed a strong relationship between knowing the correct transactions for BASIC statements and being able to solve programming problems.

These results have both specific and general implications. At a specific level, these results suggest that learning BASIC requires that the learner's incorrect conceptions be replaced with more useful ones. In addition, the transactional analysis of BASIC seems to provide a useful framework for describing user's conceptual knowledge of BASIC and upon which to build a meaningful instructional program. At a general level, these results suggest that the analytic tools of cognitive psychology can be productively applied to situations involving complex learning and cognition. These results support Rensnick and Ford's (1981) call to develop psychologies of subject matter areas.

Note

1. "Semantic knowledge" and "conceptual knowledge" are used interchangeably. A distinction should be made between the use of the term "conceptual knowledge" in this chapter and the use of the term "mental model" in other chapters. "Conceptual knowledge" is used to refer to a user's low-level knowledge of actions, locations, and objects relevant to families of programming languages (including the concept of a random variable) and high-level knowledge of programming structures, such as what various kinds of procedures do. "Mental model" refers to a user's internal representation of the states and events that occur within a specific machine or system. This chapter relies partly on transactional analysis (Mayer, 1979a, 1985) as a way of describing a user's conceptual knowledge.

References

Bayman, P. (1983). Effects of instructional procedure on learning a first programming language. Unpublished doctoral dissertation. University of California, Santa Barbara.

Bayman, P., and Mayer, R. E. (1983). A diagnosis of beginning programmers' misconceptions of BASIC programming statements. *Communications of the ACM*, 26, 677–679.

Bayman, P., and Mayer, R. E. (1984). Instructional manipulation of users' mental models for electronic calculators. *International Journal of Man-Machine Studies*, 20, 189–199.

Card, S. K., Moran, T. P., and Newell, A. (1980). Computer text-editing: An information processing analysis of a routine cognitive skill. *Cognitive Psychology*, 12, 32–74.

Carroll, J. M., and Thomas, J. C. (1982). Metaphor and the cognitive representation of computing systems. *IEEE Transactions on Systems, Man, and Cybernetics*, 12, 107–116.

Clement, J. (1982). Students' preconceptions in introductory mechanics. *American Journal of Physics*, 50, 66–71.

Du Boulay, B., and O'Shea, T. (1981). Teaching novices programming. In M. J. Coombs and J. L. Alty (Eds.), *Computing Skills and the User Interface*. London, Academic Press.

Du Boulay, B., O'Shea, T., and Monk, J. (1981). The black box inside the glass box: Presenting computing concepts to novices. *International Journal of Man-Machine Studies*, 14, 237–249.

McCloskey, M. (1983). Intuitive physics. *Scientific American*, 248(4), 122–130.

McCloskey, M., Caramazza, A., and Green, B. (1980). Curvilinear motion in the absence of external forces: Naive beliefs about the motion of objects. *Science*, 210 (No. 4474), 1139–1141.

Mayer, R. E. (1975). Different problem-solving competencies established in learning computer programming with and without meaningful models. *Journal of Educational Psychology*, 67, 725–734.

Mayer, R. E. (1976). Some conditions of meaningful learning for computer programming: Advance organizers and subject control of frame order. *Journal of Educational Psychology*, 68, 143–150.

Mayer, R. E. (1979a). A psychology of learning BASIC. *Communications of the ACM*, 22, 589–593.

Mayer, R. E. (1979b). Can advance organizers influence meaningful learning? *Review of Educational Research*, 49, 371–383.

Mayer, R. E. (1981). The psychology of how novices learn computer programming. *Computer Surveys*, 13, 121–141.

Mayer, R. E. (1985). Learning in complex domains: A cognitive analysis of computer programming. *Psychology of Learning and Motivation*, 19, 89–130.

Mayer, R. E., and Bayman, P. (1981). Psychology of calculator language: A framework for describing differences in user's knowledge. *Communications of the ACM*, 24, 511–520.

Moran, T. P. (1981a). An applied psychology of the user. *Computing Surveys*, 13, 121–141.

Moran, T. P. (1981b). The command language grammar: A representation for user interface of interactive computer systems. *International Journal of Man-Machine Studies*, 15, 3–50.

Norman, D. A. (1983). Some observations on mental models. In D. Gentner and A. L. Stevens (Eds.), *Mental Models*. Hillsdale, NJ, Erlbaum.

Resnick, L. B., and Ford, W. (1981). *The Psychology of Mathematics for Instruction*. Hillsdale, NJ, Erlbaum.

Shneiderman, B., and Mayer, R. E. (1979). Syntactic/semantic interactions in programmer behavior: A model and experimental results. *International Journal of Computer and Information Sciences*, 8, 219–238.

Young, R. M. (1981). The machine inside the machine: Users' models of pocket calculators. *International Journal of Man-Machine Studies*, 15, 51–85.

Young, R. M. (1983). Surrogates and mappings: Two kinds of conceptual models for pocket calculators. In D. Gentner and A. L. Stevens (Eds.), *Mental Models*. Hillsdale, NJ, Erlbaum.

5 Paradox of the Active User

John M. Carroll and
Mary Beth Rosson

1 Introduction

One of the most sweeping changes ever in the *ecology* of human cognition may be taking place today. People are beginning to learn and use very powerful and sophisticated information processing technology as a matter of daily life. From the perspective of human history, this could be a transitional point, dividing a period when machines merely helped us do things from a period when machines will seriously help us think about things. But if this is so, we are indeed still very much within the transition. For most people, computers have more possibility than they have real practical utility.

In this chapter we discuss two empirical phenomena of computer use: (1) people have considerable trouble learning to use computers (e.g., Mack, Lewis, and Carroll, 1983; Mantei and Haskell, 1983) and (2) their skill tends to asymptote at relative mediocrity (Nielsen et al., 1986; Pope, 1985; Rosson, 1983). These phenomena could be viewed as being due merely to "bad" design in current systems. We argue that they are in part more fundamental than this, deriving from conflicting motivational and cognitive strategies. Accordingly, (1) and (2) are best viewed not as design problems to be solved, but as true paradoxes that necessitate programmatic tradeoff solutions.

A motivational paradox arises in the "production bias" people bring to the task of learning and using computing equipment. Their paramount goal is throughput. This is a desirable state of affairs in that it gives users a focus for their activity with a system, and it increases their likelihood of receiving concrete reinforcement from their work. But on the other hand, it reduces

We are grateful to John Whiteside and Phyllis Reisner for critiquing an earlier version of this chapter. We also received helpful comments from our lab's reading group (John Black, Rich Catrambone, Bob Mack, Jean McKendree, and John Richards).

their motivation to spend any time just learning about the system, so that when situations appear that could be more effectively handled by new procedures, they are likely to stick with the procedures they already know, regardless of their efficacy.

A second, cognitive paradox devolves from the "assimilation bias": People apply what they already know to interpret new situations. This bias can be helpful, when there are useful similarities between the new and old information (as when a person learns to use a word processor, taking it to be a supertypewriter or an electronic desktop). But irrelevant and misleading similarities between new and old information can also blind learners to what they are actually seeing and doing, leading them to draw erroneous comparisons and conclusions, or preventing them from recognizing possibilities for new functions.

It is our view that these cognitive and motivational conflicts are mutually reinforcing, thus exaggerating the effect either problem might separately have on early and long-term learning. These paradoxes are not defects in human learning to be remedied. They are fundamental properties of learning. If learning were not at least this complex, then designing learning environments would be a trivial design problem (Thomas and Carroll, 1979). Our discussion is based on studies of the learning and routine use of word processing systems, and we speculate on potential programmatic tradeoff solutions to the paradoxes in this domain and generally.

2 The Active User

A colorful, and apt, image of the world of the new user of a computer system is found in the often quoted phrase of William James: "a bloomin' buzzin' confusion." People in this situation see many things going on, but they do not know which of these are relevant to their current concerns. Indeed, they do not know whether their current concerns are the appropriate concerns for them to have. The learner reads something in the manual, sees something on the display, and must try to connect the two—to integrate, to interpret. It would be unsurprising to find that people in such a situation suffer conceptual—or even physical—paralysis. They have so little basis on which to act.

And yet people do act. Indeed, the typical pattern we have observed is that people simply strike out into the unknown. If the rich and diverse sources of available information cannot be interpreted, then some of these will be ignored. If something *can* be interpreted (no matter how specious the basis for this interpretation), then it will be interpreted. Ad hoc theories are hastily assembled out of these odds and ends of partially relevant and partially extraneous generalization. And these "theories" are used for further prediction. Whatever initial confusions get into such a process, it is easy to see that they are at the mercy of a diverging feedback loop: Things quite often get worse before they get better.

Designers of computer systems and training technology surely would have liked things to have been different. The easiest way to teach people something is, after all, to tell them directly. However, what we see in the learning-to-use-a-computer situation is that people are so busy trying things out, thinking things through, and trying to relate what they already know (or believe they know) to what is going on that they often do not notice the small voice of structured instruction crying out to them from behind the manual and the system interface.

A similar picture appears in considering the more experienced users of computer systems. Here, the best characterization is not one of striking out into the unknown. Rather, it is one of relying on the *known* to get things accomplished. Users tend to make use of the functions they know about to get a result, regardless of the efficacy of the mehod entrained. Designers of reference and help systems count on users to recognize opportunities for new methods, and to search out the information needed to implement them. But users often figure out how to use what they already know to achieve new goals. They have little desire to explore new functions or to search out information, if they can use methods they are already comfortable with to achieve the same goal.

What is wrong? We would argue that the learning practices people adopt here are typical, and in many situations adaptive (Scribner, 1984). The problem in this particular learning situation is that learners are *innocent* in the extreme. Each feature of a computer system may indeed have a sensible design rationale from the viewpoint of the system's engineer, but this rationale is frequently far beyond the grasp of the new user, or indeed even a user familiar with the basic function of the system. "Word processor," so far as we know, is not a natural concept. People who do not know about word processors have little, possibly nothing, to refer to in trying actively to learn to use such things. Innocence turns reasonable learning strategies into learning problems (Carroll and Mack, 1984).

3 The Production Paradox

It is good to want to get something done. One would only ever *want* to learn to use a new tool if one wanted first to get something done. But wanting to get something done can also be a problem, if one lacks the prerequisites: You have to learn to do in order to do. Merely wanting to use a new tool may be necessary, but it is not sufficient.

3.1 Problems for New Users

Training and reference materials often are designed under the assumption that people who need to learn something will be willing to read about it, to practice skills in a sensibly structured sequence of exercises, and finally to assemble these conceptual and skill components into a mature competence and understanding. Further, it is assumed that when people seek to learn more about a domain, they will again be willing to engage in these activities to develop and refine their expertise. But these assumptions are empirically unsound. Learners at every level of experience try to avoid reading. In structured practice, they often accidentally or deliberately get off track and end up in lengthy and complex tangles of error recovery or self-initiated exploration. (For details, see Carroll and Mazur, 1986; Mack, Lewis, and Carroll, 1983).

New users are not "blank slates" for training designers to write upon. Indeed, the most accurate way to think about new users is as experts in other, noncomputer domains. Secretaries trying to learn to use a word processor are not starting from ground zero in any relevant sense. They are experts at routine office tasks. (Unfortunately, but in all likelihood, they are far more expert than the designers of their word processing system!) The same point can be made for any other class of new users as they come to learn an application system designed to be a tool for them in their work. When a domain expert tries to use a tool designed specifically to support his or her work activities, the orientation is to do real work, *not* to read descriptions and instructions, or to practice step-by-step exercises.

New users tend to jump right in when introduced to application systems. If an operation is referred to in their training materials, they want to try it out at once. Rote descriptions and practice are resisted, and even when complied with, prove difficult to follow and assimilate. In a training system studied in Carroll and Mazur (1986), there is a list of icons in the training guide identifying the applications available, but users are not allowed to try the applications represented. After an hour or so of training, one learner complained, "I'm getting impatient. I want to do something, not learn to do everything." Half an hour later, he exclaimed, "I could have typed 3,000 words by now!" Users become very frustrated when training "introduces" them to a function but expects them to refrain from using it to perform a real task. Another learner balked when instructed by an on-line tutorial to read a passage but not do anything, exclaiming "I'm tempted to do it anyway and then see if I can get out."

Often, users respond to these desires to try things out, to get things done. But jumping the gun like this, and relying on exploratory learning strategies instead of the step-by-step rote structure of a manual or on-line tutorial, can be costly. Carroll and Mazur (1986) described a learner who explored a Wastebasket function by throwing away one and then another of the applications available on the system. This hypothesis testing approach did in fact enable her to induce correctly the Wastebasket operation, but at a fairly high price—she could not restore these applications. In other cases, the heuristic reasoning strategies users bring to bear do not even produce the correct conclusions. Another learner began drawing conclusions about work diskettes as soon as he saw the term: "Work diskette. Does that mean it won't work without a work diskette?" Later, he got an error message—"Work Diskette needs recovery. Use recovery task."—and confidently concluded that he had initially placed the diskette in the wrong slot of the disk drive—which was a totally irrelevant consideration in this case. Loosely reasoned hypotheses are of course frequently wrong, yet they are attractive to users in that they allow rapid (albeit reckless), learner-directed progress on real tasks.

3.2 Problems for Experienced Users

For more experienced users, the Production Paradox is more subtle. It is not merely a matter of an urgent and yet premature need to produce, but rather a matter of balancing investment of time in learning versus throughput. The issue is one of whether it is worth the time to suspend throughput via already learned, but perhaps inefficient, methods, to engage in learning, which only in the long run might facilitate greater throughput.

Most computer systems and their reference libraries are designed with an inherently rational view of users in mind. They provide a range of functions from basic to advanced, under the assumption that with experience, users will naturally acquire the procedural knowledge that most effectively fulfills their needs. Indeed, much of the early work in system evaluation has been guided by this assumption—that the asymptotic level of behavior is one relatively free of errors and inefficient strategies (e.g., Card, Moran, and Newell, 1980, 1983). However, this assumption is called into question by recent work examining routine text editor use (Rosson, 1984a,b).

In this work, users were both surveyed about their use of a text editor and monitored during their daily use of the system. The users varied in their experience with the editor, as well as in their experience with other editing systems, and in their job type. This editor provides a number of advanced functions for streamlining use, and one of the issues of interest was the extent to which such a function is picked up by experienced users.

In general, we found that many users were not discovering and using functions that could have made their jobs easier. A good example comes in the analysis of *macro* use; macros are stored programs that allow for extensions and modifications of the basic editor function. Many macros are available on a public disk, and one thing we examined was the use of this "extra" function. We discovered that a large number of users had not incorporated any of the macros into their daily activities; this was true despite the fact that the most popular macros were ones providing very basic extensions to general editing functions, not routines serving special-purpose functions that could be viewed as appropriate only for sophisticated users. Thus, although there appeared to be a general need for this added function (analysis indicated that use of the macros was indeed associated with more rapid editing activity), the less sophisticated users (in this case, these were secretarial and administrative users) made virtually no use of these public macros. We speculated that this was due to the number of steps required to find out about and use the extra function, steps that might well seem too much trouble to a user focused on generating end products.

Additional evidence that users fail to become experts is the appearance of "pockets of expertise" in user populations (Rosson, Gould, and Grischkowsky, 1982; Draper, 1984): Instead of becoming generalized experts themselves, users learn a basic set of knowledge, presumably relying on local experts to help them out when special needs arise. In some situations, this sociological phenomenon may work out nicely—where a work situation is structured in such a way that specific users are assigned topics to master, and other users are made aware of when and whom to consult. However, in the general case, its success hinges on users' willingness to take the time to find and consult an appropriate expert when a particular need arises rather than making do with their more primitive skills. Unfortunately, we have no reason to believe that users will take the time and effort to find and consult human experts any more than they would a reference manual.

4 Approaches to the Production Paradox

As we stated in our introductory remarks, we do not see the Production Paradox as a problem to be solved *tout court.* We do see several approaches to the paradox, but each is limited; indeed the three approaches we describe below are actually inconsistent with one another if taken to logical conclusions.

One approach is to ease the focus on tangible end products for users. While it may be natural for users of computing equipment to adopt an end-product motivational orientation, this may not be inevitably monolithic. Other motivational sets may be suggested or induced. A second approach is to minimize the consequences of an end-product focus by reducing the motivation necessary for learning. Learning that requires less motivation of the user might occur successfully even for users focused principally on generating end products. As a third approach, we can try to design computing systems to better support the end-product focus; we can give the people what they want.

4.1 Attacking the End-Product Focus

At an extreme, the end-product focus can have the effect of subjugating *intrinsic* sources of reward (achievement, satisfaction of curiosity, control of the environment) to *extrinsic* sources of reward (printed output, hits in a data base query). Nevertheless, it is known that intrinsic rewards—when they can be made salient to people—can be far more potent motivators than extrinsic rewards (e.g., Greene and Lepper, 1979). Thus, one approach to the Production Paradox is to make the intrinsic rewards of successfully learning and using a computing system more salient to users.

Computer games have been investigated from this perspective. Malone (1981a,b) argues that these games can be effective learning environments for children by stimulating curiosity, fantasy, and challenge as intrinsic sources of reward. One might imagine incorporating aspects of a game environment into the interfaces of ordinary application programs. For example, a version of the system could be made available for "playing"; learners would receive points according to their ability, first, to accomplish tasks at all, and second, to accomplish them in an optimal fashion. Carroll and Thomas (1982) suggested that routine applications could be presented under multiple interesting cover stories; the operator might be interacting with a flight simulator, but in doing so actually managing a process control application.

Intrinsic motivation might also be effectively stimulated by incorporating more abstract elements of game environments into interface designs. One way that games motivate participants is by conjuring a world in which uncertainty is acceptable. In the well-known game of Adventure, players attempt to navigate a complex underground cave filled with assorted treasures and dangers. At the very outset though, they do not even know this, and as they go along they constantly encounter new and unexplained elements in the game. They remain in a discovery mode, never quite sure whether they are making progress or hopelessly lost. The game's interface dialog is structured to instill the attitude that this is all right, that uncertainty, discovery, and risk are inevitable. There is a rationale for this: People prefer activities whose outcomes of success and failure are uncertain (Weiner, 1980), and outcome uncertainty has been found to maintain greater interest in an activity (Berlyne, 1967). All this is in sharp contrast to typical application interface dialog, which implicitly projects an end-product focus to users, ruling out uncertainty, discovery, and risk (Carroll, 1982a).

McKendree, Schorno, and Carroll (1985) are currently experimenting with these ideas in a management setting. One version of their Personal Planner system provides prompting dialog that merely challenges the user to try things out. Other versions of the system provide more conventional prompting dialog that identifies correct and incorrect user responses. We expect that providing increased feedback and specifically increasing the extent to which feedback is contingent on user goals and explicit behavior will increase achievement satisfaction.

Attacking the end-product focus directly has apparent limitations. When one ponders the proposals that have been made, it seems evident that they will not work for all cases—some procedures might be too intricate for dialogs that rely exclusively on piquing the user's curiosity; some users might find it difficult to relax their end-product orientation. Moreover, the strategy can backfire; there are good effects of an end-product focus, and these too may be undermined by suggesting alternate motivational orientations—users might think of the system as a toy, or construe their real tasks in needlessly nondirective ways. In sum, it seems that other approaches will also be required.

4.2 Mitigating the Effects of an End-Product Focus

A second approach to dealing with the Production Paradox would be to make learning a less motivationally demanding task. There are two ways we might reduce the motivational "cost" of learning—make the learning safer and more risk-free, or make the relevant information easier to find. If trying out a new function is perceived as risk-free, a learner may be more willing to try it; it is less likely to interfere with the goal of producing something. Several design approaches have been taken in promoting the "safety" of systems during training. These fall into two classes—controlling the consequences of any given action by the user, and controlling the actions available to the user.

An extreme example falling into the first class is the "reconnoiter mode" proposed by Jagodzinski (1983). Here, users would be able to enter a mode that simulates the results of some proposed actions, but none of the activity has any permanent consequence for the task. The problem here, of course, is that the simulated activity does not move the user toward a goal in any real sense—it only allows him or her to "try out" something that when repeated outside of reconnoiter mode might have the desired effect.

Another approach to controlling the consequences of actions requires that each operation have an obvious inverse. Thus, if there is a command to "drop" a file, there should be a complementary command to invert that operation and "pick up" a file—and the names of the commands should make this opposition salient (Carroll, 1982b). In such an environment, a person can try something out at a very low cost; if the result is not what was desired, the operation can be reversed, leaving no lasting consequence. A generalization of this approach is the so-called "undo" command, which is intended to be an inverse to any operation (or sequence of operations). Of course, this sounds simpler than it is: What is the appropriate "grain" of undo (a typed character, a command, a user task)? What state should you be in if three undos are executed in sequence? (See Gordon, Leeman, and Lewis, 1984.) Currently there are only approximations of undo available.

A second class of solutions moves the control up a level, so that the options available are controlled, rather than their consequences. So, for example, one can design or retrofit an interface so that advanced functions and/or potentially errorful troublespots are unavailable to beginners (or more generally to users diagnosed as not yet ready for them). This is sometimes called a "staged" interface. Staging the presentation of a function can limit the range of errors that inexperienced users can fall into, and therefore make experimenting with the system less risky. An example is a system that refrains from displaying parameter options when a workable default value is available (e.g., Smith et al., 1982). While such "progressive disclosure" restricts the range of activity available to the user, it restricts in parallel the number of error conditions that can occur.

Work in our laboratory has developed a "training wheels" approach that combines the two classes of solutions (Carroll, 1983). A training wheels interface displays all of the function choices of a full function system, but disables advanced and provocative incorrect choices during the early stages of a user's learning. Making one of these choices merely elicits a disablement message indicating that the selected function is not available during training, leaving the user in the same system state. Thus, while the learner is allowed to make an "error" (choosing an incorrect option), the consequences of the error are minimized.

We have carried out several experimental evaluations of the training wheels system. We asked learners to use either the training wheels system or the complete commercial system to learn to type and print out a simple document. The results of these studies were quite encouraging; learners using the training wheels system got started faster, produced better work, and spent less time not only on the errors that our design blocked, but on the errors we did not block—indicating a generalized facilitation of learning. Moreover, the magnitude of these advantages increased over the course of the experiment. Finally, the training wheels learners performed better on a system concepts test we administered after the experiment (see Carroll and Carrithers, 1984).

An important complement to making learning safe is to make information about a new function easy to find and understand. Users focused on a particular task may be much more likely to enter into "learning mode" for a time, searching for new knowledge, if they believe that the knowledge will be easy to come by. One way to encourage this perception would focus on the reference materials available to a user. In the system studied in Rosson (1984a), the reference material (manual, reference card, and help screens) is organized in a linear, alphabetical fashion. This is true despite the face that a large proportion of the 140 commands are never used interactively; they are issued only from within macros or stored procedures. As a result, a user looking for information on commands useful to him or her at the terminal must wade through a number of commands unlikely ever to be used by other than a very sophisticated user. A relatively inexpensive improvement would be to take into account actual use patterns, rather than simply alphabetical ordering, in organizing the material.

A more expensive approach would be to use the computer as an active partner in learning. One might imagine a system that is able to determine the most effective path for reaching any given goal. When users recognize limitations in their current knowledge, they could query the system for a better method. An even more radical approach would be to allow the system to take the initiative, thus removing the requirement that users be motivated to look for learning opportunities (e.g., Shrager and Finin, 1982). Of course, such methods assume considerable intelligence on the part of the system, at a level yet to be provided in any real system. But even partial systems of this sort—a system that recognizes and understands only a limited set of common inefficient methods, for example—could contribute considerably to the goal of making the discovery and use of a new function easier.

The various approaches to reducing the motivation required of the user that we have reviewed must be qualified in terms of their potential and current limitations. Many of these proposals have yet to be implemented for serious testing; reconnoiter mode and undo do not really exist in non-approximate forms. And although some work has been done on systems able to observe users and make suggestions, at this point the domains studied have been rather restricted. Further, the proposals that have been implemented have generally not been studied very thoroughly in terms of their behavioral concomitants. While progressive disclosure makes a priori sense, we know of no empirical work examining its effectiveness. The training wheels approach has only been studied for a single computer application (word processing) and a single interface style (menu-based control).

A host of behavioral questions remains open. How can systems transit between stages so as to most facilitate transfer of old knowledge and incorporation of new knowledge? What effects will the blocking of error consequences have on learning in the long run? Preliminary results from Carroll and Kay (1985) suggest that certain types of protective interfaces may have a negative effect on subsequent learning, indicating that the nature of the "block" will be critical. If not presented carefully, a system that volunteers suggestions for improvement may be so disruptive as to wipe out any benefits to learning. And of course, there is the danger that by making learning too easy, we shall make it too passive. If all problems are automatically analyzed, and suggestions for improvement directly provided, users' motivation to learn may be reduced even further, due to lack of challenge. Clearly, the issues here are complex, and it is unlikely that a single approach will be sufficient.

4.3 Designing for the End-Product Focus

We need not take the learner's focus on tangible products to be the problematic aspect of the Production Paradox. As a complement to designing around the end-product focus, that is, by making the system itself more intrinsically interesting or more safe to navigate and easy to learn, we can directly exploit the user's desire for a product by using it to drive learning. We can take the production bias as our starting point, and attempt to design systems and learning environments that actually depend on such an orientation.

An example is the Guided Exploration cards studied by Carroll et al. (1985). This training approach challenges the assumption that a linearly structured training manual format is the most appropriate training tool. The cards are more task oriented than manuals in that each card addresses a particular functional goal that users can understand on the basis of their understanding of office tasks (irrespective of computers). The cards are designed to keep learners focused on and involved in the learning task by being intentionally incomplete, often relying on hints. The cards are also more simply organized than manuals. Each card attempts to address its functional goal without reference to material covered on other cards. Finally, each card includes specific checkpoint information (to help learners detect and diagnose errors) and error recovery information (to help them get back on track). In addition, there is a general "What if something goes wrong?" card that describes remedies that apply anywhere.

We performed experimental evaluations of Guided Exploration cards and state-of-the-art self-study training manuals. Learners using the Guided Exploration cards spent substantially less time, yet still performed better, on a transfer of learning posttest than learners using the commercially developed self-study manual. Taking learning efficiency to be achievement per unit time, we found that the cards were nearly three times as efficient as the manual. Moreover, qualitative analysis of learning protocols shows that the Guided Exploration cards worked as they were designed to work; they increased attention to the task, they encouraged learners to explore (and to do so successfully), they helped learners recognize and recover from errors, and they provided a better understanding of learning goals.

While this work was carried out for novice user groups, many of the objectives and techniques of the work should apply to more experienced users as well. Indeed, some systems now include "job aids" cards, which are in many ways a generalization of Guided Exploration cards. Other possibilities can be imagined. For example, one might design reference material for advanced function in a text processing system that is organized according to real-world goals rather than according to system function. In such an environment, a user's first exposure to a macro facility might come in discovering how to update a bibliography, with the result being a better association to actual needs. Work such as this underway at the University of California (e.g., O'Malley et al., 1983). The approach there has been to request goal-oriented comments from users during their interactions with a system, and to base recommendations for structuring reference materials on an analysis of these goals.

A separate area, now barely beginning, is the design of advice-giving systems—systems that are designed to help the user better articulate his or her own goal (Coombs and Alty, 1984). While this approach shares some similarities with the intelligent help systems described in the previous section, a distinction exists in the level at which suggestions are made. Instead of offering advice about ways to "tune" a method for achieving a given result, these systems would attempt to assist a user in developing and organizing task-oriented goals from the start.

Like the other approaches we have considered, attempts to design for the end-product focus carry limitations. The proposals that have actually been implemented and studied all rely on the user having appropriate goals. But clearly this assumption may not hold. If the user of Guided Exploration cards has a defective analysis of what he or she is trying to do, or if the analysis is at a different level than that provided by the card titles, this training approach may fail. And while we have suggested that intelligent problem solving aids may contribute to this piece of the process, it is not at all clear that such systems can truly be developed. Finally, even if we assume the availability of appropriate goals, end-product approaches may ultimately impair breadth of learning. An organization of knowledge by particular task procedures may produce isolated modules of understanding that will be difficult to combine when novel tasks are encountered.

5 The Assimilation Paradox

If we knew *nothing* at all, it is difficult to imagine how we could make any progress at learning *anything* at all. Almost every new idea that we learn comes to us through the graces of things we have already mastered. Nevertheless, this unavoidably good learning strategy cannot be the whole story—or indeed we would *never* learn anything truly new (Bartlett, 1932; Piattelli-Palmarini, 1980).

5.1 Problems for New Users

In discussing the Production Paradox, we made the point that even new users should be thought of as experts, albeit not in the computer domain. As such, their natural approach to a new tool is to try to use it—not simply to learn about it. As experts, new users also know a lot, though what they know is not necessarily relevant to the computer domain. Nevertheless, even a little knowledge can be a dangerous thing, particularly in a situation that invites the inference that it is relevant when it is not. This is a typical problem for new users of computer systems.

New users of word processing applications often try to understand their systems by reference to what they already know about typewriters (Carroll and Thomas, 1982). The metaphor of a typewriter can be useful in this context. But it can also lead to trouble. New users are often surprised that the Space Bar, Backspace key, and Carriage Return can change the format of their documents (including deleting characters and inserting special format characters into the document), as well as performing their more familiar typewriter functions. Learning is of course facilitated by the typewriter metaphor, but those places where the metaphor breaks down strain this advantage (see also Douglas and Moran, 1983).

We have seen similar problems in studying learners interacting with systems based on the "desktop" metaphor, where users are invited to make the comparison of an office system's directory objects to physical desktop objects like stationery, stationery pads, and folders. In one extended episode a person tried to create some test documents and then to store them. He started with a "folder," and was somewhat unsure what to do with it. He found operations for "making a stationery pad" and "tearing off stationery," which seemed consistent with his original goal, and tried them. Unfortunately, the interface metaphor strains a bit here; what he got was a stationery pad of folders from which he tore off a folder. This never quite sank in and for almost an hour he labored, selecting and making stationery pads, tearing off stationery, but never creating and storing a test document. The episode finally produced only a confused question: "Why can I sometimes make a stationery pad and not tear off stationery and other times I can tear off stationery but not make a stationery pad?"

Another aspect of this problem is that by relying on metaphors, learners impair their ability to anticipate correctly the function of the system they are learning. For example, if one conceives of an office workstation as a supertypewriter, then it is doubtful that one will tumble to an anticipation of its capabilities for formatting alternative fonts or for integrating text functions with graphics, database, and spreadsheet functions.

5.2 Problems for Experienced Users

Again, for experienced users the problem is somewhat more subtle. Experienced users, by definition, either have experience on another system or systems, or they have prior experience on the current system. In both cases, they have established patterns of behavior and understanding that can interfere with the establishment of new patterns. Thus, people who have some experience with traditional half-duplex systems (which require pressing an Enter key to send buffered interactions to a host processor) may have trouble adjusting to full-duplex systems (in which each keystroke is an interaction with the processor, and in which Entering is not necessary); they expect to need Enter (much like a novice application user might expect word processing functions to behave like the typewriter's Space Bar and Backspace). In the survey work of Rosson (1984b), one of the most frequent classes of responses to the question "What things about ⟨the editor⟩ were especially difficult to learn?" described functions in the editor similar to, but slightly different from, those available in a previously used editor.

This type of learning problem is called *negative transfer*, the inhibition of later learning by prior learning of related material. The classic demonstrations of the phenomenon have been in the context of unrelated word lists (e.g., Underwood, 1957), and the effects are much less robust in real-world situations. However, it is clear that there is some disruption caused by the mapping of new command names or function keys to identical or similar function goals. Fortunately, while the interference can be frustrating during initial learning, it tends to be a short-lived problem, one that disappears if the learner discontinues use of the old system. And in general, its negative effects are more than compensated for by the positive transfer that occurs for more general system concepts (Singley and Anderson, 1985).

There is another component of the assimilation paradox, however, that can have long-lasting effects. Prior knowledge not only can mislead users about how a system will work, but also can in a sense put blinders on them, preventing them from fully anticipating the function available. This negative effect of prior knowledge can be especially debilitating because often a learner may be completely unaware of the problem.

Evidence of these limiting effects of prior knowledge is seen in the routine editing behavior analyzed by Rosson (1984b). So, for example, one feature of the editor used by individuals in this study is a set of program function (PF) keys that can be used to speed up editing activities through assignment of frequently used functions to single keypresses. We discovered that larger function key repertoires were in fact associated with faster work rates; however, there was no tendency for key repertoire to be greater for the users most experienced with this particular system. Instead, use of the keys appeared to be a function of users' experience with other editors—specifically, experience with other *screen-oriented* systems seemed to encourage use of a greater number of PF keys. We believe that users' experience with other systems that rely heavily on function keys allowed them to recognize similar possibilities in this system. In contrast, users familiar only with more traditional command-driven systems were blinded to the many opportunities for extending their editing methods that these programmable keys provide.

6 Approaches to the Assimilation Paradox

As in the case of the Production Paradox, we shall describe three different approaches to the Assimilation Paradox. One approach is to attack the assimilative tendency, to try to get people to deal with the system on its own terms, as it were, and not "as if" it were similar to something else they already know about. A second approach tries to compromise, simplifying the assimilation processes required of (or offered to) users, and therefore, it is hoped, mitigating the force of the paradox. Finally, a third approach manipulates the assimilative opportunities for the user, deliberately highlighting inconsistencies between the current situation and the prior knowledge engaged in order to stimulate new learning.

6.1 Attacking Assimilation

As we remarked above, we doubt that the tendency for people to try to learn assimilatively can be altered. Nevertheless, effort could be directed at limiting the apparent similarity of a new experience to some prototype of past experiences. If we think of this relativistically, we might expect that the trackball as a pointing device for text applications would be less susceptible to inappropriate assimilation than are step-keys for cursor pointing. The latter work very much like typewriter pointing via the Carriage Return, Space Bar, and Backspace. As a result, users might be less likely to begin with misconceptions about how a trackball works, and might be more likely to imagine, and to learn, novel aspects of its function.

One could also take an instructional approach, specifically directing the learning experience, advising against assimilation at least in certain cases. Interface metaphors, like the desktop and typewriter comparisons mentioned earlier, have only recently been incorporated into system training and documentation. Perhaps we need to qualify these explicit invitations to assimilative learning strategies. Halasz and Moran (1982) assume this, suggesting that users be provided with explicit models of the system, highly accurate and arbitrarily complete descriptions, usually in some abstract format, like a flowchart or a graph (e.g., du Boulay, O'Shea, and

Monk, 1981; Moran, 1981; Young, 1981). Indeed, they suggest that the user be warned against apparent metaphors and analogies in favor of this more literal conceptual model.

One thing that explicit system models have in common with analogical models is that both focus on concepts that users need to master in order to have "understood" the system—as opposed to the operational procedures that users must execute in order to use the system. This distinction suggests another approach to attacking assimilation, namely, to forgo attempts to encourage "conceptual" models at all—literal or analogical. Instead, user training and interaction could be aimed strictly at the procedures that a user must execute, minimizing the conceptual material incorporated into these descriptions. An example is the teaching of recursive programming to students learning Lisp. Pirolli, Anderson, and Farrell (1984) found that students learned recursive programming much more quickly if directly provided with the programming procedures than if provided with a conceptual model of recursion.

There are apparent limitations to approaches that try to eliminate assimilation. For example, can a designer really provide the user with a conceptual model that does not evoke assimilation, as advocated by Halasz and Moran? Carroll and Mack (1985) argue that when such a model is codified in any way (e.g., on paper as a graph or a chart), as it would have to be in order to function as an instructional tool, its interpretation will require prior knowledge about such representational formats and their characteristic interpretation. To the extent that this process is not automatic and determinate, it will be assimilative. Thus, there is no sharp dichotomy here and no way to eliminate assimilation in toto.

It is also not clear that strictly procedural materials can really be developed. The examples available so far either provide implicit conceptual content (e.g., trading on understood conventions for flowcharts and graphs) or confound conceptual content per se with difficulty of material (Pirolli, Anderson, and Farrell reduced conceptual content by eliminating conceptual material on recursion, but in doing so eliminated a notoriously difficult concept as well). Perhaps the most severe limitation is that non-assimilative materials—if they can be developed—may be inappropriate for real users. Detailed descriptions and step-by-step directions, such as those one might find in a state-of-the-art self-instruction manual, are often close approximations to the explicit model approach of Halazs and Moran or to the pure procedural approach, but they are inconsistent with the propensities and capacities of actual learners trying to master computing systems (the Production Paradox).

6.2 Mitigating the Effects of Assimilation

A second approach to the Assimilation Paradox would be to accept assimilation as a given of learners and learning, and to try to design systems in such a way that potential negative effects are minimized. One way to do this is to simplify the assimilative process by reducing the "assimilative gap." For example, one could take a strong view of metaphors in which the metaphor comparisons would have to be completely obvious and true; if the word processor appears to be "like" a typewriter, then it indeed would be operable in exactly the same way as a typewriter. Extending this idea, one could approach computer system design in general from the perspective of naive and intuitive expectations, designing the appearance and operation of systems so that they optimally accord with user expectations. What the user sees and predicts when introduced to the system is guaranteed to be correct by the designer.

One example of such an approach is the principle of *direct manipulation* described by Shneiderman (1983). He argues that wherever possible, the operations available to a user should be based on visual metaphors. So, for example, instead of issuing commands to modify textual material indirectly, word processors should allow users to move directly to text to be edited and press buttons to produce the desired changes. This approach may not be extensible, however; it is by no means clear that there will be appropriate visual analogs to computer system function in the general case. Further, the approach is based on the fundamental assumption that a visual analog will indeed provide the best match to learners' naive expectancies about system function. The validity of this assumption has yet to be demonstrated.

A related approach incorporates naive expectations about system operation, but develops the understanding of users' intuitions through empirical observation rather than through analysis and assumption. Mack (1984) provides an example of this approach in his design of a word processing system based on a prior study of naive users' expectations about how such a system would work. In observing learners' interactions with the resulting system, however, Mack discovered that the goal of matching naive intuitions is a difficult one to meet. Intuitions are often very complex, inconsistent, and even irrational. Further, not all users have the same intuitions, suggesting that designing an intuitive interface for the general case may be an impossible task. Mack's solution to this was to use behavioral observations as a starting point for his design, relying on an empirically driven iterative process to point to modifications and additions not suggested by the initial corpus of naive expectations.

The problem of nonconvergent user expectations is not merely an issue of "early learning," something users outgrow. Mayer and Bayman (1981; see also Bayman and Mayer, 1984) asked students to predict the outcomes of keypress sequences on a calculator. All of the students were experienced users of calculators, but nonetheless their prediction responses varied considerably. For example, some predicted that an evaluation occurs immediately after a number key is pressed, some predicted that evaluation occurs immediately after an operation (e.g., plus) key is pressed, and some predicted that an evaluation occurs immediately after equals is pressed. The variability and the inaccuracy of these predictions varied as a function of the student's prior training in programming, but it is open as to whether this is a smoothing effect of experience or of aptitude.

Other research has explored the possibility of addressing nonconvergent expectations by providing increased flexibility. Furnas et al. (1984) analyzed naive users' intuitions about function names and found considerable variation among users. They developed a limited natural language facility with multiple levels of keyword synonyms for an information retrieval application (Gomez and Lochbaum, 1984). Good et al. (1985) used a similar approach in developing an electronic mail application. These interfaces could simultaneously meet the different expectations of different people.

A major limitation of approaches that seek to reduce the assimilative gap directly has been the size of the example systems developed. So, for example, all major examples of direct manipulation interfaces are small systems with relatively little function (experimental simulations or hobbyist personal computers, for the most part). Intuitive design approaches have also addressed small-scale systems environments. There has yet to be a demonstration that this empirically driven mapping between interface and intuitions will work for more complex real-world systems. Finally, there remains the possibility of a more general cost of eliminating the assimilative gap; if learners are no longer required to "work" for their new knowledge, they may fail to engage in the active processing critical to building a rich and flexible understanding.

6.3 Designing for Assimilation

A final approach to the Assimilative Paradox exploits the accommodation that can occur when assimilation fails. The terms assimilation and accommodation are associated with the theory of Jean Piaget (1954), in whose view the two are natural complements—learners assimilate experience into mental structures as possible, and then accommodate mental structures to experience as necessary. Computer interfaces and accompanying materials can be deliberately cast to stimulate direct comparisons between the current situation (the system itself so to speak) and whatever prior knowledge is engaged by the current situation, thereby highlighting key similarities and differences. These comparisons must be engineered to stimulate inferential processing, hypothesis testing, and active learning (Carroll and Mack, 1985; Whiteside and Wixon, 1985).

Consider the computer interface metaphor, often referred to, that "a text editor is a super typewriter." Not all properties of a typewriter can be carried over to a developing concept of a text processor. Some can (the layout and character-transmission function of the keys); some cannot (character keys cannot straightforwardly be overstruck using a text editor); and some can be mapped from the typewriter base, but somewhat problematically (e.g., with respect to the storage of information, the tape recorder provides an alternative—and in some ways more accurate—metaphor). The comparison of a text editor with a typewriter carries *all* of these implications. The obvious similarities in function and form justify the metaphor in the first place; text editor learners almost never puzzle over what will happen when they strike a character key. In the context of such canonical and salient correspondences, the *dissimilarities* between the text editor and a typewriter become open questions—impelling further thought and leading then to further learning.

For example, keying two characters at the same location on a conventional typed page results in an overstrike. However, text editors do not produce overstrikes (in this way). They either insert (i.e., place the new character adjacent to the old one, and adjust the text line accordingly) or replace (i.e., place the new character where the old one was—deleting the old one). Conventional typewriters, of course, do not have an insert or replace capability; this is a clear dissimilarity in the metaphor. But this incomplete fit is not a functional limitation on the metaphor. Salient dissimilarities—in the context of salient similarities—stimulate thought and afford a concrete opportunity for developing an enhanced understanding of the electronic medium (e.g., the concept of dynamic storage).

Consider an example from a computer system that is based on the metaphor of a desktop. In this system objects and their manipulations are represented concretely (at least on the surface); for example, to create a new document file, a user is prompted to initiate an action roughly described as "tearing off paper," in the context of an icon representing a pad of paper. One user we observed took the prompt quite literally. He tried to execute the action of "tearing" by sweeping the cursor across the icon representing the paper. In fact, the metaphor is misleading in this case because actions applied to objects like files (or applications) must be selected in a more conventional fashion, from menus that describe the actions. Was the metaphor a failure? In fact, the experience was informative; the user understood that the desktop metaphor has certain boundary conditions, but more important, he had a specific insight into the concept of selection and the fundamental role it plays in this interface (see Carroll and Mack, 1985).

The cognitive engineering challenge that inheres in designing for assimilation is formidable. In this approach, we design not merely to enhance simplicity, but to manage the presentation of complexity, to stimulate and guide an active problem solving orientation and thereby to elicit better learning and more skilled and fulfilled routine performance. Much evidence indicates how these processes can go awry when they are not guided effectively. Thus, Scandura et al. (1976) described a student who came to the conclusion that the equals and plus keys on a calculator had no function by observing that the keys caused no visible change in the display. Norman (1983a) described learners who superstitiously pressed the clear key on calculators several times, when a single keypress would do.

A key problem with designing for assimilation is determing how and when assimilative opportunities should be provided to learners. A classic approach has been to provide learners with advance organizers (Ausubel, 1960) that engage and direct appropriate prior knowledge. The idea is that making relevant prior knowledge available at the outset allows it to be brought to bear on the variety of problems that the user actually encounters, hence increasing the chance that the learning will be meaningful. This approach has been used in studies of learning computing (Foss, Rosson, and Smith, 1982; Mayer, 1976). It is difficult, though, for the designer to predict whether the prior knowledge engaged by the advance organizer will still be salient to the user when an opportunity for assimilation occurs.

7 Is Effective Learning Possible?

In couching our discussion in the language of paradoxes, we have not intended to convey hopelessness, just complexity. A paradox, in this sense, is a problem utterly refractory to a simple, comprehensive, logical treatment. Human learning is in this sense paradoxical. We do not believe that there is a simple, comprehensive, logical treatment of human learning in the offing, now or ever. But if the problem is complex, it is surely not hopeless. We have raised a number of suggestions as to how the paradoxes of learning can be addressed. However, as we have pointed out along the way, these solutions themselves have problems.

A premise of our discussion has been that the paradoxes of learning must be taken seriously, not as defects or errors but as fundamental patterns of learning. One could question this premise, and clearly there are no demonstrative arguments either way, but it seems to us that the inevitability of both paradoxes is plausible. If learners were less focused on action, the Production Paradox could be avoided. But the cost would be that the connection between knowledge and performance goals would be far less stable, far less direct. If learners were to rely less on prior experience, the Assimilation Paradox could be avoided. But here the cost would be a far less stable and direct connection between prior learning and new learning achievement. Both the paradoxes point to a single—and perhaps disturbing—fact of mental life: *Adults resist explicitly addressing themselves to new learning* (see also Knowles, 1973; Kidd, 1977).

If we are correct, the paradox of the active learner entails specific a priori limitations on how much we can accelerate learning—limitations that apply irrespective of design intervention. Our only course, however, is to address the paradox through design, resigning ourselves to inevitable tradeoffs (Norman, 1983b). In our discussion of approaches to the Production and Assimilation Paradoxes, we have considered solutions from three often conflicting perspectives: direct attacks on the underlying learning tendency, ways to limit the effects of the tendency, and attempts to take advantage of the tendency in a creative way (see table 5.1).

In discussing the Production Paradox, we suggested that one solution might be to try to reduce learners' production bias by making the system more intrinsically interesting. But it is not clear that all systems can be presented in this fashion, and even if they could, we cannot be sure that the effects of such an approach would be uniformly beneficial—users might well come to see the system not as a useful tool, but rather as a toy to play with on occasion. The other solutions have their own problems; if we try to get around learners' motivation to produce rather than learn, by reducing the cost of learning—perhaps through error blocking and guided discovery of function—we run the risk of making learning too passive, or of setting up learning situations that may not transfer to subsequent use scenarios. And finally, if we accept learners' end-product focus, and try to design systems and training materials to take advantage of it, we risk either

Table 5.1
Summary of the Active User Paradox

	Approach	Example
Production Paradox: Users focus on end products at the expense of prerequisite learning		
Attack:	Make learning the system intrinsically rewarding	Systems as games Performance feedback
Mitigate:	Make learning the system easy	Training wheels Undo
Design for:	Exploit the user's desire for a product by using it to drive learning	Guided Exploration cards
Assimilation Paradox: Users apply prior knowledge even when it does not apply		
Attack:	Repress potential connections to prior knowledge	Explicit system models
Mitigate:	Make or describe the system as truly similar to something familiar	Direct manipulation Natural language
Design for:	Exploit the accommodation that can occur when assimilation fails	Incomplete metaphors

guessing at inappropriate goals for users or relying on users to structure their own goals, a task for which they may be poorly prepared.

Our analysis of solutions to the Assimilation Paradox also pointed to limitations in each case. If assimilation is attacked directly, through designs too novel to assimilate, or through explicit instructions intended to eliminate assimilation, any learning that does take place may be quite fragile, due to its lack of connection with the learner's wealth of past experiences. And if we try to mitigate the problem by reducing the assimilative gap as much as possible, we may set ourselves up for designs that are trivial and offer little new in the way of function. Further, the "learning" involved here would again be extremely passive, requiring little cognitive effort on the part of the user, and might well lead to a less comprehensive understanding. Last, it seems attractive to contemplate designing for assimilation, attempting to incorporate concepts that have a natural link to prior knowledge, while stretching the mind by introducing inconsistencies at appropriate stages. However, the development of metaphors and other learning guidance for this is difficult, and only now beginning to have an impact on user interface designs.

The paradoxes themselves are best thought of as indicative of fundamental orientations to learning, as properties of the learning. Of concern to us as design scientists, however, is the status of the solutions we have described. We have pointed to specific limitations in each case, and it is by no means clear that they can be resolved in any satisfactory way. It is important to note, though, that many of the limitations in these solutions stem from our analysis of the state of the art in interface design. We are not rejecting in principle the possibility that breakthroughs in design might speak to these problems in ways we cannot anticipate now. But frankly, we doubt it.

8 Learning and Design

We have argued that the issues associated with these paradoxes are complex enough, and the tradeoffs implied by the various solutions significant enough, that any single approach will not be sufficient. Rather designers will need to sample creatively from complementary or indeed even competing approaches. In this section, we briefly describe a method for undertaking such an eclectic process, illustrated by recent work on training manual design (for greater detail, see Carroll, 1984; Carroll and Rosson, 1985).

The first stage of design is analytic. It consists of the eclectic sampling of design elements implied by state-of-the-art empirical work, as well as by formal analyses of the design problem (e.g., as in Moran, 1981, and Reisner, 1984). An important constraint, though, is that the sampling be user centered; it must be done in the context of specific considerations engendered by the particular design domain at hand: Who are the users? What are their special interests, needs, and difficulties? How does the particular system address these? None of this is front page design news. It makes perfect sense to have an understanding of what you are designing and who you are designing it for before you begin work—and to take advantage of whatever theoretical base is currently available (guidelines, user complexity metrics, etc.). Often, though, designers focus on a single approach to usability problems (e.g., the use of visual metaphors). We argue instead that they should be encouraged to incorporate complementary or even contradictory principles into their initial analysis.

The second stage of design involves detailed empirical testing of the subskills that will determine users' success with the system. This subskill analysis should also center on the activities of the intended users: What subskills are necessary for a typical user to perform a typical task on the system? Thus, a planning application intended for personnel managers to use in preparing salary and promotion plans must be tested on a set of typical personnel managers who are asked to use it to prepare typical salary and promotion plans. Relevant subskills might be an ability to describe the steps needed to accomplish a given task, a paraphrase understanding of menu selections and prompts, and an ability to recover from some of the more likely error states.

Because the goal of subskill testing is to gather detailed information about design elements rapidly, the testing should be qualitative rather than quantitative in nature, producing diagnostic rather than performance measures. Interpretation should focus on inadequacies in both the function provided by the system and the interface for the user. For example, close observation of managers interacting with our hypothetical personnel planning application might reveal both that salary and promotion plans need to share data in particular ways (a function problem) and that typical personnel managers misunderstand certain specific prompts in the system dialog (an interface problem). This information must then be fed back into the design process so that the next iteration can remedy the problems. Subskill testing is inevitably a process of discovery and one in which the original design undergoes important changes.

While reiterative subskill testing guarantees a sort of local optimization of the design, it is not directed at providing an objective benchmark assessment of the final success of the design. Nonetheless it is useful in the end to know just how good a design really is, for instance, relative to other contrasting designs or relative to particular usability goals. For example, can the final planning application for salary and promotion plans be used for routine tasks by typical personnel managers after one hour of training? Can it be learned faster than the current state-of-the-art alternative systems? Criterion testing is an important third stage of design, providing a means of empirically validating the results of the eclectic, iterative approach taken in the first two stages. We turn now to a description of a case study in which this three-stage approach was employed.

The development of the Minimal Manual (Carroll, 1984; Carroll et al., 1986) exemplifies the eclectic design process we have described. The initial design of the manual was a response to a number of observations about how naive users learn to use word processing systems, and many of these observations have already been discussed in illustrating the Production and Assimilation Paradoxes. But it is the design response to these paradoxes that is of particular interest here, because it reflects a sampling of approaches that might at first seem in conflict.

The Minimal Manual design work addressed the Production Paradox by simultaneously attempting both to *attack* and *support* the end-product bias. Thus, the manual included "On Your Own" sections that encouraged users to apply the procedures they had just worked through to new problems of their own choosing, leaving the instructions intentionally incomplete in an effort to promote intrinsic interest in the learning process through a performance challenge. This aspect of the design directly competed with another aspect, which was to *support* the end-product bias by streamlining prerequisites and focusing training activity on the production of real work output. In this case, two apparently conflicting strategies were consciously combined to yield a richer design solution.

The design approach adopted for problems stemming from the Assimilation Paradox was similar. A major feature of the Minimal Manual design was the removal of the conceptual material often found in training manuals, and a focus instead on concrete procedures. This constitutes an *attack* on assimilation through an emphasis on procedural rather than conceptual knowledge. However, this approach was combined throughout with instances of designing *for* assimilation through the careful use of metaphoric references. So, in describing procedures for removing unwanted line-end characters from the data stream, the manual specifically introduced the "blank line" metaphor as a way of identifying the problem. It then went on to identify the difference between the metaphoric reference (a physical blank line) and the word processing problem (the presence of a line-end character). Ideally, pointing to such a divergence would serve not only to aid learners in correcting this specific problem, but also to initiate processing leading to more general insights into the control of page layout via special formatting characters (Carroll and Mack, 1985).

After its initial design, the Minimal Manual underwent subskill analysis and testing. In some cases, this testing confirmed that the design principles had corrected problems observed in other training manuals. So, for example, the emphasis on procedural rather than conceptual material significantly reduced the problems learners encountered in achieving the important subskill of getting to the typing area. This activity requires traversing several menus, and can seem quite complex when described within a conceptual framework; the Minimal Manual reduced this to a few simple steps (in part by sheer deletion of conceptual material).

It is important, though, to note that the subskill testing also uncovered points at which the basic procedural approach was not optimal. One such point was the assignment of a document name, a fairly simple procedure, but one that appeared to confuse learners conceptually. This problem was treated by the addition of two brief conceptual sections. One developed a metaphor based on the practice of labeling physical office file folders to introduce the requirement that data objects like documents have names; the other developed a metaphor based on the practice of naming babies before they are born to introduce the requirement that data objects must be named before they can be used at all. This material, while it represented a departure from simple procedural descriptions, filled an important need. Without the early qualitative testing, the need may not have been discovered.

After the iterative design process, guided by subskill testing, the Minimal Manual underwent criterial testing (Carroll et al., 1986). In one experiment, learners used one of five training methods (including two variations of the Minimal Manual) for up to seven full working days. The Minimal Manual proved to be substantially faster than the other manuals for the basic topic areas it covered—and to produce learning achievement at least as good as the other methods. The Minimal Manual only covered basic topics, where the commercial manuals covered advanced topics as well. In a later phase of the experiment, Minimal Manual learners were transferred to the sections on advanced topics of a commercial manual. It is notable that they still were substantially faster, but in this comparison their performance on learning achievement tests was better by a factor of eight. In sum, this experiment provided evidence that the final Minimal Manual design was an order of magnitude more effective than comparable state-of-the-art commercial manual designs, and as such represents a successful application of an eclectic design process.

The paradox of the active user imposes serious constraints on designs of computing environments for people to use. We have presented an analysis of the paradox from cognitive and motivational standpoints, and we have described a variety of programmatic approaches to its resolution. Nevertheless, it is not our view that any cookbook engineering solution is likely to develop and "solve" this problem *tout court.* Rather, we believe that this paradox inheres in human-computer interaction, that it derives from fundamental properties of human behavior and experience, and that addressing it through usability research and design will be an ongoing project for the foreseeable future. The social and technological urgency of this project entails an outstanding opportunity and challenge to cognitive science by placing it in a public spotlight in which the power of its theory and methodology will be assessed by the absolute yardstick of practical efficacy.

References

Ausubel, D. P. (1960). The use of advance organizers in the learning and retention of meaningful verbal material. *Journal of Educational Psychology*, 51, 267–272.

Bartlett, F. C. (1932). *Remembering: An Experimental and Social Study*, Cambridge, Cambridge University Press.

Bayman, P., and Mayer, R. E. (1984). Instructional manipulation of users' mental models for electronic calculators. *International Journal of Man-Machine Studies, 20*, 189–199.

Berlyne, D. (1967). *Structure and Direction in Human Thinking*, New York, John Wiley.

Card, S. K., Moran, T. P., and Newell, A. (1980). The Keystroke-Level Model for user performance time with interactive systems. *Communications of the Association for Computing Machinery*, 23, 396–410.

Card, S. K., Moran, T. P., and Newell, A. (1983), *The Psychology of Human-Computer Interaction*, Hillsdale, NJ, Erlbaum.

Carroll, J. M. (1982a). The adventure of getting to know a computer. *IEEE Computer*, 15/11, 49–58.

Carroll, J. M. (1982b). Learning, using an designing command paradigms. *Human Learning*, 1, 31–62.

Carroll, J. M. (1983). Presentation and form in user interface architecture. *Byte*, 8/12, 113–122.

Carroll, J. M. (1984). Minimalist training. *Datamation*, 30/18, 125–136.

Carroll, J. M., and Carrithers, C. (1984). Training wheels in a user interface. *Communications of the Association for Computing Machinery*, 27, 800–806.

Carroll, J. M., and Kay, D. S. (1985). Prompting, feedback and error correction in the design of a scenario machine. *CHI'85 Human Factors in Computing Systems Proceedings*, New York, ACM SIGCHI.

Carroll, J. M., and Mack, R. L. (1984). Learning to use a word processor: By doing, by thinking, and by knowing. In J. C. Thomas and M. Schneider (Eds.), *Human Factors in Computer Systems*, Norwood, NJ, Ablex.

Carroll, J. M., and Mack, R. L. (1985), Metaphor, computing systems, and active learning. *International Journal of Man-Machine Studies*, 22, 39–57.

Carroll, J. M., and Mazur, S. A. (1986). LisaLearning. *IEEE Computer*, 19/11, 35–49.

Carroll, J. M., and Rosson, M. B. (1985). Usability specifications as a tool in interative development. In H. R. Hartson (Ed.), *Advances in Human-Computer Interaction*, Norwood, NJ, Ablex.

Carroll, J. M., and Thomas, J. C. (1982). Metaphor and the cognitive representation of computing systems. *IEEE Transactions on Systems, Man and Cybernetics*, 12, 107–116.

Carroll, J. M., Smith-Kerker, P. L., Ford, J. R., and Mazur, S. A. (1986). The Minimal Manual. IBM Research Report, RC 11637.

Carroll, J. M., Mack, R. L., Lewis, C. H., Grischkowsky, N. L., and Robertson, S. R. (1985). Exploring exploring a word processor. *Human Computer Interaction,* 1, 283–307.

Coombs, M., and Alty, J. (1984). Expert systems: An alternative paradigm. *International Journal of Man-Machine Studies,* 20, 21–43.

Douglas, S. A., and Moran, T. P. (1983). Learning text editor semantics by analogy. *CHI'83 Human Factors in Computing Systems Proceedings,* New York, ACM SIGCHI.

Draper, S. W. (1984). The nature of expertise in UNIX. In B. Schackel (Ed.), *INTERACT'84: Proceedings of the First IFIPS Conference on Human-Computer Interaction,* Amsterdam, North-Holland.

du Boulay, B., O'Shea, T., and Monk, J. (1981). The black box inside the glass box: Presenting computing concepts to novices. *International Journal of Man-Machine Studies,* 14, 237–249.

Foss, D. A., Rosson, M. B., and Smith, P. L. (1982). Reducing manual labor: Experimental analysis of learning aids for a text-editor. *Proceedings of Conference on Human Factors in Computer Systems,* Gaithersburg, MD, National Bureau of Standards.

Furnas, G. W., Landauer, T. K., Gomez, L. M., and Dumais, S. T. (1984). Statistical semantics: Analysis of the potential performance of keyword information systems. In J. C. Thomas and M. Schneider (Eds.), *Human Factors in Computer Systems,* Norwood, NJ, Ablex.

Gomez, L. M., and Lochbaum, C. C. (1984). People can retrieve more objects with enriched key-word vocabularies. But is there a human performance cost? In B. Schackel (Ed.), *INTERACT'84: Proceedings of the First IFIPS Conference on Human-Computer Interaction,* Amsterdam, North-Holland.

Good, M. D., Whiteside, J. A., Wixon, D. R., and Jones, S. J. (1985). Building a user-derived interface. *Communications of the ACM,* 27, 1032–1043.

Gordon, R. F., Leeman, G. B., and Lewis, C. H. (1984). Concepts and implications of interactive recovery. IBM Research Report, RC 10562.

Greene, D., and Lepper, M. R., Eds. (1979). *The Hidden Costs of Reward,* Hillsdale, NJ, Erlbaum.

Halasz, F., and Moran, T. (1982). Analogy considered harmful. *Proceedings of Conference on Human Factors in Computer Systems,* Gaithersburg, MD, National Bureau of Standards.

Jagodzinski, A. P. (1983). A theoretical basic for the representation of on-line computer systems to naive users. *International Journal of Man-Machine Studies,* 18, 215–252.

Kidd, J. R. (1977). *How Adults Learn*, New York, Association Press.

Knowles, M. S. (1973). *The Adult Learner: A Neglected Species.* Houston, Gulf Publishing Company, American Society for Training and Development.

Mack, R. L. (1984). Understanding text-editing: Evidence from predictions and descriptions given by computer-naive people. IBM Research Reoprt, RC 10333.

Mack, R. L., Lewis, C., and Carroll, J. M. (1983). Learning to use office systems: Problems and prospects. *ACM Transactions in Office Information Systems,* 1, 254–271.

McKendree, J. E., Schorno, S. S., and Carroll, J. M. (1985). Personal Planner: The Scenario Machine as a research tool. Videotape demonstration, *CHI'85 Human Factors in Computing Systems Proceedings,* New York, ACM SIGCHI (short version distributed by SIGGRAPH).

Malone, T. W. (1981a). What makes computer games fun? *Byte,* 6/12, 258–277.

Malone, T. W. (1981b). Toward a theory of intrinsically motivating instruction. *Cognitive Science,* 4, 333–369.

Mantei, M., and Haskell, N. (1983). Autobiography of a first-time discretionary microcomputer user. *CHI'83 Human Factors in Computing Systems Proceedings,* New York, ACM SIGCHI.

Mayer, R. E. (1976). Some conditions of meaningful learning for computer programming: Advance organizers and subject control of frame order. *Journal of Educational Psychology,* 67, 725–734.

Mayer, R. E., and Bayman, P. (1981). Psychology of calculator languages: A framework for describing differences in users' knowledge. *Communications of the Association for Computing Machinery,* 24, 511–520.

Moran, T. P. (1981). Command language grammar. *International Journal of Man-Machine Studies,* 15, 3–50.

Nielsen, J., Mack, R. L., Bergendorff, K., and Grischkowsky, N. L. (1986). Integrated software usage in the professional work environment: Evidence from questionnaires and interviews. *CHI'86 Human Factors in Computing Systems Proceedings,* New York, ACM SIGCHI.

Norman, D. A. (1983a). Some observations on mental models. In D. Gentner and A. L. Stevens (Eds.), *Mental Models,* Hillsdale, NJ, Erlbaum.

Norman, D. A. (1983b). Design principles for human-computer interfaces. *CHI'83 Human Factors in Computing Systems Proceedings,* New York, ACM SIGCHI.

O'Malley, C., Smolensky, P., Bannon, L., Conway, E., Graham, J., Sokolov, J., and Monty, M. (1983). A proposal for user centered system documentation. *CHI'83 Human Factors in Computing Systems Proceedings,* New York, ACM SIGCHI.

Piaget, J. (1954). *The Construction of Reality in the Child,* New York, Basic Books.
Piattelli-Palmarini, M. (1980). *Language and Learning,* Cambridge, MA, Harvard University Press.

Pirolli, P. L., Anderson, J. R., and Farrell, R. (1984). Learning to program recursion. *Proceedings of the Sixth Annual Conference of the Cognitive Science Society,* Boulder.

Pope, B. (1985). A study of where users spend their time using VM/CMS. IBM Research Report, RC 10953.

Reisner, P. (1984). Formal grammar as a tool for analyzing ease of use: Some fundamental concepts. In J. Thomas and M. Schneider (Eds.), *Human Factors in Computing Systems,* Norwood, NJ, Ablex.

Rosson, M. B. (1983). Patterns of experience in text editing. *CHI'83 Human Factors in Computing Systems Proceedings,* New York, ACM SIGCHI.

Rosson, M. B. (1984a). The role of experience in editing. In B. Schackel (Ed.), *INTERACT'84: Proceedings of the First IFIPS Conference on Human-Computer Interaction,* Amsterdam, North-Holland.

Rosson, M. B. (1984b). Effects of experience on learning, using, and evaluating a text-editor. *Human Factors,* 26, 463–475.

Rosson, M. B., Gould, J. D., and Grischkowsky, N. (1982). Field observations of IBM Displaywriter use. Unpublished research, IBM Watson Research Center.

Scandura, A. M., Lowerre, G. F., Veneski, J., and Scandura, J. M. (1976). Using electronic calculators with elementary children. *Educational Technology,* 16, 14–18.

Scribner, S., Ed. (1984). Cognitive studies of work. *Quarterly Newsletter of the Laboratory of Comparative Human Cognition,* 6 (1 and 2).

Shneiderman, B. (1983). Direct manipulation: A step beyond programming languages. *IEEE Computer,* 16(8), 57–69.

Shrager, J., and Finin, T. (1982). An expert system that volunteers advices. *Proceedings of the National Conference on Artificial Intelligence,* Pittsburgh, Carnegie-Mellon University, pp. 339–340.

Singley, M. K., and Anderson, J. R. (1985). The transfer of text-editing skill. *International Journal of Man-Machine Studies,* 22, 403–423.

Smith, D., Irby, C., Kimbal, R., Verplank, B., and Harslem, E. (1982). Designing the Star user interface. *Byte,* 7/4, 242–282.

Thomas, J. C., and Carroll, J. M. (1979). The psychological study of design. *Design Studies,* 1/1, 5–11.

Underwood, B. J. (1957). Interference and forgetting. *Psychological Review,* 64, 49–60.

Weiner, B. (1980). *Human Motivation,* Chicago, Rand McNally.

Whiteside, J., and Wixon, D. (1985). Developmental theory as a framework for studying human-computer interaction. In H. R. Hartson (Ed.), *Advances in Human-Computer Interaction*, Norwood, NJ, Ablex.

Young, R. (1981). The machine inside the machine: Users' models of pocket calculators. *International Journal of Man-Machine Studies*, 15, 51–85.

6 Cognitive Resources and the Learning of Human-Computer Dialogs

Philip J. Barnard

1 Introduction

1.1 The Need for Applicable Theory

A requirement for developing theories that are applicable to the understanding of operator error and advancing the resolution of real-world problems has been a major objective of applied human information processing since its postwar inception in problems of memory, attention, and perceptual motor control (e.g., see Broadbent, 1958). The argument in support of theory is straightforward. It is simply not feasible to perform formal experiments for resolving all issues that are likely to arise within the context of a particular design problem and its associated development cycle. The behavioral consequences of novel designs nevertheless need to be foreseen. Theoretical syntheses of known performance characteristics are therefore required to supplement or replace intuitive design or ad hoc evaluations.

It should be acknowledged at the outset that bridging the gulf in cognitive psychology between theory and application is far from straightforward. All too often specific cognitive theories are restricted in scope to a small class of simplified and well-delineated laboratory paradigms. Move outside the scope of the defined paradigm and predictive power is lost—either because the theory is inaccurate or because it is unclear how a prediction should be arrived at in the novel context. Obviously, people working in different conceptual frameworks have their own agendas for building bridges. The particular agenda for this chapter will seek to address three general issues associated with the development of applicable cognitive theories. They each represent different ways in which the bridge between cognitive psychology and its application might usefully be strengthened.

First, theories in cognitive psychology are typically partial theories focused on a specific component of mental life—for example, speech perception, short-term memory, or problem solving. In addition, specific theories of human information processing tend to concentrate on a particular aspect of the computer metaphor. For example, within the theoretical tradition of short-term memory research, primary emphasis is placed on the modeling of information processing facilities (e.g., stores/buffers), their organization, and the general-purpose operations involved in the control, encoding, and retrieval of information. In this kind of tradition relatively little reference is made to the knowledge-based processes that construct and manipulate the content of mental representations of meaningful material. In contrast, psycholinguistic research tends to concentrate on precisely these forms of computational activities, while making only restricted reference to the wider properties of the information processing architecture in which those computational processes might be embedded (for a more extended discussion of these issues see Barnard, 1985).

In these respects, theories in cognitive psychology tend to be unintegrated both with respect to the use of the computer metaphor and in relation to the different components of mental life. The fragmentary and paradigm-bound nature of cognitive theory has, of course, been widely discussed (e.g., Allport, 1980), as has the apparent inability of experimental research to deliver cumulative theoretical developments (e.g., Crowder, 1982) or unifying principles for human information processing (e.g., Johnson-Laird, 1978). However, in the kind of rich task environments characteristic of cognition in human-computer interaction, the processes of perception, memory, understanding, problem solving, and action are brought into play in a fully orchestrated manner. These would seem to require an *integrated* theoretical approach to the cognitive resources involved.

Second, our empirical knowledge of cognitive phenomena tends to be confined to tasks that require subjects to develop special-purpose behavior for that task. For example, in studies of speech perception, subjects may be asked repeatedly to monitor a speech stream for the presence or absence of a particular phoneme. While justifiable in the context of a particular theoretical paradigm, such repetitious judgments are not normally required to understand and respond to a communication. It must therefore be assumed that subjects have to construct special-purpose mental representations to cope with the particular conditions of the experiment and to control the responses it requires.

This should not be viewed as a general request to orient empirical work toward studying cognition "in the wild," to use Landauer's (1985a) apt description. Some "real" tasks in human-computer interaction involve cognitive demands that are almost as peculiar as those posed by abstract experiments. The point is more specific. In cognitive tasks of even moderate complexity, mental processes and knowledge are purposefully coordinated to control extended sequences of behavior. These sequences are integrated both over time and in relation to an often dynamically changing environment. For these circumstances evidence concerning the performance of the human cognitive system is woefully lacking. This could prove to be a major factor underlying our apparent difficulties in generalizing theories across laboratory conditions or to a practical application. The primary empirical emphasis tends to have been placed upon isolating the underlying properties of individual processes rather than focusing upon their wider coordination, integration, and control.

Third, attempts to bridge the gulf between theory and application have tended to have a somewhat piecemeal and heuristic character. The piecemeal character of the bridging process is again related to the restricted scope of individual theories. For the complex tasks of human-computer interaction, many theoretical perspectives are potentially relevant. Appropriate ones must be selected. This is often a matter of personal experience, preference, and "skilled" judgment. Few theories are sufficiently developed to incorporate fully explicit means of mapping from the core constructs of the theory to the complexities of an applications environment. Specific attempts to forge such links often leave much unstated. The best applied psychologists appear to acquire a great deal of implicit knowledge and very often apply that knowledge heuristically without necessarily being able to communicate how they do it.

For example, faced with the problem of analyzing issues associated with managing multiple activities at an interface, theories of memory, attention, and planning may all be relevant (cf. Miyata and Norman, 1986). However, a good deal depends upon the insight and skill of the researchers involved in identifying and expressing potentially relevant relationships between cognitive theory, performance, and system design. At the level of identifying usability issues for a particular system, different researchers may well exhibit some overlap in the issues on which they focus. However, they also tend to develop their own more idiosyncratic usability themes (Hammond et al., 1984b). If mature relationships are to be established between cognitive theory, user performance, and system design, then the mappings one to another must be explicit. Without such explicitness, there is little chance that human factors practitioners will be able to evaluate a situation and apply appropriate constructs with both accuracy and consistency.

For applied psychology in general, these kinds of issue are by no means new (e.g., Card, Moran, and Newell, 1983). Furthermore, it seems unlikely that they will be either simply or speedily resolved (cf. Broadbent, 1958, 1971). Indeed, for different topics and problems they may require markedly different resolutions. Finding ways and means of addressing them in the context of knowledge intensive tasks nevertheless represents a substantial challenge for modern cognitive psychology.

1.2 Current Approaches

A number of quite distinct research approaches are being established in the specific context of human-computer interaction. Some approaches are primarily empirical. Others regard an understanding of cognitive problems and issues as a productive route to "inventing" new designs to replace older, more problematic ones (e.g., Landauer, 1985b; 1987). Others share a fundamental belief in the importance of developing applicable theories that are predictive. Following the influential approach of Card, Moran, and Newell (1983), it is now also becoming widely accepted that predictive needs for design purposes are best served by approximate models rather than by theories that are necessarily formally adequate (e.g., see also Norman, 1986).

Several approaches have, for example, emphasized methods for the codification of knowledge. Thus, formal grammars have been utilized as tools to represent the complexity of different types of human computer dialogs (e.g., Moran, 1981) with a view to predicting their usability (e.g., Reisner, 1982; Payne and Green, 1983). Similarly, the knowledge required to use a particular system can be codified in a working production system and the properties of the resulting model utilized to derive predictions for learning or intersystem transfer times (e.g., Kieras and Polson, 1985; Polson, 1987). Other models, at typically lower levels of analysis, have emphasized methods for the codification of actions and mental processes. With the keystroke level model of Card, Moran, and Newell (1983), methods for tasks are codified in terms of their constituent physical and mental actions. Estimates of the temporal attributes of each constituent are then used to predict how long an expert user would take to execute the method.

Obviously, much needs to be done before the promissory note of approximate predictive models is exchanged for mature design tools. As each type of model evolves, strengths and weaknesses will emerge together with new problems to resolve (e.g., see Newell and Card, 1985).

While the advantageous properties of the strongly predictive approaches should by no means be undervalued, it is equally important to consider their potential limitations.

For example, just as the process of designing computer systems involves a whole range of trade-offs (Norman, 1983), so does the process of developing applicable models. By their very nature, predictive models require some form of direct mapping between a set of explicit constructs and some quantifiable aspect of behavior. Since that behavior is complex, a subset must be selected and some "appropriate" level of model formulated. The designer of a behavioral model must make a selection in a depth/breadth trade-off. Where there is a strong requirement to quantify, the modeling trade-off is typically resolved by selecting a small set of core constructs and mapping them in depth onto a restricted set of circumstances.

In this respect, predictive models for human-computer interaction mirror the first of the general issues, raised earlier, concerning the unintegrated character of much cognitive theory. Where the primary emphases of a model are placed upon the codification of knowledge and learning, assumptions concerning the functional constraints on human information processing may play only a minor role in the derivation of predictions. In contrast, where the primary emphases are upon mental processes and performance time, the situation may be reversed. The key assumptions are likely to relate to information processing constraints with little or no part played by assumptions concerning the content of the information undergoing processing.

This situation is well illustrated by reference to the overall approach described by Card, Moran, and Newell (1983). They encapsulate much of what is known about human information processing constraints in a specific processing architecture (The Model Human Information Processor). This incorporates sensory, cognitive, and effector "processors," together with a working memory and a long-term memory. Each constituent is assigned relevant parameters, such as cycle time or storage capacity. It is not difficult to establish the part played by such a general-purpose mechanism in the derivation of specific predictive models for searching or typing. However, it is much more difficult to see how this particular theoretical viewpoint relates to the ways in which the contents of mental representations are constructed, manipulated, and acted upon. The model human information processor, in and of itself, has little to say about how a set of computer commands might be represented in memory and an appropriate one retrieved to execute a particular function.

Within that approach these issues must be addressed by applying the

GOMS (Goals Operators Methods and Selection rules) family of models. However, the form and content of these models is relatively unrelated to the form and content of the model human information processor itself. Specific developments of this approach may, of course, utilize broad assumptions concerning working memory load (e.g., Polson and Kieras, 1984). However, key theoretical connections are missing for relating the model human information processor to the higher-level representational descriptions of tasks and knowledge. For example, what substantive mental processes are involved in the translation of a visual representation, of a word or icon into a representation of the meaning of its underlying referents? There is a good deal of theoretical knowledge concerning these and other mental processes. The overall form of the Model Human Information Processor provides few clues as to how to go about integrating this information with the cycle times associated with visual and cognitive processors or with a particular GOMS representation.

The GOMS family of models was designed to support the explicit analysis of user tasks at different levels of description. The intention was to provide a framework that would support the practical application of the models and their extension to new problems. In this context, the absence of certain kinds of strictly theoretical connections does not mean that the approach lacks unity or coherence. However, taken together with a requirement for quantitative prediction in an applied setting, their absence can have profound consequences. In particular, the absence of an integrated and explicit specification of mental processes can make it difficult to extend this approach to many topics in user cognition. The cognitive processes involved in understanding, memory, and problem solving are not readily analyzable in terms of simple, quantitative indices of performance. Although there are important quantitative differences in the functioning of these mental processes, there are equally important qualitative differences.

Examples of qualitative differences in the character of human cognitive performance are not hard to find. One classic example concerns the nature of the errors made in recall tasks. In short-term recall for words, people will tend to confuse words that have a similar phonological structure. In longer-term recall they tend to confuse words that have a similar meaning (e.g., see Baddeley, 1966). Another classic case concerns the relationship between the syntactic complexity of sentences and the ease with which they are understood. Syntactically complex sentences can be more difficult to understand than syntactically simple ones. However, such performance differences tend to be reduced or eliminated when the underlying meaning of the sentence can be established on the basis of other semantic or pragmatic clues (e.g., see Herriot, 1969). Examples of these kinds of qualitative difference in human-computer dialog will be discussed in subsequent sections.

Ultimately, our models must be able to foresee and accommodate the quantitative and qualitative differences in user performance. If the basic attributes of user performance vary substantially from one task context to another, then different quantitative models may be required for each set of circumstances. Once this is acknowledged, it seems clear that we must have some principled basis for knowing which model is likely to be most appropriate for which set of circumstances. This again raises the second issue outlined in the previous section. Given the paradigm-bound nature of our empirical knowledge, relatively little is known about the general performance of the complete cognitive system under circumstances where its various activities are purposefully coordinated. As a result, there is little principled information that might guide selection among detailed models. Indeed, in the absence of some integrative theoretical apparatus there is a danger that such models might proliferate wildly. This in turn could place in some jeopardy the wider enterprise of providing "simple" behavioral tools that are readily usable in the context of system design and development.

In order to address these broader issues it would seem unhelpful to adopt a research paradigm in which a particular model is initially specified in depth and its predictions tested in a restricted set of circumstances. For the more integrative function, a broader approach to cognitive modeling would seem to be required. However, any alteration to the depth/breadth trade-off in cognitive modeling has an associated cost. The role of theory alters from being strongly and quantitatively predictive to one in which partial theories help us to interpret and understand the different phenomena that we observe. Norman's developing distinctions (1984, 1986) between different stages of user activity in the performance of an action (e.g., planning, execution, evaluation) play precisely this kind of role. Any relaxation of the requirement to be quantitatively predictive means that other ways have to be found to make explicit the various interrelationships between theory, cognitive phenomena, and system design.

The remainder of this chapter outlines one way in which these issues can be addressed. Section 2 is devoted to a summary description of a particular theoretical framework, *interacting cognitive subsystems* (Barnard, 1985). This framework specifies a distributed processing architecture for human perception, cognition, and action. In addition, it specifies the nature and properties of mental representations together with the actual processes that transform one kind of mental representation into another. In these respects, it can be regarded as an "enhanced" model human information processor of the type proposed by Card, Moran, and Newell (1983). Whereas those authors concentrated on the properties of process*ors*, the core constructs here concern the nature, organization, and function properties of computational process*es* together with their associated memory structures. The aim is to provide an explicit and integrated set of information processing resources. These can then be utilized for a *cognitive task analysis* that has a common basis for exploring both the demands for representing knowledge and the information processing constraints involved in its use.

In section 3 illustrative behavioral results from several experiments are interpreted in terms of this framework. The experiments were not motivated by the theoretical framework. Rather, the intention was to explore a variety of issues associated with the content and constituent structure of dialogs in order to discover the nature of important phenomena that might require explanation. The data were obtained in simplified experimental settings in which novices learned different forms of interactive dialogs. Although the settings were simplified from a systems point of view, from a behavioral point of view they may be regarded as relatively complex task environments in which the various components of user cognition are orchestrated in purposeful sequences of behavior.

Many of the interpretations suggested in section 3 are underspecified and will undoubtedly prove inaccurate. The nature of the enterprise in this section is to sketch some potential links between possible theoretical principles and applied issues. The intention is not to forge direct links between theory and the design of specific products. Section 4 concludes the chapter by briefly considering one way in which this latter issue might be addressed. Here an effort is made to be explicit about the conditions under which particular kinds of user performance might be expected. Gradual accumulation of information of this sort could form a basis on which to build an expert system tool to aid problem solving in design. Such a tool would have qualitative properties complementary to quantitative predictive models.

2 A Theoretical Approach to Cognitive Task Analysis

2.1 The Resources of Interacting Cognitive Subsystems

The theoretical approach adopted here makes a number of general assumptions. It assumes that perception, cognition, and action can usefully be analyzed in terms of well-defined and discrete information processing modules; it assumes a separation of mental representations stored in episodic memory records from the content-specific processes that construct and utilize them; and it assumes a significant capability on the part of the human cognitive system for parallel processing of information.

The modularity of processing resources is described at two basic levels. First, the complete human information processing system is subdivided into a set of functionally independent subsystems each of which operates in a specific domain of processing (cf. Baddeley, 1982). This level is outlined in figure 6.1, which distinguishes sensory, representational, and effector subsystems. Associated with each subsystem is an "image record" that preserves, in parallel with the subsystem's processes, episodic memory traces appropriate to each domain. Sensory subsystems process incoming sense data in their domain (e.g., vision, acoustics) and transform it into specific mental "codes" that represent the structure and content of the incoming data. These encodings are handled by subsystems that specialize in the processing of higher-level representations with specific properties. For example, the "Morphonolexical" subsystem incorporates specific processes for handling the surface structure of language, while the "Object" subsystem specializes in the processing of visuospatial structures. Similarly, the "Propositional" and "Implicational" subsystems support the processing of more abstract semantic and conceptual representations. Effector subsystems process output from representational subsystems and compute appropriate instructions to control motor output (e.g., articulation, limbs, etc.).

The second level of analysis concerns the organization of processes within a particular subsystem. Although subsystems operate in different domains of processing, it is assumed that they all share a common internal organization of processing resources. Each subsystem incorporates a set of parallel processes and an episodic memory structure, the image record. The basic internal organization of all subsystems is shown in figure 6.2. Any given subsystem can only process information represented in a specific mental code. This is the defining code of the domain and is indicated in figure 6.2 by the variable I. A single primary process, the "copy" process, serves the function of creating an episodic record of all information input to that subsystem. This image record extends back in time and is not subject to any definable capacity limitations.

A set of parallel secondary processes serve the function of recoding information. These are shown as the transformation of the defining code into output codes (e.g., $I \rightarrow J$; $I \rightarrow K$). In the case of the acoustic sub-

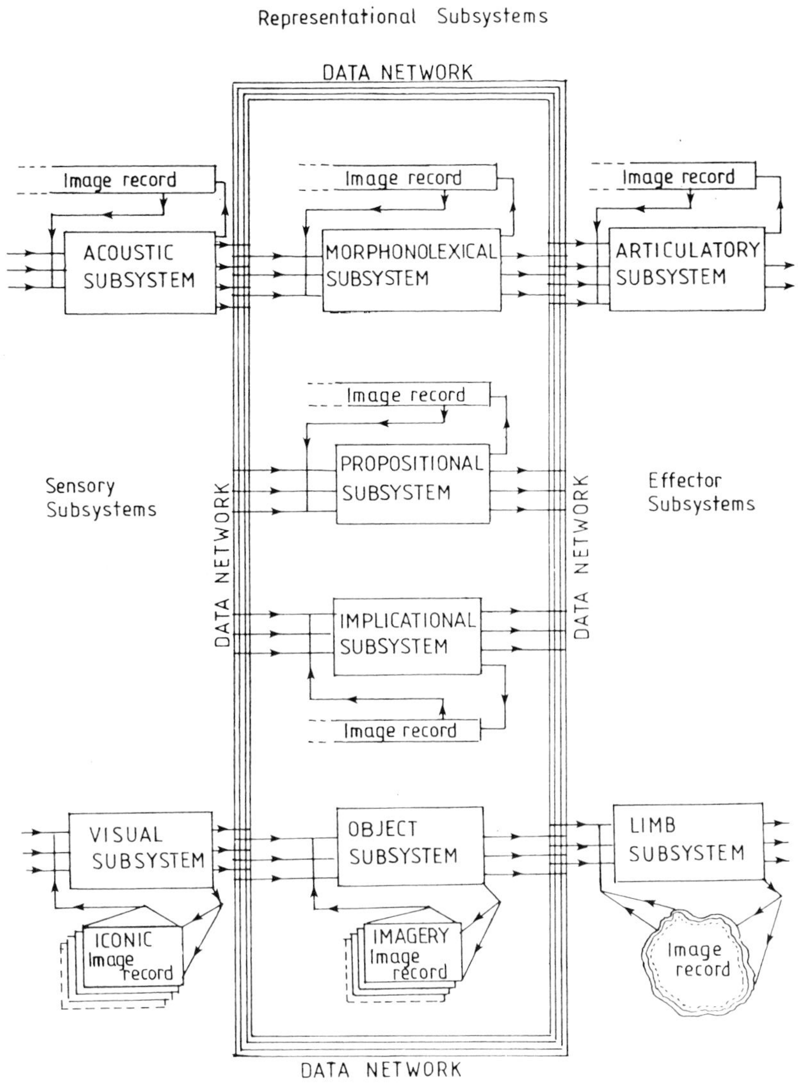

Figure 6.1
An architecture for perception, cognition, and action (Barnard, 1985).

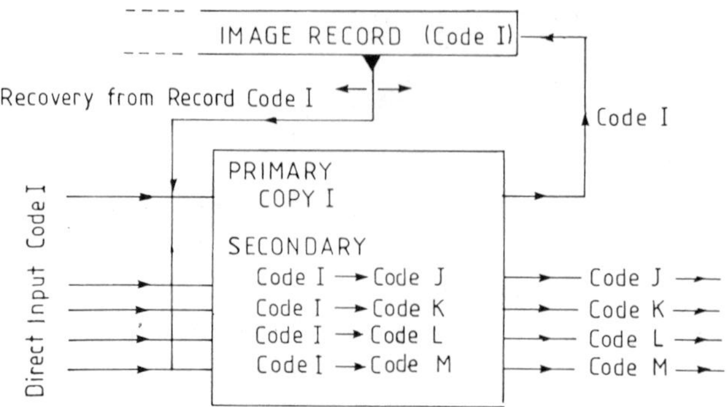

Figure 6.2
A structure for cognitive subsystems (Barnard, 1985).

system, secondary processes operating in parallel could construct a lexical output for further processing by the relevant representational subsystem. Simultaneously it could transmit a representation of locational information on which basis an effector subsystem could control the action of orienting the head toward the acoustic source.

Each secondary process can usefully be thought of as a functionally independent production system. If a particular pattern of conditions is met in the pattern of data input to a subsystem (in code I), then a particular process (I → J) will transform it into an output representation (in code J). The operation of a subsystem is constrained by a number of information processing principles. A secondary process can, for example, only process a single data stream at a time. Thus, when two people are speaking simultaneously, the relevant process in the acoustic subsystem would only be able to represent the lexical content of one of the messages. The primary copy process can, however, represent in the image record *all* data input to that subsystem. In addition, the secondary processes that recode information from one representation to another can only carry out that recoding if the temporal properties of direct input are compatible with the temporal properties of the output code.

The fact that the primary copy process creates a record of all input to a particular subsystem has the consequence of enabling the secondary processes to operate either on direct input or on information represented in that subsystem's image record. This has three theoretically significant properties. First, it permits two modes of processing activity. In one mode, secondary processes directly recode input to the subsystem. The other mode is buffered processing in which a secondary process is effectively

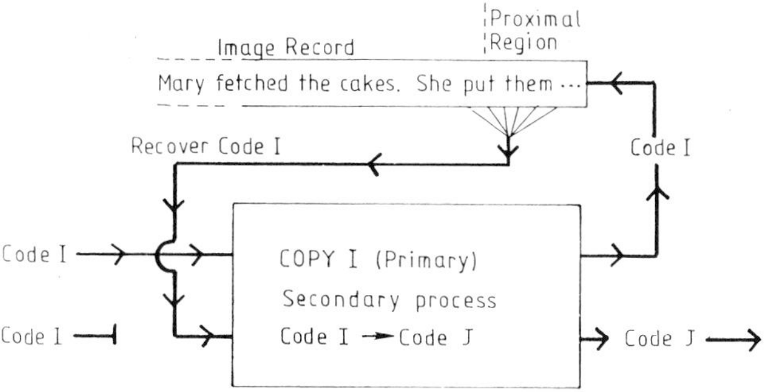

Figure 6.3
Buffered processing, illustrated for one of the peripheral auditory/verbal subsystems (AC, MPL, or ART).

operating in series with the primary copy process (figure 6.3). This allows a secondary process to operate on an extended representation at the most recent or proximal end of an image record. It also enables a secondary process to compensate for certain incompatibilities between the temporal properties of direct input and the temporal properties of output. Buffered processing is thus viewed as more robust and is associated with conscious attention to processing activity in that domain.

The second property concerns memory retrieval. In buffered processing a secondary process utilizes information at the proximal end of the image record. However, it is assumed that secondary processes can also configure to access information at the nonproximal regions of the image record. In effect, the conditions required for effecting a particular recoding can be met either in one of the forms of immediate processing or by access to stored representations of past input. The process of information recovery envisaged is like that proposed by Norman and Bobrow (1979). A description of the information to be recovered from nonproximal parts of the image record is activated, generally by input from another subsystem. The description is then utilized to examine the contents of the record structure. Records matching that description can then be operated on by a secondary process to produce an output from the subsystem concerned. In this view, memory retrieval and the recoding of current input are performed by the same process resources. Since any one secondary process can only recode one stream of data, it can only be involved in one of these activities at a given time.

The third property of a parallel organization of processes within a subsystem concerns "learning." In order to effect a particular recoding, a secondary process must embody appropriate procedures for recoding a particular incoming information pattern into an output representation. Since the primary copy process is organized in parallel, information can be represented in an image record in the absence of appropriate procedures for recoding it. Indeed, the theoretical framework assumes that the main function of episodic memory records is to furnish the basic data from which such procedures develop. It is in this sense that the recoding processes are viewed as secondary to the primary copy process. An ability to preserve records of auditory/verbal input is viewed, not in terms of a general-purpose short-term memory store, but rather as a fundamental prerequisite for the proceduralization of linguistic knowledge. Similarly, records of input to visual or propositional subsystems provide a basis for the proceduralization of appropriate recodings for those domains of processing.

A more complete justification and description of the framework has been elaborated elsewhere for the analysis of short-term memory tasks (Barnard, 1985). For the applied scientist, the potential relevance of such abstract descriptions to the problems of human computer dialogs may appear opaque. However, the initial description of memory and processing resources together with principles that govern their operation provides an explicit framework within which a cognitive task analysis can be developed. Clearly, analyses of even the most simple tasks will require many additional assumptions—particularly concerning the role of knowledge embodied in individual processes and the representations they create. These are best approached in the context of a particular illustration.

2.2 Configurations of Cognitive Resources in Word Processing

Figure 6.4 elaborates the basic architecture of figure 6.1 by incorporating primary and secondary processes within each subsystem. For the purposes of illustration only a relevant subset of secondary processes need be considered here. The example concerns a situation in which a user is revising a paper on a word processor. In reading a paragraph a particularly difficult sentence is noted. This is deleted and a rephrased version entered. Figure 6.4 essentially freezes the state of information in relevant subsystems at the point at which the user completes the reading of the difficult sentence. The analysis proceeds by tracing the configuration of processes involved in reading and interpreting the sentence—deleting it and typing in fresh input.

The text itself must obviously be processed through the visual subsystem, where the primary copy process creates an image record of all

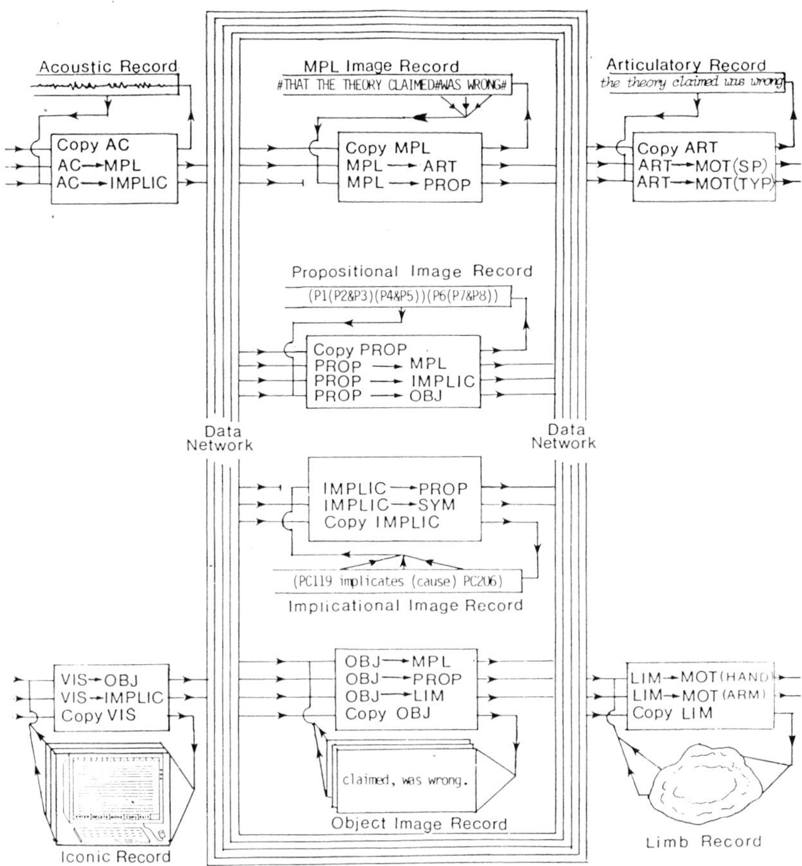

Figure 6.4
An illustration of the different types of representation built into the interpretation of text presented on a VDU.

the information in the visual field. The full display thus appears as the representation in the proximal end of the image record. In parallel the VIS → OBJ process recodes the raw visual data into a higher-order representation reflecting a more abstract structural description of visual form. This process of recoding involves information reduction. For example, the higher-level object code would not represent gradations of brightness but would distinguish the form of upper- and lowercase letter shapes. Since secondary processes can only recode a single data stream at a time, the actual recoding would also be selective. With the recoding of a visual representation, selectivity would operate spatially and only part of the visual field would be undergoing recoding. The object-level description of the selected area of the visual field is passed over the data network, where it is copied into the image record of the object subsystem.

A secondary process (OBJ → MPL) in the object subsystem then recodes the orthography of words into a speech-based code, the morphonolexical (MPL) code, which represents the surface structure of language. This latter code specifies lexical items in phonological form and marks the higher-order constituents (e.g., phrases and clauses) within the linguistic string. In the normal course of understanding spoken speech, this surface structure representation would be computed from an initial acoustic representation (AC → MPL). However, reading demands cross modal recoding, and the exact way in which this is achieved is itself the subject of theoretical controversy. Within the present framework, the temporal properties of normal visual processing are assumed to be incompatible with the normal time base for auditory speech processing. Accordingly, MPL representations originating in the object subsystem are copied into the image record of the MPL subsystem, where the secondary processes must adopt a buffered configuration (see figure 6.3) to interpret the incoming representation.

It is important to note that it would not have been possible for the OBJ → PROP process to represent the linguistic meaning of visually presented sentences. The linguistic knowledge required to construct propositional representations of sentences is viewed as confined to the MPL subsystem, where the MPL → PROP process constructs a representation of the meaning of the text in propositional format. In MPL → PROP recoding, the details of surface structure form, such as specific lexical items and their order, are discarded. The resulting representation is transmitted over the data network and copied into the image record of the propositional subsystem. Hence, the propositional image record contains abstract semantic symbols to represent the meaning of recently interpreted text (P1(P2 & P3) . . .).

The propositional subsystem incorporates a secondary process that interprets relations among propositions. In this recoding (PROP → IMPLIC) details of the individual propositions are lost and the highest-level cognitive representation of the text is constructed, the "implicational" code. This code specifies relations among interlinked knowledge structures at a level of description similar to Minsky's (1975) "Frames" or Schank and Abelson's (1979) "Scripts." In order to avoid confusion with the specific properties of other formulations, the implicational level of representation will be described as involving "propositional complexes" (PC119 implicates PC206). The PROP → IMPLIC process involves interrelating propositions in the text both among themselves and in relation to prior experience as represented in the propositional image record. This process is therefore inferential in nature. The representation transmitted over the data network and copied into the implicational image record thus reflects the overall conceptual structure or "model" arising out of the actively interpreted meaning of the text.

The cognitive activities associated with understanding text on a VDU are thus viewed as involving a number of discrete processes that successively recode the visual image of the text through a number of representational levels until an implicational representation of its content is formulated. The interpretation of the text may nevertheless develop further. The implicational subsystem incorporates a secondary process that computes detailed propositional structures from propositional complexes (IMPLIC → PROP). This process can elaborate the interpretation of the text, and any propositions actually output would be transmitted over the data network and copied into the image record of the propositional subsystem. Thus, propositional content would come together both as a result of the interpretation of the physical text (MPL → PROP) and via reciprocal inferential mapping between the propositional and implicational subsystems (PROP → IMPLIC & IMPLIC → PROP).

As the "difficult" sentence is being reread by the user of the word processor, the form and content of the derived propositions and propositional complexes might, for example, prove inconsistent with an accessed representation of the writer's original intentions. Under such circumstances the IMPLIC → PROP process might represent the propositional content of the discrepancy and a subsequent PROP → IMPLIC & IMPLIC → PROP cycle might then construct a representation specifying that the sentence be deleted and rewritten. The propositional contents of this representation can be equated with the intention to delete—or a "goal" in conventional task analyses. The representation would then have to be mapped through output processes appropriate for the interface to that particular word processor.

For the purposes of illustration, suppose that the interface involves a linear menu of command words at the bottom of the display and a mouse-based dialog. The sentence would be deleted by pointing at the command word "delete" and then moving the mouse to select appropriate start and end points. For an inexpert user, further computational cycles through PROP → IMPLIC & IMPLIC → PROP processes might be required to elaborate a representation of the action sequence. In addition, the configuration of resources outlined above for reading would also be involved in scanning the menu for the appropriate command. However, the propositional representation of the intention "to delete" would have to be mapped onto the object (PROP → OBJ) and limb subsystems (OBJ → LIM) to control the motor act of mouse selection (LIM → MOT). During this process feedback concerning cursor location would be made available to the representational subsystems via VIS → OBJ and OBJ → PROP processes. Each step in the sequence would be evaluated and controlled by the higher-level propositional and implicational representations.

As soon as the evaluation by PROP → IMPLIC and IMPLIC → PROP processes confirms that physical deletion has occurred, these processes would establish that the next thing to do is to rewrite the text. Possibly by a combination of rereading prior sentences and/or accessing prior episodic representations stored in their image records, these same processes would elaborate a fresh propositional representation for the new sentence (IMPLIC → PROP). A configuration of processes would then be required to map this representation onto direct effector action.

Each of the representational subsystems outlined in figure 6.4 incorporates parallel secondary processes for recoding both "incoming" and "outgoing" representations. The propositional representation computed in the implicational subsystem can therefore be transmitted over the data network, where the propositional subsystem would assign it a surface structure form (PROP → MPL). This in turn would be transmitted and recoded in the MPL subsystem into an extended articulatory representation (MPL → ART). The actual act of typing characters would then be controlled by the articulatory subsystem's ART → MOT_{typ} process operating in a buffered configuration with its associated image record. It might also reasonably be assumed that some spatial aspects of motor control requires concurrent processing via the PROP → OBJ, OBJ → LIM, and LIM → MOT processes. In addition, auditory feedback from keystroke activity would be copied automatically into the acoustic image record, but

Table 6.1
Three process configurations for understanding text, deleting it, and creative typing[a]

"Understanding"	"Deleting"	"Creative Typing"
*VIS → OBJ::	(::PROP → IMPLIC::	(::PROP → IMPLIC::
::OBJ → MPL::	::IMPLIC → PROP::)$_n$	::IMPLIC → PROP::)$_n$
(::COPY MPL →	::PROP → OBJ::	::PROP → MPL::
MPL → PROP::)$_{buf}$	::OBJ → LIM::	::MPL → ART::
(::PROP → IMPLIC::	::LIM → MOT*	(::COPY ART →
::IMPLIC → PROP::)$_n$	Plus "Feedback" via	ART → MOTtyp*)$_{buf}$
	*VIS → OBJ::	
	::OBJ → PROP::	

a. * denotes "external" input/output; :: denotes transmission over the data network; (. . .)$_{buf}$ denotes buffered processing within a subsystem; and (::. . . .::)$_n$ denotes probable reciprocal processing between subsystems.

further processing of this information would presumably be suppressed. Table 6.1 summarizes the configurations of processes outlined above for understanding text, deleting it, and creatively typing fresh input. In each case processes from a number of subsystems are brought into play in an integrated fashion. Although the wider architecture permits significant parallel processing, the table focuses on only those processes that may be regarded as central to a particular cognitive activity. Not all possible forms of representational feedback are included, nor all possible forms of parallel output processing. Some of the processes appear in only one of the configurations; others, in more than one. However, for any one phase of cognitive activity all of the processes listed are operating concurrently and any one process is only doing one thing at a time.

Although different forms of cognitive activity may invoke different underlying patterns of processing activity, a particular kind of overt behavior may also be controlled by different underlying configurations of processes. For example, in table 6.1 the configuration of activity for creative typing assumed that motor output was mediated by buffered processing of an articulatory representation. This particular assumption is likely to be inappropriate for highly skilled behavior, where an expert copy typist would presumably make use of a more direct configuration (C2) for mapping for visual input to motor output:

C2 *VIS → OBJ::OBJ → LIM::(COPY LIM → LIM → MOT)$_{buf}$*

In addition, the assumption that a specifically articulatory representation is used to control motor output is arguable. This particular assumption seeks to capture the more general idea that an inexpert two-finger typist engaged in creative composition may need to maintain an extended representation of the surface structure of the intended text while it is decomposed and sequenced for output. For this purpose the representations processed by the specifically verbal subsystems are assumed to have appropriate properties. However, other candidate configurations could equally well fulfill this criterion.

For example, a similar buffering capability could be achieved by assuming a cross-modal secondary process in the MPL subsystem giving a direct mapping to the limb subsystem (e.g., C3). Alternatively, the speech code might be broken down into propositional elements for spelling (MPL → PROP, it is an "f," an "o," an "r") and subsequent output controlled via the object and limb subsystems (C4):

C3 ::PROP → MPL::(COPY MPL → MPL → LIM)$_{buf}$::LIM → MOT*

C4 ::PROP → MPL::MPL → PROP::PROP → OBJ
::OBJ → LIM::(COPY LIM → LIM → MOT)$_{buf}$*

These hypothetical configurations would have different detailed consequences for the microstructure of output and are open to empirical evaluation. However, where the microstructure of motor output is not the focus of attention, as with an analysis of the higher-level properties of dialog, the assumed configuration can be truncated to reflect the core assumption that some output configuration ([..]eff) is controlled by a productively generated surface structure representation (PROP → MPL):

C_{mpl} ::PROP → MPL::MPL → [..]eff

The modular specification of resources within individual subsystems thus provides an overall conceptual framework within which configurations of processing activity can be constrained in a principled manner. As in table 6.1, different phases, or types, of cognitive activity can be contrasted in terms of the configuration of resources involved. Within the same framework, it is also possible to represent a number of alternative process configurations that might plausibly support a particular type of behavior. The framework enables these alternatives to be specified explicitly in a way that enables their empirical ramifications to be explored.

2.3 A Theoretically Motivated Cognitive Task Analysis

Most forms of task analysis take as their point of departure a descriptive analysis of the constituent structure of action, or of the knowledge underlying those actions. Specification of the constituent processing resources of cognition provides an alternative point of departure. The present approach will seek to develop an analysis of *cognitive tasks* from a description of information processing transactions that occur internally between the subsystems of cognition. The form of this analysis will be motivated by the theoretical framework outlined and illustrated above.

Let us briefly review. This framework specifies functionally independent subsystems whose constituent processes operate within larger configurations of cognitive resources. Within a particular configuration processes must operate in a coordinated manner. Each subsystem incorporates secondary processes that transform information from an input mental representation into an output representation. These processes embody procedural knowledge. In addition, each subsystem includes an image record. An episodic trace of representations inputed to that subsystem is created in this record via a primary "copy" process. The actual data undergoing recoding by the secondary processes may be sourced from direct input to the subsystem concerned or by accessing information preserved in its associated image record. Within this overall approach there is no general-purpose central working memory shared by the different resources; nor is there a central executive controlling the pattern of activity. The subsystems are viewed as self-controlling via representations computed by specific processes and passed from one subsystem to another over a data network.

For any given task, the characteristics of overt behavior should thus be systematically related to the architectural properties of subsystems. Behavior will be constrained by the way in which processes and memory records are configured to support particular types or phases of cognitive activity. However, the operation of any configuration should also be related to the form and content of the particular representations undergoing processing. These representations will be constrained by the procedural knowledge incorporated within individual processes, by "prior experience" of specific instances stored in image records, and by the way in which these constraints interrelate to determine the dynamic control of processing activity. Taken together, these constitute a basis for elaborating a form of task analysis in which the properties of overt behavior are a complex function of multiple constraints:

Behavioral Properties ← Fn (Process Configuration & Procedural Knowledge & Record Contents & Dynamic Control)

Tasks of even moderate complexity will make use of a vast amount of procedural knowledge within the processes that make up a particular configuration. In addition, these tasks may involve frequent access to numerous representations stored in episodic records. However, the framework provides a potential means of approximating over individual representations. By definition, each secondary process operates on an *information structure* in a particular mental code and outputs an *information structure* in a different mental code. Information structures with the same form are preserved in the image record associated with the subsystem concerned. Thus, potential approximations concerning knowledge use can be pursued by seeking to establish general relationships between the properties of these mental codes and the characteristics of overt behavior.

One form of potential relationship concerns the origins of errors of different types. A semantic confusion involving the issuing of "quit" rather than "exit" is likely to originate in the process that generates a name from a propositional information structure (PROP → MPL). In the context of just having scanned a file directory, users might err by confusing two file names that have similar form in a morphonolexical information structure (e.g., Nine.txt instead of Mine.txt). In this case the error may result from the recovery or recoding of a recently encountered surface form (e.g., via MPL → ART).

Other potential relationships between overt performance and the representations undergoing processing might concern the consequences of a lack of procedural knowledge of a particular type. For example, suppose a user of a graphics presentation package is confronted with a totally novel set of rather abstract icons. It would seem reasonable to assume that the available repertoire of procedures within the object subsystem would not enable the direct mapping of the incoming information structure onto its intended meaning (OBJ → PROP) or even onto a "name" that accurately reflected that meaning (OBJ → MPL).

Under such circumstances, more general procedural knowledge might come into play and pass on a descriptive representation of key features of the icon (e.g., its a cross-hatched region). This would then place a demand on inferential processes (PROP → IMPLIC & IMPLIC → PROP) to sort out a putative interpretation in the context of the task, and in the context of other icons within the set. Such inferential activity would have quantitative consequences, in that it would take time to complete these additional information processing transactions, and qualitative effects on the course of overt user-system dialog (e.g., access to help facility/trial and error). Thus, the procedural knowledge embodied within one component of a configuration may have general consequences for the representations processed by other components and implications for the overall dynamic control of the pattern of cognitive activity.

Some of the additional information processing transactions resulting from restricted procedural knowledge may require accessing specific information structures represented in the image records associated with individual subsystems. The basic theoretical framework assumes that these information structures are laid down as an automatic consequence of processing activity. Of course, these records might routinely be accessed to recover information structures relevant to a particular dialog exchange (e.g., the specific name of a file to be deleted). However, the framework assumes that the records have a more fundamental role in learning. Such records are viewed as a prerequisite for the development of new procedures within a particular secondary process. These assumptions provide a basis for exploring potential relationships between subsystem operation and the development of performance as learning progresses.

In the earliest phases of learning a novel command language, numerous memory records would be laid down during the course of user-system interactions. Relevant records would be created during the interpretation of instructions and help frames, the productive generation of command strings for output, and the interpretation of system and error states. Many of these would be created as a result of purely internal processing demands. In the course of planning, retrieval, and problem solving there would be a considerable amount of processing activity among the MPL, propositional and implicational subsystems $((::\text{MPL} \rightarrow \text{PROP}::\text{PROP} \rightarrow \text{MPL}::)_n$ and $(::\text{PROP} \rightarrow \text{IMPLIC}::\text{IMPLIC} \rightarrow \text{PROP}::)_n)$. Records in the different subsystems would contain information relevant to the surface form of dialog (MPL), its meaning (PROP), and more complex interrelationships with prior knowledge structures relevant to the tasks, the system, and its operation (IMPLIC).

In many of these records, constituents of a particular information structure would come together in novel combinations. Simply reading a definition in a help frame would, for example, create an information structure in the MPL record. This information structure would link the command term to a phrase that, when processed (MPL → PROP), would specify its intended meaning. In the absence of a specific procedure capable of directly generating the command term, the PROP → MPL process may recruit more general procedural knowledge to generate an MPL description that can be passed over the data network where a subsequent process (MPL → [..]eff) could utilize that description to access the MPL image record and recover the name itself.

As experience with the command language evolves, the number of relevant memory records with the same, or similar, form and content would naturally increase. Frequent access, use, and inferential processing of these representations would eventually lead to the addition of new, fully automated procedures to the repertoire incorporated within a particular process (e.g., PROP → MPL). Thus, the pattern of cognitive activity underlying the performance of an unskilled novice should differ radically from that of an expert. The behavior of a novice user should reflect the characteristics of additional information processing transactions. These would be required to overcome the constraints imposed by restricted repertoires of procedures and record contents in specific subsystems of cognition. In the case of an expert, the activation of fully automated procedures for mapping an information structure from one code to another would lead to greater cognitive economy in terms of the number of internal information processing transactions required.

On the basis of what is known about the general course of skill development (e.g., see Fitts, 1964), acquisition of fully automated procedures requires considerable experience and practice. It would, for example, seem most unlikely that many new procedures would be added during the first few hours of learning. However, the first few hours of experience often give rise to the most substantial improvements in performance. These improvements are most likely to be related to the accessing and use of a rapidly increasing number of memory records. Accordingly, the initial characteristics of novice performance and its subsequent development may be best approached by considering potential interplays between preexisting procedural knowledge, the accessing of memory records, and the overall dynamic control of processing activity.

Although the above illustrations have concentrated upon examples drawn from human computer interaction, the basic form of task analysis, and the theoretical framework on which it is based, is defined in such a way as to have general applicability. The cognitive resources underlying performance in human-computer dialogs are assumed to be the same as those that would be involved in the understanding and production of the English language or in the learning of a second language, such as French. While the particular representations involved would obviously differ across tasks, the basic principles governing the underlying operation of the cognitive system should be the same.

The overall strategy will be to develop the analysis in a top-down manner on the basis of empirical evidence. This will be pursued here by reviewing findings from several experiments that manipulated factors likely to influence the learning of human-computer dialogs. Many of the properties of user behavior exhibited in these experimental settings can be captured by the kind of hypothetical principles outlined above. In addition, specific patterns of results can be used to abstract and justify more detailed claims concerning the possible effects on overt behavior of systematic interrelationships among process configurations, procedural knowledge, record contents, and the dynamic control of processing activity.

3 Interpreting Experimental Evidence in Terms of Cognitive Task Analysis

3.1 A Core Configuration for Processing Lexical Command Structures

The particular experiments reviewed below all examined the performance of novice users and have all been concentrated upon phenomena associated with the structure and content of lexical dialogs requiring keyboard actions. For these dialog tasks, the primary processing activity will occur within the configurations of resources required to understand system states from visual input and generate output on the basis of lexical form:

$$\begin{aligned} C_{\text{task}} \quad & *\text{VIS} \rightarrow \text{OBJ}::\text{OBJ} \rightarrow \text{MPL}::(\text{COPY MPL} \rightarrow \text{MPL} \rightarrow \text{PROP})_{\text{buf}} \\ & (::\text{PROP} \rightarrow \text{IMPLIC}::\text{IMPLIC} \rightarrow \text{PROP}::)_{n} \\ & ::\text{PROP} \rightarrow \text{MPL}::\text{MPL} \rightarrow [\,..\,]\text{eff} \end{aligned}$$

The first illustration focuses upon the effects on performance of the constraints imposed by preexisting procedural knowledge in the learning of command names. The second focuses upon the utilization of information stored in image records in the learning of extended command sequences. The final illustration extends the analysis of the role of image records in learning to a more complex case. In this more complex case, the contents of different image records interact in the control of processing activity. Each illustration is actually drawn from a series of studies. Since a large body of evidence is involved, the treatment must necessarily be highly selective. Little reference will be made to the practical justification of individual studies or their relationship to the broader literature on a particular topic. These can be established by reference to the source material.

3.2 Preexisting Procedural Knowledge and the Learning of Command Names

In many kinds of system dialog users are faced with the general problem of referring to system objects and functions by name. In order to do so they must be able to interpret (MPL → PROP), or generate (PROP → MPL) these names. The extent to which users can effectively perform or learn these mappings should be related in a principled manner to their preexisting repertoires of procedures for handling lexical information structures. A recent study by Grudin and Barnard (1984) contrasted the learning of command name sets that differed systematically in the extent to which users could be expected to call upon their preexisting knowledge of lexical form and meaning.

This particular study utilized a simplified text editing system with ten commands. The basic task involved retrieving a proverb that contained four "errors." These were edited and the correct proverb stored. Users had to infer the relevant operation by examining the current state of the proverb field or the proverb itself. The appropriate command name for the required operation had to be typed in. However, the system prompted the user as to the specific arguments required by individual commands. If users were unsure what to do, they could access a two-level help facility providing, first, a menu of command names, and then, a full listing of names together with their operations.

The cognitive demands imposed by this task include learning about the basic system facilities, the operations it performed, and the command names required to invoke them. Learning was monitored over three editing sessions, and an independent groups design was used to compare performance with five different command vocabularies. These were specific names whose natural semantics were related to the actual command operations, an abbreviation scheme (the first three different consonants in the specific name), names that were semantically unrelated to operations associated with them, pseudowords (invented words that conform to the normal rules of lexical form), and consonant strings of the same length as the abbreviations. The full command sets are reproduced in table 6.2.

The basic pattern of performance obtained by Grudin and Barnard was quite clear and consistent across measures. There were substantial effects of learning for all command sets. Overall, editing performance was most efficient with the specific command names. Performance with the abbreviations and the unrelated command names was less efficient. It was least efficient with the pseudowords and consonant strings. Just one measure, the mean times taken to edit proverbs in each session, is reproduced in figure 6.5.

A relatively straightforward account of the performance differences can be provided by considering the operation of those processes that map meaning onto form (PROP → MPL) and form onto an output sequence

Table 6.2
The command name sets[a]

Specific names	Abbreviations	Unrelated names	Pseudowords	Consonant strings
front	frn	stack	blark	ksd
back	bck	turn	lins	rlp
insert	nsr	afford	aspalm	trp
delete	dlt	parole	ragole	fnm
prefix	prf	chisel	clamen	drs
append	pnd	uncurl	extich	gpf
merge	mrg	rinse	dapse	lts
split	spl	throw	thrag	ctf
fetch	ftc	light	manst	nrb
store	str	brake	fluve	rcn

a. From Grudin and Barnard (1984).

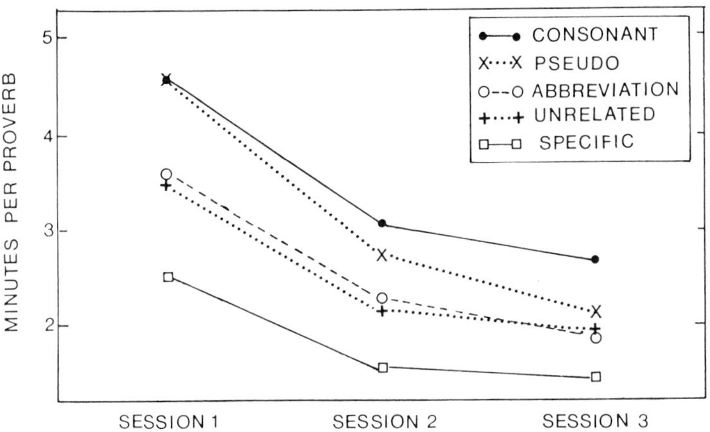

Figure 6.5
Illustrative data from the Grudin and Barnard (1984) study: the average time taken to edit proverbs.

(MPL → [..]eff). Users' preexisting repertoires of procedures for recoding information structures in these codes would seem well placed to cope with the specific command names. It can reasonably be assumed that these names are already a part of their normal productive vocabulary. Accordingly, there should be existing procedures capable of processing a surface structure representation to yield a sequence of characters for that command (MPL → [..]eff). In addition, some feature of the underlying operation was systematically related to the semantics of the command word. Procedural knowledge of those semantics should thus support the direct generation of the lexical item itself (PROP → MPL).

In fact, the only novel processing demand for the specific names is to establish their interpretation in the context of text editing (e.g., PREFIX—Adds a *character* to the beginning of a *word*). This type of requirement is not atypical of many forms of comprehension. In consequence, from the point at which the nature of the operation is inferred (IMPLIC → PROP), the output configuration could be controlled relatively automatically through the stages of production (::PROP → MPL::MPL → [..]eff). There would be little need for additional information processing transactions between subsystems to construct or recover novel representations. Indeed, some initial training with this vocabulary seemed all that was required to support efficient performance. In the main editing sessions users made few errors and rarely invoked the help facility.

With the abbreviated command set, initial control of the output configuration would be more complex. Since the abbreviations were contractions of the full command name, the mappings from a semantic specification of the underlying operation to the full command word (PROP → MPL) would be equivalent to those for the specific name set. However, there is a requirement to represent and recover novel information structures concerning the actual characters in each abbreviation.

As a consequence of initial training, information structures representing the length, identity, and order of characters required to invoke each command would be represented in the image record of the MPL subsystem. However, the processes of other subsystem would be called into play to draw inferences about the abbreviation rule (::MPL → PROP::PROP → IMPLIC::) and to generate descriptions for the recovery of information from that record (::IMPLIC → PROP::PROP → MPL_{desc}). Information recovered from the MPL image record might then be fed back to the propositional and implicational subsystems for further processing prior to an attempt at command entry or a decision to consult help. These additional information processing demands would not only take time but also tend to increase the number of overt dialog exchanges (errors and use of the help facilities).

The unrelated command names would pose similar problems for the control of the output configuration, but for a different process. Like the specific command names, the unrelated names would fall within the user's productive vocabulary. As such the mappings from surface form to output (MPL → [..]eff) would be directly processable by preexisting repertoires of procedures. However, unlike the specific names and their abbreviations, users need to be able to generate a known lexical item in a novel propositional context (PROP → MPL). In this case, additional transactions between subsystems would be required to represent and recover novel propositional information structures. Effectively, the use of abbreviations leads to additional information processing transactions to support one type of novel mapping (MPL → [..]eff), and the use of unrelated names a different type of novel mapping (PROP → MPL). With the pseudowords and consonant strings, *both* kinds of mapping are initially unknown and would need to be resolved by yet more complex control of processing activity.

The possibility of this type of relationship between preexisting procedural knowledge was introduced in an earlier section. On the basis of this type of evidence, pertinent features of the relationship can be captured a little more precisely. Performance with the specific command vocabulary is efficient because preexisting procedures support the relatively automatic control of output processing. The absence of preexisting procedures in any one secondary process within the required configuration results in an additional cognitive workload to control processing activity and govern access to information structures stored in image records—or failing that, access to a help facility via overt dialog exchanges. This gives rise to performance costs. The absence of preexisting procedures in two components of the required configuration increases the cognitive workload involved with the control of processing and is consequently associated with larger performance costs.

Obviously, a fully elaborated account of the Grudin and Barnard data would not be confined to these relationships alone. An analysis of the rate of learning is also required. For example, the precise pattern of performance with the pseudoword vocabulary indicated that users were able to put their more general procedural knowledge of the properties of lexical items to good use. Initially, performance resembled that for consonant strings, but by the third session was more comparable to that for unrelated words (see figure 6.5). This suggests that over the relatively short period of learning studied here, these novel "words" were actually becoming lexicalized. Once lexicalized, item and order information would be processable from an integrated MPL information structure (MPL → [..]eff). This would then leave residual problems of operation-name mapping (PROP → MPL) comparable to those for the unrelated command names.

In addition, users of the consonant string vocabulary were particularly disadvantaged throughout the experiment. At the beginning of the third session of editing, less than 40% of the consonant strings were accurately retrieved in a free recall task. At this stage some 80% or better of the names in all the other vocabularies were accurately recalled. For these other vocabularies (including the abbreviations), the recovery of information in image records would be facilitated by the processing of integrated lexical units. In the absence of such units, or the possibility of deriving them, the users of consonant strings would be forced to rely upon access to the MPL image record to recover the identity and order of individual characters. The fallibility of this form of retrieval would help explain the perseveration of high levels of error and use of the help system.

The vocabularies utilized in this particular study by Grudin and Barnard involve rather gross distinctions. However, evidence obtained in other studies using the same paradigm suggest that the general principles outlined here can be developed to account for more subtle effects within particular vocabulary types, such as abbreviations (e.g., Grudin and Barnard, 1985) or full words (e.g., Barnard et al., 1982). The study by Barnard et al. showed that a vocabulary of semantically general command names (e.g., MOVE, SHIFT) gave rise to different patterns of performance when compared with a specific command vocabulary of the type shown in table 6.2. An unpublished follow-up study examined performance with command sets that were made up of 50% general names and 50% specific names. Performance with these vocabularies closely approximated that for command vocabularies made up of wholly specific names. This type of empirical finding suggests that the particular semantic features associated with a class of names were perhaps less important than the potential ambiguities in name operation-mapping within the complete set.

3.3 Record Contents and the Learning of Command Structures

In the preceding illustration memory records were implicated in the learning of the internal structure and content of command names. A text editing paradigm was employed in which the identity and order of commands had to be inferred by the user on the basis of the errors in the text. In addition, the arguments required by a particular command were prompted. Other forms of dialog require users to generate more extended, and often strictly ordered, structures that incorporate several distinct constituents. Dialogs with these characteristics may be expected to furnish evidence concerning the properties and utilization of more elaborate information structures. Representative evidence concerning the learning of dialogs with these properties has been reported by Barnard, MacLean, and Hammond (1984).

This particular study employed a task involving handling electronic mail. Users were required to issue sequences of commands to handle two forms of messages, incoming messages and outgoing messages. Eight command operations were required to complete the sequence for each type of message. These had to be issued in a strictly ordered sequence or an error message would result. There were twelve commands in the set and four command operations were thus required in the handling of both incoming and outgoing messages. Hence, for each type of message, users had to learn the identity and order of command operations, as well as the names required to invoke them. In addition, half of the command operations *established* information required by another operation that carried out related *actions*. For example, the action of sending an item of mail required a prior operation to establish a full address. As with the text editing paradigm, the arguments required by commands were prompted, and users could access a multilevel help facility to obtain information on the required sequences of operations, the names, and the relationships between names and operations.

In this task context, two aspects of the required dialog were manipulated: the superordinate structure of the command sequence and the nature of the command nameset. In one form of superordinate structure, the sequence of eight commands involved issuing the four *establish* operations followed by the four *action* operations. The alternative structure involved issuing a sequence of four semantically related establish-action pairs. These two organizations are illustrated in table 6.3. One set of command names contained pairs of names that were potentially confusable (e.g., DISPLAY & SHOW; ENTER & INPUT). In the other command set an attempt was made to reduce the possibilities for confusion among names within the set.

The actual data from this and subsequent follow-up studies furnish evidence on a number of specific points. However, this treatment will focus upon those data that primarily inform the processing of superordinate structures. Figure 6.6 reproduces the basic learning curves for the mean number of commands entered without help or error. In this figure, the curves for the establish class of operation are plotted separately from those

Table 6.3
The two alternative sequences[a]

2 × 4 grouped structure (incoming messages)
*Establish the time at which the message arrived
*Establish the originator reference of the sender
*Establish the register number for keeping a copy
*Establish the mail point of the recipient
*Mark the message with its time of arrival
*Acknowledge receipt of the message (to sender)
*Keep a copy of the message in the register
*Forward the message to the recipient's mail point
4 × 2 paired structure (outgoing messages)
*Establish the company reference of the sender
*Attach the company reference to the message
*Establish the price of sending the message
*Debit the department sending the message
*Establish the file number for keeping a copy
*Keep a copy of the message in the file
*Establish the destination code for the recipient
*Forward the message to the destination code

a. From Barnard, MacLean, and Hammond (1984).

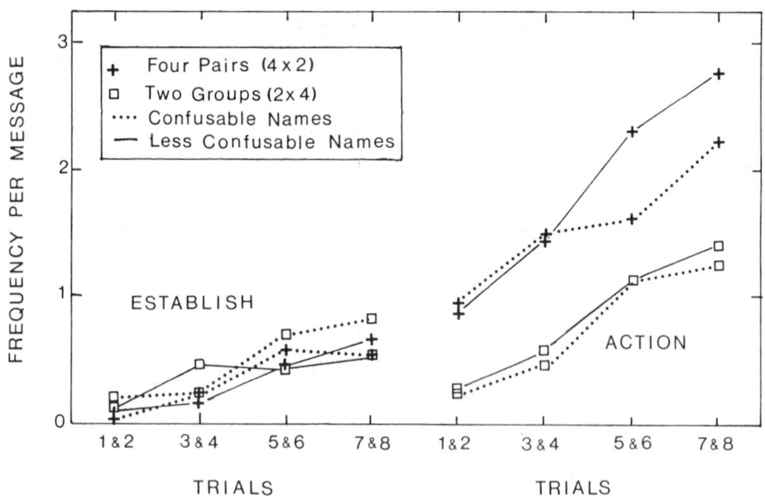

Figure 6.6
Illustrative data from the study by Barnard, MacLean, and Hammond (1984): the frequency with which commands were entered without error or access to the help facilities (maximum possible = 4).

for the action operations. For both command sets, performance with the action operations was superior in the structure involving four pairs of commands. There was no difference for the establish operations. More detailed analysis of the use of the help facilities indicated that this particular advantage for the paired structure was entirely attributable to features associated with the representation of the operations and their order rather than their names.

However, as figure 6.6 shows, performance on the establish operations was abysmal throughout learning. In fact, it appeared that users were experiencing considerable difficulty discriminating among these operations for both name sets. Accordingly, an unpublished follow-up study sought to overcome this potential floor effect by increasing the general discriminability of these operations. This was approached by replacing command verbs for establish operations with object-based names related to the information sought. Under these conditions an overall performance advantage for the paired superordinate structure emerged for both establish and action operations.

A basic account of this class of effects can be provided by considering the properties of propositional representations and their consequences for the control of processing activity. Within the framework of *interacting cognitive subsystems*, it is assumed that propositional information structures do not explicitly represent lexical form or order. Such specifications can be generated (PROP → MPL), but are not stored in the image record associated with that subsystem. In the sequences involving four pairs of commands, the first member of the pair delivered an argument for use in the execution of the second member of the pair. Initial propositional information structures would therefore share a common referent:

P1(A delivers B)..&..P2(C requires B)....P3(D delivers E)..&..etc.

The process that interprets and combines propositional content (PROP → IMPLIC) would be able to abstract the common component and construct (IMPLIC → PROP) a new propositional information structure that reflects those relationships within the sequence:

$$(P_{incoming}(P_n(P1\&P2))\ \&\ (P_o(P3\&P4))\ \&\ (P_p(P5\&P6))\ \&\ (P_q(P7\&P8)))$$

This kind of representation would be copied into the image record of the propositional subsystem as an automatic consequence of its construction in the implicational subsystem (IMPLIC → PROP::COPY PROP). The inferred propositional information structure for the grouped commands would presumably be based upon more abstract relationships among operations (e.g., collate information in the argument window, operate on the message window) and thus have the following form:

$(P_{incoming}(P_n(P1\&P2\&P3\&P4)) \& (P_o(P5\&P6\&P7\&P8)))$

These two forms of propositional information structures would have different consequences for the resolution of item and order uncertainty in the generation of sequences of action. The more detailed superordinate descriptions (e.g., P_n) for the paired sequence would facilitate the recovery of the subordinated operations to a greater extent than those for the grouped structure. With respect to order uncertainty, the "&"s in these propositional information structures are basically unordered. However, the contents of the representations provide an additional constraint. *Establish* operations need to be executed before *action* operations. This effectively resolves the order ambiguity within the four pairs and between the two groups of four operations. There remains less order uncertainty with the paired structure (four points between pairs) than with the grouped structure (four points within *each* of two groups).

Variation in the level and nature of these uncertainties associated with propositional information structures could thus be related directly to the kind of performance differences shown in figure 6.6. Unlike the illustration concerning command names, the key constraints are not obviously related to the presence or absence of particular repertoires of procedures within individual subsystems. Rather, they appear to be related to fundamental properties of the kind of propositional representation assumed here. This in turn constrains the information that can be recovered from the image record of the propositional subsystem. Such constraints are again likely to complicate the control of processing activity with consequences for the use of the help facilities and for the origins of errors.

For example, one strategy for resolving the uncertainty implicit in propositional representations would be to try to represent and recover a surface structure representation (MPL) or a list of actual command words. This kind of strategy requires the generation of an MPL description (PROP → MPL_{desc}). This description can then be used to access, recover, and output (via MPL → [..]eff) constituents represented in the MPL image record. These constituents have phonological form and are explicitly ordered. The error data suggested that this kind of strategy was more prevalent among the users of the grouped structure than among the users of paired structures.

Where the command vocabulary included pairs of synonymous command names (DISPLAY/SHOW), a proportion of the command errors were confusions among these terms. The absolute and relative frequencies of this class of confusion errors were greater for command sequences involving four related pairs of operations than for those sequences involving two groups of four operations. Words like DISPLAY and SHOW have similar semantic specifications. Hence, confusions would be readily generated if output were to be controlled on the basis of the recovery of information from the propositional image record (via PROP → MPL). These same words do not have a common phonological specification. Hence a reduced occurrence of such errors would be consistent with more frequent control of output via recovery of information from the MPL image record (MPL → [. .]eff). This interpretation receives some additional support from a higher frequency of certain kinds of transposition errors with the grouped command sequence.

In terms of the cognitive task analysis sought here, tentative principles interrelating record contents and the dynamic control of processing activity can now be stated. The following claims are at least consistent with the type of evidence discussed above. All other things being equal, information processing transactions are minimized when output processing can be controlled from the contents of a single image record. Additional information processing transactions will be required when the demands of a particular task cannot be met in this way. The nature and extent of these additional transactions will be related to the specific properties of the mental codes involved.

There are, of course, other cases in human-computer dialogs where constitutents need to be entered in a strict order. Command-argument sequences are a case in point. These also appear to give rise to structural effects that are dependent upon multiple constraints imposed by task demands, command vocabularies, and alternative sequencing schemes (e.g., see Barnard et al., 1981; Hammond et al., 1984a). However, features of these particular studies suggested that the patterns of performance might differ systematically between dialogs involving strict sequencing of elements and those in which the order of elements was optional.

3.4 Further Evidence Concerning Process Interactions Involving Multiple Image Records

Empirical issues associated with optional sequencing of operations as opposed to fixed sequencing were pursued in a different empirical paradigm. This paradigm involved menu dialogs in which users invoked commands via programmed function keys. The operations carried out by these keys were indicated by a menu of command names. This form of dialog clearly

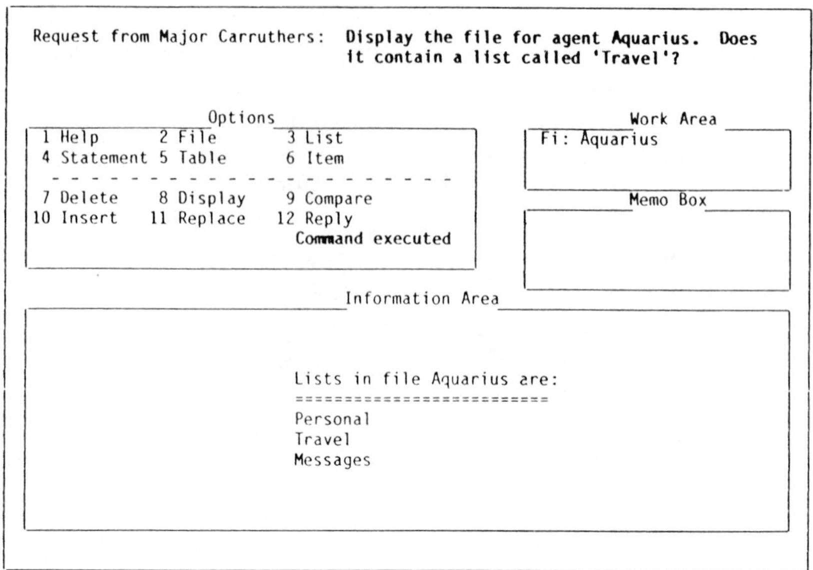

Figure 6.7
An illustration of the display used in the menu selection study (from Barnard and Hammond, 1982).

differs from those discussed above in that the control of output processing (::PROP → MPL::MPL → [..]eff) does not require a name to be produced. Although, the overt actions differ, the assumption will be retained that the command names are processed. On this basis it will also be assumed that surface structure representations are still involved in the control of keyboard actions (MPL → [..]eff).

The study itself, summarized in Barnard and Hammond (1982) and in Hammond and Barnard (1984), focused upon a data base retrieval task. Information in the data base was structured into a set of objects (files, lists, tables, statements, and items) that could be operated on by an equal number of functions (display, compare, delete, insert, and replace). Users were required to answer a sequence of questions. They did so by selecting appropriate functions and objects from menus. Figure 6.7 illustrates one form of screen structure for this task. In the first phase of the study users could answer the questions by selecting a single function and object. In the second phase of the study more complex questions required two function/object selections. The order of entering functions and objects was either optional or fixed. The optional case will be considered first.

In the optional case a single unified menu listed both functions and objects. Users had to select one function and one object, but the selections could be made in either order. The actual pattern of selections was studied under several conditions. For two groups of users, the objects were listed in the upper part of the menu panel and the functions in the lower part (as in the figure). For the other two groups the functions were located above the objects.

The two groups receiving each type of menu organization were given different initial briefings concerning the system. One type of briefing provided an explicit description of the types of objects held in the data base. In this briefing, the names of the functions were simply listed without further explanation. In the alternative briefing, the operation of functions was explicitly defined and the names of the objects simply listed. For all users half of the questions were phrased in such a way that the function required was mentioned first (Display the file for agent Aquarius. Does it contain a list called travel?). The remaining questions mentioned the object first (The file for agent Aquarius should be displayed. Does it contain . . . ?).

In principle, the dialog exchanges required to answer the questions could actually be completed successfully on the basis of relatively simple-minded cognitive strategies. For example, users could seek to match words in the question with menu items. Nevertheless, the orders that users actually selected appeared to be under systematic influences. Overall there was a strong bias toward selecting a function before selecting an object. However, the extent to which users did so was biased by the initial briefing. Users whose briefing explicitly described the functions showed an immediate bias toward selecting functions before objects. This was maintained throughout the first phase of answering simple questions. In contrast, for the very first question, those users whose initial briefing was focused upon the objects were more likely to select the object before the function. This was a very transient effect. These users rapidly changed to a bias toward selecting functions before objects. Indeed, after half a dozen questions, these users were actually *more* likely to enter a function before an object than those users who had been explicitly briefed on the functions.

The extent of the bias toward entering functions first was also influenced by the arrangement of the menu panel. When averaged over the other factors involved, placing the functions above the objects enhanced the bias toward selecting functions first. Placing the objects above the functions reduced the extent of that bias. An influence of comparable magnitude to that exerted by the structure of the menu was also observed for the structure of individual questions. Although this particular effect was statistically unreliable, the trend was in the same direction. The probability of entering a function first tended to be enhanced when the function occurred before the object in the actual surface structure of the question and was reduced when the object was mentioned before the function.

Thus, under conditions where users were free to select functions and objects in any order, several factors interrelated to determine their precise pattern of choices. The production of English imperatives usually involves topicalization on the required action rather than its object (e.g., Shut the door!). The recruitment of preexisting procedures for generating imperative forms within a configuration of processes supporting sequence planning (e.g., ::IMPLIC → PROP::(::PROP → MPL::MPL → PROP::)$_n$) would tend to lead to representations whose contents were topicalized on action constituents. The principal bias toward selecting the function first may thus be primarily attributable to preexisting procedural knowledge. However, the processing activity involved in reading the question and the options in the menu panel would give rise to specific representations in the image records of the MPL and propositional subsystems (*VIS → OBJ::OBJ → MPL::(COPY MPL → MPL → PROP::)$_{buf}$).

In the context of a particular dialog exchange, there would thus be several recently created information structures in the image records of the propositional and MPL subsystems. In the specific context of the first question, the set of recently created representations would also include information structures derived from the initial briefing. The form and content of these representations would have many features in common with the actual form of representation required to control output processing. Specific instances would be either consistent or inconsistent with the underlying procedural bias. Were these representation to be accessed in the course of planning activity, their content could override the bias built into preexisting output procedures.

User performance was also studied under the same basic conditions but where the system, rather than the user, controlled the order of selecting functions and objects. In this form of dialog, two separate menus were presented in sequence. Each menu gave either a choice of functions or a choice of objects. Two groups of users were asked to make a choice among functions before making a choice among objects. For the other two groups the order was reversed. In the sense that users would encounter one set of options before another, this is not unlike organizing functions above objects (or vice versa) within a single unified menu. In both cases a sequence would be represented in image records as a consequence of information processing activity. Manipulation of the question structures and the briefing instructions was exactly the same as that described above.

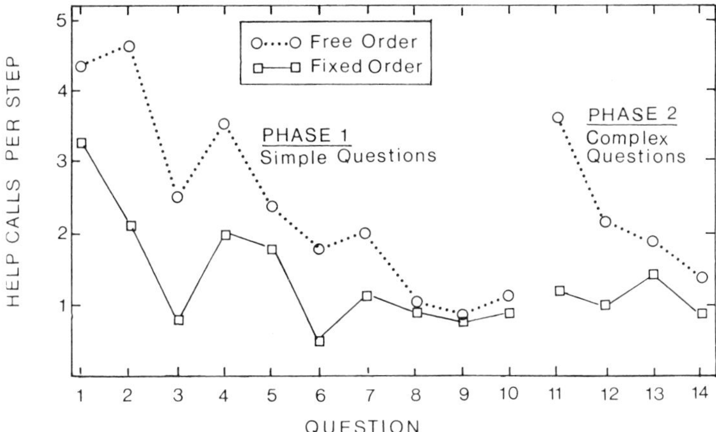

Figure 6.8
The use of the help facility for fixed and free order selections across the two phases of question-answering (from Barnard and Hammond, 1982).

With the fixed order of selection, neither the initial briefing information nor the question structure resulted in marked or systematic effects on the efficiency of performance. Furthermore, the order of selecting functions and objects had virtually no effects at all. Given a free order of selection, and consistent with the likely properties of preexisting procedural knowledge, users exhibited a bias toward selecting functions first. On this basis, a requirement to select objects first might have been expected to have some detrimental effects on performance when compared to a requirement to select functions first. However, key characteristics of performance with the fixed order of selection proved to be markedly different from that for the free order of selection. Data that are representative of these differences are reproduced in figure 6.8 (use of the help facility).

This figure illustrates two basic points. First, initial performance with the fixed order of selection was superior to that for the free order of selection. Second, users in the fixed order conditions transferred from simple to complex questions with relative ease. At this point, the questions changed from requiring one function/object exchange to two such exchanges. Although users in the free selection conditions had attained a level of performance comparable to that for the fixed order of selection, they nevertheless appeared to have considerable difficulties managing this transition.

In all of the conditions studied, the form and content of the actual user-system exchanges were closely related. Basic principles seeking to account for these data thus need to explain why prior briefing and the order of encountering information (e.g., from menus or from questions) influence the characteristics of overt behavior in one circumstance but not in another. They also need to explain the gross differences in performance between the fixed and free dialogs. In particular, they would need to explain the different transfer effects.

The information processing demands of the two forms of dialog task are clearly different. As with the analysis for the electronic mail task, it will be assumed that users construct a propositional information structure (via ::PROP → IMPLIC::IMPLIC → PROP::) to represent relevant features of the basic task. This information structure would be preserved in the image record of the propositional subsystem. The contents of representation should include constituents concerning the reading and interpretation of the question—(P_{ques}(....)), the first menu selection—($P_{select1}$(....)), and the second selection—($P_{select2}$(....)). Embedded within each of these would be a representation concerning scanning the menu for the PF key number and actually striking it P_{act}(.....). At this level the representations for fixed and free order dialogs would be equivalent. The following elaboration is for the free order of selection:

$$(P_{task}(P_{ques}(\ldots.) \,\&\, (P_{select1}(P_a(\;) \,\&\, P_b(\;) \,\&\, P_{act}(\ldots.))) \,\&$$

$$(P_{select2}(P_c(\;) \,\&\, P_b(\;) \,\&\, P_{act}(\ldots.))))$$

In the first selection a decision has to be made concerning the category with which to initiate the dialog exchange. This would call upon P_a(SELECTION 1 CAN BE ⟨FUNCTION⟩ OR ⟨OBJECT⟩) and then upon the selection of the instance, for example, P_b(⟨FUNCTION⟩). In making the second selection, some knowledge of the prior selection, such as P_c(SELECTION 2 CANNOT BE ⟨LAST VALUE OF P_b for SELECTION 1⟩), is required to control the selection of the instance P_b(⟨OBJECT⟩). Since order uncertainty is associated with the disjunctive form of P_a( ), additional information processing transactions among subsystems would again be required to resolve a value for P_b( ). This would provide conditions under which other information structures preserved in image records may bias the particular selection made. These could be derived from the initial briefing; the menu structure; or the structure of the question posed.

Under conditions where the order of selection is determined by the system, the propositional representation needed to control action would be very much more straightforward. The constituents represented by P_a( ) and P_c( ) would not be required since the value of P_b( ) is constrained by the actual menu currently displayed. With fewer constituents, and particularly in the absence of a disjunctive one, fewer information processing transactions would be required to generate overt dialog exchanges. This contrast would account for the initial performance advantage of the fixed order dialog relative to the free order dialog. As was the case with the electronic mail task, a basis pattern of data can be utilized to infer potentially systematic relationships between generalizable properties of the contents of particular image records and the dynamic control of processing activity.

In the case of the transfer effects, the simple doubling of the number of explicit function-object selections did not appear to be the root cause of the problem for the users in the free dialog condition. In fact, the posttransfer difficulties exhibited under conditions of free order selection appeared most related to the making of the second selection within each of the two exchanges. In effect, having made one selection, they appeared uncertain as to how to complete the exchange. This pointed to some interaction between the interpretation of the complex question posed and their past experience with the system.

The complex questions actually differed from the simple ones in two ways. First, the function names in the menu no longer mapped quite so directly onto key words in the questions. Second, since the questions described two exchanges, reference was made to many more concepts. The interpretation of the complex questions thus involved greater ambiguity at the level of identifying potential functions or objects. In seeking to resolve these ambiguities, one obvious strategy would be to match a description of the current situation to the contents of image records concerning previously used combinations of objects and functions.

During their initial experience of the system, representations of command sequences would automatically have been stored in the image records of subsystems concerned with the control of output. This occurs as a consequence of the automatic operation of the primary copy processes. In the case of the dialog involving a free order of selection, these representations would vary from instance to instance depending on the biases operating. The representations preserved would thus be structurally *inconsistent*. With the fixed dialog order the representations would have been structurally *consistent*. Discounting occasional anomalies, either a function would always have preceded an object or vice versa. Hence, this particular transfer effect can be readily understood if it is assumed that accessing operations across consistent structures are more likely to succeed than those across inconsistent structures.

4 Mapping from Theoretical Principles to System Design

In the introduction to this chapter three general issues were raised concerning bridging theory and application. The first concerned the limitations imposed by the unintegrated nature of much cognitive theory; the second concerned the restricted scope of empirical evidence and the tendency for it to stand in a paradigm-bound relation to theory; the third concerned the requirements to generate explicit mappings between the underlying principles that govern behavior and the problems of system design.

The preceding sections have suggested possible approaches to the first two issues. A theoretical framework has been presented that seeks to integrate over the various components of mental life and over the problems related to knowledge representation and the constraints imposed by the mechanics of human information processing. This model was then used to motivate a form of task analysis focused upon the nature of the transactions likely to occur within the human information processing mechanism in support of overt behavior. Both the basic theoretical framework and the form of task analysis were defined in such a way as to enable their application over a wide range of cognitive tasks. The form of task analysis covered four types of general constraint likely to interrelate to determine the characteristics of overt performance.

Some experiments were then reviewed and interpretations offered in terms of specific interrelationships between the elements of the cognitive task analysis. In these particular instances the interpretations were post hoc. Since we only currently have a restricted number of studies, it is quite possible that particular findings may not be replicated. It is even more likely that the particular principles suggested will prove incomplete, inaccurate, inexpertly thought through, or just plain wrong. The intention was to illustrate that the analytic framework has the utility of turning potentially generalizable principles that are open to further empirical test into explicit statements. For such principles to be of practical utility outside the context of laboratory research, there remains the problem of finding a strategy for bridging the gap.

The patterns of evidence obtained in the kind of research outlined above are characteristically complex, involving both qualitative and quantitative differences in performance. It would clearly be advantageous if some means could be found to use computer technology itself to help organize and interpret the interrelationships involved (e.g., see Barnard, 1984). The form and content of the cognitive task analysis is open to representation in the knowledge base of an expert system. The approach itself suggests one principled strategy for moving toward the development of such systems. This involves developing the task analysis with bottom-up constraints provided by evidence and top-down constraints provided by the theoretical framework.

From the bottom up, the kind of fragmentary evidence from individual pieces of research can at least be described in terms of the potentially generalizable conditions under which they are likely to occur. So, for example, results can be expressed as follows:

Characterization of data

Under conditions (Novice, menu dialog, order uncertainty)
Result: Selection order biased by recently processed information structures involving ordered constituents whose description matches the selection
Under conditions (Novice, command language, ordered sequence)
Result: Performance impaired when adjacent sequence constituents have few semantic interrelationships
Under conditions (Novice, command language, unordered sequence)
Result: Performance impaired as function of requirements to learn new lexical forms or meaning

Likewise, from the top down basic theoretical assumptions can be represented concerning the processing resources required for tasks, processing constraints, knowledge representation, and so on:

Core configuration for tasks

Under conditions (VDU,Kybd,Explicit Command) config is

$$*\text{VIS} \rightarrow \text{OBJ}::\text{OBJ} \rightarrow \text{MPL}::(\text{COPY MPL} \rightarrow \text{MPL} \rightarrow \text{PROP})_{\text{buf}}:: \\ (::\text{PROP} \rightarrow \text{IMPLIC}::\text{IMPLIC} \rightarrow \text{PROP}::)_{n} \\ ::\text{PROP} \rightarrow \text{MPL}::\text{MPL} \rightarrow [..]\text{eff}$$

Under conditions (VDU,MOUSE,ICON) config is

$$*\text{VIS} \rightarrow \text{OBJ}::\text{OBJ} \rightarrow \text{PROP}::\text{PROP} \rightarrow \text{IMPLIC}::\text{IMPLIC} \rightarrow \text{PROP}:: \\ ::\text{PROP} \rightarrow \text{OBJ}::\text{OBJ} \rightarrow \text{LIM}:: \\ ::(\text{COPY LIM} \rightarrow \text{LIM} \rightarrow \text{MOT})_{\text{buf}}*$$

Under conditions (Speech I/O) required config is

$$*\text{AC} \rightarrow \text{MPL}::\text{MPL} \rightarrow \text{PROP}::(::\text{PROP} \rightarrow \text{IMPLIC}::\text{IMPLIC} \rightarrow \text{PROP}::)_{n} \\ ::\text{PROP} \rightarrow \text{MPL}::\text{MPL} \rightarrow \text{ART}:: \\ ::(\text{COPY ART} \rightarrow \text{ART} \rightarrow \text{MOT}_{\text{sp}})_{\text{buf}}*$$

Under conditions (Copy type, expert) config is

VIS → OBJ::OBJ → LIM::(COPY LIM → LIM → MOT)$_{buf}$
:etc.

Processing constraints

Under conditions (Config x, retrieve ⟨CODE I⟩ for ⟨CODE J⟩)
PROCESS ⟨I → J⟩ occupied; ACCESS TO IMAGE RECORD ⟨I⟩ occupied
Under conditions (Process ⟨I → J⟩, Input = incomplete description ⟨I⟩)
RECONFIGURE ⟨I → J⟩ FOR ACCESS TO IMAGE RECORD
Under conditions (Process ⟨I → J⟩, DATA ⟨I⟩ fast)
RECONFIGURE ⟨I → J⟩ for BUFFERED PROCESSING
:etc.

Knowledge representation

Under condition (Propositional Code)
Description is semantic, unordered, hierarchical
Under condition (MPL Code)
Description is phonological, ordered, nonlength sensitive
Under conditions (Process PROP → MPL, Input data: Imperative)
Description of unmarked output: Verb Constituent then Object constituent
:etc.

The tactic would then be to specify a core set of intermediate principles to link the characteristics of the data to those of the theory and the domain of application. These would be derived in the manner illustrated in the previous section. The objective would be to get the knowledge base to a point where it could build a model for the cognitive task analysis from some novel specification and infer key aspects of user behavior:

Cognitive task model

Under conditions ⟨Config x⟩
⟨Key attributes of procedural knowledge⟩
⟨Key attributes of record contents⟩
⟨Key attributes of dynamic control⟩
Result: ⟨Key attributes of user behavior⟩

The initial target would be to establish enough intermediate principles to handle a restricted set of cases such as the three experimental settings discussed in the previous section. In the case of the last illustration, some partial specification of the full analysis would contrast fixed and free order menu exchanges in terms of the underlying propositional representations for the control of dialog. For the set of circumstances described, the required inferences would have to include the intermediate consequences that order uncertainty would be resolved partly on the basis verb-object ordering and partly on the basis of recently created image records, that the fixed order is relatively economic in terms of the number of internal information processing transactions required and results in consistent memory records, that the free order is less economical and results in inconsistent memory records, and so on.

The prospective output would have to specify the likelihood of differences in the initial levels of performance between FIXED and FREE orderings; for the FIXED case, the probability that design choice of FUNCTION/OBJECT orderings would not affect performance; and some indication of the circumstances under which a design choice involving FREE order of selection might give rise to transfer difficulties. This kind of output would have properties complementary to those of models aimed at the quantitative prediction of learning and performance time. The underlying cognitive task analysis might also furnish clues as to when the use of particular quantitatively predictive models was appropriate.

As a part of our current research program, we are exploring ways and means of turning this general idea into a reality. A prototype expert system has recently been implemented for the three illustrations discussed here (Barnard, Wilson, and MacLean, 1986). Of course, a superintelligent design tool is a long way off. Our actual evidence concerning the properties of user behavior remains limited and our experience at trying to represent principles appropriately within a knowledge base even more so. In addition, there are other issues concerning the ways in which such a tool might actually be used, in terms of both meeting the real needs of designers and the somewhat more reflexive problem of how to turn the knowledge *in* it into the best form of interface *for* it.

In the shorter term, however, explorations with restricted knowledge bases should help impose more discipline on the actual process of uncovering the nature and form of appropriate principles. Attempting to represent relationships when complex contingencies are involved is a notoriously difficult problem. As research tools, even restricted knowledge bases can help us uncover inadequacies in the formulation of principles and point toward perhaps more profitable lines of empirical enquiry. The present approach also has properties that are potentially cumulative. *Interactive cognitive subsystems* is a framework that addresses issues concerned with the overall coordination and control of the constituent resources of cognition. As such it embodies no commitment to, for example, a particular detailed theory of speech perception (AC → MPL). Accordingly, claims at that level can be modified as our more basic knowledge progresses without necessarily requiring the abandonment of the wider framework.

References

Allport, D. A. (1980). Patterns and actions: Cognitive mechanisms are content-specific. In G. Claxton (Ed.), *Cognitive Psychology: New Directions*, London, Routledge & Kegan Paul, pp. 26–64.

Baddeley, A. (1966). Short term memory for word sequences as a function of acoustic, semantic and formal similarity. *Quarterly Journal of Experimental Psychology*, 18, 362–365.

Baddeley, A. (1982). Domains of recollection. *Psychological Review*, 89, 708–729.

Barnard, P. (1984). Applying the products of research on interactive dialogues. In M. J. Elphick (Ed.), *Man-machine Interaction: Proceedings of the Joint IBM/University of Newcastle Seminar*, University of Newcastle-upon-Tyne, pp. 11–20.

Barnard, P. (1985). Interacting cognitive subsystems: A psycholinguistic approach to short term memory. In A. Ellis (Ed.), *Progress in the Psychology of Language*, Vol. 2, London, Lawrence Erlbaum, Chap. 6, pp. 197–258.

Barnard, P., and Hammond, N. (1982). Usability and its multiple determination for the occasional user of interactive sytems. In M. B. Williams (Ed.), *Pathways to the Information Society*, Oxford, North-Holland, pp. 543–548.

Barnard, P., MacLean, A., and Hammond, N. (1984). User representations of ordered sequences of command operations. In B. Shackel (Ed.), *Proceedings of Interact '84: First IFIP Conference on Human-Computer Interaction*, Vol. 1, London, IEE, pp. 434–438.

Barnard, P., Wilson, M., and MacLean, A. (1986). Approximate modelling of cognitive activity with an expert system: A concept demonstrator for an interactive design aid. *IBM Hursley Human Factors Report*, HF 123, September 1986, 38 pp.

Barnard, P., Hammond, N., MacLean, A., and Morton, J. (1982). Learning and remembering interactive commands in a text-editing task. *Behaviour and Information Technology*, 1, 347–358.

Barnard, P., Hammond, N., Morton, J., Long, J., and Clark, I. (1981). Consistency and compatibility in human-computer dialogue. *International Journal of Man-Machine Studies*, 15, 87–134.

Broadbent, D. (1958). *Perception and Communication*, London, Pergamon.

Broadbent, D. (1971). *Decision and Stress*, London, Academic Press.

Card, S. K., Moran, T. P., and Newell, A. (1983). *The Psychology of Human-Computer Interaction*, Hillsdale, NJ, Lawrence Erlbaum Associates.

Crowder, R. G. (1982). The demise of short-term memory. *Acta Psychologica*, 50, 291–323.

Fitts, P. M. (1964). Perceptual motor skill learning. In A. W. Melton (Ed.), *Categories of Human Learning*, New York, Academic Press.

Grudin, J., and Barnard, P. (1984). The cognitive demands of learning and representing command names for text-editing. *Human Factors*, 26, 407–422.

Grudin, J., and Barnard, P. (1985). The role of prior task experience in command name abbreviations. *Proc. CHI '85: Human Factors in Computer Systems*, New York, ACM, pp. 121–125.

Hammond, N., and Barnard, P. (1984). Dialogue design: Characteristics of user knowledge. In A. Monk (Ed.), *Fundamentals of Human-Computer Interaction*, London, Academic Press, Chap. 9, pp. 127–164.

Hammond, N., Morton, J., Barnard, P., Long, J. B., and Clark, I. (1984a). Characterising user performance in command driven dialogue. IBM Hursley Human Factors Report HF093, June 1984.

Hammond, N., Hinton, G., Barnard, P., MacLean, A., Long, J., and Whitefield, A. (1984b). Evaluating the interface of a document processor: A comparison of expert judgment and user observation. In B. Shackel (Ed.), *Proceedings of Interact '84: First IFIP Conference on Human-Computer Interaction*, Vol. 2, London, IEE, pp. 135–139.

Herriot, P. (1969). The comprehension of active and passive sentences as a function of pragmatic expectations. *Journal of Verbal Learning and Verbal Behaviour*, 8, 166–169.

Johnson-Laird, P. N. (1978). The correspondence and coherence theories of cognitive truth. *The Behavioural and Brain Sciences*, 1, 108–109.

Kieras, D. E., and Polson, P. G. (1985). An approach to formal analysis of user complexity. *International Journal of Man-Machine Studies*, 22, 365–394.

Landauer, T. K. (1985a). Some bad and some good reasons for studying memory and cognition in the wild. Paper presented at the Third George A. Talland Memorial Conference on Memory and Aging, New Seaburg, Massachusetts, March 1985.

Landauer, T. K. (1985b). Psychological research as a mother of invention. In *Proc CHI '85 Human Factors in Computer Systems* (San Francisco, April 14–18), New York, ACM, p. 44.

Landauer, T. K. (1987). Relations between cognitive psychology and computer system design. In J. M. Carroll (Ed.), *Interfacing Thought: Cognitive Aspects of Human-Computer Interaction,* Cambridge, MA, MIT Press.

Minsky, M. (1975). A framework for representing knowledge. In P. Winston (Ed.), *Psychology of Computer Vision,* New York, McGraw-Hill, pp. 211–277.

Miyata, Y., and Norman, D. A. (1986). Psychological issues in support and multiple activities. In D. A. Norman and S. W. Draper (Eds.), *User Centered System Design,* Hillsdale, NJ, Erlbaum, pp. 271–290.

Moran, T. P. (1981). The command language grammar, a representation for the user interface of interactive computer systems. *International Journal of Man-Machine Studies,* 15, 3–50.

Newell, A., and Card, S. K. (1985). The prospects for psychological science in human-computer interaction. *Human Computer Interaction,* 1, 209–242.

Norman, D. A. (1983). Design principles for human-computer interaction. In *Proc. CHI '83 Human Factors in Computer Systems* (Boston, December 12–15), New York, ACM.

Norman, D. A. (1984). Stages and levels in human-machine interactions. *International Journal of Man-Machine Studies,* 21, 365–375.

Norman, D. (1986). Cognitive engineering. In D. A. Norman and S. W. Draper (Eds.), *User Centred System Design,* Hillsdale, NJ, Erlbaum, pp. 31–62.

Norman, D. A., and Bobrow, D. G. (1979). Descriptions: An intermediate stage in memory retrieval. *Cognitive Psychology,* 11, 107–123.

Payne, S., and Green, T. R. G. (1983). The user's perception of the interaction language: A two level model. In *Proc. CHI '83 Human Factors in Computing Systems* (Boston, December 12–15), New York, ACM, pp. 202–206.

Polson, P. G. (1987). A quantitative theory of human-computer interaction. In J. M. Carroll (Ed.), *Interfacing Thought: Cognitive Aspects of Human-Computer Interaction,* Cambridge, MA, MIT Press.

Polson, P. E., and Kieras, D. E. (1984). A formal description of users' knowledge of how to operate a device and user complexity. *Behaviour Research Methods, Instruments and Computers,* 16, 249–255.

Reisner, P. (1982). Further developments toward using formal grammar as a design tool. In *Human Factors in Computer Systems, Proc. Gaithersburg Conference,* New York, ACM, pp. 304–338.

Schank, R. C., and Abelson, R. P. (1977). *Scripts, Plans, Goals, and Understanding,* Hillsdale, NJ, Lawrence Erlbaum Associates.

7 Technology Transfer: On Learning a New Computer-Based System

Donald J. Foss and
Mitchell DeRidder

Learning builds on learning. When an individual first acquires information about a computer-based system, the way in which the resulting knowledge is represented will be affected by knowledge of other, noncomputational systems. Later, when information about a second computer-based system is acquired, knowledge and use of it will likely be affected by the way in which the first system is represented. The impact of older knowledge on the acquisition and use of newer knowledge is a traditional topic in psychology—transfer of training. As we move into an era when more and more people are acquiring knowledge of multiple systems, transfer of training again looms as an important topic. In this chapter we shall be concerned with how to choose among design alternatives for a computer-based system when faced with users who already have some knowledge of related systems. We hope to suggest some principled ways in which to make such choices. We also suggest that studies of transfer can help lead us to the very principles we seek. In addition, we propose that that amount of transfer may be affected by the relationship among the goal structures of the old and new tasks. Finally, we describe an experiment on transfer of training that speaks to some of the issues we raise. This chapter begins by discussing in broad terms the goals of research in the area of human-computer interaction (HCI). Such a discussion will show why we consider the transfer paradigm to be central to our thinking on this topic.

James Bryant Conant (1951) has argued that one of the signs of a mature science is a "low degree of empiricism"—the lack of necessity to do

This work was supported by a contract from the Army Research Institute (Contract No. MdA903-82-C-0123).

The present chapter has been significantly improved over its initial version thanks to helpful comments by Phyllis Reisner, John Whiteside, and Mary Beth Rosson, each of whom saved us from howlers. We are grateful. Since we did not always take their advice, they will no doubt still find matters with which to disagree in this version.

experiments in order to answer questions. Instead, in such fields, one refers to a theory: Initial conditions are measured or specified, the theory is applied to them, and an outcome is predicted. For example, one need not launch an extensive experimental project on optics to try out new telescope designs. We know enough about optics—how in detail light interacts with materials—to design telescopes that will work as predicted. The degree of empiricism in this field is relatively low.

If we turn to the domain of "classical" human factors we find that the degree of empiricism varies substantially across the subfields, but most would agree that none of these domains remotely approaches optics in its degree of theoretical release from empiricism. Instead we find empirically based handbooks, such as Woodson (1981), that can be used to guide system designers, and we find a very useful set of analysis principles—those of functional analysis and task analysis (e.g., Meister, 1971)—that can be used to aid in the design process. But these are engineering guides; they are not general theories to which we can refer when we are faced with new problems. Of course, at the point in the design stage when one assigns tasks to a person or a machine, then an appeal is made to such aids as Fitts lists (e.g., Singleton, 1974), but such appeals are themselves justified more by the handbook approach than by the theory-driven approach.

Most contributors to this volume are interested in "cognitive" human factors, a field concerned with such topics as the organization of command languages for computer systems, producing useful tools for software design, the way one selects information to present to operators of complex systems, and, in general, how best to organize the interface between systems and their users so that the interface aids in good decision making. We do not want to argue that the field of cognitive human factors is presently in a substantially better position vis-à-vis its theory base than is the field of classical human factors. However, we think it is worth speculating about what our goals should be in this field so that we might better be able to evaluate the empirical steps we take.

1 The Ideal and a Relaxed Version of It

It is not difficult to list a set of ideals toward which we should strive; many workers have done so. Our motivation for carrying out this exercise is to find ways around them—to examine how we might relax the ideal goals in light of present-day limits on our knowledge. Imagine, then, that we are consulting with a designer on the nature of an interface. Clearly we want the interface to yield a minimum of errors in the system, to be maximally fast in operation and maximally easy to learn, to stimulate appropriately creative solutions to novel problems that the user faces, to be maximally easy to maintain, and to be personally satisfying to the operator—all while meeting our cost target. While in one sense this set of goals constitutes a truism, it is unlikely that we could ever know when we had met such absolute standards. Let us change the picture somewhat by considering instead a set of relative standards. Suppose we already have a system with highly similar top-level goals to the one we are trying to build, e.g., another text editor or nuclear power plant control room. Arbitrarily, let us say that the new system should lead to only half the errors as the existing one, must be learned in half the time, must be declared twice as satisfying by its users on an appropriately scaled questionnaire, and must lead to a benchmark set of problems being solved in one-half the time that is required when using the existing system. These are aggressive standards. We could set even more aggressive ones by declaring that an optimal interface at a given state of technology is one that would not be improved upon by 50% in some reasonable length of time—say, five years. (Of course, this criterion could only be shown to be successful after the fact.)

In order to make such aggressive improvements on the basis of theory, one very nearly would need a completed cognitive psychology; theories of perception and motor behavior, of problem solving and learning, and of their interrelationships, among other topics, would have to be substantially better developed than at present. As we shall argue further below, we would also need to know how the system at issue would be represented by its users (or, perhaps more realistically, something about the range of representations that are likely to be formed).

Let us consider our goals in light of those of our colleagues in linguistics. Chomsky (1965) has discussed issues of adequacy for linguistic theories and for grammars; his views may be able to inform our own. The goal of a "descriptively adequate" linguistic theory is to make available for each natural language a set of rules and principles (a grammar) that describes the legal sentences in that language and that gives each sentence its appropriate structure. An "explanatorily adequate" linguistic theory is one that selects a descriptively adequate grammar when provided with the primary linguistic data (e.g., the utterances that a child is likely to hear) along with the associated nonlinguistic input. Explanatory adequacy is clearly the appropriate, and highly stringent, goal for which linguists should strive. In order to have a theory with explanatory adequacy, one must have a rule for picking out from among a set of candidate grammars the one that best fits the data—the one that assigns the correct structure

Figure 7.1
A complex object.

in the intuitively clear cases, classifies together linguistic items that behave homologously, etc. In other words, there is a selection algorithm (what Chomsky called an "evaluation metric") that picks from among the candidates the most highly valued alternative. The "choice of an evaluation metric constitutes a decision as to what are 'similar processes' and 'natural classes'—in short, what are significant generalizations" (Chomsky, 1965, p. 42). The evaluation metric does not pick out an optimal grammar in some absolute sense. Rather it picks out the one that captures the generalizations made by humans as they learn their natural language. It may be useful to draw an analogy between such concepts and some aspects of human-computer interaction, even though what is acquired when one learns about such cultural artifacts is of much less generality than in the case of language.

Before returning to issues in applied cognitive psychology, though, let us remind ourselves that behavior in any given situation is likely to be the result of a number of underlying systems interacting with one another. Again, linguists have addressed this issue, for example, by attempting to separate problems about the sounds of the language from those of syntax. Larson (forthcoming) has devised a simple way to make the point. Look at figure 7.1 and imagine writing an equation to describe it. It could be done, of course. But the description is, in some sense, "simpler" if we note that figure 7.1 is the result of intersecting three commonplace figures each of which can be described by familiar equations (see figure 7.2). With other linguists, Larson argues that describing language is likely to be simpler, and more likely to be psychologically accurate, if we assume that there are multiple underlying systems producing the observed behavior. Of course, it is commonplace among scientists to assume that observables are explained by the interaction of underlying unobserved processes. Efforts to apply congitive psychology are likely to be aided if we remember this commonplace tenet.

The analogy that we would like to draw between work in linguistics and in HCI is a simple one, based on the above-noted obvious fact about the

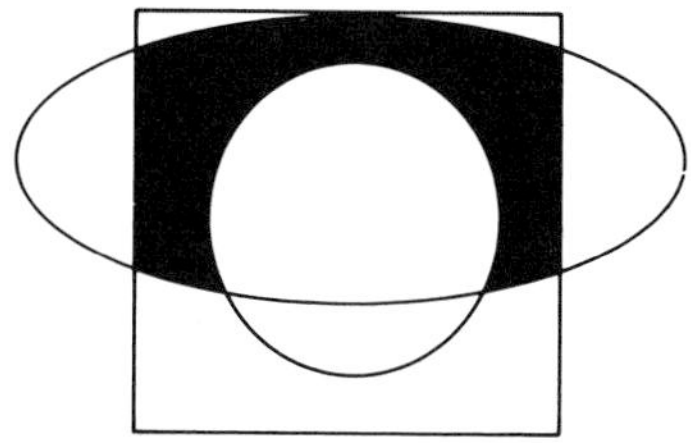

Figure 7.2
Complexity results from the interaction among simple components.

present situation in the field: It is most unlikely that theories in the near future will be able to make secure recommendations about the "optimal" interface. That is, we doubt it will be possible to make a theory-driven recommendation about details of the interface when given such "primary data" as the functions to be carried out by the user of that interface along with specifications of acceptable error rates, learning times, benchmark times for problem solving, etc. It seems to us that we should aim for a different goal, though still a highly ambitious one, namely, to have a theoretical basis for choosing between alternative proposals for an interface. As we shall show momentarily, we think this will occur by formulating a hypothesis about the internal representations of the alternatives and by having a rule for choosing between them. Thus, choosing between interface alternatives will be a matter of cognitive engineering, engineering based on cognitive psychology. The decision rule might need as input to it some information (primary data) over and above a specification of the functions to be carried out with the interface and the desired benchmark times. In particular, we believe that such a rule will need information about the present knowledge of the users (especially if they know a related system) and other factors, some of which we shall mention shortly. The desire to have a principled basis for choosing between alternative interface proposals amounts to a desire to make explicit the relevant dimensions along which users conceptualize the interfaces they have learned. In this way it is analogous to the principle of explanatory adequacy discussed above.

To concretize this proposal, let us examine briefly one type of decision that we might submit to our putative decision rule, a decision about cursor movement controls on a traditional CRT screen. We have no theory for specifying in advance the optimal device or technique for positioning the cursor. However, the work of Card, Moran, and Newell (1980) with the keystroke-level model gives us a way to choose among proposed alternative devices. That model evaluates the time required to accomplish various tasks, basing its estimates on partially theory-related and partially empirically derived estimates of movement times (e.g., time to strike keys of various sizes and distance from the home position and time to move the hand to an ancillary device such as a mouse—these being estimated by use of Fitts's law of movement times). Card, Moran, and Newell value most highly a device that minimizes total time to accomplish a representative set of tasks in the system under design. In practice, then, one first proposes a cursor moving device, then analyzes in detail the required movements to accomplish a set of representative tasks (this presupposes that one knows what such a set will be), and makes time estimates for each of the movements (this is where the empirical estimates are used). One iterates through this process for each proposed device, choosing in the end the one with the lowest time estimate.

The above example is clearly restricted to one aspect of the interface, that of cursor movement. Of course, we must keep in mind the fact that there is nothing sacred about the entire concept of cursor control. A better interface may be devised with something quite different carrying out the functions we now think of as inextricably tied up with the notion of a cursor. As noted, our present (but still ambitious) goal is a theory that can help us choose among proposed alternatives; it does not give us the alternatives, let alone the optimal one. We have to think those up ourselves.

Landauer (forthcoming) has recently noted that a goal like ours is not ambitious enough. He favors a theory that could tell us how to create an appropriate inteface. In the long run we favor such theory, too. For the present, however, we will simply note that it would be a significant advance if we could predict which of a set of alternatives would lead to better performance.

The cursor movement example given above shows how a decision about one aspect of the interface depends upon theory and data from a particular subdomain, that of motor skills in the example. We can ask whether it generally will be true that decisions about various aspects of the interface will depend upon evaluation metrics defined in a variety of ways depending upon the particular subdomain of cognitive psychology at issue. If so, such metrics will still probably try to minimize operations (physical or mental). An alternative is that a single evaluation scheme will serve in all cases. If one believes that a common, monolithic "architecture" such as a production system can describe the salient aspects of cognition (e.g., Anderson, 1983; McKendree and Anderson, 1987), then one is more likely to believe that a single evaluation metric will be adequate. If one subscribes to a more modular approach, in which the subsystems follow different rules, it is likely that the evaluation metrics will be defined over different entities in different subdomains.

To this point we have been assuming that it is possible to discuss the interface more-or-less independently of the overall computational system within which it fits. Many readers may balk at this treatment, believing that sound human factors thinking requires one to consider the interface only in concert with the rest of the system. There is substantial truth in that observation. Still, as noted by others (e.g., Green, 1985) concerned with interface problems, the interface is just that—a Janus-faced structure with connections in one direction to the rest of the computational system and connections in the other direction to the human system. To some extent designers may be able to write software to do the appropriate translations between the human and computational subsystems. In such cases, the "front end" of the interface can be designed primarily with users' needs in mind. Such modular design would permit psychologists to concentrate on work that advances our understanding of the (class of) effective interface(s); consequently, good designs are more likely to be portable, and our knowledge is more likely to cumulate as we proceed.

The program we have alluded to so far has the following components. First, someone (engineer, designer, human factors expert, psychologist) proposes two or more alternative ways of accomplishing a system goal. Then an analysis is made of the perceptual, cognitive, and motor subtasks that are required of the user as he or she interacts with each of the proposed interfaces. Next, one computes the number of operations for each of these subtasks and the time they will require (or the number of calls to long-term memory they entail, or the number of errors they are likely to spawn, or ?). The choice of what is best to count is an empirical matter that will get our attention for most of the rest of this paper. Finally the evaluation metric (or metrics) is brought to bear, choosing the way of accomplishing the subtasks that yields the best score on the metric.

So far we have been implicitly proposing a program for research at least as much as, if not more than, a program for practice. The research required is "basic" research in the normal understanding of the basic/applied distinction, yet it is stimulated by an applied concern. The division between science and engineering is not a sharp one at this point. The use in practice of the framework we are outlining largely depends upon having the appropriate evaluation metric(s). How can such metrics be obtained?

2 Transfer of Training and the Evaluation Metric

Our goal is to have evaluation metrics that permit us to choose between proposed interface designs. Such measures simply cannot be obtained a priori—finding them is an empirical matter. Thus, one of our important tasks is to bootstrap our way to the metrics. We suggest that one way to attack this problem is via the classic issue of transfer of training. A choice among alternative designs will be a function of the user population as well as of the details of the interface itself. That is, users will come to the new system with a history that will affect their learning speed, the likelihood of errors and the type of errors that will occur, and their generalization abilities when they are past the initial learning phase. The user's state of knowledge at initial learning may be as important in determining performance as are the properties of the interface designs that are vying for our favor. There are, then, at least three corners to the analysis: the initial knowledge brought to the task by the learner, the knowledge required to master the first of the proposed alternatives, and the knowledge required to master the second alternative. Our task is to evaluate the ease of transfer between the initial system (call it the learner's initial knowledge state) and each of the two competing systems (the two end states). Naturally we shall pick the alternative in which positive transfer is greater and negative transfer is less. In addition, we may then be able to use this result to help us make future decisions between alternatives because we can devise an evaluation metric based on it. Of course, such a metric will have to be validated in other applications, and a theoretical explanation must be devised for why it is appropriate. Thus, we are suggesting that effective technology transfer may depend upon a technical understanding of transfer itself.

Let us consider a somewhat abstract example. Suppose that we find a difference in transfer from an inital knowledge state, S_1, to two new states, S_2 and S_3, such that transfer to S_2 is better according to some measure, such as learning time. Suppose further that S_2 and S_3 differ in a "systematic" way from S_1. We then conclude that the dimension (of representation or processing) along which S_2 and S_3 differ is germane to further decisions between alternatives. It is unlikely that this putative dimension will be so well understood as to have the metric properties of high-level scales. So let us further assume that the distance between S_1 and S_2 along the dimension is simply less than the distance between S_1 and S_3 (e.g., the scale has ordinal properties). Thus, when trying in the future to decide between two interface possibilities, one should examine them with respect to our dimension and, according to the example, should choose the alternative that is "closer" to the initial state. Note that while this procedure may correctly identify relevant dimensions that affect transfer, it still will not permit specification of the ideal interface.

3 Caveats

Before turning to some proposals about "dimensions" of importance, we feel it is wise to insert appropriate caveats at this point. First, the above analysis implies that there are simple "dimensions" along which proposed alternative interfaces will differ. Naturally, this need not be the case. The dimensions themselves may more typically be constructs of some complexity. Also, this analysis so far completely ignores the importance of consistency among the subcomponents of an interface. Thus, choosing on the basis of transfer data the better of two options for, say, moving the cursor may lead one to select an option that is inconsistent with other choices one has made earlier about how to move within the application. This may be the incorrect decision. It would be an instance of a common problem in design—optimizing a subsystem while simultaneously making the system as a whole nonoptimal. Problems of interactions among choices are notoriously difficult. It is conceivable that the above analysis can be generalized to such problems by examining various alternatives for what constitutes "consistency"—or for what aspect of interface consistency is most important—using the transfer of training technique. Alternatives could be proposed in which consistency is variously defined and studies conducted to see which definition leads to better performance. Then that definition would be used to make choices in the future.

4 Relation to Mental Models

There has been a great deal of interest of late in the construct of mental models and their importance for teaching about technical materials (e.g., the chapters in Gentner and Stevens, 1983). A mental model is an individual's organized body of knowledge for a domain. Sometimes the existing knowledge for a domain is used to teach about a new domain because of the overlap in representation or procedures between the two. For example, Gentner and Gentner (1983) describe some work in which subjects were asked to reason about electric circuits after calling to mind their knowledge about water flowing through pipes. In effect, subjects were asked to transfer their knowledge from one domain to another, and the investigators looked at the degree of positive transfer (which was not very great in the case cited). The fact that work with mental models is work on transfer has been explicitly recognized by Mayer (1981) and his colleagues. Mayer taught simple systems to subjects (e.g., a model for programming in BASIC), and then looked at how well they could learn and solve problems using the BASIC language. He found that subjects taught the simple model did no better than those not taught the model when the problems were similar to the ones used in the training session—the "near" transfer cases. However, when the new problems were dissimilar—what Mayer called the "far" transfer cases—subjects presented with the model did better than those who were not. One problem with this research is that we are given no independent definition of what constitutes "near" and "far." Kieras and Bovair (1984) also recognized explicitly the relation of mental models to transfer; they observed substantial savings when their "device model" permitted "direct and simple inference of the exact steps required to operate the device" (p. 255).

5 Dimensions of Transfer between Text Editors

Millions now have experience with text editors, and it is becoming more and more common for individuals to know and work with more than one. Most people who do know more than one editor would probably report two things, neither of them surprising: some difficulty in moving back and forth between them, and an easier time learning the second or third editor than the first one. Suppose that we give ourselves the task of predicting which of two people will learn a new editor more readily, given that each already knows a distinct one. This is nearly equivalent to a problem that we discussed earlier, that of choosing between two candidate editors when the learner knows some initial editor. The equivalence comes from the fact that in each case we are discussing a transfer paradigm and that the decision in each case will be to choose in person (or the editor) that maximizes positive transfer and minimizes negative transfer. If we can compare the initial knowledge states of the two people with that of the required end state, and if we can determine whose initial state is more "similar" to the required state, then presumably we shall be able to choose the correct individual (or editor). In the end, the two transfer cases are nearly equivalent because in both paradigms we compare internal representations and the transfer between them.

6 Dimensions of Similarity

The study of transfer of training is an old and honored tradition in psychology. Substantial theorizing has been done about the determinants of transfer, from Osgood's (1949) "transfer surface"—which predicted that the amount of transfer could be accounted for in terms of the similarity between stimuli and responses in the original task and the transfer task (see figure 7.3)—to explanations of transfer in terms of a semantic network model of memory.

Recent theorizing about human-computer interaction has provided newer frameworks within which to conceptualize the transfer problem. One approach of interest provides various levels of analysis each of which can be construed as making a contribution to the amount of transfer observed in a particular case. The framework we have in mind is that suggested by Card, Moran, and Newell (1980), the GOMS model. Since most readers will be familiar with this model, we shall sketch it only briefly.

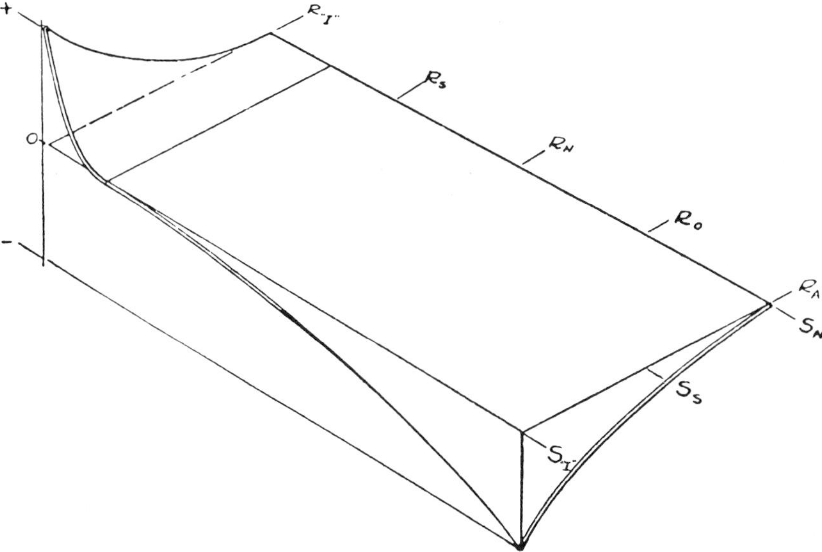

Figure 7.3
The transfer and retroaction surface. This surface was used by Osgood (1949) to summarize the then known conditions under which one could expect positive (+) and negative (−) transfer. The medial plane represents effects of zero magnitude. Response relations (from response identity through similarity to antagonistic responses) are on the x axis; stimulus relations (from identical stimuli to neutral stimuli) are on the y axis.

The acronym GOMS stands for Goals, Operators, Methods, and Selection Rules. The Goals are derived from the tasks and subtasks to be accomplished (e.g., editing a manuscript, deleting a phrase) and expressed in terms of the computer-based system (e.g., finding the appropriate location in the file such that an edit can be specified). Goals are structured hierarchically so they have subgoals, subsubgoals, etc. Goals are accomplished by stringing together the Operators that the system provides to the user (e.g., cursor positioning operators might include use of arrow keys, moving a mouse, and using a "find" command). A particular string of Operators that will accomplish a goal or subgoal is called a Method. Since it is typical for there to be more than one method possible for attaining a goal, a choice must be made among these methods. Such choices are made via a set of Selection rules. The latter are chosen according to such principles as "minimize the number of keystrokes" or "minimize the amount of information that must be stored in working memory." We shall return below to a further consideration of the GOMS framework.

6.1 Related Approaches to Transfer

Moran (1983) proposed a technique of task analysis that he called ETIT analysis; it "consists of three parts: (1) an *external task space,* (2) an *internal task space,* and (3) a *mapping* from the external task space to the internal task space (hence the term ETIT)" (p. 45). A task space is a set of terms and operators that can apply to them. The external space refers to the set of tasks that the user tries to accomplish in the world (for example, text editing tasks); somewhat more specifically, the external task space is composed of terms (e.g., words, sentences) and a set of functions over these terms (e.g., copy, move). The internal space refers to the set of tasks that the computer-based system can accomplish (e.g., inserting characters, cutting a string of characters out of the text), described in the conceptual model of the system. The third part refers to "a set of mapping rules which convert the external task description into an internal task description" (e.g., a mapping rule for changing the text might require internal operations of cutting a string of characters and inserting a new string). Moran's ETIT analysis left unspecified the detail of such operations as finding and marking the string to be cut; in general, cursor movements are at a level of detail below what he described (though this is not a limitation in principle of the proposed analysis). Moran pointed out that the mapping rules from external to internal task spaces were fewer for some editors than for others, and he suggested that editors requiring fewer such rules would be easier to learn.

In addition, Moran argued that ETIT analysis could be used to predict the amount of transfer that will occur between editors. The important aspect of the system for this purpose lies in the mapping rules; thus, he argued that positive transfer will occur when the rules correspond in the original and the to-be-learned systems. (In a footnote, Moran points out that the analysis does not take into account negative transfer caused by noncorresponding rules. Also, he suggested that transfer might also be from the internal task space of the known system to the internal space of the to-be-learned system.)

Our suggestion about transfer is similar to Moran's proposal, though we favor his footnoted idea that the amount of transfer is a function of the relation between the internal representation of the initial editor and the internal representation of the to-be-acquired one.

The ETIT analysis presented by Moran does not reflect the flow of work accomplished by a user (the detailed activities actually carried out). As he noted, however, task descriptions in the ETIT framework could be more complex, in which case work flow would be more directly represented. In related work, Polson and Kieras (1985) have brought the work flow more directly into the picture. They made predictions about transfer using a "common elements" transfer assumption, where the elements are productions in a production system. (In such a system the rules are a collection of condition-action pairs, reminiscent of stimulus-response pairings. Actions need not have an overt consequence in a production rule, but instead can change the internal state of the system. Such changes may then be the appropriate conditions for subsequent actions.) Polson and Kieras (see also Kieras and Polson, 1985) in essence write a production system for each of two editors (old and new) and then examine them for the amount of overlap in rules. "[T]ime to learn a given method [editor] is a function of the number of 'new' productions, that is the number of productions unique of the new method" (1985, p. 209). These investigators adopted the GOMS model of analysis (Card, Moran, and Newell, 1980, 1984), and their production rules represent the goals, subgoals, and selection rules involved in accomplishing an editing task.

As noted, Polson and Kieras's embodiment of GOMS uses the production system formalism and counts the number of new productions when making predictions about transfer. They do not make a distinction between productions associated with high-level goals and those associated with lower-level actions in service of those goals, recognizing that this "homogeneity of productions" is a simplifying assumption.

6.2 Planning and Execution of Plans

It is worth considering whether the effect of similarity between the old and the new systems is affected by where in the goal hierarchy the similarity resides. If the external tasks to be accomplished are identical, does the amount of transfer depend on the extent to which the internal structure of the two systems permits similarity in goal and subgoal structure? If so, the homogeneity-of-productions assumption would be incorrect. A change in the syntax between the old and new systems may result in a substantial number of differences in the production rules that describe the behavior of the users; but if all these changes are "late" in the goal structure, then they may not have the same impact on transfer as an equal number of changes in production rules that affect subgoals "higher" in the goal hierarchy.[1]

If you will recall our earlier discussion of explanatory adequacy, you will note that this discussion is concerned with the appropriate choice of an evaluation measure. To quote Chomsky again, the "choice of an evaluation metric constitutes a decision as to what are 'similar processes' and 'natural classes'—in short, what are significant generalizations" (Chomsky, 1965, p. 42). If transfer can be predicted merely by the overlap in number of productions, then the similarity between goal structures of old and new systems does not determine transfer, and such structures do not constitute a "natural class" in Chomsky's sense.

For example, consider two editors that are quite similar save that one of them uses arrow keys for cursor movement while the other uses a mouse. Suppose that to move a block of text each of these editors requires the user to (a) mark the beginning of the block by inserting a character (or clicking the mouse), (b) mark the end of the block, (c) issue a "cut" command (the syntax varies between the two), (d) move the cursor to the desired location for the block (again the syntax of the movement command varies), and (e) issue an insert command (which might be clicking a different button in the case of the mouse-based system). Although in detail the production rules would be quite different in these two cases, the overall structure of the subgoals is nearly identical. Now consider a third editor whose structure is quite different, perhaps a line-oriented editor. In it a block of text might be moved by issuing a command such as the following— **t; 550: 600,900**—which is interpreted as "Transfer the lines numbered 550 through 600 to the location after the line that is now numbered 900." Before one issues such a command one must first find and store the numbers of the initial and final lines of the block as well as the number of the destination line; in addition, one must check whether the initial and final segments of the block to be moved correspond with beginnings and ends of lines and take proper steps to correct the situation if they do not. Also, if inserting the block at a location where there is following text, such an editor may require additional steps to "make room" for the text that is to be inserted. Thus, while the top-level goal of moving text is the same for this third editor as for the previous two, it seems clear that the intermediate steps in achieving the goal are quite different for it.

If someone knows the first of the above-described editors, it may be that he or she will have an easier time learning the second one than the third one. What will transfer, on this view, is the subgoal structure that is used in accomplishing the editing tasks. The more similar such subgoal structures, the more positive transfer that will ensue. This view is tantamount to proposing that the evaluation metric should value more highly changes that preserve the subgoal structure; i.e., that it should not just count the number of production rules that differ between the two systems. (The two measures will generally be positively correlated; see note 1.)

We wish to emphasize our belief that counting productions is not an error; however, we think that looking at the subgoal structure more directly is a good hypothesis for a useful evaluation metric. (As noted, the productions written by Polson and Kieras actually derive from a prior analysis of subgoals.) Indeed, both shared subgoal structure and overlap in low-level productions may be important—perhaps in an interesting way. It seems quite possible that one can get positive and negative transfer at different "levels," where the levels correspond roughly to height in the subgoal hierarchy. Thus, in the situation where the editors share the goal hierarchy down to the low-level syntax (e.g., the cursor movement operations in our example), one would expect errors at the level of cursor movement but not at the level of choosing commands. On the other hand, command-level errors would be expected in cases where the command structure diverges earlier in the subgoal hierarchy (e.g., the transfer from the display editor to the line editor in our example). This analysis suggests that there is both *transfer of planning* and *transfer of execution* (see Foss, Smith-Kerker, and Rosson, in press, for further discussion). It has the advantage of predicting a mix of positive and negative transfer as one moves between editors, a prediction that seems intuitively correct.

Of course, the extent to which transfer will differ among editors (or between tasks within an editor) is likely to be influenced by the amount of transfer due to learning about interacting with computer-based systems, what we might call global transfer. But that, too, can be described by the overlap in the goal hierarchy of the older and newer systems. If both use the same operating system, then one would expect the transfer to be greater than if they do not simply because the total amount of overlap would be greater, and, therefore, the amount to be learned would be less.

We shall now present some data from a transfer study that bear on some of the issues we have raised. Although it was not initially designed with this question in mind, the experiment does permit a rough first look at whether amount of transfer is affected by where in the subgoal hierarchy the editors are similar. It also examines the extent to which global transfer is affected by similarity between the external task spaces in the first and second tasks. In the experiment to be described, some subjects were given an initial task that permitted them to become familiar with the operating system, cursor movement, and other general aspects of an interactive session, but they learned something other than a text editor.

7 Transfer Experiment: Acquiring a Second System

Three groups of subjects were used in this study, all of whom learned two computer-based systems. Each group studied and was tested on a (subset of a) common editor as its second task. That editor (the DEC K52 editor) is a screen-oriented one in which some of the commands are issued via the keypad. The first task varied across the three groups. One group learned a (subset of a) different screen-oriented editor (EMACS), and a second group learned part of a line-oriented editor (SOS), while a third group was given equivalent computer experience by learning part of the BASIC programming language. For this third group the typical editing functions that are associated with many BASIC environments were not made available (see below). The subset of EMACS was chosen to be highly similar to the subset used in K52, while the SOS command subset was chosen to be dissimilar to K52.

The 36 subjects in this study were college students with some modicum of typing ability (at least 16 words/minute), but with no background in computer programming or in computer-based text editing. They were assigned randomly to the three conditions with the restriction that an equal proportion of males and females were in each group (two-thirds of our subjects were male). Each subject participated in two sessions. During the initial session each subject received one-on-one instruction from an experimenter. The content was predetermined, consisting primarily of spoken descriptions of various commands and hands-on exercises designed to illustrate use of those commands. The exercises were carried out on a CRT linked via a dedicated line to a DEC-20 timesharing system.

7.1 Initial Training

Subjects assigned to the EMACS and SOS conditions were presented with similar exercises; in fact, these two groups made the same modifications in copies of a single essay stored in a text file. The exercises required the subject to display various parts of the essay on the CRT screen, to search for patterns of characters in the file, and to make a number of changes in the essay. To aid the experimenter in explaining the file-modification tasks to the subjects, illustrative visual aids were developed. Although the same set of changes was required of each group, the changes were accomplished by different means depending upon the command set available. The changes included (1) insertion, deletion, and replacement of lines and characters; (2) replacement of words, including multiple replacements; and (3) repositioning blocks of text. To minimize the similarity between SOS and K52, the SOS command set was limited to its line-oriented capabilities. Also eliminated from the SOS command set was any capability to refer to the default, or "current," line position that the editor tacitly maintains. In contrast, the command set for the EMACS editor emphasized its screen-oriented properties. Scoring forms were devised in order to permit systematic recording or errors made during the exercises.

The lesson on programming in BASIC provided a working understanding of the concepts and commands needed to write simple programs. The I/O capabilities covered were the interactive input of integer data and the output of integer variables, as well as integer and string constants. Logical expressions and arithmetic assignments were discussed, as were loops and branches. A series of programs illustrating these capabilities was devised as part of the instruction. The subject's role in writing these programs was specified fully in the lesson plan. That role ranged from simply typing as the experimenter dictated, to composing the programs with assistance provided only as necessary. The editing capabilities used were limited to insertion at the end of programs, the replacement of lines on a one-for-one basis, and the listing of the entire program.

7.2 Test

Training in the use of the K52 editor was provided by a series of 14 lessons, preceded by several minutes of introductory material, recorded on a tape recorder. The first lesson described the nature and function of blanks and end-of-line characters in text files, while the remaining lessons tersely described the process of invoking the editor and the functions of various keypad commands. Also briefly described were strategies for using the editor's main buffer to relocate blocks of text and to perform multiple replacements of patterns.

We devised a one-to-five-page paper-and-pencil "knowledge check" for each of the lessons. Most of the information tested in a given knowledge check came from the immediately preceding lesson, though some integration across lessons was also required. The test items asked for (a) descriptive information about particular commands or sets of commands, (b) predictions about how a file would look after the execution of a command (in many cases some of the information required for a correct response was intentionally omitted from the lesson in order to elicit inferences and guesses from the subjects), and (c) a statement about the next command or set of commands required in order to carry out some desired editing operation.

Each subject was tested individually in two sessions 48 hours apart. The first session, during which the initial training (on EMACS, SOS, or BASIC) took place, lasted up to $1\frac{1}{2}$ hours; the second session, the K52 test session, lasted up to $2\frac{1}{2}$ hours. During the second session the experimenter scanned each of the knowledge checks as it was completed to verify that the subject had attempted every item, as instructed. The time spent by the subject on each test was recorded. No feedback on item-specific information was provided during the second session, but subjects concerned about their performance were assured that they were doing well.

7.3 Results

Performance on the K52 test items was scored as either correct or incorrect, and these dichotomous data were then classified into one of 14 categories. One set of categories was derived from questions that asked subjects to predict how a given file would look after a particular command was executed. These questions were scored for performance at predicting the "primary" and the "side effects" of the commands (e.g., these were separate categories in the scoring procedure). The primary effect of a command was defined as that effect, or set of effects, for which a user would choose to invoke that particular command; e.g., the ⟨erase word⟩ command would be used to delete a word to the left of the cursor. Possibly accompanying such a primary effect would be (a) character side effects, in which characters to the right and below would shift position in response to a primary effect, and (b) cursor side effects, defined as the movement of the cursor (or lack thereof) that is incidental to a primary effect. Other categories were

Table 7.1
Average performance on transfer task

	Time (seconds)	Accuracy (%)
Basic	301	58
SOC	304	65
EMACS	345	67

defined by such issues as whether or not the correct command in K52 had an analog command in EMACS, whether or not the contexts in which such commands were used were also similar to the EMACS contexts, and others. In addition, the time that subjects took for each of the knowledge checks was measured.

We conducted an overall analysis across the 14 tests, where each subject's percent correct and time taken on each of the tests were used as the basic data. Table 7.1 shows the average results. An analysis of the percent correct data, by test, found a highly significant effect due to initial training, $F(2,26) = 26.68$, $p < .01$. A planned comparison demonstrated that the average percent correct for the EMACS group (67%) was greater than the pooled averages of the SOS and BASIC groups (65% and 58%, respectively), $F(1,26) = 28.43$, $p < .01$. Another comparison found a difference in performance between the latter two groups, $F(1,26) = 24.94$, $p < .01$. It seems apparent on inspection that the significance of the first planned comparison is due to the lower scores obtained by the BASIC subjects. This was borne out by a post hoc Newman-Keuls test on the means. It found a significantly lower level of performance in the BASIC group than in the other two groups ($p < .01$), and found no other comparisons to be significant. When this analysis was carried out with subjects rather than tests as the unit, the differences failed to reach significance.

The analysis on the time data, by tests, also found a significant effect due to training group, $F(2,26) = 17.04$, $p < .01$. A planned comparison found that the average time per test for the EMACS subjects (345 seconds) was significantly *longer* than the pooled average of the SOS and BASIC subjects (304 and 301 seconds, respectively), $F(1,26) = 33.92$, $p < .01$. The analysis with subjects as the unit did not reach significance.

We examined whether performance on the K52 tests was influenced by the similarity of the operations (and their context) to those of the EMACS editor. If so, then those who were trained on EMACS during the first

Table 7.2
Percent correct on primary effects test

	Familar command Familar context	Familar command Unfamilar context	No EMACS Analog
Basic	61	54	46
SOS	67	60	52
EMACS	72	59	64

Table 7.3
Transfer study, percent correct on tests of side effects

	CursA[a]	CursN	CharA	CharN	EOL	NEOL
BASIC	63	54	66	36	51	76
SOS	72	70	71	46	65	80
EMACS	70	68	78	46	58	81

a. See text for explanations of column headings.

session should do better than those who were trained on SOS or BASIC. Some data bearing on this issue are shown in tables 7.2 and 7.3. Table 7.2 shows percent correct on the primary effects measure when subjects were asked to predict the result after the application of a command, where that command either does or does not have an analog in EMACS. In addition, for cases where there was an analog, some uses occurred in similar screen contexts, while others occurred in contexts that were not so similar; table 7.2 also shows the results under these circumstances. Inspection of that table shows that there is no apparent advantage of the EMACS group over the SOS group. (Recall that whether or not a command or its context is "familiar" is defined solely in terms of the EMACS group.) There was a bit of evidence that subjects from the EMACS group were better at describing the primary effects of some action commands. On this measure the EMACS group got 67% correct, the SOS group 60%, and the BASIC group 56%; however, since this result was not statistically significant, it is likely just a chance observation.

Table 7.3 shows the data from some analyses of the side effects. In that table "Curs" refers to cursor side effects and "Char" to character side effects; "A" indicates that there was an EMACS analog to the K52 command, while "N" indicates that there was no EMACS analog. The EOL column refers to side effects that were associated with Ends of Lines, while NEOL refers to side effects not associated with Ends of Lines. (The latter two spawned substantially different percents of side effect errors. Again, however, the EMACS group gave no evidence of having an advantage over the SOS group, even though the latter had no real analog in the K52 editor.)

7.4 Discussion

The results of the study did not strongly support the hypothesis that the amount of positive transfer would be affected by the similarity among subgoals of the first and second editors. Had that been the case, we would have observed more positive transfer from the EMACS editor than from the SOS editor in the analysis of primary effects. In addition, we would have observed effects of similarity in the analyses of side effects. Instead, we saw significant amounts of transfer from both editors (by task) when compared to the BASIC group. (And since the amount of overlap in productions was almost certainly positively correlated with similarity among subgoals, we also did not observe here strong evidence that the amount of transfer was predicted by overlap in the number of productions.) We did find evidence of positive transfer from each of the editors to the third one.

There are, though, at least three significant reasons to believe that the above is not the last word on the subject. One is the results on the time measure. Those data are somewhat paradoxical; the EMACS group actually took longer to answer the questions on the K52 knowledge tests than did either of the other two groups. This was so even though the EMACS group did as well as or better than the other groups on the knowledge checks. One possible explanation for this finding rests on the similarity of subgoals between the EMACS and K52 editors. Because the EMACS subjects learned a goal structure more similar to K52 than did subjects in the SOS condition, those in the former group may have been tempted to respond with similar (e.g., EMACS-like) but incorrect commands and to err in predicting some of the side effects. They may also have recognized the fact that they were likely in error and made the effort to correct themselves, a time-consuming process. Admittedly this is an ad hoc explanation for the phenomena that we observed, but some such explanation seems required since the time differences were fairly large.

A second reason for caution about conclusions derives from the design of the study. As mentioned earlier, the experiment was not specifically designed to contrast a "subgoal" hypothesis with that of a "counting productions" hypothesis. We have already noted that one would have to design the editors carefully if one wished to pit these views against one another. Both new systems would be built according to the subgoal thesis, but many low-level rules would change in one system, while a few higher-level rules would change in the other. Such was not the case in the present study.

In addition, and this may be important, the experiment did not use an actual on-line test with the K52 editor. A paper-and-pencil test was used for convenience. Work using an on-line test might have a much better chance of detecting positive transfer due to similarity in goal structure across editors. Indeed, recent work by Singley and Anderson (1985)—using on-line keystroke data—has shown that the amount of transfer between two line-oriented editors is greater than that between a line editor and a screen editor.[2] In addition, they observed significant transfer from line to screen editors. These authors propose a two-component model of transfer. According to that model, transfer is determined by a general component (composed of the overlap of two production sets) and a specific component (the remainder of one of the sets of productions). This model clearly is in the tradition of those we have reviewed above, and merits further study.

8 Summary

In this chapter we have been concerned with how to choose a new computer-based system when faced with users who already have some knowledge of related systems. We argued that it is extraordinarily unlikely that we shall be able to design in advance an optimal system because of the lack of a theory to guide such a design. We suggested that it might be easier (though still very difficult) to make a reasoned choice among alternative designs on a theoretically grounded basis. In order to do this we need a metric for making such choices. We then proposed that studies of transfer of training might help to identify the relevant dimensions along which an evaluation metric could be defined. In order to aid in selecting the dimensions, we discussed the GOMS and ETIT approaches and suggested that transfer might fruitfully be conceptualized by keeping distinct the notions of goal structure and command syntax. Such a distinction may be useful, we said, because transfer may be differentially affected by these two. With the external task held constant, the goal structure may transfer more or less intact (yielding positive transfer), while changes in the syntax of commands and exactly what each accomplishes may lead to negative transfer. Thus, a transfer metric might do well to take into account both kinds of differences between the old and new systems. (One difficulty with this abstract analysis is that selection rules in the GOMS framework are themselves sensitive to the details of command syntax. For example, if the syntax of a command is such that many keystrokes are required to accomplish it, then the selection rules and the internal task space will be adjusted to avoid that command. In other words, the goal structure and the syntax appear to interact in a significant way.)

We presented the results from an experiment that made a first-pass attempt to examine whether similarity among goal structures across text editors has an effect on transfer. We did not find striking effects. We did find that there were effects of having learned an editor on learning an editor (not surprising), but that these effects were not large relative to subjects who had learned quite a different computer-based system, rudiments of the BASIC programming language. We concluded by giving some reasons why the test was not as sensitive as it might have been as far as examining the major hypothesis.

We shall end by noting that the present work is exploratory; we feel that the present path seems worth exploring a bit further into the thicket of problems since the question of design choices is not going to go away and the advantage of having a principled reason for making the choices is substantial. For the present, then, we must make the traditional call for further empirical efforts—remembering, of course, Conant's dictum that these efforts should be in the service of reducing the degree of empiricism in the future.

Notes

1. Changes in subgoals "higher up" would no doubt propagate changes in productions until that subgoal was met; e.g., it would change the productions lower down, as well. This means that for the total change in productions to be the same in the two cases, a small number of higher-level goals would have to be changed in order to equal a large number of changes in syntax at lower-level goals.

2. We thank Mary Beth Rosson for calling this study to our attention.

References

Anderson, J. R. (1983). *The Architecture of Cognition*, Cambridge, MA, Harvard University Press.

Card, S. K., Moran, T. P., and Newell, A. (1980). Computer text-editing: An information processing analysis of a routine cognitive skill. *Cognitive Psychology*, 12, 32–74.

Card, S. K., Moran, T. P., and Newell, A. (1984). *The Psychology of Human-Computer Interaction*, Hillsdale, NJ, Lawrence Erlbaum Associates.

Conant, J. B. (1951). *Science and Common Sense*, New Haven, Yale University Press.

Chomsky, N. (1965). *Aspects of the Theory of Syntax*, Cambridge, MA, MIT Press.

Foss, D. J., Smith-Kerker, P., and Rosson, M. B. (in press). On comprehending a computer manual: Analysis of variables affecting performance. *International Journal of Man-Machine Studies.*

Gentner, D., and Gentner, D. R. (1983). Flowing waters or teeming crowds: Mental models in electricity. In D. Gentner and A. L. Stevens (Eds.), *Mental Models*, Hillsdale, NJ, Lawrence Erlbaum Associates.

Gentner, D., and Stevens, A. L. (1983). *Mental Models*, Hillsdale, NJ, Lawrence Erlbaum Associates.

Green, M. (1985). The University of Alberta User Interface Management System. *Siggraph '85 Proceedings*, pp. 205–213.

Kieras, D. E., and Bovair, S. (1984). The role of a mental model in learning to operate a device. *Cognitive Science*, 8, 255–273.

Kieras, D. E., and Polson, P. G. (1985). An approach to the formal analysis of user complexity. *International Journal of Man-Machine Studies*, 22, 365–394.

Landauer, T. (forthcoming). Relations between cognitive psychology and computer system design.

Larson, R. (forthcoming). *Modern Grammatical Theory: A Primer to the Government—Binding Theory.*

McKendree, J., and Anderson, J. R. (1987). Effects of practice on knowledge and use of basic Lisp. In J. M. Carroll (Ed.), *Interfacing Thought: Cognitive Aspects of Human-Computer Interaction*, Cambridge, MA, MIT Press.

Mayer, R. (1981). The psychology of how novices learn computer programming. *Computing Surveys*, 13, 121–141.

Meister, D. (1971). *Human Factors: Theories and Practice*, New York, Wiley.

Moran, T. P. (1983). Getting into a system: External-internal task mapping analysis. *Proceedings of the CHI 1983 Conference on Human Factors in Computing*, Boston, 1983.

Osgood, C. E. (1949). The similarity paradox in human learning: A resolution. *Psychological Review*, 56, 132–143.

Polson, P. G., and Kieras, D. E. (1985). A quantitative model of the learning and performance of text editing knowledge. *Proceedings of the CHI 1985 Conference on Human Factors in Computing*, San Francisco, 1985.

Singleton, W. T. (1974). *Man-Machine Systems*, Harmondsworth, England: Penguin Books.

Singley, M. K., and Anderson, J. R. (1985). The transfer of text-editing skill. *International Journal of Man-Machine Studies, 22*, 403–423.

Woodson, W. E. (1981). *Human Factors Design Handbook*, New York, McGraw-Hill.

8 A Quantitative Theory of Human-Computer Interaction

Peter G. Polson

1 Introduction

This chapter describes a quantitative theory of human-computer, interaction, presents empirical tests of the theory's predictions, and discusses the application of the theory to the design process. The theory was originally developed by David Kieras of the University of Michigan and myself (Kieras and Polson, 1985; Polson and Kieras, 1984, 1985). The goals of our research program are to develop and verify a comprehensive, quantitative theory of human-computer interaction and to explore the applied implications of the theory. This chapter summarizes and extends theoretical and empirical results presented in these papers and describes a proposed design methodology for user interfaces, incorporating the theory as an evaluation tool.

1.1 Limitations on Current Practice

Lack of a predictive, quantitative theory of human-computer interaction imposes constraints on human factors practice. Current practice focuses on the evaluation of prototypes, often limiting human factors considerations to a very late stage in the design cycle. Most if not all of the design decisions that have fundamental impact on usability parameters, such as

This chapter presents the results of a collaborative research program conducted by David Kieras of the University of Michigan and myself. The press of other responsibilities prevented Dave from collaborating with me on the authorship of this chapter. He deserves equal credit for the work presented in this chapter. Many of the good ideas are his. He is of course absolved from blame for mistakes and any awkwardness in exposition. I am grateful to John Whiteside, Phyllis Reisner, and John Bennett for detailed, critical reviews of an early version of this chapter. This research was supported by International Business Machines Corporation. The opinions and conclusions contained within this research are those of the author and not necessarily those of IBM.

training time and productivity, have been made by the time the prototype has been developed.

In addition, most human factors considerations are not quantified using metrics that have predictive value. Design, by its very nature, is a multidimensional optimization process with schedule, cost, performance, and other considerations trading off against each other (Bennett, 1984). A manager will be unwilling to extend a development schedule by weeks or months if he or she cannot quantify improvements gained by investing additional resources in the development of the user interface.

1.2 Outline of Chapter

The chapter is divided into three major sections. The first section presents a summary of the assumptions of the theory (Kieras and Polson, 1985), a description of the simulation methodology, and a description of the models. Earlier papers (Polson and Kieras, 1984, 1985) gave abbreviated presentations of the models and the derivations of quantitative predictions. This chapter provides more extensive descriptions of the models and the derivations.

The second section reports empirical results that test quantitative predictions made by the theory. Two series of experiments are described. The first deals with the acquisition of utility procedures for a word processor (e.g., check spelling, duplicate a diskette). A second series of experiments evaluates the theory's ability to account for the acquisition and performance of text editing skills.

The third section explores the implications of the theory for the development of a design process that attempts to optimize usability parameters like training time and productivity. This hypothetical design process is based on two assumptions. First, the development process has to use evaluation tools that make quantitative predictions for usability parameters. The second assumption, following Gould and Lewis (1985), is that design of user interfaces is an iterative process. A design team develops a tentative design, evaluates it with respect to goals for usability parameters, modifies the trial design, and evaluates the new version. The cycle continues until an adequate user interface has been developed.

2 A Quantitative Theory of Human-Computer Interaction

Kieras and Polson (1985) present the foundations of a theory of human-computer interaction that makes quantitative predictions for usability parameters like training time and productivity. The scope of the theory includes routine tasks like editing text and executing utility functions (e.g., deleting or copying a file). No attempt is made to represent fundamental cognitive processes such as memory retrieval or reading comprehension. Kieras and Polson (1985) observe that simulation of fundamental processes would dramatically increase the complexity of the simulation, and they assume that including these processes would provide little additional information about human-computer interaction.

Quantitative predictions are derived from computer simulations of the execution of tasks. A simulation program has two components: (1) a model of a user performing the task and (2) a model of the system generating its input-output behavior. The model of the user is formalized as a production system. A main focus of this chapter is on production system models and their empirical validation as models of user performance. However, the model of the system's input-output behavior is a critical component of the simulation. The system model enables the developer or theorist to validate the user model by showing that it generates the correct sequence of operator actions and responds properly to simulated outputs from a system during execution of a task. The input-output behavior of a system is formalized as a generalized transition network; the formalism is described in Kieras and Polson (1983, 1985).

A production system model generates a hypothesized series of cognitive operations and the sequence of user actions required to complete the task. The psychological and formal assumptions of these models are collectively referred to as Cognitive Complexity Theory. The *basic assumption* of the theory is that the *content, structure,* and *amount of knowledge* required to perform a task on a system determine training time and productivity. The following sections describe the content and the structure of a user's knowledge, the representation of this knowledge as a production system, and the assumptions necessary for deriving learning and performance predictions from the representation.

2.1 The Content of a User's Knowledge

2.1.1 Classification

Kieras and Polson (1982, 1985) assume that a user's knowledge can be partitioned into *job situation, how-to-do-it,* and *how-it-works* knowledge. Job situation knowledge is a user's knowledge of the tasks that can be performed with a system. How-to-do-it knowledge is knowledge of how to carry out the actual procedures necessary to complete each task. How-to-do-it knowledge is further decomposed into the four categories defined by the Card, Moran, and Newell (1980, 1983) GOMS model: goals, operations, methods, and selection rules. How-it-works knowledge is a user's understanding of how a system functions (Kieras and Bovair, 1984a; Norman, 1982); this knowledge may be based on analogies and can be fragmentary and/or incomplete.

2.1.2 *Goals, Operations, Methods, and Selection Rules*

The GOMS model describes a user's how-to-do-it knowledge in terms of *goals, operations, methods,* and *selection rules.* Furthermore, the goals are organized into structures of interrelated goals, and control structures like do-until describe the flow of control.

Goals are the representation of a user's intention to perform a task, a subcomponent of a task, or a single cognitive or physical operation. Examples of goals are edit-manuscript, locate-next-edit, and delete-word.

Operations are a user's representation of elementary physical actions (e.g., pressing a single key or typing in a string of characters) and various cognitive operations (e.g., storing the name of a file in working memory).

Methods are sequences of operations that accomplish some intermediate-level subgoal. Examples are methods for entering a parameter into a menu, going from one menu to another, or deleting a word from a manuscript. Methods are complex in that they can contain submethods.

Selection rules specify the conditions under which it is appropriate to execute a given method. Selection rules are compiled pieces of problem-solving knowledge and assert the goal to execute a given method under the appropriate circumstances.

2.2 The Structure of a User's Knowledge: Goal Structures

The GOMS model and Cognitive Complexity Theory assume that a user decomposes a complex task into a sequence of subtasks. There is a goal or subgoal defined by the intention to complete the task and each subtask. The decomposition is represented as a goal structure that defines the interrelationships among the subtasks and specifies the sequencing of subtasks required to complete the task.

For example, Card, Moran and Newell (1980, 1983) have shown that the task of manuscript editing can be decomposed into a series of *unit tasks.* Each unit task involves *locating the next edit* in a marked-up manuscript, *making the indicated change,* and then *verifying the change.* Thus, the goal to *edit a manuscript* decomposes into a series of subgoals to *perform each unit task*. This subgoal is further decomposed into subgoals associated with locating, editing, and verifying.

Methods are a user's knowledge of how to achieve subgoals defined by various subtasks. The structure of a user's knowledge of a method is also described by a goal structure associated with each method. There are subgoals associated with each submethod, user action, and cognitive operation. The details of a particular interface determine these goal structures.

2.2.1 *High-, Middle-, and Low-Level Goals*

Task and method goal structures define the overall organization of a user's knowledge of how to accomplish a task on a system (Kieras, personal communication). The *high-level* goals, defined by the task decomposition, are extremely general (e.g., edit-manuscript). The *low-level* goal structures are specified by the methods that are defined by the details of a particular user interface. There is also a potentially critical *middle-level,* consisting of goals that represent the interface between a user's decomposition of a task and methods that accomplish each subtask.

2.2.2 *Task- and Interface-Specific Knowledge*

An important point to emphasize is that a user's how-to-do-it knowledge is a mixture of *task-specific* and *interface-specific* information. The goal structures defined by the task decomposition and various methods can be combined into an overall goal structure for the task. The top-level is task-specific, the middle-level is a mixture of both kinds of knowledge, and the low-level is determined by the user interface. Technological changes show up most strongly at this lowest level.

For example, faster terminals and systems make screen editors possible. A screen editor defines methods and thus low-level goal structures that are different from line-oriented editors. However, the top- and middle-level goal structures remain similar because the task decomposition does not change and the user is still deleting words, inserting characters, and so forth.

2.3 A Formal Representation of How-to-Do-It Knowledge

Kieras and Polson (1985) represent a user's how-to-do-it knowledge as a production system. Production systems, first proposed by Newell and Simon (1972) as a model of the human information processing system, have become an almost generic theoretical formalism in cognitive psychology. Numerous production system models of cognitive processes have been developed. Examples include problem-solving models (Newell and Simon, 1972; Karat, 1983), models of text comprehension (Kieras, 1982), and models of learning (Anderson, 1982). For the last several years, John Anderson (1976, 1983) has embarked on an ambitious theoretical program that has led to the development of a general theory of human cognition based in part on the production system formalism.

Kieras and Polson's decision to use the production system formalism thus enables them to build on a very solid foundation of theoretical and empirical analyses of cognitive skills. Furthermore, quantitative predictions for training time, transfer, and productivity are easily derived from production system models.

This section presents a basic description of production systems and the assumptions underlying the derivation of quantitative predictions. A detailed description of the notation and function of the production system developed by Kieras and Polson (1985) is presented in the following.

2.3.1 *An Overview of Production System Models*

The production system formalism represents the user's knowledge as a collection of rules and includes processing mechanisms that interpret the rules generating a sequence of cognitive operations and user actions. A production system is made up of three components: a collection of *rules*, a *working memory*, and an *interpreter*. A rule is a condition-action pair of the form

IF (condition) THEN (action).

The working memory contains representations of current goals, notes about current activities, and the external environment, for example, prompts and other information on a CRT display.

If the pattern of goals, notes, and external information in working memory *matches* the condition of a specific rule, the rule is said to *fire*, and the action of the rule is *executed*. The action is complex, containing several elementary actions. Possible elementary actions include adding and deleting goals and notes in working memory and user actions like entering a character string.

The interpreter operates in *cycles* alternating between *recognize* and *act* modes. The system begins in the recognize mode. During this mode, the conditions of all rules are matched against the content of working memory. All rules that match will fire, but the set of rules is written so that typically one rule fires during a cycle. The system then makes a transition to the act mode, in which the actions of the fired rule are executed. These actions modify the working memory by adding and deleting goals and notes and possibly modifying the environment as the result of a user action. The system then returns to the recognize mode, completing a cycle. The conditions of all rules are again matched with working memory. Observe that a different rule will fire, because the last rule that fired modified the contents of working memory.

A typical rule for a newly trained user generates a single cognitive operation or user action. The condition describes the pattern of information in working memory that specifies the execution of the cognitive operation or user action. The pattern of subgoals typically includes subgoals to perform the cognitive step or user action, to execute a method, and to execute a subtask, and a goal to perform the task. The rule is one of several that have to be executed in the proper sequence in order to complete the method. The sequential behavior of the model is controlled by manipulating the pattern of subgoals. The rule just fired deletes the subgoal to complete the current step and adds to working memory the subgoal to execute the next step. The changing pattern of subgoals, notes, and environmental information in working memory determines the sequence of rule firings, generating actions required to complete the method.

2.4 Quantitative Predictions

2.4.1 Learning, Transfer, and Productivity

Predictions for usability parameters can be derived from the production system architecture described in section 2.3.1. Training time is a function of the number of *new rules* that a user must acquire in order to perform a task. A series of related tasks may have identical methods or subsequences of user actions in common, and transfer across these common components can cause large reductions in training time. Kieras and Bovair (1986) have developed a common elements theory of transfer based or Thorndike (1931) within the context of the production system formalism. It is assumed that rules common to two tasks represent common elements and that these common rules can be incorporated in the representation of the second task in a training sequence at little or no cost in training time. Thus, training time for a task in the middle of a training sequence is a function of the number of new rules to be learned in order to master the current task.

Productivity is the sum of the execution times of the rules that must fire in order to complete a task. The execution time for a single rule is a constant firing time, the activation time, plus the sum of the times to carry out the operations in the action. For example, the action of a rule that makes a number of working memory manipulations can take longer to execute. In summary, the execution time for a task can be decomposed into two components: (1) the number of cycles to complete the task times the activation time and (2) the sum over these cycles of the operation execution times.

2.4.2 *Quantification*

Training time is assumed to be a function of the number of new rules, n, a user must learn in order to perform the task:

$$\text{Predicted training time} = t \cdot n + c,$$

where t is the training time per production and c is the time required to complete the parts of the task not involving the acquisition of new rules (e.g., the criterion run). Both t and c are estimated from the data and assumed to be constant over tasks and serial positions in a training sequence.

Let the total number of rules, m, be the sum of the number rules in a task model and the rules in the representations of methods called by the model. A common elements theory of transfer at the level of individual rules is assumed. Common rules are defined by identical sequences of user actions and cognitive operations for identical prompts. Once learned, common rules transfer perfectly to subsequent tasks and require 0 seconds to incorporate into the representation of a new task. A new rule requires t seconds to learn. The number of new productions, n, equals m minus the number of common rules. Training time is calculated using the expression in the previous paragraph.

Quantitative predictions for execution times are derived from predictors like number of cycles and total number of goals and notes added to working memory and other statistics calculated during the simulated execution of tasks. On the basis of results from Experiment 5, it is assumed that

$$\text{Execution time} = \text{NCYCLES} \cdot a + \text{WMIN} \cdot b + i,$$

where NCYCLES is the number of cycles required to complete the task, a is the activation time per cycle, WMIN is the total number of add-goal and add-note actions, b is the time for an add action, and i is an intercept parameter assumed to be 0. The parameters a, b, and i are estimated using multiple regression techniques.

2.4.3 *Parameter Estimation*

The learning and performance parameters in the five experiments described in the following sections were estimated using regression techniques from the cell means. This was done for three reasons. Cognitive Complexity Theory has no mechanisms that permit it to predict variances due to a hypothesized learning process or to characterize individual differences. Thus, the theory is capable only of predicting cell means. Second, this method simplifies the analysis. Third, the typical method for dealing with individual differences is to use the individual observations, regressing out between-subject differences by using subject means and then fitting the model. However, this method is not completely satisfactory because the means and large standard deviations are highly correlated, and there are large decreases in the cell standard deviations as a function of practice.

The danger is that the results presented in the following sections may hold only for the aggregate and not characterize the behavior of any individual subject. Kieras and Bovair (1986) derived production system models for the acquisition of operating procedures for a simple control panel device. They estimated parameters using individual observations regressing out between-subject differences using subject means, and they found results that compare well to those reported in the following.

2.5 A Summary of a Formal Description of the Simulation

The complete simulation system including the production system interpreter and the system description interpreter are programmed in INTERLISP running on a Xerox 1108. This section describes the production rule notation and the operation of the production system interpreter in more detail.

The production system interpreter and the system description interpreter interact through a data base. The data base is a set of clauses that describe the state of the system and the contents of working memory. Each clause is a list of constants separated by spaces; each constant is a string of characters.

2.5.1 *Description of Notation*

The notation used in the simulation programs is shown in figure 8.1. Constants, labels, and variable names may be of arbitrary length and contain hyphens and periods. Figure 8.1 shows a generic production; the parentheses shown are part of the notation. Each production has a label that is not functional and is used for tracing and debugging. The condition is made up of a list of patterns and is prefaced by an IF. Each of the patterns is a test for the presence of a corresponding clause in the database. All patterns must match in order for the condition to be true and the production to fire. An AND is implied.

```
(Label
        IF    ((GOAL pattern)
                (NOTE pattern)
                (SCREEN pattern)
                (USER MESSAGE IS pattern)
                (NOT(any pattern))   )
        THEN
              ((Add GOAL or NOTE pattern)
                (Delete GOAL or NOTE pattern)
                (MakeComment pattern)
                (LookMSS pattern)
                (DoKeystroke pattern)
                (TypeIn pattern)
                (StopNow))      )
```

Figure 8.1
A generic production giving examples of the possible elements of the condition and action of a single production. Pattern is a list, separated by spaces, of constants, wild cards, and variable names.

By convention, the first term in a pattern or clause is a constant and specifies the type of information in the list. Clauses or patterns with the first term of GOAL or NOTE represent the contents of working memory. Clauses or patterns with the initial constant SCREEN represent information displayed on a CRT.

The actions *add* and *delete* add and delete clauses from the database, respectively. *LookMSS* retrieves information from the simulation's representation of the marked-up manuscript. *DoKeystroke* transmits a single specified keystroke to the system simulation.

2.5.2 *Pattern Matching*

Pattern matching occurs during the recognize part of the cycle. This process determines what rule will fire and provides a parameter-passing mechanism. The patterns that make up the condition of a rule are matched to the data base. If all patterns match, the rule fires. The patterns are made up of constants, wild cards, and variables.

If a pattern is a list of constants, it is matched only if there is an identical list of constants in the database. For example, the pattern (GOAL DELETE WORD) matches only if the clause (GOAL DELETE WORD) is in the database.

The string ??? is a wild card, and it can appear one or more times in a pattern. This string will match any item in the corresponding position. For example, the pattern (GOAL ??? WORD) will match any one of the following clauses: (GOAL DELETE WORD), (GOAL COPY WORD), and (GOAL MOVE WORD).

Variables may appear in pattern definitions. The character * indicates that the following symbol is a variable. All variables are automatically unbound at the end of the act portion of the cycle. The variable binding process in the pattern-matching mechanism implements parameter passing in the production system. For example, consider a rule containing the pattern (NOTE DOCUMENT-NAME IS *NAME) with an action (TYPE-IN *NAME). If the rule fires when the clause (NOTE DOCUMENT-NAME IS SMITH-LETTER) is in the database, the constant SMITH-LETTER will be bound to *NAME, and the rule will enter the document name SMITH-LETTER into the simulated system.

Negation can be used in the definition of a pattern. Let p be a pattern not involving negation. The pattern NOT(p) matches if p does not match.

2.6 Relationships between GOMS and Production System Models

2.6.1 *Goals and Goal Structures*

Goals in the production system formalism correspond directly to goals in the GOMS model. The goal structures are not directly represented in a production system. They are defined by patterns of goals in working memory that are generated during successive recognize-act cycles. The production system model is constructed so that the task decomposition specified by the goal structure of the GOMS model is represented by the patterns of goals on successive cycles. On any cycle, working memory contains the goal to complete the task and subgoals to execute the current subtask, method, and step in the method. The pattern of goals in working memory on the next cycle is the same except for the subgoal associated with the next step in the method. At the completion of the current method, the subgoals associated with the last step in the method and the method itself is deleted and the subgoals to execute the next method in the current subtask and the first step of the new method are added to working memory.

2.6.2 *Methods*

In the GOMS model, methods are implemented as subroutines. There is no corresponding construct in the production system formalism because neither working memory nor the rule memory is partitioned into noninteracting subsets. However, subroutines can be emulated by asserting a goal that only occurs in every rule representing the body of the method. Parameters are passed using the pattern-matching mechanism and information contained in notes stored in working memory. One returns from a method by deleting goals and other control information associated with the method. Then a note is added to working memory asserting that the method has been completed. A rule in the "calling routine" has the note as one of its patterns, and this rule fires when this note is added to working memory.

2.6.3 Selection Rules and Operations

Selection rules are typically single rules with conditions that test for the pattern of goals and environmental information that call for the execution of a given method. The acting of this rule adds the goal to perform the method and notes containing parameters to working memory. Operations are implemented as various kinds of elementary actions that appear in the action component of individual productions.

3 Experimental Tests of the Theory

The first set of three experiments evaluated the learning and transfer assumptions of the theory using the acquisition of utility procedures for a stand-alone, floppy-disk-based word processor. The second set was two experiments studying the acquisition and execution of text editing methods. These experiments tested the performance assumptions as well as the learning and transfer assumptions of the theory. Experimental evidence, from a rich variety of tasks, permits generalization across tasks and training methods. The discussion for each set of experiments includes descriptions of the task and training methods, the theoretical analysis, and comparisons of observed and predicted measures.

3.1 Utility Procedures Experiments

In three experiments, subjects learned a series of utility procedures such as inserting a diskette, changing document format parameters, duplicating a document, printing a document, and copying a diskette for a popular stand-alone word processor. The first and second experiments provided preliminary evidence for the learning and transfer assumptions of the theory; a preliminary analysis of these results was presented in Polson and Kieras (1984). The third experiment evaluated predictions derived from the transfer assumptions concerning context and training order effects (Polson, Muncher, and Engelbeck, 1986).

3.1.1 *The Tasks*

Most tasks involved loading a specified diskette containing documents into the right slot of a diskette unit and then performing a utility task. The diskette unit was simulated as a series of diagrams and prompts presented on a CRT screen. The loading of the diskette was simulated by pressing function keys and typing the diskette name into the terminal. Each utility task involved traversing through a series of menus to a menu associated with the task. The task was completed by filling in parameters on the menu and then exiting the menu, which caused the specified operations actually to be carried out. The utility tasks were performed on a high fidelity simulation of the word processor that was presented to the subjects on a Visual Technology VT200 terminal controlled by a program written in FORTRAN 77 run on a Digital Equipment Corporation VAX 11/780.

3.1.2 *Common Training Procedures*

The same training procedures were used in all three experiments. Subjects were first given general instructions about how to use the menu system and how to enter menu choices and parameters. Each task was learned by a serial anticipation method. At each step in a task, the user was required to anticipate the next correct action. If the correct action was made, the system responded in a manner identical to the actual word processor. Instruction was presented only if subjects made two consecutive errors. On the first error, the system provided feedback identical to the actual word processor for incorrect user actions. The system would not execute correct user actions that would have taken subjects off the minimum path for the particular utility procedure being learned; users were told that the response was not correct for this particular procedure.

On a second error or inappropriate correct action, the menu was replaced by a feedback screen that described the user's goal, where he or she was in the procedure, and the correct next step. The feedback screen was displayed until the subject pressed the space bar, at which point the appropriate menu and prompts reappeared on the screen and the subject was required to anticipate correctly the current step. The training procedure continued until the user could successfully perform the utility task three successive times without making any errors or entering responses inappropriate for the trained task.

3.1.3 *Production System Models*

This section presents details of the theoretical analysis and resulting models for the tasks used in experiments 1–3. All tasks were simple sequential

Table 8.1
Common methods for all utility tasks in experiments 1, 2, and 3

Goal description	Number of rules in model of method
Load diskette containing documents into right slot of simulated diskette unit.	12
Go to next menu.	5
Select item from a menu.	5
Enter parameter into a menu.	5
Enter diskette name.	5
Enter document name.	5

procedures that employed a small collection of common methods. The production system (PS) model for a task is a series of from 9 to 25 rules with 1 rule representing each step. Steps involved making a menu transition, verifying a menu transition, or entering diskette and document names or parameter values. Most steps required several user actions and cognitive operations and were performed by a method. Each action and operation in a method was represented by a single rule. The common methods are listed in table 8.1 along with the number of rule in the PS model for each method. Each method performed the subtask described in the description of its associated goal. The PS model for the method of making a menu transition is shown in figure 8.2.

3.1.4 Goal Structure

The instructions specified a decomposition for each task, and it is assumed that the goal structure was defined by this decomposition. The top-level goal was to perform the task. There were from one to three second-level goals that were specified in the description of each task given to subjects. For the typical task, there were two second-level subgoals. The first was to load the diskette containing documents into the right slot of the diskette unit, and this goal was satisfied by using a specialized method. The second second-level subgoal was to complete the utility task. This subgoal had a series of subgoals, one for each step defined in the instructional materials. For most utility tasks, each of these steps was accomplished by one of the methods listed in table 8.1. However, some utility tasks had unique components. Lower-level goals explicitly controlled the execution of these unique steps in this case.

```
(GO-TO-NEXT-MENU.P1
   IF   ((GOAL PERFORM GO-TO-NEXT-MENU METHOD)
         (SCREEN PROMPT TYPE ID LETTER TO CHOOSE ITEM PRESS ENTER)
         (NOT (GOAL DO ???))   )
   THEN
        ((ADD GOAL DO TYPE-ID-LETTER))   )
(GO-TO-NEXT-MENU.P2
   IF   ((GOAL PERFORM GO-TO-NEXT-MENU METHOD)
         (GOAL DO TYPE-ID-LETTER)
         (SCREEN PROMPT TYPE ID LETTER TO CHOOSE ITEM PRESS ENTER)
         (NOTE ID LETTER IS *LETTER))
   THEN
        ((DoKeystroke *LETTER)
         (DELETE DO GOAL-TYPE-ID-LETTER)
         (ADD GOAL DO VERIFY-ENTRY))   )
(GO-TO-NEXT-MENU.P3
   IF   ((GOAL PERFORM GO-TO-NEXT-MENU METHOD)
         (GOAL DO VERIFY-ENTRY)
         (NOTE ID LETTER IS *LETTER)
         (SCREEN PROMPT TYPE ID LETTER TO CHOOSE ITEM PRESS ENTER
          *LETTER)   )
   THEN
        ((DELETE GOAL DO VERIFY-ENTRY)
         (ADD GOAL DO PRESS-ENTER))   )
(GO-TO-NEXT-MENU.P4
   IF   ((GOAL PERFORM GO-TO-NEXT-MENU METHOD)
         (GOAL DO PRESS-ENTER)
         (NOTE ID LETTER IS *LETTER)
         (SCREEN PROMPT TYPE ID LETTER TO CHOOSE ITEM PRESS ENTER
          *LETTER)   )
   THEN
        ((DoKeystroke ENTER)
         (ADD GOAL DO VERIFY-ITEM-HIGHLIGHTED)
         (DELETE GOAL DO PRESS-ENTER))   )
(GO-TO-NEXT-MENU.P5
   IF   ((GOAL PERFORM GO-TO-NEXT-MENU METHOD)
         (GOAL DO VERIFY-ITEM-HIGHLIGHTED)
         (NOTE ID LETTER IS *LETTER)
         (NOTE NEXT MENU IS *MENU
         (SCREEN HIGHLIGHTED *LETTER *MENU )   )
   THEN
        ((DELETE GOAL PERFORM GO-TO-NEXT-MENU METHOD)
         (DELETE GOAL DO VERIFY-ITEM-HIGHLIGHTED)
         (DELETE NOTE ID LETTER IS *LETTER)
         (DELETE NOTE NEXT MENU IS *MENU)
         (ADD NOTE GOING TO *MENU))      )
```

Figure 8.2
PS model for the common method for making a one-step menu transition.

3.1.5 *The PS Model for The First Task, Experiments 1 and 2*

The first task learned by subjects in experiments 1 and 2 required subjects to load a diskette, check spelling for a document, and return to the main menu. The model for a task is shown in figure 8.3. The three second-level subgoals defined in the instructions are (1) load a diskette containing documents into the right slot of the diskette unit, (2) perform the check spelling task, and (3) return to the main menu. Performing the check spelling task involved five steps: (1) going from the main menu to the spelling task menu, (2) verifying the transition, (3) selecting check spelling, (4) entering the document name and (5) entering the diskette name. The PS model contains 10 rules and uses five methods: load a diskette containing documents, make a one-step menu transition, select an item from a menu, enter document name, and enter diskette name.

3.1.6 *Predicted Training Time*

For the first task learned by a subject, the number of new rules is the number of rules in the task model plus the sum of the number of rules in each of the methods called by the task model. The load diskette and check spelling task has a total of 42 rules, 10 for the task model and 32 for five methods. Thus, predicted training time equals $42 \cdot t + c$, where t, training time per rule, and c, the intercept, are estimated from the data using regression techniques.

3.1.7 *Transfer*

The number of new rules for tasks in the second and later serial positions in a training order is the total number of rules minus the common rules learned in the process of mastering tasks in earlier serial positions. The number of new rules for each task in experiments 1 and 2 is shown in table 8.2. Table 8.3 gives the details of the calculations of the number of new rules.

Each column in table 8.3 shows the number of rules that must be learned for a task in a given serial position in a training order. The rows are the components of the task model and the common methods. The common components of a task model are the rules that represent subsequences of identical user actions and cognitive operations shared by two or more tasks. Each entry is the number of rules that must be learned in order to master the common method or subsequence of rules unique to the task. * means that a subsequence or method is not part of the task. An entry of zero means that the common component was learned earlier in the training sequence. The sum of the numbers in each column is the number of new rules to be learned in order to master the task.

```
(TASK1.1
      IF    ((GOAL PERFORM TASK1)
             (NOT (GOAL LOAD-INITIAL-WORK-DISKETTE))
             (NOT (GOAL CHECK-SPELLING))
             (NOT (GOAL GO-TO-TASK-SELECTION-MENU))
             (SCREEN TASK SELECTION MENU))
      THEN
            ((ADD GOAL LOAD-INITIAL-WORK-DISKETTE)
             (ADD GOAL PERFORM LOAD-DISKETTE-INTO-RIGHT-SLOT METHOD)
             (ADD NOTE DISKETTE TO BE LOADED IS WORK DISKETTE))   )
(TASK1.2
      IF    ((GOAL PERFORM TASK1)
             (GOAL LOAD-INITIAL-WORK-DISKETTE)
             (NOTE DISKETTE LOADED))
      THEN
            ((DELETE GOAL LOAD-INITIAL-WORK-DISKETTE)
             (DELETE NOTE DISKETTE LOADED)
             (ADD GOAL CHECK-SPELLING)
             (ADD GOAL GOTO-SPELLING-TASKS-MENU)
             (ADD GOAL PERFORM GO-TO-NEXT-MENU METHOD)
             (ADD NOTE ID LETTER IS D)
             (ADD NOTE NEXT MENU IS SPELLING-TASK-MENU))   )
(TASK1.3
      IF    ((GOAL PERFORM TASK1)
             (GOAL CHECK-SPELLING)
             (GOAL GOTO-SPELLING-TASKS-MENU)
             (NOTE GOING TO SPELLING-TASK-MENU))
      THEN
            ((DELETE GOAL GOTO-SPELLING-TASKS-MENU)
             (DELETE NOTE GOING TO SPELLING-TASK-MENU)
             (ADD GOAL VERIFY TRANSITION TO SPELLING-TASK-MENU))   )
(TASK1.4
      IF    ((GOAL PERFORM TASK1)
             (GOAL CHECK-SPELLING)
             (GOAL VERIFY TRANSITION TO SPELLING-TASK-MENU))
             (SCREEN SPELLING TASKS MENU))
      THEN
            ((DELETE GOAL VERIFY TRANSITION TO SPELLING-TASK-MENU)
             (ADD GOAL SELECT CHECK-SPELLING)
             (ADD GOAL PERFORM SELECT-ITEM-FROM-MENU METHOD)
             (ADD NOTE ITEM IS CHECK-DOCUMENT)
             (ADD NOTE ID LETTER IS A))   )
(TASK1.5
      IF    ((GOAL PERFORM TASK1)
             (GOAL CHECK-SPELLING)
             (GOAL SELECT CHECK-SPELLING)
             (NOTE ITEM SELECTED)
      THEN
            ((DELETE SELECT CHECK-SPELLING)
             (DELETE NOTE ITEM SELECTED)
             (ADD GOAL ENTER DOCUMENT-NAME)
             (ADD GOAL PERFORM ENTER-DOCUMENT-NAME METHOD)
             (ADD NOTE DOCUMENT IS THE DOCUMENT))   )
```

Figure 8.3
PS model for the first task in experiments 1 and 2: Load a diskette containing documents into the right slot, check spelling, and return to the main menu.

```
(TASK1.6
      IF    ((GOAL PERFORM TASK1)
             (GOAL CHECK-SPELLING)
             (GOAL ENTER DOCUMENT-NAME)
             (NOTE DOCUMENT NAME IS ENTERED))
      THEN
            ((DELETE GOAL ENTER DOCUMENT-NAME)
             (DELETE NOTE DOCUMENT NAME IS ENTERED)
             (ADD GOAL ENTER DISKETTE-NAME)
             (ADD GOAL PERFORM ENTER-DISKETTE-NAME METHOD)
             (ADD NOTE DISKETTE IS THE DISKETTE))    )
(TASK1.7
      IF    ((GOAL PERFORM TASK1)
             (GOAL CHECK-SPELLING)
             (GOAL ENTER DISKETTE-NAME)
             (NOTE DISKETTE NAME IS ENTERED))
      THEN
            ((DELETE GOAL ENTER DISKETTE NAME)
             (DELETE NOTE DISKETTE NAME IS ENTERED)
             (ADD GOAL VERIFY DOCUMENT CHECKED))    )
(TASK1.8
      IF    ((GOAL PERFORM TASK1)
             (GOAL CHECK-SPELLING)
             (GOAL VERIFY DOCUMENT CHECKED)
             (SCREEN *NAME CHECKED FOR SPELLING))
      THEN
            ((DELETE GOAL VERIFY DOCUMENT CHECKED)
             (DELETE GOAL CHECK-SPELLING)
             (ADD GOAL GO-TO-TASK-SELECTION MENU)
             (ADD GOAL PERFORM GO-TO-NEXT-MENU METHOD)
             (ADD NOTE ID LETTER IS E)
             (ADD NOTE NEXT MENU IS TASK-SELECTION-MENU)    )
(TASK1.9
      IF    ((GOAL PERFORM TASK1)
             (GOAL GO-TO-TASK-SELECTION-MENU)
             (NOTE GOING TO TASK-SELECTION-MENU))
      THEN
            ((DELETE GOAL GOTO-TASK-SELECTION-MENU)
             (DELETE NOTE GOING TO TASK-SELECTION-MENU)
             (ADD GOAL VERIFY TRANSITION TO TASK-SELECTION-MENU))    )
(TASK1.10
      IF    ((GOAL PERFORM TASK1)
             (GOAL VERIFY TRANSITION TO TASK-SELECTION-MENU)
             (SCREEN TASK SELECTION MENU))
      THEN
            ((DELETE GOAL VERIFY TRANSITION TO TASK-SELECTION-MENU)
             (DELETE GOAL PERFORM TASK1)
             (StopNow))    )
```

Figure 8.3 (continued)

Table 8.2
Task descriptions for experiments 1 and 2[a]

Serial position in training order (experiment 2)	Task description	Number of rules		
		Task model	Total	New
1(1)	Load diskette. Check document for spelling errors.	10	42	42
2(*)	Load diskette. Change default first typing line.	12	39	17
3(2)	Load diskette. Check document header.	15	52	15(20)
4(3)	Load diskette. Change the name and comment of a document.	12	49	12
5(*)	Load diskette. Change the default spacing from double to single.	12	39	9
6(4)	Load diskette. Duplicate the diskette.	25	52	23
7(5)	Load diskette. Print a document.	10	42	10

a. *means not included in experiment 2.

Table 8.3
Components of tasks in experiments 1 and 2 and calculation of the number of new rules for each position in the training sequence[a]

Task, task subsequence, or common method	Task number-serial position (experiment 2)						
	1(1)	2	3(2)	4(3)	5	6(4)	7(5)
Task							
Unique to task	10	9	13	12	9	23	10
Common subsequence A	*	3	*	*	0	*	*
Common subsequence B	*	*	2	*	*	0	*
Methods							
Load diskette	12	0	0	0	0	0	0
Go to next menu	5	0	0	0	0	0	0
Select item from menu	5	0	0	0	0	0	0
Enter parameter	*	5	0	0	0	*	*
Enter diskette name	5	*	0	0	*	0	0
Enter document name	5	*	0	0	*	*	0
Number of new rules	42	17	15(20)	12	9	23	10

a. * means not part of task; 0 means component learned earlier in training sequence.

3.1.8 *Experiments 1 and 2: Method*

Both experiments involved the acquisition of a fixed series of utility tasks listed in table 8.2. The data reported here are from two experiments analyzing the effects of providing subjects with mental models of a word processor (Polson et al., 1983). The experimental manipulation had no effect on training or later retention performance, and the data from experimental and control groups were combined in order to evaluate the learning and transfer predictions of Cognitive Complexity Theory.

Subjects participated in two 2-hour sessions. Only the first will be described here. The first day involved two phases, an instruction phase and a training phase. During the instruction phase, subjects were given a general description of the overall structure of the experiment, an instructional manipulation not discussed here, and then detailed instructions on how to use the menu system. The training phase began immediately afterward. Subjects learned either seven (experiment 1) or five (experiment 2) utility tasks listed in table 8.2.

Subjects were recruited from the local community via newspaper ads. They were paid $12 for their participation in the experiment. There were 24 and 19 subjects in control and experimental groups, respectively, in experiment 1, and 22 subjects in each group in experiment 2. Subjects had no computer or word processing experience.

3.1.9 *Experiment 1 and 2: Results*

The observed and predicted means for each task averaged across the two experimental conditions are shown in the top panel of figure 8.4 for experiment 1 and in the bottom panel for experiment 2. Earlier analyses found no differences between conditions in each experiment and no differences in performance on tasks common to both experiments. Therefore, predictions for training time were calculated estimating single values of t and c common to both experiments and experimental conditions and tasks.

The parameters were estimated using regression techniques from the means of each experimental condition and task in the two experiments: experiment 1, 14 means; experiment 2, 10 means. The values of the number of new rules for each task are shown in table 8.2. The estimated value of t, training time per rule, is 20.2 seconds per rule, and the estimated value of the intercept, c, is 247.0 seconds. The number of new rules accounts for 90% of the variance in the 24 means.

3.1.10 *Experiment 3*

This next study provides a much more rigorous test of the theory, focusing on the assumptions underlying the transfer process. The transfer processes

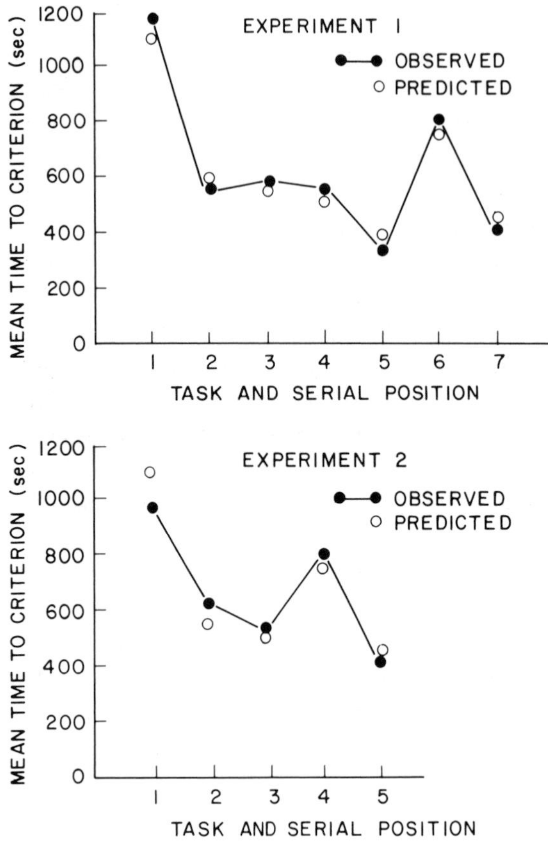

Figure 8.4
The observed and predicted mean times to criterion averaged over experimental and control groups for experiment 1 (top) and experiment 2 (bottom) plotted as a function of serial position in the training order.

Table 8.4
Task descriptions for experiment 3

Task ID number	Description	Number of rules in: Task model	Total
1	Change default first typing line from 5 to 7.	11	26
2	Change default from double to single.	11	26
3	Load diskette. Change first typing line for document from 5 to 7.	16	53
4	Load diskette. Change spacing for document from double to single.	16	53
5	Load diskette. Duplicate diskette using quick method.	25	52
6	Load diskette. Duplicate diskette using careful method.	25	52
7	Print a document.	9	24
8	Check a document for spelling errors.	9	29
9	Change the name of a document.	11	36

in Cognitive Complexity Theory make strong implicit assumptions about improvements, in performance across tasks and other transfer mechanisms (Polson, Muncher, and Engelbeck, 1986). First, improvements in performance are mediated *solely* by common rules; there are no *generalized* learning-to-learn effects. Second, common rules are always recognized and utilized in novel contexts. However, there is evidence from the associative learning and transfer literature that this assumption is not necessarily correct. Polson (1972) showed that salient common elements were not necessarily utilized in a paired associate transfer task. In addition, encoding specificity effects (Tulving and Thompson, 1973) are both powerful and pervasive.

3.1.11 *Tasks*

These assumptions were evaluated by manipulating the order in which subjects learned pairs of utility tasks across four experimental conditions. The utility tasks are listed in table 8.4. There were three pairs of tasks. Members of a pair were always presented in a fixed order, shared an identical initial sequence of steps, and could have a large number of common final steps. The first four tasks listed in table 8.4 all manipulated format parameters. Tasks 1 and 2 changed default format parameters and had a common initial subsequence of menu selections. Tasks 3 and 4 manipulated format parameters for a specific document and shared a different initial subsequence that included loading a diskette into the diskette unit.

Tasks 1 and 3 changed the first typing line from 5 to 7 for the default and a specific document, respectively. Tasks 2 and 4 changed the line spacing from single to double for the default and a specific document, respectively. For each of the different format parameter manipulations, there was an identical final sequence of menu selections and parameter entries. Assumptions about the lack of context effects were evaluated by showing that knowledge about common methods transferred independently of the context in which they were learned and that productions describing various combinations of common initial and final sequences transferred independently of the learning context.

Tasks 5 and 6 were two versions of duplicate diskette procedures. The tasks were both difficult and highly similar. Thus the first member of the pair should have been very difficult to learn. The extra difficulty was due to the fact that in the middle of a sequence of menu selections and parameter entries, the user had to remove a diskette from the left slot and then load another diskette into the slot. This is a novel sequence of actions and thus is represented by a unique series of rules.

Nonspecific transfer effects were evaluated by having a control group learn a series of three unrelated tasks—tasks 7, 8, and 9 in table 8.4—followed by the four format parameter manipulation tasks. If nonspecific transfer is a significant component of the overall transfer process, the four format tasks should be significantly less difficult than predicted by the common elements transfer model. The three initial unrelated tasks do share some common methods with the final four tasks, and thus some transfer is predicted by the theory.

3.1.12 Transfer Predictions

Tables 8.5 and 8.6 present the details of the calculations of the number of new rules for each task learned by experimental group 1 and the control group, respectively. The rows list the components of each task model including the common subsequences discussed in the previous paragraphs and the number of rules associated with each component. Table 8.7 shows the training orders for the four experimental groups and the control group and the number of new rules for each serial position in each of the five groups. The training orders for the four experimental groups were generated by the factorial combination of the position of the two duplicate document tasks (beginning or end of the training sequence) and the ordering of the two pairs of format parameter manipulation tasks (default-document or document-default).

Table 8.5
Components of tasks in experiment 3, group 1, and calculation of the number of new rules for each position in the training sequence[a]

Task, task subsequence, or common method	Task number (serial position)					
	1(1)	2(2)	3(3)	4(4)	5(5)	6(6)
Task						
Unique to task	1	1	1	1	5	5
Initial common subsequence A	3	0	*	*	*	*
Initial common subsequence B	*	*	8	0	*	*
Final common subsequence A	7	*	0	*	*	*
Final common subsequence B	*	7	*	0	*	*
Subsequences common to duplicate	*	*	*	*	20	0
Methods						
Load diskette	*	*	12	0	0	0
Go to next menu	5	0	0	0	0	0
Select item from menu	5	0	0	0	0	0
Enter parameter	5	0	0	0	*	*
Enter diskette name	*	*	5	0	0	0
Enter document name	*	*	5	0	*	*
Number of new rules	26	8	31	1	25	5

a. * means not part of task; 0 means component learned earlier in training sequence.

3.1.13 *Method*

The same basic procedures used in experiments 1 and 2 were employed in this experiment. Subjects participated in one 2-hour session. They first received general instructions about how to use the terminal, make menu selections, and respond to prompts. They then learned six or seven tasks. Subjects who served in partial fulfillment of a course requirement were recruited from introductory psychology courses. Fifteen subjects were randomly assigned to each condition.

3.1.14 *Results*

Figure 8.5 shows the observed and predicted mean times to criterion for each task in the five conditions listed in table 8.7. Two sets of analyses were done on the data. The first was an analysis of variance, verifying that the effects of training order shown in figure 8.5 were significant. An analysis of variance for tasks by groups on the times to criterion for tasks for the four experimental groups showed significant differences between

Table 8.6
Components of tasks in experiment 3, control group, and calculation of the number of new rules for each position in the training sequence[a]

Task, task subsequence, or common method	Task number (serial position)						
	7(1)	8(2)	9(3)	1(4)	2(5)	3(6)	4(7)
Task							
Unique to task	9	9	11	1	1	1	1
Initial common subsequence A	*	*	*	3	0	*	*
Initial common subsequence B	*	*	*	*	*	8	0
Final common subsequence A	*	*	*	7	*	0	*
Final common subsequence B	*	*	*	*	7	*	0
Methods							
Load diskette	*	*	*	*	*	12	0
Go to next menu	5	0	0	0	0	0	0
Select item from menu	*	5	0	0	0	0	0
Enter parameter	*	*	5	0	0	0	0
Enter diskette name	5	0	0	*	*	0	0
Enter document name	5	0	0	*	*	0	0
Number of new rules	24	13	16	11	8	21	1

a. * means not part of task; 0 means component learned earlier in training sequence.

Table 8.7
Training orders for experiment 3

Group	Task number (number of new productions): serial position in training order						
	1	2	3	4	5	6	7
1	1(26)	2(8)	3(31)	4(1)	5(25)	6(5)	
2	3(53)	4(8)	1(4)	2(1)	5(25)	6(5)	
3	5(52)	6(5)	1(16)	2(8)	3(9)	4(1)	
4	5(52)	6(5)	3(26)	4(9)	1(4)	2(1)	
Control	7(24)	8(13)	9(16)	1(11)	2(8)	3(21)	4(1)

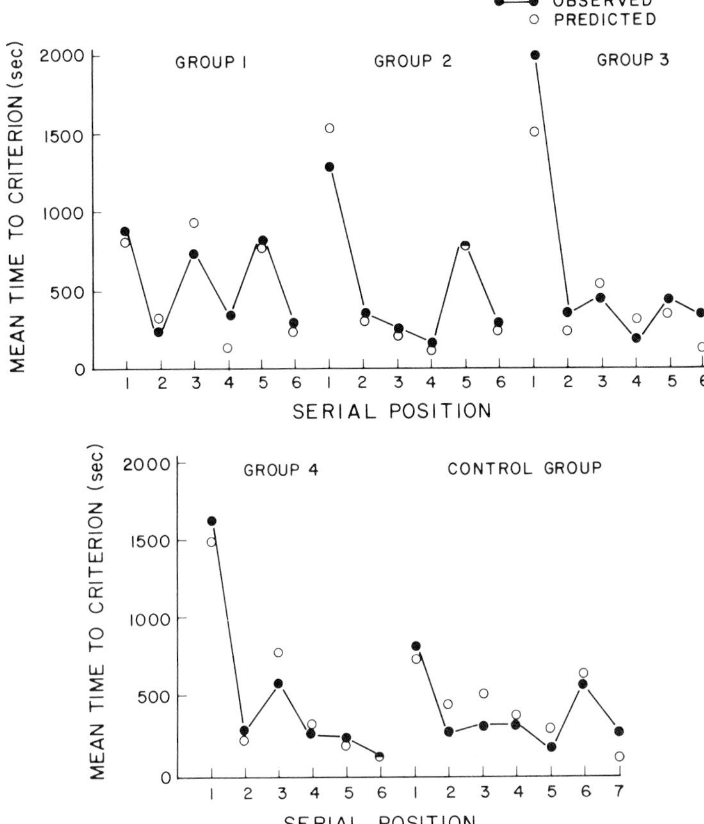

Figure 8.5
The observed and predicted mean times to criterion for the four experimental groups and the control group plotted as a function of serial position in the training order from experiment 3.

tasks, and a significant interaction for tasks by groups. The groups, however, were not found to be significantly different. The second analysis involved fitting the production system model to the mean training times using regression techniques.

The transfer assumptions were evaluated on the basis of the model's fit to the mean times criterion for each task in each condition. The predictions shown in figures 8.5 and 8.6 were calculated using regression techniques. There was a single predictor—the number of new rules. The number of new rules for each task in each serial position of the five different training sequences is shown in table 8.7. Tables 8.5 and 8.6 show the details of these calculations for experimental group 1 and the control group. The analogous tables were generated for the remaining three experimental groups by filling in the columns as dictated by the specific sequences of tasks show in table 8.7. The model accounted for 88% of the variance of the 31 means. The learning time per new rule, t, was 27.2 seconds. The intercept, c, was 97.0 seconds. The observed and predicted values for all 31 means are shown in figure 8.5.

The top panel of figure 8.6 shows the observed and predicted values averaged over the four experimental groups and plotted as a function of serial position. The fit is excellent, and the theory is able to account for the sawtooth learning curve induced by the highly similar pairs of tasks. Since the model contains no nonspecific transfer mechanism, significant nonspecific transfer effects should show up in such a figure with observed performance better than that predicted in later serial positions. Examination of the top panel of figure 8.6 does not show such deviations; thus nonspecific transfer is not a large component of the improvement in performance across serial positions. The bottom panel of figure 8.6 shows the training times of the six experimental tasks averaged over serial positions in the four experimental training orders.

3.1.15 *Summary*

Models derived from Cognitive Complexity Theory provided good to excellent fits of the data from the first three experiments. The only disturbing aspect of the results is the variations in the parameters t and c. These parameters are sensitive to the characteristics of the task in the first serial position of a training sequence. Typically, there are a large number of new rules to learn because the user must acquire a majority of the common methods as well as the first task. The data for this first task are also highly variable. Finally, the values for both the times and number of productions are large and thus have a strong influence on both t and c.

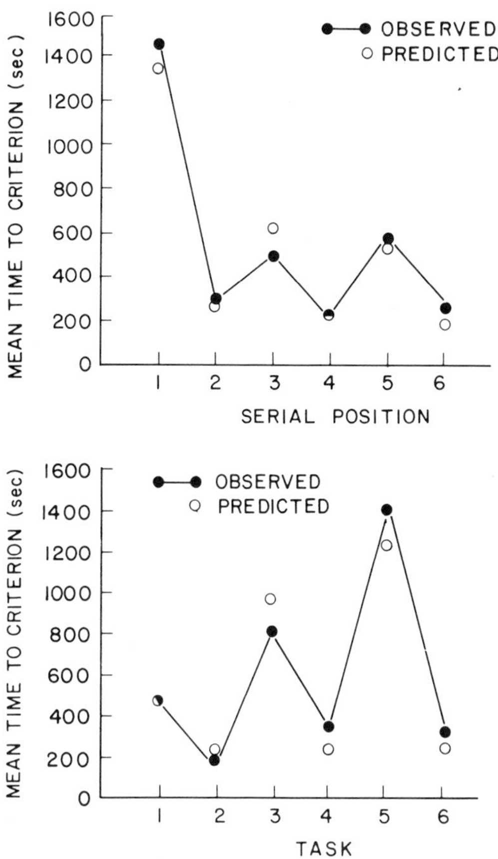

Figure 8.6
The observed and predicted mean times to criterion for the four experimental groups averaged over groups plotted as a function of serial position (top) and averaged over groups plotted as a function of task (bottom).

The two sets of parameters would be similar if it had been assumed that there was a single underlying method for entering diskette and document names. The current transfer theory does not permit generalization across these two methods because different prompts appear in their conditions, and no generalization across context defined by different relevant prompts is permitted. The necessary generalization requires that the theory have the semantic knowledge necessary for recognizing that diskette and document names are very similar entities and that it is legitimate to generalize across the different prompts generating a common method.

The results from experiment 3 provide reasonable support for the transfer assumptions of the model. The fits to individual experimental conditions shown in figure 8.5 are more variable than one would like, and the theory makes more aggressive transfer predictions than are supported by the data, although none of the deviations are significant. When the data are aggregated across the four experimental groups by serial position or task as shown in the two panels of figure 8.6, the fit is excellent. The results from the control group shown in figure 8.5 and the data aggregated across serial positions in the top panel of figure 8.6 provide no support for the conjecture that generalized transfer effects are an important contributor to performance of these utility tasks.

In conclusion, these results suggest that Cognitive Complexity Theory's learning and transfer assumptions are at least good approximations. There are suggestions in the data, in particular where the theory predicts that only one new production has to be learned, that the theory's transfer predictions are too aggressive. Such results could be accounted for by the probabilistic, all-or-none transfer assumption described by Greeno and Scandura (1966) and Polson (1972).

3.2 Text Editing Experiments

This subsection reports data from two experiments that evaluated Cognitive Complexity Theory's learning and performance assumptions on a manuscript editing task. The screen editor for the word processor used in the first three experiments was the model for the editor used in these experiments. Experiment 4 evaluated the learning and transfer assumptions using training order manipulations similar to those employed in experiment 3. Experiment 5 evaluated the performance predictions of the theory by having a limited number of subjects practice the manuscript editing task for 8 days after they had mastered the editor.

3.2.1 *The Training Task*

The subject's initial task in both experiments was to learn to use the screen editor to perform manuscript editing. Editing was described to the subject as involving moving the cursor to the beginning of a change in the manuscript and then carrying out the operation specified in the markup. This initial cursor positioning was done using cursor keys; there was no find function. The editing operation was executed by pressing a key labeled with the specified function and then selecting the range.

3.2.2 *Editing Functions*

There were five editing functions: INSERT, DELETE, MOVE, COPY, and TRANSPOSE. Pressing the INSERT key caused the line to be broken, and text was then entered and terminated by the ENTER key. DELETE was executed immediately at the end of a select range function on depression of the ENTER key. The COPY and MOVE functions were nearly identical and used the cursor keys to specify the target location. At the end of the select range operation, the user moved the cursor to the target location and pressed ENTER, causing the material to be moved to or copied to the target location. TRANSPOSE involved the specification of two ranges. The command began like MOVE or COPY. The cursor keys were used to position at the beginning of the second range, which was selected using the method described previously. On depression of the ENTER key at the end of the second select range operation, the two segments of text were transposed.

The range was specified using the cursor keys or a single-character find function available during the select range component of any editing operation. When the subject pressed a character key on the keyboard, the cursor jumped to the matching character in the text, highlighting the intervening characters. The subject then pressed ENTER, signaling the end of the range selection operation.

All editing functions ended with a verification phase. A prompt appeared on the bottom of the screen requesting the subject to press an ACCEPT or REJECT key. ACCEPT caused the program to continue. REJECT undid the operation and repositioned the cursor at the end of the range of the previous edit.

3.2.3 *Apparatus*

The experiments were controlled by two FORTRAN programs that interacted with each other. The first program implemented the screen editor described previously. The second program was a computer-assisted instruction (CAI) system that controlled the training procedure, including presentation of instructional material and presentation of feedback on errors. There were two CRTs. The material to be edited appeared on one, and the subject inserted text and pressed command keys on its keyboard. The second CRT presented all instructions and feedback under the control of the CAI package.

The CAI package presented the instructional materials and then turned control over to the editor. When the subject completed an edit and depressed the ACCEPT key, the editor transmitted a description of the subject's actions to the CAI package, where it was evaluated. If the subject was correct, there was no interruption in the procedure, and the subject was permitted to go on to the next edit. If an error was made, the CAI package had the logic necessary to identify the error and provide explicit feedback.

3.2.4 Theoretical Analysis

The manuscript editing task has a more complicated control structure than the simple linear structure of the utility tasks. This analysis of the manuscript editing task is essentially identical to that presented by Card, Moran, and Newell (1980, 1983, chapter 6). The top levels of the goal structure for the production system model are based on their (1983, chapter 6) analysis.

Card, Moran, and Newell assume that a majority of human-computer interaction tasks can be decomposed into a sequence of *unit tasks.* In the case of manuscript editing, the unit task is decomposed into the *acquisition, execution,* and *verification* of each change indicated in the manuscript. Acquisition of the unit task involves positioning the cursor at the beginning of the range of the next edit and then deciding which of the five editing functions should be carried out. Executing the edit involves pressing the proper function key, entering the required text in the case of the insert function, or carrying out the necessary series of select range and cursor positioning operations required by the other four methods. The verification step involves checking the edit and pressing the ACCEPT key. Figure 8.7 is a GOMS analysis of the top-level goal structure and control structure of the model using a notation very similar to that employed by Card, Moran, and Newell (1983, chapter 6).

The model uses seven methods: one for each of the five editing functions, a cursor-positioning method using the arrow keys, and a select range method using the single-character find function. The top-level goal structure is shown in the upper panel of figure 8.7. The top-level control structure is a do-while loop that exits when there are no more unit tasks. The simulation retrieves the coordinates of the start of the range of the

```
GOAL: EDIT-MANUSCRIPT
    GOAL: EDIT-UNIT-TASK (Repeat Until no More Unit Tasks)
       GOAL: ACQUIRE-UNIT-TASK
         GOAL: LOOKUP-TASK-LOCATION
         GOAL: MOVE-TO-TASK-LOCATION
                USE-MOVE-CURSOR-METHOD
         GOAL: LOOKUP-TASK-FUNCTION
       GOAL: EXECUTE-UNIT-TASK
                [select: USE-INSERT-METHOD
                         USE-GENERAL DELETE-METHOD
                         USE-COPY-METHOD
                         USE-MOVE-METHOD
                         USE-TRANSPOSE-METHOD]

              GOAL STRUCTURE FOR GENERAL-DELETE-METHOD

        GOAL: DELETE TEXT
              GOAL: PRESS DELETE-KEY
              GOAL: CHECK DELETE-PROMPT
              GOAL: SELECT RANGE
                    USE-SELECT-RANGE-METHOD
              GOAL: PRESS ENTER
              GOAL: VERIFY DELETE
              GOAL: CHECK ACCEPT-PROMPT
              GOAL: PRESS ACCEPT-KEY
              GOAL: FINISH DELETE
```

Figure 8.7
The top-level goal structure for the PS model of the text editing task (top) and the goal structure of the DELETE method (bottom).

next edit from the task list, which is the model's representation of a marked-up manuscript, and calls the cursor-positioning method to position the cursor at the beginning of the range. The simulation then retrieves a description of the edit from the task list. This information is used to fire a selection rule, which asserts the goal to execute the appropriate editing method. The verification phase is part of each editing method.

The select range method is called from each of the editing methods. The cursor key and select range methods are do-while loops that terminate when the cursor is moved to a specified position. The select range method retrieves the last character at the end of the range and enters this character, repeatedly if necessary, until the range is highlighted. The goal structures for the five editing methods are linear sequences of the actions and verification steps necessary for completing each method. The goal structure for DELETE is shown in the bottom panel of figure 8.7. The goal structures for the other methods are very similar.

The PS model for manuscript editing has a structure identical to that of the GOMS model described in the preceding paragraphs. The model con-

Table 8.8
Components of tasks in experiment 4, training order 1, special delete, and calculation of the number of new rules for each position in the training sequence[a]

Task, editing method, or common submethod	Editing task (serial position)				
	Insert(1)	Delete(2)	Copy(3)	Move(4)	Transp(5)
Top-level core	7	0	0	0	0
Editing method					
Unique to method	9	13	7	7	12
Common subsequence copy/move	*	*	4	0	*
Methods					
Cursor positioning	14	0	0	0	0
Range selection	*	*	9	0	0
Number of new rules	30	13	20	7	12

a. * means not part of task; 0 means component learned earlier in training sequence.

tains representations of the task control structure, referred to as the core, and methods for cursor positioning, range selection, and the five editing methods. The training time and transfer predictions were calculated in a manner identical to those for experiment 3. Tables 8.8 and 8.9 present the details of the calculations for the number of new rules for two of the six experimental conditions. The rows are the various components of the production system model for the editing task described above. The columns are the five editing methods listed in the training order sequence. Each entry is the number of rules that must be acquired in order to master the current task in the training order.

3.2.5 *Experiment 4: Method*

The design a was 2 × 3 factorial with three training orders and two levels of delete instructions. INSERT was the first method learned by subjects in all experimental conditions. MOVE always followed COPY in all conditions. The training orders for the four methods excluding INSERT were (1) DELETE, COPY-MOVE, TRANSPOSE, (2) TRANSPOSE, DELETE, COPY-MOVE, and (3) COPY-MOVE, TRANSPOSE, DELETE.

The instructional manipulation involved giving subjects one of two different descriptions of the DELETE operation. Specific DELETE instructions described the delete operation in terms of deleting specific entities from text. There were specialized methods for deleting characters, words followed by a space, and sentences. For example, deleting a word was

Table 8.9
Components of tasks in experiment 4, training order 1, general delete, and calculation of the number of new rules for each position in the training sequence[a]

Task, editing method, or common submethod	Editing task (serial position)				
	Insert(1)	Delete(2)	Copy(3)	Move(4)	Transp(5)
Top-level core	7	0	0	0	0
Editing method					
Unique to method	9	7	7	7	12
Common subsequence copy/move	*	*	4	0	*
Methods					
Cursor positioning	14	0	0	0	0
Range selection	*	9	0	0	0
Number of new rules	30	15	11	7	12

a. * means not part of task; 0 means component learned earlier in training sequence.

described as positioning the cursor at the beginning of the word, hitting the space bar, and then hitting the ENTER key. The general DELETE instructions described the select range function independently of any text entities. Either the single-character find function or the cursor keys could be used to highlight the range.

The experiment involved an instruction phase and a training phase. In the instruction phase, subjects received instructions on the general structure of the task, the layout of the keyboard, and the use of the cursor positioning keys. In training phase, subjects learned five text editing methods. They were first given detailed instructions on how to perform the editing function, including the procedure for selecting the range. They then had to complete successfully a practice task involving editing a two-page manuscript with four edits on each page. If they made errors, they received appropriate feedback immediately after they pressed the ACCEPT key. Subjects then had to review the instructions for the method. The criterion for learning was one error-free repetition of all eight edits. After reaching criterion, subjects were immediately to the instructions for the next method.

Subjects were recruited from the Boulder Colorado, community by a newspaper ad and were paid $15.00 for participation in the experiment. Subjects were required to be able to type and to have had no computing or word processing experience. There were 15 subjects in each of the 6 experimental conditions.

3.2.6 *Experiment 4: Results*

The data from experiment 4 were used to evaluate predictions concerning learning and transfer. The average times to reach criterion on each block of practice edits was calculated; this time included the reading times for feedback screens and review of instructions. An editing method by training order by delete instructions analysis of variance found no training order or DELETE instruction effects, but the training order by method interaction was highly significant. There were large differences in the difficulty of learning a method as a function of its serial position across training orders.

There were two causes for the failure of the DELETE instructions to have any effect. The two forms of the DELETE function required that subjects learn very similar numbers of new productions when DELETE was in serial position 2 in training order 1. Subjects had learned the general select range function by the time DELETE was presented in the other two training orders. The results from these conditions is consistent with the hypothesis that subjects ignored the special DELETE instructions and used the general select range function.

Predictions were calculated for mean times to criterion for each editing method in each of the 6 experimental conditions; the model was fitted to the observed 30 cell means. The number of new rules accounted for 81% of the variance in the observed means. Training time per rule, t, was 37.0 second per rule, and the intercept, c, was 405 seconds. The observed and predicted mean times to criterion averaged over the DELETE instructions is presented in figure 8.8.

The model makes strong predictions about the shapes of the serial position curves for MOVE and TRANSPOSE as a function of their serial positions in the three different training orders. MOVE should be learned very rapidly, requiring only seven new productions, and its difficulty should be independent of its position in the training order. This prediction is a consequence of two facts. First, MOVE always followed COPY in all three training orders, and MOVE and COPY are very similar. Once COPY has been learned, MOVE can be mastered by acquiring only seven rules that are unique to MOVE. Second, additional training on rules common to COPY, MOVE, and other editing methods should have small effects on performance. The top panel of figure 8.9 shows the observed and predicted and serial position functions for MOVE. There is a very small improvement in observed times for MOVE as a function of serial position.

The model predicts that the serial position function for TRANSPOSE will be a step function with the most difficult position being serial position 2 and no difference in training times for serial position 4 or 5. TRANS-

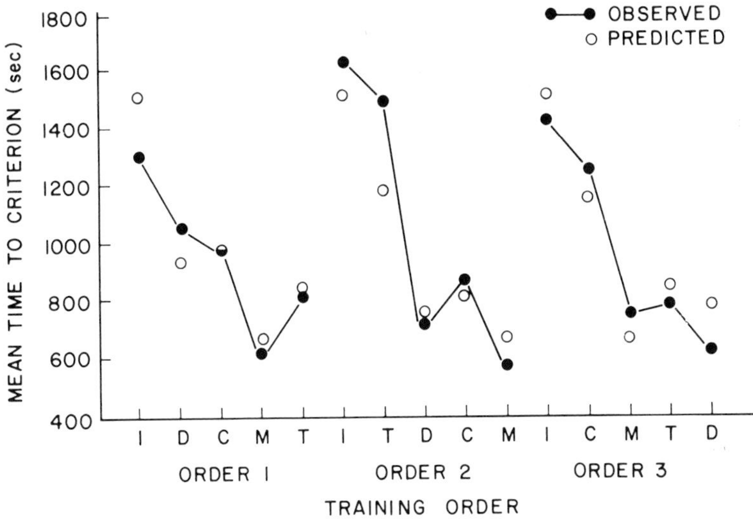

Figure 8.8
The observed and predicted mean times to criterion averaged over the two forms of the DELETE instructions plotted as a function of serial position in a training order for experiment 4.

POSE is more difficult in serial position 2 because subjects have to acquire the 9 rules representing the select range method as well as the 12 rules for the TRANSPOSE method. The observed and predicted serial position functions are presented in the bottom panel of figure 8.9. Examination of both panels of figure 8.9 shows that there is excellent correspondence between the predicted shapes of the serial position curves and the observed means.

3.2.7 *Experiment 5*

The results of this study were used to evaluate the performance predictions of the model for newly trained as well as experienced users. Subjects were first trained using the same procedures used in experiment 4; then they practiced editing for eight days. Performance predictions were derived from simulation runs in which the model edited exactly the same manuscripts used in the experiment. This study also explored the issue of representing practice effects in the theory.

3.2.8 *Performance Models for Newly Trained Users*

In a preceding section, it was shown that the production system architecture predicts that the execution time for an edit is the sum of two components:

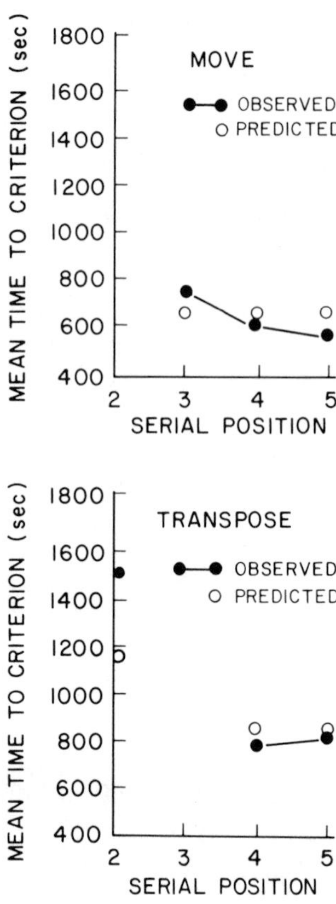

Figure 8.9
The observed and predicted mean times to criterion plotted as a function of serial position in the training orders for MOVE (top) and TRANSPOSE (bottom).

(1) the number of cycles for completing the task times a constant activation time and (2) the sum of the elementary action times over these cycles. In practice, it turns out that it is impossible to obtain independent estimates of the activation time and the times for the various elementary actions.

The simulation runs for the manuscript editing task give two highly intercorrelated sets of predictors: (1) a set correlated with the number of cycles and (2) a set correlated with the number of working memory inputs. Members of each set make independent contributions to predicting the execution times. The number of cycles and keystrokes are highly correlated, and thus it is difficult to separate activation time from execution time for keystrokes. Various statistics measuring working memory load are highly correlated. The patterns of high correlations between logically independent aspects of the model are due to the structure of the text editing task.

The results from the first day of practice in experiment 5 and theoretical considerations led us to select one predictor from each of these subsets: (1) the number of cycles and (2) the total number of goals and notes added to working memory:

$$\text{Execution time} = \text{NCYCLES} \cdot a + \text{WMIN} \cdot b + i,$$

where NCYCLES is the number of cycles required to perform an edit, a is the activation time per cycle, WMIN is the total number of Add goal and note actions, b is the time for an Add action, and i is an intercept parameter assumed to be 0. The parameters a, b, and i are estimated using multiple regression techniques. However, the values of a and b have to be interpreted with some caution. For example, NCYCLES and number of keystrokes are highly correlated, and thus an observed value for a is a mixture of activation and keystroke times.

3.2.9 *Practice Effects*

The other issue explored in this study was the representation of practice effects in the theory. Two possibilities are considered here. The first is that a and b are constant and that the production system representation becomes more efficient with practice. The second is that a and b decrease with practice and that practice does not produce changes in the PS representation of a task.

PS models for experiments 1–4 are assumed to represent the how-to-do-it knowledge of newly trained users. Two assumptions determine the structure of these PS models. The first is that only one cognitive operation or physical action is executed during a cycle. The second is that all user inputs and system responses are verified, leading to additional operations and their associated rules. Performance predictions for newly trained users were evaluated using the model developed to account for the training time from experiment 4 using the data from the first practice day of experiment 5.

It is assumed that additional experience after the first day of practice causes learning mechanisms to generate more efficient representations of the editing methods. Three assumptions are made. First, the basic activation, *a*, and execution time, *b*, parameters are independent of the amount of practice. Second, highly practiced users omit verification steps from their methods; thus, the associated verification rules are removed from the PS model. Third, additional improvements in performance are due to the composition mechanism (Anderson, 1983). Composition is a process that combines the actions of rules that fire in an invariant order into the actions of a single rule.

A second model, the expert model, was derived from the production system model for new users by omitting the verification steps and applying the composition process in cases in which rules fire in a fixed order. This second model was assumed to represent the subject's knowledge of the task on the eighth day of practice. It generated the same sequence of keystrokes as the first model did for newly trained users for any edit, but it took fewer cycles and working memory operations.

3.2.10 *Experiment 5: Method*

Experiment 5 required 9 days to complete. On the first day, subjects were trained using the training procedures from experiment 4. On each of 8 practice days, they edited a new manuscript containing 70 edits. The edits were randomized in blocks of 10 and placed on a single page, two edits of each type. The manuscript was taken from the draft of an introductory psychology textbook. The materials had been reverse-edited so that when subjects completed a given edit the text made sense. Each day began with a brief review of the instructions for the five editing methods. The correctness of each edit was checked by the CAI package after the depression of the ACCEPT key. Incorrect edits had to be redone. Eight subjects were involved in the experiment.

The seven subjects included in the analysis selected the range of an editing operation using either the method incorporated in the simulation or a simple variant of it on approximately 80% of the edits. The simulation selects the range by entering the last character in a range, repeatedly if necessary, until the range is highlighted. The one subject who was dropped from the analysis used the arrow keys to select the range of editing operations. The data from INSERTs and positioning the cursor at the beginning of the range using the arrow key were excluded because they was dominated by typing times, which are highly variable and provide little insight into the processes assumed by the theory.

3.2.11 *Experiment 5: Results*

The execution time for each of the remaining edits was measured from the last keystroke that positioned the cursor at the beginning of the range to the pressing of the ACCEPT key. The average time to perform correct edits plotted as a function of practice days is shown in figure 8.10. The average time for edits involving DELETE and TRANSPOSE operations is also plotted.

Peformance predictions and alternative explanations of changes in performance as a function of practice shown in figure 8.10 were evaluated using the data from the first and eighth practice days. The first block of eight edits, two each of DELETE, COPY, MOVE, AND TRANSPOSE, were dropped from the analysis because they were highly variable and seemed to have a large warmup component. The remaining edit times were averaged across the seven subjects and the model fit to the 48 means from the first day and 48 means from the last day.

Values of the predictors for each edit were generated by having the simulation edit the actual manuscripts that were used on the first and last practice days in the experiment. Two sets of predictors were generated for each edit, one from the PS model for newly trained subjects and the other from the model for expert subjects. The predictors were the total number of recognize-act cycles (NCYCLES) and the total number of goals and notes entered into working memory (WMIN). They were accumulated from the last arrow key keystroke before depression of the function key to the activation of the ACCEPT key.

The first analysis involved fitting common parameters for both days. The predictors for the first practice day's data were derived from the newly trained subjects' model, and predictors for the last day's practice data were derived from the experts' model. The mean editing times for the last 48 edits on each day were fitted using multiple regression techniques. The observed and predicted times as a function of editing method averaged over the 48 edits for each day are shown in figure 8.11. The following equation accounted for 80% of the variance of the means:

$$\text{Editing time (sec)} = .19 \cdot \text{NCYCLES} + .47 \cdot \text{WMIN} - .09.$$

The coefficients for NCYCLES and WMIN are highly significant ($p > .01$).

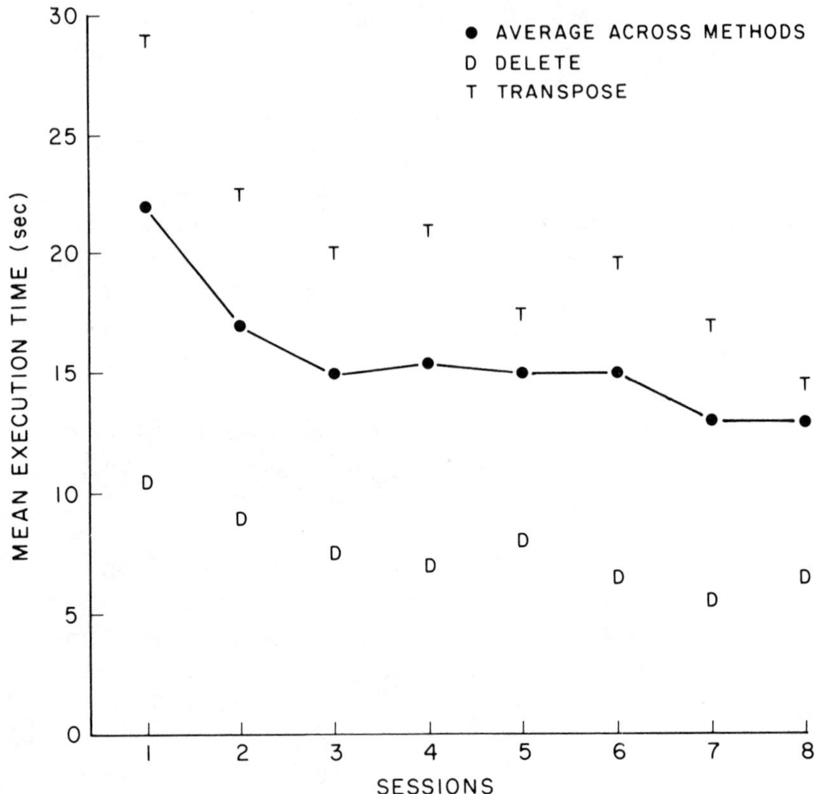

Figure 8.10
The average time to perform and edit plotted as a function of practice days. The Ds are the times for the DELETE method. The Ts are the times for TRANSPOSE.

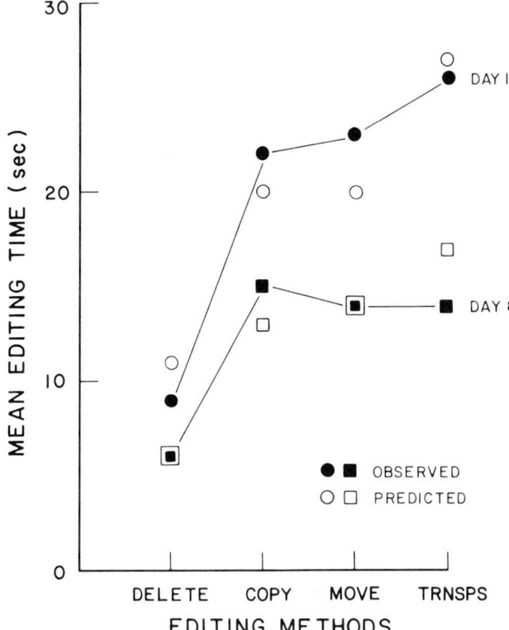

Figure 8.11
The observed and predicted mean editing times for days 1 and 8 averaged over edits plotted by editing methods.

Other analyses attempted to fit the newly trained and expert PS models to both days' data using common parameter values. Both analyses, one fitting the new trained subjects' model and the other fitting the expert subjects' model gave significantly worse fits with a 20% reduction in percentage of variance explained. Finally, both models were fitted assuming that *a* and *b* decreased with practice. Those fits were equivalent and quite satisfactory, with approximately a 5% reduction in the percentage of variance explained.

3.2.12 *Summary: Experiments 4 and 5*

Cognitive Complexity Theory makes successful quantitative predictions of learning and performance measures for a simple manuscript editing task. Furthermore, the model is able to account for the changes in performance between the first and last days of practice by assuming that parameter values are common to both days, that subjects drop verification steps with increased experience, and that the composition process leads to more compact representations of the procedural knowledge. Furthermore, the attempt to fit both the newly trained and expert models to both days' data using common parameter values leads to significantly worse fits.

There are limitations on the conclusions that can be drawn about the performance model at this time. The large number of statistics derivable from the simulation as possible predictors falls into two highly intercorrelated subsets. This is due to part to the structure of the text editing environment. There is a strong correlation between cycles, simulated keystrokes, and other associated statistics. Various working memory statistics are also highly intercorrelated. Thus, it is not possible to conclude that the equation presented previously is the unique best-fitting model for the performance data.

3.3 Conclusions

The results from the first four experiments reported in this chapter provide strong support for the learning and transfer assumptions of Cognitive Complexity Theory. The data from experiment 4 on acquisition of text editing skills are monotonically decreasing learning curves, and one might be tempted to consider the alternative explanation that nonspecific transfer could account for the data. However, the results of experiment 3 rule out such an interpretation, given the theory's ability to account for the nonmonotonic learning curves generated by the training order manipulations in this study.

Careful study of the individual panels of figure 8.5 shows that there are situations in which the transfer theory seems to make overly aggressive predictions. In three out of five of the cases for which the model predicts that a new procedure can be mastered by learning a single production, there are deviations between observed and predicted values, with the observed values being higher.

The data from the first four experiments are well described by the theory. The deviations discussed in the preceding paragraphs are second-order perturbations that become apparent only when quantitative predictions derived from the current model are compared to the observed results. The current theory makes adequate approximations that would enable a designer to predict training times for a system under study.

4 A Theoretically Based Design Methodology

This section describes a hypothetical design methodology using PS models derived from Cognitive Complexity Theory as evaluation tools in an iterative design process. The section begins with three examples illustrating the importance of being able to make quantitative predictions of usability parameters, training time, and productivity during all phases of the design cycle. Then the design process is described. In essence, a modified version of the typical stepwise refinement process is proposed in which the design team concurrently develop hardware and software as well as a user interface that minimizes cognitive complexity, usng the production system modeling technology as an evaluation tool. The proposed methodology is explicitly compared to fast prototyping (Gould and Lewis, 1985).

4.1 Quantitative Estimates of Usability

The proposed design methodology calls for the *concurrent design* of *hardware and software* as well as the *tasks* performed by the user. Many tasks require the coordinated use of several different software subsystems. A given subsystem may not have functions that permit users to perform frequently occurring subtasks easily. Related functions like delete, copy, and move may involve inconsistent methods in different subsystems. A given function may be needlessly complex, having been designed to handle an infrequently occurring special case. Today, a majority of user interfaces are designed with little attention given to what tasks users will want to carry out with the proposed system or how these tasks will be performed. In other words, no explicit attention is given to the usability of the proposed system.

The other, and equally important, aspect of the methodology is its ability to make quantitative estimates of usability parameters early in the design cycle. The achievement of usability criteria and the rational evaluation of trade-offs all require quantitative estimates of usability parameters. The following paragraphs describe three examples.

4.1.1 Usability Criteria

Development projects have explicit objectives for functionality, schedule, and cost of a new product. Recently, some authors (e.g., Bennett, 1984) have proposed that project objectives should also include usability criteria specifying training time and productivity. For example, a new user should be able to complete a specific task after 2 hours of training, while an experienced user of an earlier version of the system should be able to perform the same task after a half-hour of training. Current human factors practice provides very limited tools for evaluating the reasonableness of such specifications or for effectively managing their achievement.

User testing on prototypes provides the information necessary for evaluating usability criteria, but such tests often occur late in the development cycle. It could be expensive or impossible, because of schedule constraints, to make necessary modifications if the prototype failed by a wide margin to meet usability specifications. Cognitive Complexity Theory provides methods for generating quantitative predictions for training time and productivity early in the design cycle. Thus, the theory provides tools for effectively managing the achievement of usability objectives.

4.1.2 *Trade-Offs*

The development process always involves trade-offs between various technical, economic, and functional objectives. Cognitive Complexity Theory provides methods for quantifying training time, performance, and other usability criteria. Such quantitative estimates enable a development team to make more rational decisions concerning schedule and economic or engineering trade-offs that interact with usability considerations.

4.1.3 *Details of the User Interface*

In a recent paper, Whiteside et al. (1985) reported results evaluating training and execution times for several utility tasks on seven different commercially available systems. The sytems used a wide range of interface styles, including command languages, menus, and icons. They found that there was no one uniformly superior interface style and that there were examples of good and bad interfaces within each style. They concluded that the details of a given design, not the interface style, determine a system's usability.

Cognitive Complexity Theory provides tools for evaluating the details of a proposed interface. The methodology summarized below forces the design team to work through the details of all aspects of interactions between user and system in carrying out tasks, and it provides tools for evaluating usability criteria for trial designs early in the design cycle.

4.2 The Design Process

This subsection summarizes the design process and the use of the simulation tools. Each of the four phases of the design process involves specifying, in increasing detail, the user interface of a system as well as the sequences of user actions and cognitive operations required to complete each task performed by the system. There are two important differences between a traditional top-down, stepwise-refinement methodology and the proposed design process. The first is the *concurrent development* of both the hardware and software specifications as well as a user's representation of tasks performed by the system. The second is that the iterative nature of the complete design process. Several iterations of the stages outlined below are necessary in order to develop a highly usable interface (Gould and Lewis, 1985).

The four phases of the design process are

1. System Definition Phase: Specify the functional requirements of a system.

2. Task Analysis Phase: Specify the user's decomposition of each task performed by the system.

3. Detailed Design Phase: Specify the details of the user interface, including methods, menus, commands, etc.

4. Evaluation Phase: Evaluate the design using simulation methods.

4.2.1 *The System Definition Phase*

The specifications of user requirements, implementation environment, basic structure of the user interface, and system functionality take place during the system definition phase. Functionality is specified in terms of the applications supported by the system, including document preparation, time management, and financial analysis. The general properties of the user interface are specified in terms of constraints imposed by the implementation environment (e.g., character-oriented versus all-points-addressable displays) and the style of the interface (i.e., command language, iconic, or menu).

The design team also describes the set of tasks to be performed by users of the system. A user's knowledge of how to perform each task is represented in a PS model developed later in the design process.

4.2.2 *The Task Analysis Phase*

The task analysis phase involves specifying the top- and middle-levels of a user's goal structure for each task identified during the system definition phase. These levels are defined by a user's decomposition of a task into subtasks and the further decomposition, if necessary, of complex subtasks. Then the design team develops methods that efficiently accomplish the various subtasks. This process is to be contrasted with the more typical procedure of defining a command set and then requiring users or developers of training material to discover methods for accomplishing various subtasks.

The first two phases, the system definition phase and the task analysis phase, involve the decomposition of the functionality of a system into a collection of tasks and the specification of the top levels of the goal structure for each task. Task analysis is the initial step in other user-centered design methodologies (Card, Moran, and Newell, 1983; Rubinstein and Hersh, 1984). However, there is no well-defined methodology for task analysis, although Card, Moran, and Newell (1983, pp. 385ff.) have provided a theoretical foundation, in which the concept of unit task is introduced. Task analysis is an art that is practiced successfully by some system designers and cognitive scientists.

Task analysis is not a routine process. However, it is possible to separate the task analysis from the rest of the design cycle because the top levels of the goal structure of a model are primarily determined by the task structure and not by the details of the interface. Thus, a group with a small number of specialists could do the task analyses that would be used by developers.

4.2.3 *Detailed Design Phase*

In the detailed design phase, the design team completes the detailed specifications of the interface and the sequences of user actions necessary for accomplishing each task identified during the tasks analysis phase. The design team also develops a test suite. The test suite specifies the tasks and the characteristics of each task to be employed in the usability evaluation of the design. For example, the test suite for a manuscript editing task would specify one or more manuscripts and the changes to be made in each manuscript. The tests should be designed to exercise each method necessary for completing the various tasks specified during the system design phase.

4.2.4 *Evaluation Phase*

During the evaluation phase, the design team writes the system model and PS models for each task. It then simulates execution of all of the tasks in the test suite, deriving static and dynamic measures from the PS model for each task. These measures are used to make predictions about training time and productivity. These results are used to evaluate the design and to plan changes, implemented during the next iteration of the design process, that will improve the usability parameter of the proposed system.

4.3 Benefits of Cognitive Complexity Analysis

An analysis using the theoretically based simulation tools described here enables a design team to generate quantitative predictions for training costs and productivity early in the design cycle. Such predictions permit the effective management of usability criteria and the evaluation of trade-offs between various usability parameters and other goals (e.g., cost or schedule).

The completed simulation program has important uses in other parts of the development cycle. The system model is a formal specification of the user interface and is a detailed specification of the code that implements the interface. The system model can also be used to derive a generalized fast prototyping system, an application discussed in the next subsection. Since the production system model is a specification of the knowledge necessary for operating the system, it can be the basis for the development of training and reference documentation.

4.4 Alternative Methods—Fast Prototyping

Fast prototyping is the most viable alternative to our simulation-based evaluation methodology. Studies using test subjects give developers quantitative estimates of training time and productivity for new users. Gould and Lewis (1985) argue forcefully that successful user interfaces are the result of a design process involving an evaluate-revise cycle evolving to a good design. Cognitive Complexity Theory is *not* a design generation tool; it is an evaluation tool. Thus, the simulation methodology can be used in an iterative design process in place of fast prototyping. Changing the production system and the system models and rerunning the simulations may be a faster method for closing the loop.

4.4.1 Level of Abstraction

Fast prototyping techniques are used to evaluate a single design with respect to usability criteria or to select between two competing designs. There are no theoretical analyses providing abstract characterizations of designs independent of the details of a particular application or implementation environment. Fast prototyping does not provide the conceptual tools necessary for understanding the general properties of classes of interfaces, nor does it enable designers to separate the complexity of a task from flaws in a proposed design. The PS is a model of both the user's understanding of the task and the actions necessary for performing the task using a given interface.

4.4.2 *Modifications of the Current Design*

Deciding what changes would improve the current version of an interface design is the critical step in an iterative design process. Fast prototyping results provide little guidance if several complex changes are made in successive versions of the interface. Cognitive Complexity Theory provides a more detailed description of a user's representation of the different versions and thus provides a designer with the ability to make design revisions based on cognitive principles.

4.5 Theoretical Foundations

The design methodology outlined in the preceding subsections is based on the assumption that designers can write PS models that are at least a first-order approximation to the representations and processes employed by users to perform tasks. This subsection evaluates the foundations and assumptions underlying the modeling process. Limitations of the theory and design methodology are also discussed.

4.5.1 *A Controversial Assumption*

The most controversial assumption of the theory is that a designer can develop a model of a task that suppresses details of learning, comprehension, and problem solving mechanisms. PS models of a task can be derived from a high-level understanding of a user's decomposition of the task and detailed descriptions of the methods used to accomplish goals defined by various subtasks. Other approaches claim that issues involving learning and comprehension will have large effects on a user's representation and thus on the structure of the PS model.

4.5.2 *Limitations*

There are design issues that directly involve the details of mechanisms of perception and comprehension. The layout of displays and the selection of command names are two examples. Gould and Lewis (1985) describe a project in which fast prototyping prevented some serious errors in the choice of command names; new users misinterpreted the meanings of initial choices of commands. However, most problems involving an initial interface design can be discovered using an evaluation methodology based on

Cognitive Complexity Theory. Examples include inconsistent commands, unnecessarily complex methods, and a lack of effective methods for treating common subtasks.

Both fast prototyping and the simulation-based evaluation methodology can be used in the design process. The final iterations of the design process could be done using fast prototyping studies during which the designers evaluate display layouts and command names. The system model can be used to drive a fast prototyping system by upgrading the output so as to produce full emulations of displays.

References

Anderson, J. R. (1976). *Language, Memory, and Thought*, Hillsdale, NJ Lawrence Erlbaum Associates.

Anderson, J. R. (1982). Acquisition of cognitive skill. *Psychological Review*, 89, 369–406.

Anderson, J. R. (1983). *The Architecture of Cognition*, Cambridge, MA, Harvard University Press.

Bennett, J. L. (1984). Managing to meet usability requirements. In J. L. Bennett, D. Case, D. Sandelin, and M. Smith (Eds.), *Visual Display Terminals*, Englewood Cliffs, NJ, Prentice-Hall.

Card, S. K., Moran, T. P., and Newell, A. (1980). Computer text editing: An information-processing analysis of a routine cognitive skill. *Cognitive Psychology*, 12, 32–74.

Card, S. K., Moran, T. P., and Newell, A. (1983). *The Psychology of Human-Computer Interaction*, Hillsdale, NJ, Lawrence Erlbaum Associates.

Engle, S. E., and Granda, R. E. (1975). Guidelines for man/display interfaces. Technical Report TR 00.2720, Proughkeepsie, NY, IBM.

Gould, J. D., and Lewis, C. (1985). Designing for usability: Key principles and what designers think. *Communications of the ACM*, 28, 300–311.

Greeno, J. G., and Scandura, J. M. (1966). All-or-none transfer based on verbally mediated concepts. *Journal of Mathematical Psychology*, 3, 388–411.

Karat, J. (1983). A model of problem solving with incomplete constraint knowledge. *Cognitive Psychology*, 1983, 14, 538–559.

Kieras, D. E. (1982). A model of reader strategy for abstracting main ideas from simple technical prose. *Text*, 2, 47–82.

Kieras, D. E., and Bovair, S. (1984a). The role of a mental model in learning to operate a device. *Cognitive Science*, 8, 255–273.

Kieras, D. E., and Bovair, S. (1986). A production system analysis of transfer of training. *Journal of Memory and Language*, 25, 507–524.

Kieras, D. E., and Polson, P. G. (1982). An outline of a theory of the user complexity of devices and systems. Universities of Arizona and Colorado Project on User Complexity of Devices and Systems, Working Paper No. 1, pp. 1–22.

Kieras, D. E., and Polson, P. G. (1983). A generalized transition network representation of interactive systems. *Proceedings of the CHI 1983 Conference on Human Factors in Computing*, Boston, MA, ACM.

Kieras, D. E., and Polson, P. G. (1985). An approach to the formal analysis of user complexity. *International Journal of Man-Machine Studies*, 22, 365–394.

Newell, A., and Simon, H. A. (1972). *Human Problem Solving*, Englewood Cliffs, Prentice-Hall.

Norman, D. A. (1982). Some observations on mental models. In D. Gentner and A. Stevens (Eds.), *Mental Models*, Hillsdale NJ, Lawrence Erlbaum Associates.

Polson, P. G. (1972). A quantitative analysis of the conceptual processes in the Hull paradigm. *Journal of Mathematical Psychology*, 9, 141–167.

Polson, P. G., and Kieras, D. E. (1984). A formal description of users' knowledge of how to operate a device and user complexity. *Behavior Research Methods, Instruments, and Computers*, 16, 249–255.

Polson, P. G., and Kieras, D. E. (1985). A quantitative model of the learning and performance of text editing knowledge. *Proceedings of the CHI 1985 Conference on Human Factors in Computing*, San Francisco, ACM.

Polson, P. G., Muncher, E., and Engelbeck, G. (1986). A test of a common elements theory of transfer. In M. Mantei & P. Orbeton (Eds.), *Proceedings CHI'86 Human Factors in Computer Systems* (pp. 78–83). New York: Association for Computing Machinery.

Polson, P. G., Kieras, D. E. Engelbeck, G., and Willer, N. L. (1983). Effects of a mental model on acquisition of operating procedures. A paper read at the Annual Meeting of the Psychonomics Society, San Diego, CA.

Rubinstein, R., and Hersh, H. (1984). *The Human Factor*, Burlington, MA, Digital Press.

Smith, S. L., and Mosier, J. N. (1984). Design guidelines for user-system interface software. Final Report ESD-TR-84-190, Bedford, MA, Miter Corp.

Thorndike, E. L. (1931). *Human Learning*. New York: Appleton-Century-Crofts.

Tulving, E., and Thomson, D. M. (1973). Encoding specificity and retrieval processes in episodic memory. *Psychological Review*, 80, 352–373.

Whiteside, J., Jones, S., Levy, P. S., and Wixon, D. (1985). User performance with command, menu, and iconic interfaces. *Proceedings of the CHI 1985 Conference on Human Factors in Computing*, San Francisco, CA.

Woods, W. A. (1970). Transition network grammars for natural language analysis. *Communications of the ACM*, 13, 591–606.

9 Effect of Practice on Knowledge and Use of Basic Lisp

Jean McKendree and
John R. Anderson

Practice Effects

Cognitive psychology is being called upon to guide designers of computer systems toward more effective interfaces and training methods. Basic research on learning of skills has the potential to influence the direction of these projects and to have an impact on the productivity of old and new users. Research in human-computer interaction has generally concentrated on characterizing various tasks and on the methods available for accomplishing these tasks via the computer. The enticement of the technology often has been the guide to the design and direction of these research projects. Many domains and questions have been addressed, but fundamental issues in theory or application are seldom made clear. The need now is for an explicit modeling of the processes involved in performing the given tasks and in interacting with the chosen interface. Detailed performance models should be able to provide guides for further research and to make predictions about relevant dimensions in man-machine interaction.

Card, Moran, and Newell (1983) assert that the usefulness of psychology to the design of human-computer interfaces "centers on this notion of performance models." They note that such a model must explain the transition from problem solving to cognitive skill that is seen in the progression from novice to expert. The expert has accumulated knowledge that can guide problem solving to the point that the search for possible answers is vastly reduced. They conclude that "examination of the transition... shows that the mechanisms whereby search is reduced are (1) accumulation of control knowledge and (2) the formation of new, large scale operators, which effectively partition the problem space into a reduced problem space and a skill space."

Control knowledge serves to guide decisions so that solutions become more efficient. The learner attempts to find more optimal methods and to use knowledge to constrain the search for possible operators. When enough knowledge and experience are accumulated to define a partial method for a problem, search is effectively eliminated. The newly acquired method, discovered by search guided by control knowledge, becomes part of the skill space of the evolving expert. Card, Moran, and Newell discuss the acquisition of this control structure by one user. This was an expert text editor given a novel task. Over the course of the first 35 trials spent repeating the same task, the user came to use the optimal sequence of operators and became much faster as a result. While this is certainly a factor in the earliest stages of skill acquisition, it largely ignores the concurrent and subsequent speedup due to the second of their hypothesized mechanisms: the formation of larger operators.

Their model of expert users assumes that they have acquired the methods already for accomplishing a task and have reached the minimal time per operator. In other words, the model does an admirable job of predicting expert use of methods and at least addresses the novice's acquisition of these methods through discovery. It does not address the transition from the time of discovering the method to the point when expert performance time is attained. There may be only a small amount of control knowledge to be found in a repeated task. After the "reduced problem space" of methods is acquired, the important component influencing performance for the intermediate-level user becomes the formation of larger operators. The mechanisms that produce and then gradually speed up these operators are the subject of this chapter.

The present study investigates these basic questions about learning through the acquisition of simple programming skills. Programming skill has recently begun to be a subject of research in skill acquisition. It involves a complex interaction of skills, such as problem representation, algorithm design, code generation, and debugging. All of these cognitive tasks should be better understood and integrated in order to assess human-computer interactions and designs more effectively. Many of the studies of programming have looked at aspects of languages or at structures used in programming in an attempt to enhance performance of programmers or to discover expert-novice differences (Adelson, 1981; Gannon, 1976; Green, 1977; Mayer, 1976). However, it has proved notoriously difficult to establish these differences using current experimental methodology (Sheil, 1981). Perhaps an understanding of more basic units from which these skills are produced would aid in focusing on the relevant dimensions in the more complex tasks.

We have set out to investigate the effects of practice on learning beginning with a theoretical framework. One definition of learning is any change in a system that allows it to perform more efficiently and effectively on subsequent repetitions of the same or similar tasks (Simon, 1983). Practice on a task generally results in faster and more accurate performance. Therefore, practice somehow induces learning in the system seemingly without need for conscious effort or awareness on the part of the performer. There have been numerous studies describing phenomena associated with practice, particularly in instructional areas, such as effects of spaced versus massed practice on retention and recall (Gay, 1973; Reynolds and Glaser, 1971; Hintzman, 1974), and effects of practice on performance time (Neisser, Novick, and Lazar, 1963; Winkleman, 1974). Learning theories naturally included the fact that repetition improved memorability, but few suggested any explanatory mechanisms until recently.

One of the most robust effects of practice found has been the reduction in time to perform a task. The decrease in time for performance on a task has been found to follow a power function of the number of times a task has been performed. This equation is of the general form

$$T = AP^{-b},$$

where T is the performance time, P is the number of units of practice, A is a coefficient reflecting the initial speed when $P = 1$, and b determines the rate of speedup. This power law has been found to hold true over a variety of tasks from basically perceptual-motor skills, like the Seibel task (Rosenbloom and Newell, 1982), to complex problem solving skills, like playing solitaire (Newell and Rosenbloom, 1981).

The present study attempted to find empirical support for predictions about practice effects made by the ACT* production system model of learning (Anderson, 1983). This production system model assumes a representation of a problem that is present in working memory during problem solving. This representation is compared to existing knowledge structures that take the form of conditions to be matched in order to carry out an associated action. This type of information processing model of learning and skill acquisition suggests some mechanisms that can predict basic results of previous practice experiments. Specifically, we apply the ACT* model to questions of repetition and the resulting speedup in performance time. The ACT* model indicates that increasing familiarity with a series of procedures speeds performance because of the actor's ability to consolidate a sequence of operations into a single cognitive step. Sequences which previously required meticulous recall during solution of a problem become collapsed into a single cognitive action. This *composition of knowledge* produces a much faster solution time by creating efficient operators for handling particular problems.

An example from basic algebra will illustrate the process of composition. Given the task of solving $3x + 4 = 10$, the learner might have productions like these:

IF the goal is to solve an equation of the form
    ax + b = c
THEN subtract b from both sides
    AND solve ax = d.

IF the goal is to solve an equation of the form
    ax = d
THEN divide both sides by a.

The solver will work through the steps serially, producing the intermediate step $3x = 6$, which will then be used in the next step. There may be other steps, such as performing the subtraction of $10 - 4 = 6$, particularly when the student is first learning the skills of math. After solving the problem successfully, the learner can eventually eliminate the explicit steps and can form a new, composed production like

IF the goal is to solve an equation of the form
    ax + b = c
THEN subtract b from both sides
    AND divide by a.

A second example involving generation of simple Lisp functions will show this process in the domain of the current study. If the learner were given the task of returning the second element in a list, he might start out with a set of productions like the following:

IF the goal is to find the second element of a list
THEN eliminate the first element
    AND return the first element of the new list.

IF the goal is to eliminate the first element of a list
THEN apply the function CDR to the list.

IF the goal is to return the first element of a list
THEN apply the function CAR to the list.

Having figured out the initial algorithm (by whatever means), the system applies the productions serially, setting the new subgoals and explicitly recalling the separate Lisp functions for achieving them. Having solved the problem, the system can eliminate the explicit steps and will eventually form a composed production. This new production might look like

IF the goal is to find the second element of a list
THEN apply the function CDR
AND apply the function CAR.

In these examples, the subgoals have been subsumed in the top-level goal and the actions can be performed without the explicit recall necessary before composition took place. This will allow the correct actions to be executed more quickly and with fewer memory requirements.

A second process interacts with the composition of operators to enhance speedup. This process, called *proceduralization,* involves incorporating factual knowledge into productions. This serves to apply knowledge directly that previously had to be recalled explicitly into working memory and then applied interpretively. This is apparent in math when the student can recall the answer to addition facts without having actually to perform the addition operations. In Lisp, this occurs when a person no longer has to recall or read the definition of a function in order to apply it. Instead, the actions associated with applying the function are executed automatically when the goal is set and the production conditions are matched by the current problem representation. These two mechanisms, composition and proceduralization, produce a speedup with practice particularly in the initial stages of learning. At later stages, the speedup will continue at a gradually lessening rate as working memory capacity increases with strengthening of accumulated knowledge.

The third process that serves to govern the rate of speedup in this model is *strengthening of productions* when they are used. As production strength increases for the newly built productions, they will be able to be applied more consistently and more rapidly. This process, in fact, turns out to be the limiting factor for rate of speedup of performance (see Anderson, 1982, for a more detailed discussion).

This combination of learning processes predicts that while subjects should speed up on all tasks involving the components of a skill, they should speed up most rapidly on the tasks faced most frequently. Each task involves a specific sequence of mental operations. As these operations are practiced they will become faster due to strengthening. However, the specific combinations of operations that are practiced repeatedly will be composed into larger operators and will gain an extra boost in speed. Therefore, frequency of specific combinations is going to have an impact on performance time and accuracy, in addition to the general effect of practice.

In order to test these predictions empirically, the task environment must create a number of conditions. First, the task must be complex enough to require extended practice before reaching its asymptote in order to assure that effects will be observable. Second, the task should contain discrete components that can be placed in combinations requiring sequences of several steps. This will allow observation of the effect of repeating sequences of steps in contrast to applying individual ones. This may reveal the process by which individual steps in various combinations become collapsed with practice. Finally, the task must be composed of sufficient components to allow variation in frequency as well as combination. The combinations seen frequently can be directly compared to the ones seen infrequently since they will be built of the same basic components placed in different relations.

This paper presents a study that systematically tested the learning of a skill in a limited domain. The domain used in this study was the evaluation of basic Lisp functions seen alone and in combinations. The Lisp domain is complex enough to require a reasonable amount of practice to reach a level of proficiency at evaluation. Also, there is sufficient structure to restrict the number of possible responses and to allow an analysis of the steps used in formulating an answer. Because larger functions are easily built out of basic ones, they provide a means of evaluating effects of combinations independent of individual step differences.

By requiring subjects to evaluate Lisp functions seen with varying frequencies over a period of several days, the quantitative effects of practice on this domain can be studied. The frequent and infrequent combinations built of identical components allow an investigation into the mechanisms behind the proposed composition of operators. The processes suggested by the ACT* production system model of learning predict that high-frequency problems should have shorter solution times and higher accuracy than low-frequency problems. By testing these sorts of predictive theories, cognitive psychology can begin to build models that can guide design and evaluation of interfaces and interactive systems.

1 Method

1.1 Subjects

Subjects were 20 Carnegie-Mellon undergraduates with no previous experience with Lisp. They were given one class credit and $15.00 plus bonuses. These bonuses were given for points awarded on the basis of both speed and accuracy.

1.2 Procedure

The subjects reported to the experiment for four consecutive days. On the first day, they were given a brief introduction to four basic Lisp functions. Since one of the four functions in Lisp has a mnemonic name but the other three do not, we chose to change the three so that all four had mnemonic names. Two of the functions, FIRST and REST, return part of a list. FIRST returns the first element in a list and REST returns the list without the first element. (These functions are called CAR and CDR, respectively, in Lisp.) These will be referred to as *extract functions.* The other two, INSERT and LIST, (corresponding to CONS and LIST in Lisp) join elements. These will be called *combine functions.* INSERT puts an element given as its first argument into the beginning of the list given as its second argument. For example, (INSERT (a) (b c)) would return ((a) b c) as its answer. LIST makes a new list out of the two arguments. Thus, (LIST a (b c)) would give (a (b c)) as the answer.

The instructions also explained that the experiment would contain combinations of two and three of the basic functions. After reading this, the subjects went through 10 practice trials with the experimenter. These trials contained one problem with each of the basic four functions alone and six problems involving pairs of functions. No triple combinations were included in the practice trials.

The trials were presented on a terminal via a DEC system PDP 11/34 computer. The problems were given and the subjects were required to type in the answer. There was no time limit on the trials and subjects were given immediate feedback about the correctness of their answers. If the answer was incorrect, the correct answer was shown and the subject could study it as long as desired. The subject received 30 points at the beginning of each trial. For every 1/2 second that passed, 1 point was subtracted until the "Return" key was pressed or until no points remained. Thus, the subject could receive no less than 0 points for a correct answer. Forty points were subtracted for a wrong answer. At the end of four days, the points were totaled and the subjects were given a bonus of $1.00 for every 500 points.

There were several measurements collected on each trial. Every keystroke was timestamped by the computer and these times were recorded. The total number of keystrokes was also recorded along with a subject's answer and the correctness of the answer. After the first and last sessions, subjects were given a transfer task that involved generating functions similar to those they had practiced evaluating. They were given the variables and the answer that the function should yield and were instructed to write a function to give the desired answer. The nature of the stimulus materials for the main task and the transfer task is explained in greater detail and with examples in the next section.

1.3 Materials

The trials consisted of four possible single functions and various pair and triple combinations. There were 150 trials each day for four days. The subject saw the function to be evaluated along with its arguments on the screen and had to type in the answer. A typical problem involving one of the four basic functions FIRST, REST, INSERT, or LIST would look like

(FIRST v1)

v1: (h d s)

The subject should apply the function, retrieve the first element in the list, and type in h.

Pairs were constructed by embedding one function within another. When the embedding function was a *combine function* like INSERT, the embedded function was placed as the first argument. For instance, a typical pair problem would be

(INSERT (FIRST v1) v2)

v1: (x w)
v2: (y z)

Applying FIRST would give x and INSERTing it into (y z) would give the answer (x y z). By crossing the four possible embedding functions with the four possible embedded functions, there are 16 possible pairs. However, some possible pairs were eliminated because applying these pairs results in performing a step and then undoing it. For example, (FIRST (INSERT V1 V2)) would involve inserting V1 into V2 and then extracting V1 again to return it as the answer. These *extract-combine* functions were eliminated, leaving 12 pairs.

The basic functions, FIRST, REST, INSERT, and LIST, were all seen by themselves an equal number of times. Pairs of functions were seen either *frequently* or *infrequently*. For instance, the FIRST-REST combination might be seen frequently, while the REST-FIRST pair would be infrequently presented. Half of the subjects saw one set of functions frequently and half saw the opposite pairs frequently.

The triples involved taking an embedded pair and embedding it within a third function. An example triple is

(LIST (INSERT (FIRST v1) v2) v3)

Such a function can be seen as being composed of two pairs; in the example given, FIRST is embedded in INSERT and INSERT is embedded in LIST. The triples were presented with frequencies that preserved the relative frequency of the pairs. That is, if LIST-INSERT were a high-frequency pair and INSERT-LIST were low-frequency, the triples including the first pair would be seen more often. The triples can be categorized into four types based on the frequency of their constituent pairs. These were both pairs high frequency, just the first high, just the second high, or both low frequency. For example, a high-low frequency triple would be constructed by taking a high-frequency pair, like FIRST-REST, and combining it with a low-frequency pair such as REST-REST. The triple constructed would be

(FIRST(REST(REST v1)))

The four basic functions can be combined into four different sequences of triples. These are *extract-extract-extract*, *combine-extract-extract*, *combine-combine-extract*, and *combine-combine-combine* functions. Within each of these four types, there are eight triples: two made of high-frequency pairs, two made of low-frequency pairs, and four made of one high- and one low-frequency pair. This results in 32 triples.

As with the pairs, the first argument of any *combine* function in a triple was more complex than the second argument. For example, a typical one of these problems was

(LIST (LIST (FIRST v1) v2) v3)

v1: (d (g n))
v2: v
v3: (b)

The subject should apply the FIRST function to get the d from the first argument. Then this, LISTed with the second argument, gives (d v) and finally, LISTing this with the last argument, the (b), gives the final answer. The subject should type ((d v) (b)).

A complete list of the functions to be evaluated is given in table 9.1

Table 9.1
Lisp functions and frequencies

FIRST	16	INSERT-FIRST-FIRST	9
REST	16	INSERT-FIRST-REST	3
INSERT	16	INSERT-REST-REST	3
LIST	16	INSERT-REST-FIRST	1
FIRST-FIRST	12	LIST-REST-REST	9
FIRST-REST	4	LIST-FIRST-FIRST	3
REST-REST	12	LIST-REST-FIRST	3
REST-FIRST	4	LIST-FIRST-REST	1
INSERT-FIRST	12	INSERT-LIST-REST	9
INSERT-REST	4	INSERT-LIST-FIRST	3
LIST-REST	12	INSERT-INSERT-FIRST	3
LIST-FIRST	4	INSERT-INSERT-REST	1
INSERT-LIST	12	LIST-INSERT-FIRST	9
INSERT-INSERT	4	LIST-INSERT-REST	3
LIST-INSERT	12	LIST-LIST-FIRST	3
LIST-LIST	4	LIST-LIST-REST	1
FIRST-FIRST-FIRST	9	INSERT-LIST-INSERT	9
FIRST-FIRST-REST	3	INSERT-INSERT-LIST	3
FIRST-REST-REST	3	INSERT-LIST-LIST	3
FIRST-REST-FIRST	1	INSERT-INSERT-INSERT	1
REST-REST-REST	9	LIST-INSERT-LIST	9
REST-FIRST-FIRST	3	LIST-INSERT-INSERT	3
REST-REST-FIRST	3	LIST-LIST-INSERT	3
REST-FIRST-REST	1	LIST-LIST-LIST	1
		Random	12
Total			300

along with the frequencies of each seen over two days by one group. The second group had the same stimuli, but with reversed frequencies for the pairs and corresponding changes for the triples. Note that although the frequencies of combinations varied, the numbers of times that each of the basic functions was used are equal.

Each subject solved 150 problems per day. It took two days (300 trials) to complete the set of problems in table 9.1. In these 300 trials, subjects solved problems involving 64 basic functions, 96 pairs of functions, and 128 triples. In addition, they saw 12 "random" function combinations. These were combinations of two or three functions that were not repeated. Each of these combinations was seen only once during the entire experiment. The major difference with these combinations was that the complex argument occurred in the second position. For example, one of these problems would have looked like

(LIST v1 (FIRST v2))

v1: b
v2: (n x)

The subject should have responded with (b n). These functions were included as a baseline to determine the speedup pattern for combinations of functions that were not repeated at all. Also, these functions prevented subjects from making the overgeneralization that complex arguments in Lisp always occurred in the first position. Each subject saw the 300 trials in random order. The arguments had been randomly generated for each problem so that no two problems were identical, but each subject within a group saw the same set of problems and arguments.

The subjects were given a transfer task after the first and fourth days of evaluation problems. The transfer task involved generation of simple functions given the arguments and the desired answer. An example problem was

v1: (l s)
v2: k

answer: (l k)

The subject should have written (LIST (FIRST v1) v2). There were 16 of these problems on each of the two days: 4 requiring only one of the basic functions and 12 requiring generation of one of the pairs of functions.

2 Results and Discussion

The two groups of subjects differed in terms of the combinations seen for high- versus low-frequency conditions. Since the individual functions were seen equally often in each group and there were the same types of combinations, no differences were expected between the groups. In fact, there were no significant differences between two groups seeing the counterbalanced combinations. The number of keystrokes ($F(1,19) = .41$, $p < .53$), the time to first keystroke ($F(1,19) = .04$, $p < .85$), the time to final keystrokes ($F(1,19) = .13$, $p < .73$), and the error rate ($F(1,19) = .32$, $p < .62$) all failed to indicate a difference between the groups.

The total time spent on the task decreased each day, reflecting the general nature of the power law. This time was found by summing the solution times for all 150 trials each day. The total time for the first day was 3534 seconds, or 58.9 minutes, and by the last day was 1716 seconds, or 28.6 minutes. The equation fitted to the time across the four days is

$$\mathrm{TT(sec)} = e^{8.16}P^{-.55} = 3498P^{-.55}, \tag{1}$$

which gives the total time in seconds to evaluate all 150 problems in a session. The exponent −.55 is similar to the one found for the geometry proof justification task studied by Neves and Anderson (1981). This indicates a faster rate of learning than found on simpler tasks, such as the Siebel task used by Rosenbloom and Newell to study chunking of operators.

The analysis of the power law speedup by Anderson (1982) would predict this difference in rate of speedup between simple versus complex tasks. According to that analysis, speedup in performing a complex task like Lisp evaluation is produced by a combination of strengthening of individual productions and collapsing of multiple productions into a single one. Thus, the −.55 exponent found in this experiment reflects both collapsing and strengthening of productions used. In contrast, performance of a simple task speeds up primarily because of the strengthening process alone. These simple tasks would not involve complex sequences of productions that could be collapsed in the compilation process.

The "random" functions can be used to indicate the effect of general speedup. These combinations are also built from the basic functions, but each is seen only once over the course of the experiment. The final times for these functions are included in table 9.2. These combinations are solved more quickly with practice, indicating a general effect of practice. The

Table 9.2
Summary of final times in seconds for function types by frequency

	Day			
Function type	1	2	3	4
BASIC	11.50	7.72	5.42	5.07
Pairs				
HIGH FREQUENCY	17.86	12.63	9.57	9.35
LOW FREQUENCY	18.42	12.98	11.00	10.75
Triples				
HIGH FREQUENCY	24.63	18.68	14.06	14.18
LOW FREQUENCY	24.79	20.62	15.07	15.71
RANDOM	21.28	20.32	16.33	17.07

rate of the speedup is not as great for these functions as for the other combinations seen repeatedly; the decrease is from 21.3 sec to 17.1 sec, a 19.7% decrease, over four days, compared to a decrease from 24.8 sec to 15.3 sec or 38.3% for the low-frequency triple combinations.

The speedup for the combinations should be affected both by the general practice and also by the differing frequencies with which they were seen. This is a reflection of the combined effects of strengthening and collapsing of productions.

2.1 Frequency of Combinations

Combining basic functions into pairs and triples allows frequency of combinations to vary while keeping the frequency of the components equal. This allows a separation of effects due to collapsing of productions from effects due to strengthening of productions. Any advantage of the high-frequency combinations would be a reflection of the collapsing of production steps.

A repeated measures ANOVA on total solution time for high- versus low-frequency combinations across the four days indicated that the overall frequency effect is significant for both pairs ($F(1,16) = 9.78$, $p < .006$) and triples ($F(1,19) = 11.26$, $p < .003$). The times for the low-frequency triples were found by collapsing the intermediate- and low-frequency triples and comparing these composite scores to the high-frequency triples. The frequency effect, when broken down into the various types of combinations for post hoc comparisons, is in the predicted direction but is not significant for the *combine-extract* pairs ($F(1,16) = .01$, $p < .91$). The frequency effect is significant for both the *extract-extract* pairs ($F(1,16) = 4.75$, $p < .04$) and the *combine-combine* pairs ($F(1,16) = 21.38$, $p < .0003$). For the triples, the *extract-extract-extract* combination ($F(3,57) = 4.32$, $p < .008$), the *combine-combine-extract* combination ($F(3,57) = 11.53$, $p < .0001$), and the *combine-combine-combine* combination ($F(3,57) = 4.15$, $p < .01$) all showed a significant frequency effect on total solution time. Again, the times for the *combine-extract-extract* triples were in the predicted direction, but the effect was not significant. A summary of the solution times for high- and low-frequency combinations is shown in table 9.2.

The number of keystrokes does decrease from the first to the last day ($F(3,57) = 8.71$, $p < .0001$) and is different between high- and low-frequency combinations ($F(1,19) = 48.62$, $p < .0001$). However, the number of keystrokes is greater for the high-frequency functions, which would tend to decrease the frequency effect. This difference in keystrokes is significant only across correct trials; the number of keystrokes did not differ significantly if all trials were used. Correct trials only were used in the analysis. It is possible that that the greater number of keystrokes is a result of the subject's realizing more often that an answer to a high-frequency problem was wrong initially and hitting the "Delete" key several times to correct the answer. This would increase the number of keystrokes somewhat without influencing the time as much as would normal typing of keys. However, it was not possible to extract this information from the original data.

The frequency effect holds also for the error rates across high- and low-frequency combinations for both pairs ($F(1,19) = 7.17, p < .01$) and triples ($F(1,19) = 7.86, p < .01$). By the last day, the subjects are getting 87.7% of the high-frequency pairs correct and 80.8% of the low-frequency pairs. They are correct on 78.1% of the high-frequency triples and on 72.5% of the low-frequency triples on the last day. As the subjects are exposed to the frequent problems, they not only become faster over the days, but more accurate than they are on the less frequent function combinations.

2.2 Error Data

A more qualitative analysis of the types of errors was done for the basic and paired functions. This yielded 473 errors on the first day and 211 on the fourth day. These were categorized into error types, and the results are summarized in table 9.3.

Anderson and Jeffries (1983) have modeled novice Lisp errors in terms of undetected working memory failures. As functions increase in complexity, it appears that subjects lose partial results when applying functions. Some errors can be detected by "critics" if the result is not a sensible Lisp answer, but the errors are often overlooked if they produce a potentially legitimate form. The errors that are filtered in a manner consistent with the "repair theory" of Brown and VanLehn (1980) are fairly low-level errors, such as unbalanced parentheses or the use of an element that was not present in the problem statement. Even subjects with no Lisp experience were able to detect 75–80% of these types of errors in a study by Anderson and Jeffries. It is consistent with these observations that very few of the errors found in our study were due to these ill-formed expressions. Only 9.2% of the errors analyzed were due to unbalanced parentheses on the first day. This went up to 14.1% on the last day primarily because of the overall

Table 9.3
Percentage and types of errors on basic and paired functions on the first and last days

	Day 1 (n = 473)	Day 4 (n = 211)
BASIC		
Overall error rate	22.5	11.5
		Extract
Parentheses added	2.1	3.0
Parentheses dropped	3.5	1.5
Misapplication	5.6	7.9
		Combine
APPENDed elements	9.2	7.8
INSERT-LIST confusion	2.8	3.2
Parentheses added	1.4	0.0
Parentheses dropped	.7	1.5
Unbalanced parentheses	1.4	3.2
Typographical errors	3.5	6.2
PAIRS		
		High frequency
Overall error rate	36.7	12.3
APPENDed elements	9.2	7.8
INSERT-LIST confusion	7.0	6.3
Parentheses dropped—REST	11.3	6.2
—other	1.4	0.0
Parentheses added	4.9	4.7
Unbalanced parentheses	5.7	4.7
Misapplied extract function	4.2	4.7
Typographical errors	6.3	7.9
		Low frequency
Overall error rate	39.5	19.2
APPENDed elements	7.0	3.2
INSERT-LIST confusion	1.4	3.2
Parentheses added	1.4	0.0
Parentheses dropped—REST	4.2	4.7
—other	0.0	1.5
Unbalanced parentheses	1.4	4.7
Misapplied extract function	2.3	4.7
Typographical errors	2.1	1.5

decrease in other types of errors. None of the errors involved the use of elements not found in the problem statement.

Most of the errors were of a more conceptual nature. These errors primarily reflected a misapplication of a function or the use of an incorrect argument in a function. This type of error became more frequent as the complexity of the problem increased from a single, basic function to a combination of two; also more errors were being made on infrequently seen functions.

Overall error rates on the basic functions were 22.5% for the first day, dropping to 11.5% by the last day. The most common error on both days was a specific misapplication of INSERT or LIST. The subjects treated both these functions like the Lisp function APPEND (which they had not learned). Subjects exhibiting this error would simply create a list of all the individual elements in the arguments. For instance, given the problem

(INSERT (LIST v1 v2) v3)

v1: a
v2: (b)
v3: (c)

the subject would produce (a b c). This error accounted for 25.4% of all errors on the first day and 18.8% of all errors on the fourth day. The classic confusion in Lisp between INSERT and LIST was apparent in 11.2% of errors on the first day and 12.7% of those on the last day. It appears that the subjects have not formed a clear picture of what the *combine* functions do. They often simplify application of INSERT or LIST into a single, incorrect action. Error rates on INSERT were 35% for the first day and 14% on the fourth day; for LIST, 26% on the first day and 18% on the fourth day. These rates were for the problems where these functions were seen alone.

The *extract* functions seemed to be confused less often by the subjects. Overall error rates on these were for FIRST, 15% on day 1, dropping to 5% on day 4, and for REST were 14% on day 1 and 9% on day 4. Of the errors made, the most common on single *extract* equations was returning the last element for REST instead of all but the first element. Given a problem like

(REST v1)

v1: (r j v z)

a subject showing this error would answer z. This accounted for 3.5% of the errors made on the first day and 4.7% on the last.

However, when REST is included in a problem with a pair of functions, the error pattern changes. The most common error becomes dropping the outer pair of parentheses from the part of the answer produced by REST before applying the second function. For example, given

```
(INSERT (REST v1) v2)

v1: (a (b c))
v2: (d)
```

the subject would answer ((b c)d) rather than (((b c))d). This error accounts for 15.7% of all errors made on the pair problems, but only for 2.1% of errors on REST seen alone. By the last day, these error rates are 10.9% for the pairs and 1.5% of errors on REST seen alone. This indicates that the subjects knew the proper application of the function, but as the complexity of the evaluation task increased and partial results had to be retained in memory, features began to be lost. Since the resulting answers are syntactically correct Lisp expressions, the errors are less likely to be caught than if the same features were missing for a simpler function evaluation. The embedding of inside elements is not a predictable feature of the problems and therefore is not as easily proceduralized during practice.

2.3 Transfer Task

Subjects were given a transfer task in which they were to write the functions to produce a desired answer. All the problems involved basic functions or pairs that they had seen in the evaluation task immediately before. This transfer task provided indications of the scope of the learning acquired in the first task. Performance on the transfer task showed practically no improvement from the first day to the last day. On the first day, 29.3% of the problems had errors versus 26.6% on the fourth day. A third of the errors each time were due to a confusion between the functions INSERT and LIST, a classic difficulty for Lisp novices. A summary of the types of errors on both days is shown in table 9.4. In contrast to the relative lack of change in the error rates for the generation task, error rates on the evaluation of single and paired functions began at 34% errors on the first day and dropped to 15% by the fourth day. The ACT* model again would predict that practice effects should be very specific to the current task. The transfer task, though involving the same abstract knowledge as the

Table 9.4
Summary of errors made on transfer task requiring function generation

	Percentage of errors	
Type of error	Day 1	Day 4
INSERT/LIST confusion	33.9	23.5
Reversed order of application	14.6	17.6
Missing extract function	14.6	21.6
Extra extract function	4.8	5.9
Missing combine function	15.6	15.6
Extra combine function		
LIST	8.7	11.7
INSERT	1.0	0.0
Miscellaneous	6.8	3.8
Overall error rate	29.3	26.6

evaluation task, is clearly not the same task for the subjects. Though they understand quite well how to evaluate the functions by the fourth day, subjects are not better able to generate simple functions than they were on the first day.

2.4 Mathematical Model

The observed solution times for evaluation of basic Lisp functions and combinations showed systematic changes with practice over days and over varying frequencies. We then attempted to characterize these changes using a mathematical model based on predictions made from a theory of skill acquisition. The ACT* model would predict a general component of practice due to production strengthening and a specific component due to the frequency of particular combinations affecting the collapsing of production steps. We felt that the effects of these two processes would have different mathematical forms. As argued in Anderson (1982), the speedup due to strengthening should take the form of a power function. Thus, assume that there is a processing time associated with each function that will decrease according to a power function. In contrast, the speedup due to production composition should conform to an exponential function. That is, we assume that on each trial there is a constant probability, p, that a composition will occur, resulting in a procedure requiring a fraction, c, of the previous time needed to perform the operations. Thus, the expected proportional improvement with each trial is $p(1 - c)$. The expected time after f trials is

$$RT = (1 - p(1 - c))^f T, \tag{2}$$

where T is the time on the first trial. On setting

$$d = (1 - p(1 - c))$$

the equation becomes

$$RT = d^f T. \tag{3}$$

In addition to the mental time associated with function evaluation, there will be some time associated with each keystroke in the final answer. The average number of keystrokes for each problem type was found and multiplied by the time per keystroke parameter in the model.

The total time to evaluate a function will be a physical time involving number of keystrokes and a mental time reflecting speedup due to composition and strengthening:

$$RT = \text{physical} + \text{mental}.$$

The physical time will be the product of the number, n, of keystrokes and the time per keystroke, k. The mental time will be the product of the number of mental operations, N, and the time per operator, K. This gives this equation

$$RT = nk + NK. \tag{4}$$

The subjects' typing speed will decrease with the number of units of practice, u. This decrease will take the form of a power function with exponent of speedup a. In addition, the number of mental operations will go down with the frequency, f, of a particular combination. We assume that each time a combination is repeated, the expected number of steps goes down by the fraction c. The time per operation is a power function of units of general practice, u. Thus, the form of the equation we chose to fit becomes

$$RT = nku^{-a} + c^f(mu^{-b}). \tag{5}$$

We took the units of general practice, u, to be days and the frequency of a particular function or combination to be the number of times it had been seen by the end of each day. In the equation, b is the exponent of general speedup due to practice on the Lisp task, and m is the sum of the setup times for each basic function making up the combination.

The STEPIT program (Chandler, 1965) was used to find the best-fitting values for the parameters. These values were found to be

Parameter	Value
Cost per keystroke, k (sec)	1.39
Exponent of speedup on typing, a	−.28
Setup times for basic functions (sec)	
FIRST	3.59
REST	2.66
INSERT	2.87
LIST	3.70
Proportion of reduction due to forming a composition	.019
Exponent of speedup on Lisp, b	−.25

The correlation of the observed to the predicted values in this model is .96. The chi-square measure computed between the model and the data was $X^2(379) = 183.1$.

The values for the setup times for the four basic functions are very similar, as are the exponents of speedup for typing and for the Lisp evaluation. Therefore, we refigured the model by collapsing these separate parameters. The equation becomes

$$\begin{aligned} \mathrm{RT} &= nku^{-b} + c^f(mu^{-b}) \\ &= (nk + mc^f)u^{-b}. \end{aligned} \tag{6}$$

The loss in accuracy of the fit was minimal; the X^2 measure increased from 183.1 to 198.2. The correlation coefficient was .95. This simplification is a reasonable approximation of the previous equation. The values found using only these four parameters were

Parameter	Value
General exponent of speed-up, b	−.26
Cost/keystroke, k (sec)	1.42
Cost/function, m (sec)	3.16
Proportion reduction due to forming a composition	.020

A comparison of the data and the model is shown in figure 9.1.

The value of cost per keystroke, 1.42 seconds, seems rather large if this measure were simply an indication of typing speed. This is the value for the first day, but on applying the exponent of speedup for typing, this value

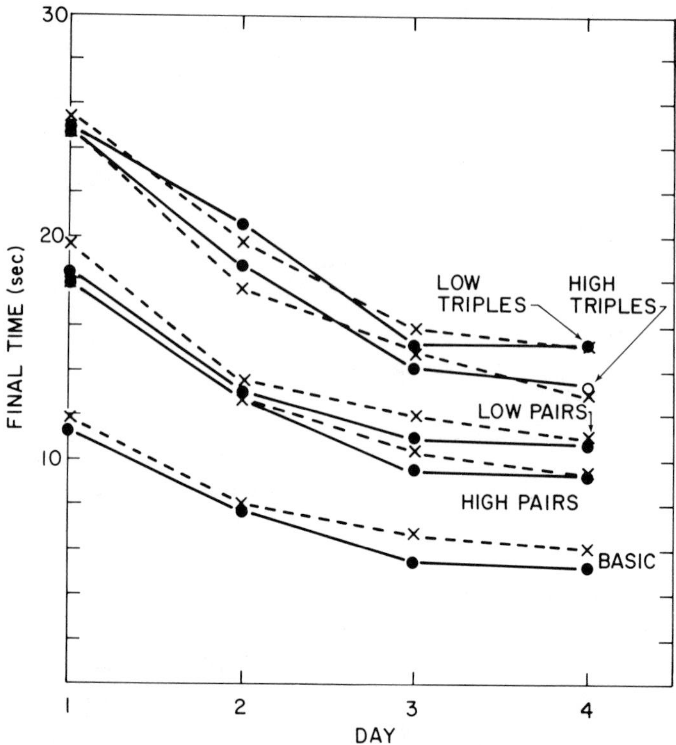

Figure 9.1
Observed and predicted final times for high and low combinations: solid line (with ●), observed; dashed line (with ×), predicted.

becomes .99 seconds by the last day. This parameter is being influenced by the time to encode information to be typed and to prepare a motor plan, indicated by the fact that the actual typing episodes occurred in bursts with interkeystroke times of much less than .99 seconds. Card, Moran, and Newell (1983) found average values of between .5 and .75 seconds per keystroke for practiced subjects typing random letters. The task in the current study involves reproducing parts of random letter strings, so the value calculated by our model for the fourth day is consistent with their results.

The speedup in mental time has components due to composition and due to strengthening. The composition component involves a time reduction of .02 each time the function combination is repeated. While this number seems small, the cumulative effect can be quite large. For instance, high-frequency pairs are practiced 4*6 = 24 times over the four days.

This means that they are reduced to $.98^{24} = .616$ of their original time. In contrast, the speedup from the first day to the last day due to strengthening is $4^{-.26} = .70$. Thus, in some cases, the speedup due to composition to specific problems can exceed the speedup due to general practice.

3 Summary

Systematic effects of frequency of practice were found for the task of evaluating simple Lisp problems. These problems were composed of the same basic four functions, but combinations of them were seen with varying frequency. The difference in number of presentations of analogous pairs was not great, 24 versus 8 times, and yet there are differences found in performance time measures and in error patterns. These differences carry over at least to some extent to the combining of pairs to make triples.

The general and specific practice effects were fitted well by a mathematical model based on the predictions of the ACT* theory of skill acquisition. This model indicated that the composition of operators is very problem specific and can account for differences in performance on problems that seem very similar on the surface.

These results lend empirical support to the theoretical speculations about the knowledge level to which compilation processes apply. The steps of the procedures appear to be encoded in productions at a very specific level at the beginning. Practice mechanisms then act to combine these steps into productions involving more information and action as the skill becomes mastered. Our results also indicate that the combining of operator sequences is indeed a process underlying a part of the speeding up of performance time consistently found with practice. This action of collapsing production steps combines with the general practice effect of strengthening existing productions. These processes combine to produce the speedup in performance that has been documented and described for many skills, but that is not well understood in terms of the mechanisms producing it.

We frankly were surprised how well the simple mathematical model did in fitting a complex pattern of data from many different conditions. That model assumed that

1. Evaluation in all cases involves a serial set of basic operations.
2. Each operation speeds up at a fixed rate independent of context.
3. Sets of operators collapse into single operators, producing an additional benefit.

The fact that this model fitted the complex pattern found in the data is strong evidence for the general conception of skill acquisition we have advanced. These theories can then be applied to the problems of complex skill learning involved in human-computer interaction domains.

The model we presented deals with the transition from complete novice to relatively expert performance. We have offered empirical evidence for the ACT* theory of skill acquisition, which has subsequently been used to model acquisition of text editing skills (Singley and Anderson, 1985) and to guide the design of intelligent tutoring systems for Lisp and geometry (Anderson et al., 1984; Anderson, Boyle, and Yost, 1985). We feel, as do Card, Moran, and Newell, that detailed performance models such as these are useful for supporting and verifying general theories of skill acquisition and cognition (Anderson, 1985) and that these types of theories will be essential in building a general theory of interface design.

References

Anderson, J. R. (1983). Acquisition of cognitive skill, *Psychological Review*, 89, 369–406.

Anderson, J. R. (1983). *The Architecture of Cognition*, Cambridge, MA, Harvard University Press.

Anderson, J. R. (1985). Skill acquisition: Compilation of weak-method problem solutions. CMU Technical Report.

Anderson, J. R., and Jeffries, R. (1983). Novice LISP Errors: Undetected losses of information from working memory, CMU Technical Report.

Anderson, J. R., Boyle, C. F., and Yost, G. (1985). The Geometry Tutor. *Proceedings of IJCAI*, Los Angeles, CA.

Anderson, J. R., Boyle, C. F., Farrell, R., and Reiser, B. J. (1984). Cognitive principles in the design of computer tutors, CMU Technical Report.

Atkinson, R. C., and Juola, J. F. (1973). Factors influencing speed and accuracy of word recognition. In S. Kornblum (Ed.), *Attention and Performance IV*, New York, Academic Press.

Brown, J. S., and VanLehn, K. (1980). Repair theory: A generative theory of bugs in procedural skills. *Cognitive Science*, 4, 379–426.

Card, S. K., Moran, T. P., and Newell, A. (1983). *The Psychology of Human-Computer Interaction*, Hillsdale, NJ, Lawrence Erlbaum Associates.

Chandler, J. P. (1965). STEPIT Modelling Program. Quantam Chemistry Program Exchange, Indiana University Chemistry Dept., Bloomington, IN.

Gannon, J. D. (1976). An experiment for the evaluation of language features. *International Journal of Man-Machine Studies*, 8, 61–73.

Gay, I. R. (1973). Temporal position of reviews and its effect on the retention of mathematical rules. *Journal of Educational Psychology*, 64, 171–182.

Green, T. R. G. (1977). Conditional program statements and their comprehensibility to professional programmers. *Journal of Occupational Psychology*, 50, 93–109.

Hayes-Roth, F., Waterman, D. A., and Lenat, D. B. (1983). *Building Expert Systems*, Reading, MA, Addison-Wesley.

Hintzman, D. L. (1974). Theoretical implications of the spacing effect. In R. L. Solso (Ed.), *Theories in Cognitive Psychology: The Loyola Symposium*, Hillsdale, NJ, Lawrence Erlbaum Associates.

Mayer, R. E. (1976). Comprehension as affected by the structure of problem representation. *Memory and Cognition*, 4, 249–255.

Michalski, R. S., Carbonell, J. G., and Mitchell, T. M. (1983). *Machine Learning: An Artificial Intelligence Approach*, Palo Alto, CA, Tioga Publishing Co.

Neisser, U., Novick, R., and Lazar, R. (1963). Searching for ten targets simultaneously. *Perceptual and Motor Skills*, 17, 955–961.

Neves, D. M., and Anderson, J. R. (1981). Knowledge compilation: Mechanisms for the automatization of cognitive skills. In J. R. Anderson (Ed.), *Cognitive Skills and Their Acquisition*, Hillsdale, NJ, Erlbaum.

Newell, A., and Rosenbloom, P. R. (1981). Mechanisms of skill acquisition and the law of practice. In J. R. Anderson (Ed.), *Cognitive Skills and Their Acquisition*, Hillsdale, NJ, Erlbaum.

Reynolds, J. H., and Glaser, R. (1971). Effects of repetition and spaced practice upon retention of a complex learning task. In M. D. Glock (Ed.), *Guiding Learning*, New York: John Wiley.

Rosenbloom, P. R., and Newell, A. (1982). Learning by chunking: a production system model of practice. Technical Report No. 82–135, Department of Computer Science, Carnegie-Mellon University.

Schneiderman, B. (1980). *Software Psychology*, Cambridge, MA, Winthrop.

Sheil, B. A. (1981). The psychological study of programming. *Computing Surveys*, 13, 101–120.

Simon, H. (1983). Why should machines learn?, In R. Michalski, J. Carbonell, and T. Mitchell (Eds.), *Machine Learning*, Palo Alto, CA, Tioga Publishing Co.

Singley, K., and Anderson, J. R. (1985). The transfer of text-editing skill. *International Journal of Man-Machine Studies*, 22, 403–423.

Winkleman, J. H. (1974). The repetition effect in mental arithmetic. PhD dissertation, University of Oregon.

10

Cognitive Analysis of People's Use of Software

Judith Reitman Olson

This chapter studies the mental activities involved in computer-supported tasks. Because using computers to aid complex tasks is an interesting domain in which to study cognition and because there are practical benefits in developing easy-to-use and easy-to-learn software, there is an increasing interest in studying human-computer interaction.

Tools for the study of human-computer interaction are of two general types, experimental laboratory methods that externalize as much of the mental behavior as possible and analytical methods based on representations of the system's functioning and the user's underlying mental processes. Both tools are important. Analytical methods synthesize disparate results into a unifying theory and allow a basis for prediction in new situations; experimental methods produce data for tests of these theories and new behaviors for theories to explain. On a more practical side, theories provide bases for design decisions in the absence of specific data; behavioral data give concrete tests of the efficacy of a new or existing system.

A recent review by the National Research Council's Committee on Human Factors collects, defines, and compares the current laboratory methods in human-computer interaction (Anderson and Olson, 1985). This chapter reviews the second type of tool, analytical methods. These methods are those that are based on theories of the interaction, including how computer systems work; how computer users perceive, remember, plan and act; and how humans' cognitive strengths and limitations affect their behavior with the system.

Two audiences, researchers and practitioners, can benefit from this review. Researchers who have selected the domain of human-computer interaction to study complex problem solving because of its richness, specifiability, and modifiability need a way to represent the person's external and internal activities before they can say how certain mental processes and capacities interact. For example, it is hard to say how perceptual processes interact with the contents of short-term memory without an explicit representation of the moment-by-moment use of each in a particular problem. Practitioners who design and evaluate software need to know how to make software easier to use and easier to learn. It would help to have a concrete representation of the moment-by-moment involvement of the user's cognitive capacities, such as knowing how many things need to be learned and retrieved reliably from long-term memory when one learns a piece of software that is similar to one already known, or how hard it is to perceive information on a screen full of similar, closely spaced information.

Thus, the goal in this chapter is to review, critique, and synthesize various concrete, explicit representations of human-computer interaction. In brief, it appears that such representations in the literature to date are *fragments* of the representation sought. They represent one aspect of the user-system loop, and/or they represent human cognitive limits. What we seek here is either a merged representation or a set of representations that can serve both researcher and practitioner.

1 General Aspects of the Problem

There are three aspects of the interaction of users and computers to be reviewed here. They are conceptually different and may each require a different representation for analysis.

- The behavior of the *computer system*. Of concern here are the requirements of the *task* to be performed and the characteristics of the computer *software system*, how it responds to actions of the user.
- The person's *processing*. What does the person need to retrieve (e.g., appropriate goals and subgoals)? How does a person choose actions and act? This is a representation of the ongoing mental and motor activity of the person interacting with the software.
- The person's *cognitive capacity, the strengths and limitations* in processing information. For example, humans have perceptual and learning strengths and short- and long-term memory limits.

2 Levels of Analysis

In this review we consider two general levels of analysis of human-computer interaction. At the most global level, people need help in accomplishing certain global tasks because of their cognitive limits. People design and purchase computer systems to help them remember facts, calculate, and do repetitive chores. Having a clear representation of the computer system, the users' goals and processes, and cognitive strengths and limits helps analysts design and purchase effective systems.

At the more local level, people interact with computer systems to accomplish certain specific tasks, such as performing "what if" analysis on financial spreadsheets, organizing thoughts for a paper or presentation, etc. Having a clear representation of the computer system, the task to be performed, and the person's problem solving processes and cognitive capacities allows the designer of software to design an easy-to-use product and allows the researcher more carefully to witness cognitive processing in real-world problem solving tasks.

Stated more colloquially, this paper will review and integrate representations of the cognitive processing that occurs when people use computers at two levels:

- at the global task level, where we are concerned with the system's *functionality*—what it can do to help the user,
- at the local task level, where we are concerned with the system's *usability*—how easy it is to learn and use.

3 Cognitive Capacities

In all the representations reviewed, the goal is to assess them for their ability to allow clear indication of how the system affects major cognitive strengths and limitations of the users, or, for the researcher, how clearly they illuminate the functioning of the users' cognitive components. What cognitive components are we looking for and what are their limitations and particular powers?

In brief, people have severe limits as to memory, accurate calculating, and patience. They have strengths in visual scanning, integration of patterns in time and space, and learning highly integrated, complex material.

More specifically, the major cognitive characteristics of concern to this review are listed below, a list whose core is similar to that of Fitts (1951) in an early review of man-machine interaction (reported in Price, 1985). Strengths are indicated with a +, limitations with a −.

Perception	+ Perceiving parallel inputs, being able to process visual information rapidly and to coordinate multiple sources of information.
	+ Perceiving patterns with fuzzy information in them, tolerating error.
	— Perceiving small differences in detailed information.
Short-Term Memory	— Holding recently experienced information temporarily until needed (e.g., remembering a value to be entered in a particular cell in a spreadsheet). The capacity of short-term memory is limited and items are easily lost after the passage of time and interference from subsequent events.
	— Holding information retrieved from long-term memory, such as keeping track of one's place in the execution of a plan. This capacity is limited, and may be shared with the storage of temporary new information. It is vulnerable to loss from time and interference.
Long-Term Memory	+ Making inferences about concepts or rules from sets of similar but not identical past experiences. Inducing rules from experience. Abstracting regularities in time and space.
	+ Storing common patterns efficiently. Patterns such as frequently used action sequences or frequently seen patterns are stored as "chunks."
	+ Retrieving relevant information quickly.
	— Discriminating small differences in experiences. Because we are tolerant of errors, the storage of information in long-term memory is not always veridical. We confuse similar items, and have difficulty permanently learning fine distinctions.
	— Acquiring information in long-term memory rapidly.
	— Being patient with repetition.

Two major summaries of human limits and capacities relevant to human-computer interaction exist in the literature. A short (75-page) summary of human processing limitations and capabilities appears as a chapter in Card,

Moran, and Newell (1983); a lengthier (150 pages) review of capacities appears as an introduction in of Bailey (1982). The summary in Card, Moran, and Newell is specific, with good examples of how certain limits and capacities are reflected in specific task/system design considerations. Unfortunately, most of their subsequent work considers only the timing characteristics of performance on computer systems, not the errors or learning times. They do not make use of the perceptual, short- and long-term memory capabilities listed above, bur rather consider only the *time* to retrieve, to perceive, or to move. The Bailey review is much more comprehensive, but less well tied to the specifies needed for a particular design or theoretical questions. The attempt here is to include the full range of human cognition, and review representations of human problem solving behavior and computer responses, noting how these cognitive characteristics are affected by features of computer interfaces.

Cognitive strengths and limitations guide both a person's choice of tools in accomplishing a task (the global analysis) and the person's timing and errors in performing the steps of the task (the local analysis). Both levels are reviewed in the following sections.

4 Cognitive Analysis of Global Tasks

Most of the work on global human-computer interaction comes from the domain of office analysis. The study of office work, and more recently the study of how to design computer systems to meet people's information processing needs, includes representations of work and classification of the types of human capabilities that are required in this work. Early studies focused on measuring such things as job satisfaction and productivity. More recently, however, studies have focused on the more practical end of designing or purchasing computer-based systems to increase office efficiency, in terms of either fewer people to hire or quicker processing of information. Most often, researchers stop after they have displayed the aspects of what happens in an office; few of these displays are analyzed for their fit to users' cognitive strengths and weaknesses.

4.1 Representations of the Task and Computer System

There are two aspects of the environment that are of concern to us: the task that must be accomplished and the system that supports the task. Office analysis begins with a representation of what information is being processed where. Essentially, office analysis maps the steps in which information enters, gets changed, and leaves part of a company, such as a department (e.g., the marketing department), or follows a function through its various interdepartmental steps (e.g., payroll processing).

The basis of office analysis, the *task*, then, is the pictorial or verbal representation of the information that goes through an office and the transformations that take place of that information at each step. Since the goal of the analysis is the design or purchase of a system or a reorganization of the work, there are no representations of the *system* itself. The desired outcome of analysis is a description of a proposed system's requirements.

There are three major types of representations of the environment in office analysis:

- Verbal Description,
- Office Specification Language,
- Flow Diagrams.

In all, descriptions can be made at a variety of levels of specificity, from broad stroke flow of task components (e.g., the payroll record sheet goes from the employees for input to the supervisor for approval to payroll for record keeping and payment initiation), to specific, detailed tasks (e.g., accessing the personnel payroll record, judging the acceptability of vacation time taken, entering the new days worked, printing a record, storing IRS data, etc.). Regardless of level, however, the description consists of what information resides where, and what happens to it at each step.

For the Office Analysis Methodology from Waterloo (Conrath et al., 1981), particular emphasis is placed on separating the activities in which information is *communicated* from those that change or *process* the information. For each step in *communication* of the information, note is made of the information's *content*, whether the communication asks or answers, gives or receives, or persuades or negotiates. The *source* of the communication and its *destination* are recorded as well as the *medium* of transfer. *Processing* includes reading-listening-observing, interpreting, completing forms, searching-retrieving, and coding-classifying. The final description of the office and its activities is a verbal narrative of the above listed features. This method has been useful for uncovering interesting aspects of office communication patterns. However, because it does not classify activities in terms of the processing required of humans or computers, it is not well suited to the purpose of studying human problem solving with computers or the design or selection of a new computer system to support work.

MIT's Office Analysis Methodology (OAM) similarly describes the

Work Order Issuing
Work Order Desk

Initiation: Request for maintenance work arrives.

Work Order Clerk

D-1.	Codes the request as requiring a printed work order or a standing work order.
D-2.	Transfers data describing the work requested to the work order from the request.
D-3.	(If it's an informal request slip) Destroys the request slip.
D-4.	Files the Work Order Desk copy of the work order in the active work order file.

Termination: Work order clerk sends the shop copies of the work order, invoking either the printed work order task group or the standing work order task group. [Other descriptions like this for different procedures.]

Figure 10.1
Example of an Outlined Verbal Description of a task from the Task Analysis Methodology office analysis procedure (from Sasso, 1985).

information at each workstation in an office (Sirbu et al., 1983). The description of the activities, however, is much more specific, being coded in what is called the "Office Specification Language" (OSL). This language is a record of specific aspects of the work: specification of the *mission* of the office, the set of *functions* as an aggregation of *procedures,* each of which has *events, steps,* and initiating or terminating *states.* It describes the *objects* being transformed and the *resources* managed by the office. The representation of the office is either a description in OSL or a narrative based on the details of the OSL.

The specification of the work in an office in this rigorous fashion makes the resultant description much more complete and uniform across offices. However, since the processes themselves are not classified into which would be difficult or easy for people to do, it leaves the identification of which stations are good candidates for support/automation to the judgment of the office analyst. The method is not well suited for our purposes.

A more recent addition to the set of office analysis procedures is the Task Analysis Methodology from the University of Michigan (Sasso, 1985; Sasso, Olson, and Merten, 1985). Like the earlier analyses, there are specific characteristics of the work processes and location that are recorded. Like the MIT OAM, the steps, objects, and initiating and terminating states or conditions are noted. What sets the Michigan approach apart, however, is that 26 types of processes are to be noted, processes such as *selecting, sorting, distribution,* and *retrieval.* These specific processes are amenable to analysis for their fit to human strengths and limitations.

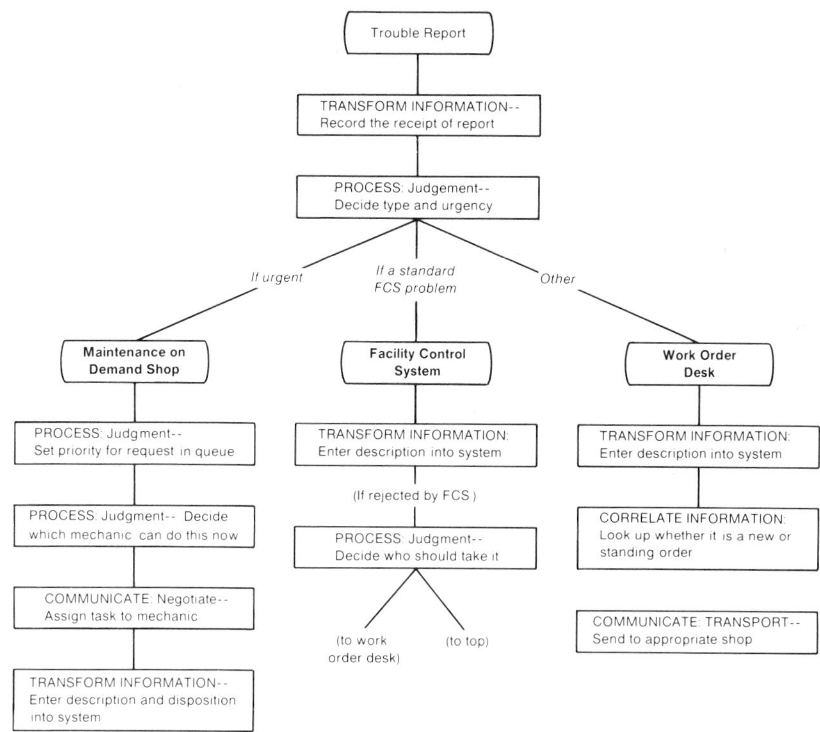

Figure 10.2
Flow Diagram of office activities for maintenance function (adapted from Sasso, 1985).

A second advance of the Michigan methodology is the form of the final description of the office activities. There are two forms of description, an Outlined Verbal Description (see figure 10.1), and a Flow Diagram of the major activities (see figure 10.2). Though the first is necessary in order to show the detail of the actual activities, and could lead to requirements for the design of a particular piece of software support, it is the second, the Flow Diagram, that is particularly appealing to the global analysis of human-computer interaction. A Flow Diagram can serve as the basis for indicating which stages should be supported/automated according to what we know about human strengths and limits.

4.2 Representing the Fit of Systems to Cognitive Strengths and Weaknesses

The second major aspect of office analysis involves an examination of the office description, leading to suggestions of which steps can be automated and supported by a computer system or reorganized for efficiency. This analysis should be guided by consideration of the human worker's cognitive strengths and limits; we should look for areas in which to support or replace the work on the basis of what the user finds cognitively tedious or difficult.

Several existing schemes for classifying descriptions for what should be automated seem to correspond to human strengths and weaknesses. The historical precedent for this kind of analysis comes from Machlup (1962) in his analysis of the nation's knowledge producing labor force. Machlup's categories of information processing include

Transport	Move information from one physical location to the next.
Transform	Change the medium in which the information is held, e.g., entering information via a keyboard entry.
Process	Change format but not content, e.g., as in filling out a standard form.
Interpret	Create new format, adding information intended by the originator.
Analyze	Add enough original information as to leave little of the original message.
Create	Generate information.

These categories are purposely ordered to reflect what Machlup considered to be increasingly intellectual endeavors. Those at the bottom of the list could be viewed as activities that are better suited for human processing. At the top of the list, the tasks are better suited for computer support or complete automation.

Other annotation schemes exist that reflect our knowledge of human processing strengths and weaknesses. Lieberman, Selig, and Walsh (1983) extend Machlup's categories by adding more computer-based aspects. They include information storage, retrieval, and disposal. The most explicit categorization of office tasks in terms of human information processing comes from Komatsubara and Yokomizo (1982). They suggest annotating tasks for their demands on perceptual discrimination (as in sorting), use of short-term memory (such as in doing simple arithmetic), simple judgments, logical thinking, imaginative thinking, and delicate complex movements. Though Komatsubara and Yokomizo's research goals were to correlate office procedures with worker satisfaction, the scheme could be used in office analysis for automation and support.

A recent taxonomy of office work specifically addresses the users' cognitive strengths and weaknesses and has the goal of suggesting support and automation for the office. Helander (1985) associates major office interaction types (focusing on transactions, documents, telephone, and face-to-face tasks), human attributes (perceptual motor skills, rule-based decision making, analysis and problem solving, and social skills), office tasks (inputting or transcribing, . . . , persuading or negotiating), and current office automation tools (optical character recognizers, . . . , expert systems).

Helander's scheme focuses on the following cognitive capacities:

Perceptual Motor Skills	For tasks that input or transcribe information, perform transaction accounting (logging), filing, and retrieving.
Rule-Based Decision Making	For tasks including planning and scheduling, evaluating and controlling, and informing and reporting.
Analysis and Problem Solving	For tasks that include researching and creating, and deciding and authorizing.
Social Skills	For supervising, counseling, persuading, and negotiating.

Both Helander's scheme and that of Komatsubara and Yokomizo emphasize the human capabilities involved, ignoring those aspects of information transformation for which the computer is especially well adapted. The scheme below merges these views with that of Machlup to cover both human and computer information processing activities and to guide allocation of task to each.

Communicate: Transport Information

The movement of information from one physical location to the next.

Transform Information

Change information storage medium.

Process: Algorithmic Decision Making

Sort information according to prespecified, stable rules.

Process: Judgment-Based Decision Making

Sort information according to multiple, complexly related dimensions.

Correlate Information
Retrieve information from several sources and merge aspects of each into a new record.

Analyze Information Look for patterns in retrieved information.

Communicate: Negotiate
Persuade, decide, teach, learn.

Create Information Organize, synthesize, add new information.

Those steps that require transportation, transformation, simple but accurate retrieval, algorithmic decision making, or merging are allocated to computer support or automation because they require actions that are difficult, inaccurate, or tedious for the human. Those that require recognition of patterns, appropriate multiattribute retrieval, judgmental decision making, learning, or creation of information are to be allocated to human processing because they capitalize on human strengths.

4.3 An Example of a Global Representation and Annotation

The above review suggests that office analysis should be based on a representation of the office in a Flow Diagram or Outlined Verbal Description, as in Sasso, examined for efficiency to suggest reorganization, and annotated with how the information transformation at each stage involves human cognitive capabilities and limits, as synthesized above. This method can serve as a basis for both the practical goal of designing new software/hardware support and for the theoretical goal of analyzing the interplay of cognitive processes in real-world problem solving in the office.

To illustrate the represention of the information flow and the assignment of processes to either human or computer, we take an example from the work on office analysis from Sasso (1985). The office illustrated is part of the maintenance process at a company. The request for maintenance, depending on whether it is urgent or not and whether it is specifically under the control of the Facilities Control System or not, is dispatched to the appropriate site or maintenance person. A part of the Outlined Verbal Description for this task is illustrated in figure 10.1. Figure 10.2 shows a higher-level Flow Diagram of the information flow in this task. Both are appropriate representations of the task, each showing a different level of detail.

After a representation is constructed, the next step is to search the representation for potential inefficiencies. In this office, for example, information about a report of trouble is transformed in four different places.

Furthermore, a rough decision is made early whether the Facilities Control System (FCS) can fix the problem, after which the FCS itself either accepts or rejects the problem description. An additional efficiency could be made if this duplication could be eliminated. Figure 10.3 shows the more efficient reorganization of these tasks.

The next stage of analysis annotates each task with whether the computer or human should do the processing. Figure 10.4 annotates the work flow representation with those steps that can be computerized and those that the human must do. In this example, decisions about how urgent a problem is requires judgment or expertise. Decisions about priorities similarly require human judgment. Dispatching mechanics to particular repair areas and problems also requires human judgment and negotiating skills. Entering information into the FCS, however, may be automatable (with optical character recognizers) or require only a clerk to enter information via a keyboard. All other processes, involving logging both timing information and characteristics of problems, locations and skills of mechanics, determination of whether the work orders are "standing" or "new," and the shipping of information to appropriate locations is supportable with computer hardware and software.

Thus, by finding an appropriate representation of the work flow in an office, annotating it with the kinds of processing done to the information, and matching with it what we know about human strengths and weaknesses (particularly the limits in memory, accuracy in calculating, and patience with tedium), we can analyze a complex information processing system and recommend practical alterations.

The kind of analysis gives the practitioner a firm, theoretical basis for looking for potentially profitable reorganizations of work and suggestions for the kinds of computer support that may be helpful. The output of this process leads well into traditional systems analysis and design procedure for doing cost/benefit analyses and feasibility studies and subsequent design requirements. The major advantage of this process is that it helps the analyst *generate ideas* about how to make offices more efficient and is based on theory of human strengths and weaknesses.

What are the benefits to the researcher? Annotated representations of information flow and processing are based on theoretical strengths and limitations of human problem solving. With this scheme, one can make predictions about behavior, such as the efficiency of processing or the kinds of software that will be purchased, that are experimentally verifiable. That is, if a system is built that, for example, makes decisions that seemed to be simply algorithmic and find that the flow of work in the office is disrupted instead of increased, one must examine more carefully the functions that

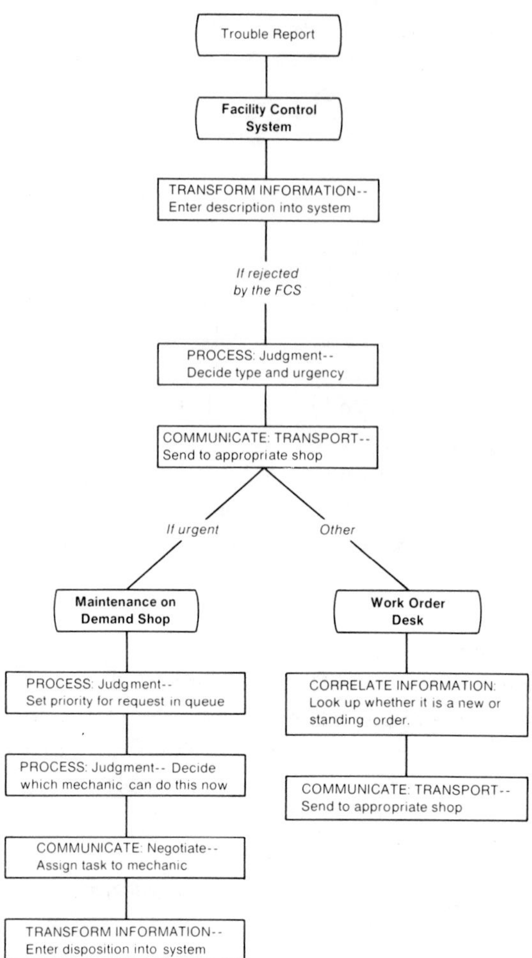

Figure 10.3
Reorganized Flow Diagram for maintenance function.

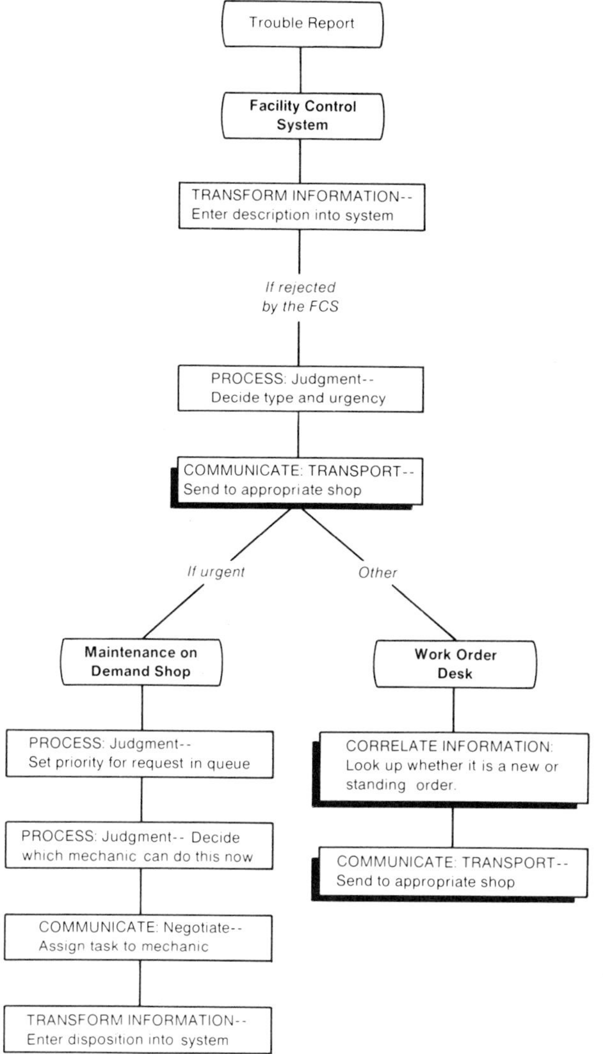

Figure 10.4
Annotated Flow Diagram with processes suitable for automation noted in shadowed boxes.

were performed earlier by the human processor and learn what other cognitive aspects were functioning that are now missing in the computer supported environment.

For example, because I send all my word processing from a home keyboard to the central computing printer, and send mail via networks across the country, my secretary no longer knows what I am doing or generally where I am. When she answers the phone, she has nothing stored in long-term memory that will help her answer the caller's request about where I might be reached. A task representation that indicates that the secretary merely enters keystrokes (transforms the medium) when typing a manuscript is inadequate. The secretary apparently also stores timing events of my activity and some knowledge about what I do. By doing office analysis and predicting certain behaviors, the researcher understands better the multiplicity of cognitive capacities that are involved in real-world information processing tasks.

5 Cognitive Analysis of Local Tasks

The analysis of specific task performance in human-computer dialogs has come a long way from the days when the major design prescription stated merely, "Know the user." A number of specific representations of the system and the user have emerged in the last five years. For our purposes, the goal of having good representations of the system and the user's behavior is to be able to identify where in an interaction human cognitive strengths and limits are affected. In what follows, we review major representations of the user's task on a particular system and the cognitive processing required to accomplish a goal, then assess each for its ability to indicate the involvement of cognitive strengths and limitations of perception and short- and long-term memory.

5.1 Representations of the Tasks and the Computer System

The task to be accomplished and the interface requirements of the software system have been represented in two major formats:

- Formal Grammars (e.g., Reisner, 1981, 1984; Moran, 1981),
- Generalized Transition Networks (Kieras and Polson, 1983, 1985),

As used in this domain, formal grammars consist of collection of "rewrite rules" that specify all the possible legal commands to the computer system. They are hierarchical representations of the major components required in the commands and of the alternative ways each component can be specified. This scheme allows a large number of legal strings (sentences in the grammar) to be represented compactly. It is a representation that indicates well both the major parts of a command (parts connected by a +) and the options the user has in choosing a method to use (parts separated by a | to indicate an option).

For example, to delete a certain block of text (using a command called **Dn**), one system's task requirements are specified with the following rewrite rules:[1]

Use Dn	——> **Identify** first line + **enter** Dn command + **press** ENTER
Identify first line	——> **Get** first line on screen + **Move** cursor to first line
Get first line on screen	——> use "**Locate**" **strategy** | use **scroll strategy**
"Locate" strategy	——> **Move** cursor to command input field + **type** "locate" command + **press** ENTER
Move cursor to command input field	——> use cursor keys | **press** PFCURSOR | null
Type "locate" command	——> **Type** "locate" keyword + **type** line number
Type "locate" keyword	——> L+O+C | L | L+O+C+A+T+E
Type line number	——> type number.

A pictorial representation of the relationship between these rewrite rules is shown in figure 10.5.

Moran's Command Language Grammar (CLG) is like a formal grammar in that it hierarchically decomposes the user's task on a particular system into its parts. The CLG additionally includes a description of the levels of this representation: At the highest level, focus is on the user's major intent, called the Task level; the lower levels, Semantic and Syntactic levels, focus more on the objects and actions involved to accomplish the task (Moran, 1981). At each level, careful specification is made of

- the *objects* that are being changed (e.g., specifying the object's name, what its constituents are, and a definition of its purpose),
- the *methods* that are used, collections of individual operations or acts that perform an integrated task (e.g., to get information in a message system, the user starts the system, the system shows the directory, the user looks

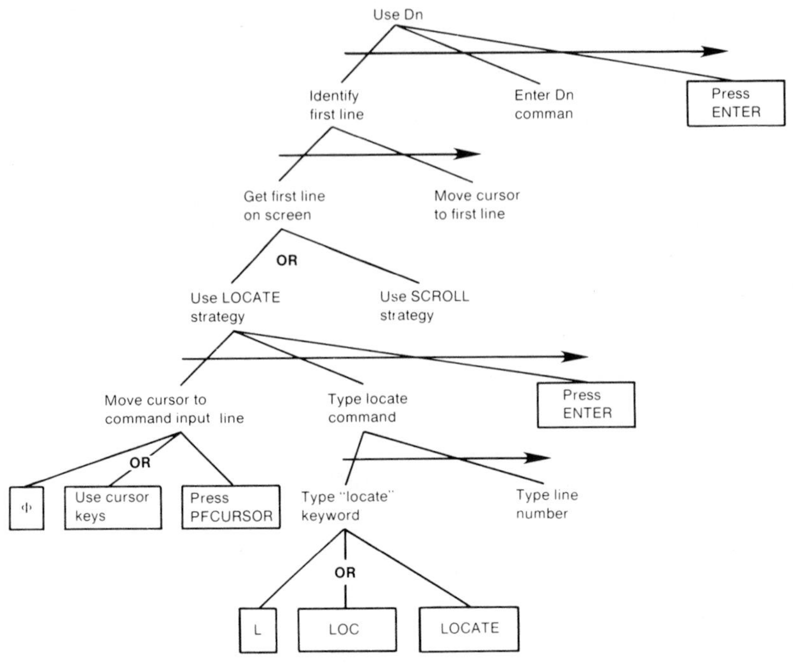

Figure 10.5
A pictorial view of the relationship between the rewrite rules for specifying a portion of the **Dn** command in a formal grammar. Arrows indicate a sequence of components; an "or" indicates a choice between alternative actions; and rectangles indicate external actions.

at the directory for a message, the user reads the message, and the user deletes the message and stops the system),

- the elementary *operations* that make up a method (e.g., "to show" means to display an object in a particular location of the screen).

Both of these representations concretely and specifically represent the actions that the user must take in order to accomplish a certain goal in this particular system. Once represented, these actions acn be analyzed for their ease of use and completeness. Both representations are oriented toward the tasks the user is trying to accomplish.

A very different representation of what the system is and what it does is displayed in a Generalized Transition Network (GTN) (Kieras and Polson, 1983, 1985). The GTN is an augmented recursive transition network that shows the system's possible states (e.g., what is presented on the screen), the possible actions the user can take in that state (e.g., commands that can be entered or menu items selected), and a connection to the next state that the system will be in as a result of that action. An

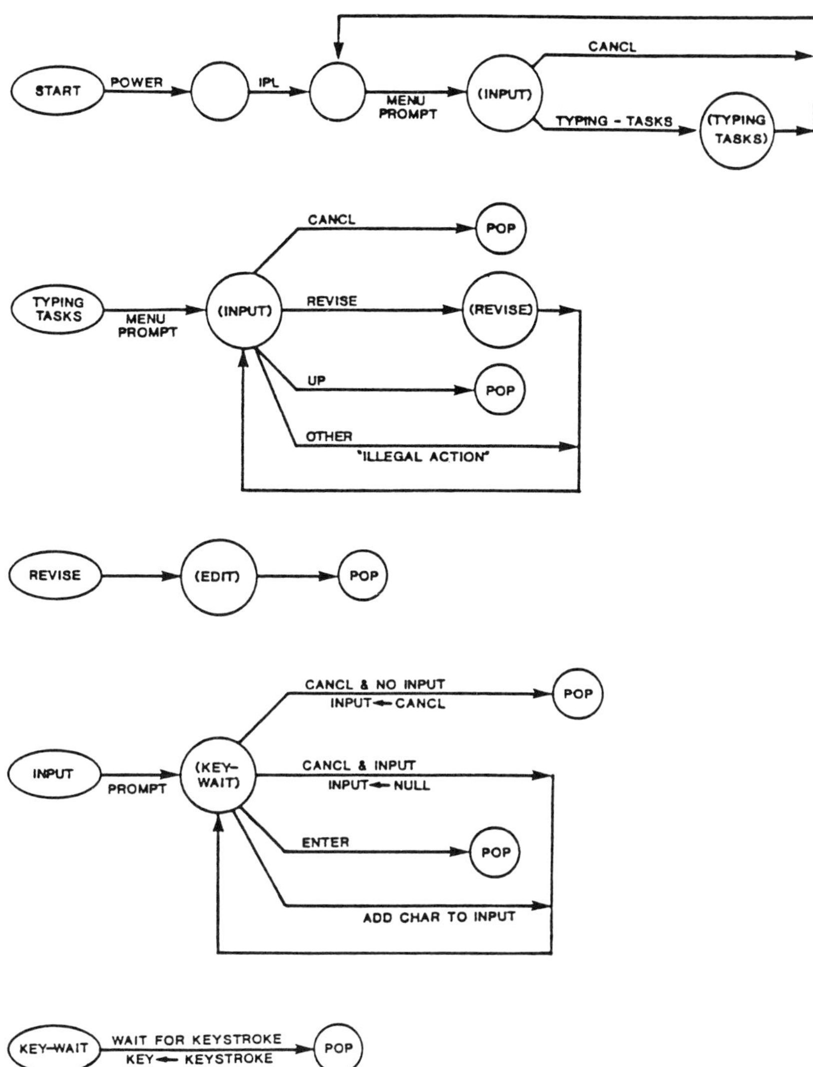

Figure 10.6
An example of a Generalized Transition Network representation. The portion shown specifies the steps one goes through in signing on to a system (from Kieras and Polson, 1983).

example of a GTN is shown in figure 10.6. It represents the beginning stages of signing onto a computer system and entering a text editor program. Each oval or circle is a state of the system annotated with a simple label of the general task being accomplished. The action the user takes is indicated on the top of the arc, the system's reaction (such as a particular menu or a prompt appearing on the screen) on the bottom of the arc connecting the nodes. Each state that has its label enclosed in parentheses indicates that that state is annotated at a more detailed level elsewhere. Thus, in Figure 10.6, "typing task," "input," "key-wait," and "revise" are annotated in other networks in the figure (see Kieras and Polson, 1983, for more details).

The representation in GTN notation has many of the characteristics of the command grammars of Reisner and Moran. The nested or recursive nature of the GTN is similar to the relationship between higher-level to lower-level rewrite rules, methods, or operations in formal grammars. Sequencing of operations and states is represented by arcs in the GTN, "+" in formal grammars, and the programminglike ordering of operators in the methods specified in the CLG.

The GTN, however, does not represent objects being manipulated or the options a user has to accomplish a goal, as represented in the choices separated by a "|" in formal grammars and the alternative methods in CLG. The lack of a specification of the alternative methods prevents an analyst from examining aspects of the user's decision making in choosing one method over another to accomplish a goal (based on certain characteristics of the current situation). Only the CLG specifies the *conditions* under which certain methods are to be chosen.

Formal grammars, on the other hand, do not represent what the user sees on the screen at each moment, what the clues are for choosing the next action. And there is no specification of the "mode" the system is in, the global context indicating that a whole new set of actions is appropriate. This feature is important for assessing a system's load on the user's perception and memory abilities.

The GTN representation has the advantage that it is a very visual representation, amenable to the analyst being able to sight complexities in the software (e.g., cases where no prompt is presented on the screen for successive required actions). The CLG and formal grammar representations, on the other hand, better specify the goal nature of the task being accomplished, amenable to the assessment of the user's use of long- and short-term memory. More of this will be discussed in the section on assessing how well each of these representations shows an impact on the user's cognitive strengths and limits.[2]

5.2 Representations of the Processing Involved

Specific models of the human interaction with the computer all bear a strong family resemblance. They are predicated on the notion that the user systematically moves toward a specified goal or goals[3] by recalling those actions that fill a goal, choosing one of these action sequences, and executing it (Newell and Simon, 1972). Most of the current representations of the user in human-computer interaction adopt this view, including that of Norman in chapter 12 of this volume.

Three related but slightly different pictures of the processing details have emerged:

- the GOMS model (Card, Moran, and Newell, 1983) and the related Keystroke Model (Card, Moran, and Newell, 1980a,b),
- Production Systems (Kieras and Polson, 1985),
- Goal Structure graphs (Kieras and Polson, 1985).

The GOMS model divides the user's knowledge into (1) Goals, (2) Selection rules, (3) Methods, and (4) Operators. The lowest-level motor and mental actions are called Operators; Methods are combinations of the primitive operators, sequences of activities that accomplish a goal or subgoal; Selection rules govern the choice of a method given certain conditions of the current problem; and Goals and subgoals are the achievements these actions are intended to accomplish. Given a task to accomplish, the user constructs highest-level goals. Goals are divided into subgoals, which trigger selection of methods and activation of operators. Each act or sequence of acts fills a subgoal and often changes the environment (in this case, the computer system), which in turn triggers the next cycle. Important to this processing are two memories: the collection of goal-to-subgoal mappings, selection rules, and action sequences stored in long-term memory; and the existence of a "goal stack," much like a short-term memory, a set of temporary memory locations where goals and subgoals are kept until satisfied.

The representation of this knowledge in the GOMS model representation is illustrated below. In this example, the Goals and Methods are accessed to accomplish the task of editing a marked manuscript. For the sake of brevity, specific Methods and Operators are not included here. A full representation further specifies rules for Selecting each of the Methods when there is a choice.

```
GOAL: EDIT-MANUSCRIPT
        GOAL: EDIT-UNIT-TASK          repeat until no more tasks
                GOAL: ACQUIRE-UNIT-TASK
                        GET-NEXT-PAGE   if at end of page
                        GET-NEXT-TASK
                GOAL: EXECUTE-UNIT-TASK
                        GOAL: LOCATE LINE
                        [select: QS-METHOD
                                 LF-METHOD]
                        GOAL:   MODIFY-TEXT
                        [select: S-COMMAND
                                 M-COMMAND]
                                 VERIFY EDIT
```

This representation is specific enough to allow prediction of the details of users' behavior in accomplishing specific tasks. The Keystroke Model in particular assigns a time to each of the mental and motor actions above, predicting the total time it will take a user to perform a task on a particular system.

Kieras and Polson (1985) have built production system models of people using computer systems, with the explicit purpose of predicting users' learning and performance times and errors. The knowledge in these production systems consists of representations that embody the details of the GOMS model and its variants, specified in an computer executable language, such as LISP. The user's knowledge about how to use a system is represented in a production system, in a collection of IF-THEN rules. At each moment, the environment is examined, the best fitting IF condition is selected, and the associated THEN action is executed. A key feature of these production systems is a "goal stack" or "working memory" in which the system temporarily holds goals, subgoals, and intermediate values necessary for the conduct of the task. The environment that is examined so that is can be matched with the best-fitting production consists of the current input from the external environment and the contents of the working memory. The actions generated by the production are of two kinds: external actions such as keystrokes, and internal actions, such as putting a new subgoal on the goal stack or deleting one that was just satisfied.

The following is an example of part of a production system representation of the highest-level goals of performing text editing on a manuscript:

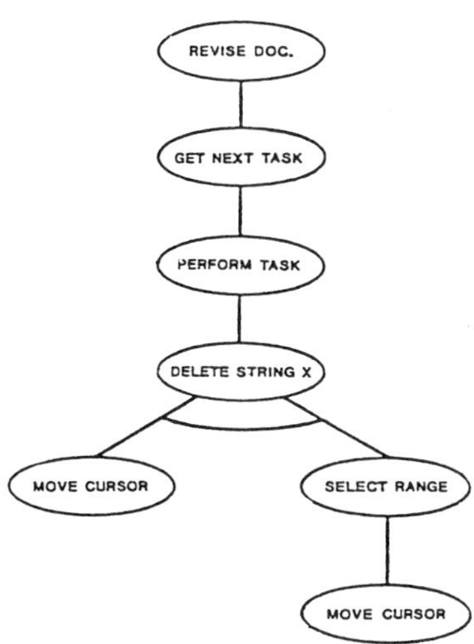

Figure 10.7
A Goal Structure graph representation of the relationships between goals and their subgoals. The portion shown involves deleting a string from a text document.

```
(SETUP-UNIT-TASK
IF (AND    (TEST-GOAL EDIT MANUSCRIPT)
           (NOT (TEST-GOAL PERFORM UNIT TASK)))

THEN ((GET-NEXT-UNIT-TASK)
          (ADD-GOAL PERFORM UNIT TASK)))

FINISHED-WITH-EDIT
IF        (AND      (TEST-GOAL EDIT MANUSCRIPT)
                    (TEST-NOTE NO MORE TASKS))

THEN      ((DELETE-GOAL EDIT MANUSCRIPT)
          (DELETE-GOAL PERFORM UNIT TASK)
          (DELETE-NOTE NO MORE TASKS)
          (PRINT-MSG '"I AM FINISHED EDITING THE
          MANUSCRIPT")
          (STOP-NOW)))
```

A more pictorial representation of goals and subgoals in a production system is shown in what is called a Goal Structure graph, for which see figure 10.7. This representation shows the highest-level Goals and Methods of a problem. If it incorporated the Selection rules and Operators used, it would look very similar to the pictorial representation of formal grammars of the type shown in figure 10.5.

Table 10.1
Five representations of the user or the system show different aspects of the cognition involved in using the system (each cell includes how the analyst would measure that aspect in that representation)

	Perception	STM	LTM
Formal Grammars		Sentence length (?)	Number of rules Number of terminal symbols Standard measure of complexity
GTN	Format of information on screen	Number of unprompted states	Number of unprompted states
GOMS		Number of items on the goal stack	
Production Systems		Contents of working memory: average, peak, duration of contents	Number of rules Similarity among and between rules
Goal Structure		Number of subgoals in working memory	

6 Representations of the Fit of Systems to Cognitive Strengths and Limits

All of the above representations of the system and the user were generated with the goal of predicting which aspects of the interface will affect users' performance. Most focus on the system's overall difficulty, in terms of the long-term memory load in learning all the rewrite or production rules. Several have explicitly discussed the load on short-term memory, in terms of keeping track of subgoals in the "goal stack" or working memory. Only one represents perceptual aspects, in representing some of the information that is presented on the screen. Below we review how well the above representations serve as bases for analyzing human strengths and limitations in human-computer interaction. Then we review three additional representations of a specific aspect of the difficulty of interacting with computers—users' initial *translations* of their goals into terms and actions that the computer understands.

Table 10.1 shows in general which representations of the system and the users' processing display which human strengths and limits.

6.1 Long-term Memory

Formal grammars and production systems include straightforward indications of the load on long-term memory: The number of rewrite rules or the number of productions represents individual things the user needs to know in order to interact successfully with the computer system. The more rules or productions, the longer the system should take to learn. Formal grammars may also indicate load on long-term memory in terms of the number of terminal symbols that must be learned. The number of terminal symbols indicates how many different individual actions must be learned, regardless of how they are combined in the service of goals. In addition, formal grammars allow the computation of standard measures of sentence complexity as combined measures of difficulty of processing (Reisner, 1984).

Formal grammars and production systems additionally allow one to assess whether after learning one system, the learning of a second would be easy or difficult. Indeed, Kieras and Polson (1985) have used production systems successfully to predict the transfer in training from one task to another. Examination of production rules could also reveal the similarity among rules within a system, allowing predictions of confusions like those found in paired-associate learning when stimuli or responses are similar.

Generalized Transition Networks do not display the load on long-term memory. There is, however, one aspect of GTNs that does affect long-term memory. Because GTNs show what is displayed on the screen at each state, one can assess whether and in how many states a prompt is given to the user indicating which actions are appropriate next and in how many states the prompts are the same. For example, in many operating systems, the only prompt for action is a single leading symbol indicating that the system is waiting for the user's action. Different symbols indicate which subsystem the user is in, but nothing is displayed to indicate appropriate actions. The more similar the prompts and the less information in them to indicate the next action, the more the user must depend on long-term memory recall of the command names and their syntax. GTN, with its display of the screen contents, allows an analysis of the amount of those kinds of loads on memory.

6.2 Short-Term Memory

All the processing representations have a short-term memory in which to keep goals currently being worked on, notes about the subgoals, and particular values, such as the location and contents of objects to be acted upon in the system. For example, in interacting with a spreadsheet program doing a "what if" analysis, one needs to locate the key cell and change its value systematically to see what happens to a dependent values, such as the "bottom line" revenues. The subgoals of accomplishing the task plus the cell location and its explicit value held may compete for space in a limited short-term memory.

In their production system representations of task performance, Kieras and Polson (1985) have explicitly measured the average number of items in short-term memory, the peak load, and the duration that any one value or goal is held. Evaluation of the correlates of these variables to performance is currently underway. They have found a relationship between the time to perform a task and the number of "cycles" that were necessary to access and fulfill subgoals on the stack.

The GOMS model similarly includes a short-term memory with its "goal stack." The goal stack holds goals and subgoals until they are satisfied. However, because their behavioral analyses concentrated on the performance times and not errors, no behavioral correlates have yet been associated with the size the contents of the goal stack.

Discussions of behavioral correlates of using systems represented in formal grammars have indicated that sentence length may indicate difficulty. Without being explicit about what processes act on the grammar, it is hard to say whether this is due to short-term or long-term memory involvement. It could be a correlate of the contents of short-term memory in keeping track of one's place in the command sequence, or it may indicate the number of rules or their complexity in long-term memory.

Although these representations include indications of the involvement of short-term and long-term memory, they are not equally easy to construct and analyze. The Goal Structure graph representation, because it ignores a number of important features useful for actually simulating behavior, is a simple picture of the goal relationships. As such, it allows an analyst to count easily the depth of the subgoals, and thus the use of short-term memory for keeping track of goal states. Both the GOMS and production system representations require computer or hand simulations to calculate the current load on short-term memory. They are more explicit and powerful, but less portable and more cumbersome for these simple purposes.

6.3 Perception

The only representation that currently indicates the load on the user's perceptual processing is the GTN. At each state in a GTN, the information displayed on the screen is indicated. These representations can be analyzed for their fit to the user's need to find certain information: for example, about the system state (when it is waiting for a response versus when it is computing and unresponsive) or the choices in a menu about what actions to take next. These representations can be analyzed for the correlation between what the user is searching for and the meaning that the spacing, fonts, color, and locations of the target imply.

7 Translation from the User's Goals to the System's Requirements

Three smaller-scale analysis techniques address the load that the system design places on the user's memory. All compare the user's mental representation of what he or she is trying to do with a representation of the system itself. Behavioral predictions are made in each about how easy the system is to use or learn.

The most global of these analyses is the Task-to-device mapping (Kieras and Polson, 1985). To assess a particular system design for its usability, they represent what the system requires as a Goal Structure graph, and set it next to Goal Structure graph of the user's point of view. Figure 10.8 shows an example of this alignment, where the mapping of the system to the user's goals is a *mis*match. In this example, the user thinks first of deleting a phrase, then decomposes this goal into the task of moving the cursor to the beginning of what is to be deleted and indicating the range of material to be deleted by moving the cursor to the end of the range. The system, however, requires that the cursor be placed the beginning of the range *first*, and then the delete command activated, which is followed by selecting a target by moving the cursor to the end of the range. The mismatches in this mapping indicates that the user will have difficulty with the delete function; in particular, the user will often invoke the delete command with the cursor misplaced. Though certainly not an indicator of all the difficulties the user will encounter, this mapping does quickly show pictorially the points at which errors are likely to occur.

The second analysis that focuses on the translation that a user must make to interact with the system is Moran's External Task-Internal Task mapping analysis (Moran, 1983). Moran specifies the *objects* that user thinks of manipulating and the *action* verbs that the user thinks of to manipulate these objects. These objects and actions are then compared to the system's object and actions, the system's data and operations. For example, a line-oriented editor works with objects such as strings of characters within a line and acts on these strings by inserting, cutting, pasting, breaking, merging, and replacing. The user, on the other hand, thinks in terms of objects such as characters, words, sentences, and paragraphs and actions such as adding, removing, changing, transposing, and moving.

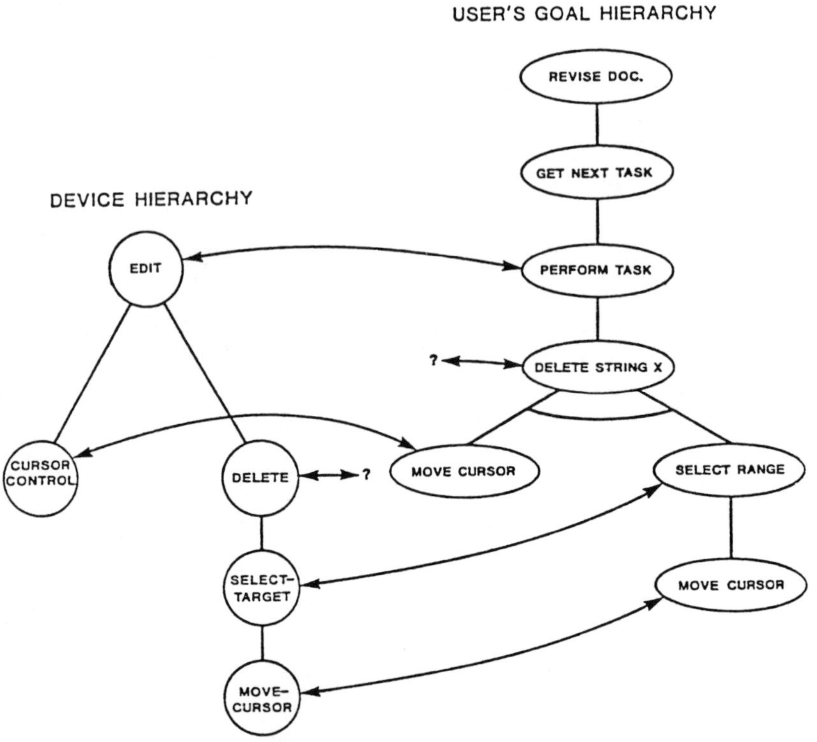

Figure 10.8
Task-to-device mapping representation of how well a user's goal structure fits the system (from Kieras and Polson, 1985).

Moran specifies the rules that the user needs to know to recast the task from the user's vocabulary into terms that the computer can understand. The number of rules necessary to make this translation is taken as a measure of difficulty. In our terms, these might be construed as some of the rules in a production system necessary in order to perform the task, and thus as a load on original learning. Moran displays the correspondence between the internal and external task constituents in tabular form, a form in which it is easy to visualize the correspondence between the two (see figure 10.9 for an example); in this table, the objects and actions in the user's vocabulary are the row and column labels, and the actions in the system's terms are in the cells.

A similar analysis of the correspondence between how the user thinks of the task and what the system requires is found in Douglas and Moran (1983). Instead of focusing on the user's view of a task in the absence of

Basic Internal Tasks for DISPED

I = *Insert String*
C = *Cut String*
P = *Paste String*

Mapping Rules for DISPED

Rule D1. *BoundaryFunction Sentence → Change String*
Rule D2. *Text → String*
Rule D3. *Add → Insert*
Rule D4. *Remove → Cut*
Rule D5. *Transpose → Move*
Rule D6. *Split → Insert*
Rule D7. *Join → Cut*
Rule D8. *Change String → Cut String + Insert String*
Rule D9. *Move String → Cut String + Paste String*
Rule D10. *Copy String → Cut String + Paste String + Paste String*

ETIT Map for DISPED

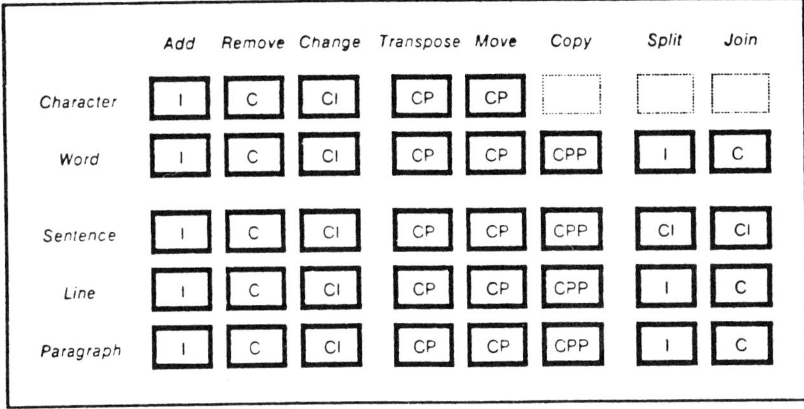

	Add	*Remove*	*Change*	*Transpose*	*Move*	*Copy*	*Split*	*Join*
Character	I	C	CI	CP	CP			
Word	I	C	CI	CP	CP	CPP	I	C
Sentence	I	C	CI	CP	CP	CPP	CI	CI
Line	I	C	CI	CP	CP	CPP	I	C
Paragraph	I	C	CI	CP	CP	CPP	I	C

Figure 10.9
An External Task-Internal Task mapping of a text editor called "DISPED" (from Moran, 1983).

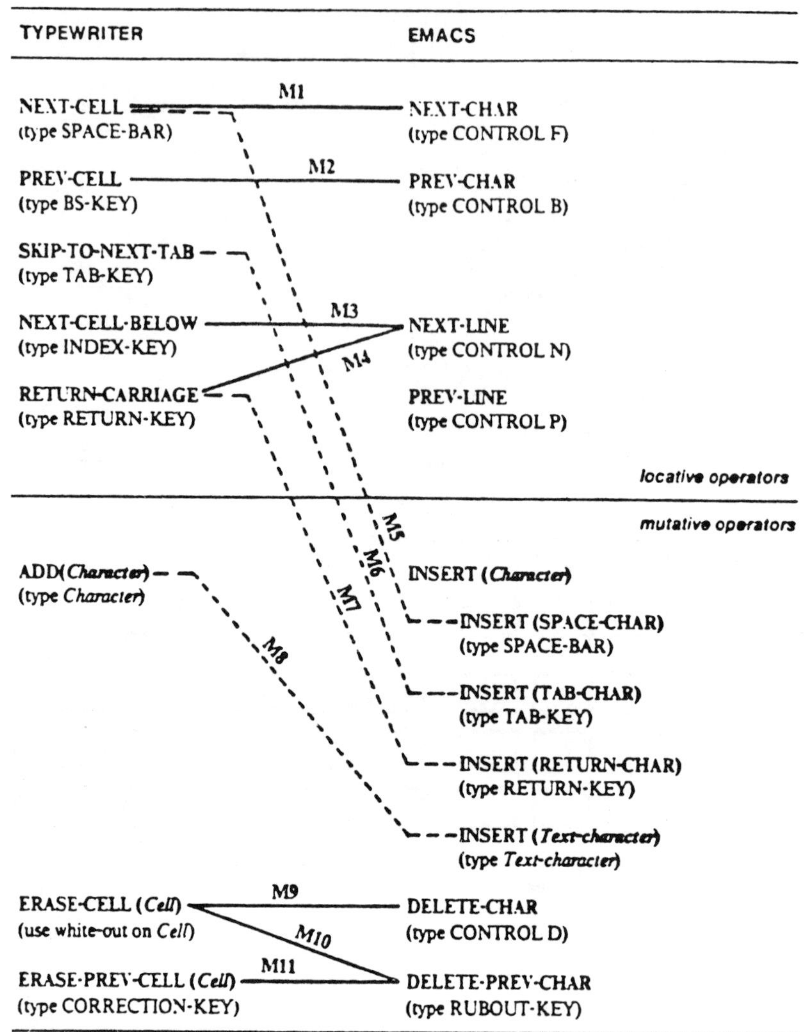

Figure 10.10
Goal-action pairs comparing a typewriter to a text editor called "EMACS." Solid lines indicate same goals, different actions; dashed lines indicate different goals, same actions (from Douglas and Moran, 1983).

any system, they focus on the analogy that the user brings to the task of learning the system. For example, many first-time users of word processors think of it in terms of a typewriter. Explicit representation is made of the *goal-action* pairs in both systems. These two sets of goal-action pairs are then analyzed across systems for similar goals that require different actions, similar actions that fill different goals, and the number of identical goal-action pairs (see figure 10.10). This juxtaposition of system representations allows easy analysis of the difficulties that a user will have in transferring from a previously learned system or by holding an inadequate analogy. It is very similar to the analysis that Kieras and Bovair (1985) do to assess the predicted transfer from one system to another, but requires less complete specification of the system. And because it concerns only simple goal-action pairs instead of complex if-then statements, it is easier to apply.[4]

8 General Discussion of the Local Representations

By far the most complete representation of the user's cognitive processing during interaction with a computer system is the production system representation. In the work of Kieras and Polson, the GTN is not used to represent the user's knowledge.[5] It is used only to represent the system, taking the user's response and presenting to the user the next screen in the interaction. The production system contains the contents of the user's long-term memory, the knowledge about what actions to take to fill certain goals, and a functioning short-term memory. The one feature that is difficult to assess in the production system representation is the difficulty a user may have in *perceiving* the information on the screen. However, there are perhaps easy extensions to the productions that, for example, search the screen for a signal that the system has received an input, search for a recognizable menu item. These productions are not now part of the system, but could be added for representing this aspect.

The GOMS model and formal grammars are simpler representations of the goals and methods that are found in the production system above. They, like all the other representations, represent *some* aspects of the interaction and ignore others. They have a distinct advantage in speed of analysis. Since they are less complete, they are faster to build. Furthermore, if the analyst is looking only to answer questions about one aspect of the interaction, the analyst can choose the representation that best illuminates that aspect. For example, as shown in table 10.1, briefer (though by no means short) analyses of short-term memory load can come from hand simulating the goal stack, analyzing long-term memory load by examining the similarity among a set of goal-action pairs, or by constructing the rules by which one translates the objects and actions of the user to those of the system.

Although the GTN is the only representation of the perceptual load on the user, only one part of the GTN is important; only the presentation of the screen contents is of interest here. The kind of perceptual analysis that seems to be required is one in which features of the information sought on the screen are mapped to the way the information is presented. The user has in mind a word or symbol he or she is looking for, and some idea as to its location on the screen. The font, color, and highlighting or blinking of the information presented may make the target more or less distinguishable from its surround. The predictability of its location given its general class (e.g., whether it is a warning message, a menu item, or an echoed input in the data section of the screen) can be determined. Detailed assessment of how difficult it is to find information being sought on the screen is an important component of usability, especially for novices, and even for experts for those aspects of a task with which they are less familiar. A new kind of analysis is needed to assess fully the perceptual load.

These representations not only display different aspects of the user's cognitive strengths and limits but are useful in different analyses. The researcher interested in real-world problem solving—for example, about how a limited capacity store is used variously for subgoals and incoming items, about the detectable similarity between productions in memory when the user is in different global contexts (using one word processor at home and another at work), or the differences between novices and experts in their searches of the environment—will require the completeness and specificity of the production system representation. Building a production system is time consuming, detailed, and controlled work. But the effort expended in programming the production system pays off in the specificity of the research results.

The practitioner, on the other hand, needs ways of representing aspects of the system in order to make timely design decisions. The representation need not be as complete, and it must be fast. The External Task-Internal Task mappings, the goal-action pair analysis, the Goal Structure graph analysis, and a new analysis of perceptual loads may be the tools that bring design rewards much more swiftly. Until higher-level tools are invented that make the building of production systems easy,[6] the practitioner will have to resort to handier methods that focus on single cognitive aspects of the user and hope that the recommendations that emerge from each are compatible.

9 Conclusions

The last five years has seen an enormous growth in interest in the analysis of users and computer systems. Many individual studies of generic design issues have been done, and done well. What is preventing significant advances in theoretical, integrative approaches is the paucity of good representations of the complexity of the interaction and the *cognition* involved. Reviewed here are those representations that are available now. It is clear that the next advances will come in representing the more user-oriented aspects of global tasks (as in office analysis), and in representing the perceptual processes involved in local computer-based tasks.

Notes

1. A portion of this function is shown; more of it can be found in Reisner (1984).

2. Discussed here are the characteristics of the formalizations as they have been used, not the full potential for each particular notation system.

3. The user could work backward from the goal to the initial conditions or both forward and backward. In the straightforward problem solved in computer systems, the search is most likely forward. All the representations include only forward search.

4. Of course, being simpler, it may also ignore other, more subtle areas of difficulty in mental processing that the complete production system will pick up.

5. The GTN could represent what the user knows of the states and options at each step in the interaction. The analyst could use it to map the correspondence of the user's knowledge to the real system. Although this is not what Kieras and Polson use it for, the extension is natural.

6. Such higher-level tools, such as the languages OPS5 and LOOPS, are now making the production of expert systems much easier and faster. Similar tools could be in the offing for production models of human users of computer systems.

References

Anderson, N. S., and Olson, J. R., Eds. (1985). *Methods for Designing Software to Fit Human Needs and Capabilities*, Washington DC, National Academy Press.

Bailey, R. W. (1982). *Human Performance Engineering: A Guide for System Designers*, Englewood Cliffs, NJ, Prentice-Hall.

Card, S. K., Moran, T. P., and Newell, A. (1980a). Computer text-editing: An information processing analysis of a routine cognitive skill. *Cognitive Psychology*, 12, 32–74.

Card, S. K., Moran, T. P., and Newell, A. (1980b). The Keystroke-Level Model for user performance time with interactive systems. *Communications of the ACM*, 23, 396–410.

Card, S. K., Moran, T. P., and Newell, A. (1983). *The Psychology of Human-Computer Interaction*, Hillsdale, NJ, Lawrence Erlbaum Associates.

Conrath, D. W., Higgins, C. A., Thackenkary, C. S., and Wright, W. M. (1981). The electronic office and organizational behavior—measuring office activities. *Computer Networks*, 5, 401–410.

Conrath, D. W., Higgins, C. A., Irving, R. H., and Thackenkary, C. S. (1983). Determining the need for office automation: Methods and results. *Office: Technology and People*, 1, 275–294.

Douglas, S. A., and Moran, T. P. (1983). Learning text editor semantics by analogy. *Proceedings of the CHI'83 Human Factors in Computing Systems*, New York, ACM, pp. 207–211.

Fitts, P. M., Ed. (1951). *Human Engineering for an Effective Air-Navigation and Traffic-Control System*, Columbus, OH, Ohio State University Research Foundation.

Helander, M. G. (1985). Emerging office automation systems. *Human Factors*, 27, 3–20.

Kieras, D. E., and Bovair, S. (1985). The acquisition of procedures from text: A production system analysis of transfer of training. University of Michigan Technical Report No. 16 (TR-85/ONR-16).

Kieras, D. E., and Polson, P. G. (1983). A Generalized Transition Network representation for interactive systems. *Proceedings of the CHI'83 Human Factors in Computing Systems*, New York, ACM, pp. 103–106.

Kieras, D. E., and Polson, P. G. (1985). An approach to the formal analysis of user complexity. *International Journal of Man-Machine Studies*, 22, 365–394.

Komatsubara, A., and Yokomizo, Y. (1982). Characteristics of office work. *Proceedings of 8th Congress of the International Ergonomics Association*, Tokyo, International Ergonomics Assoc.

Lieberman, M. A., Selig, G. J., and Walsh, J. J. (1983). *Office Automation*, New York, Wiley.

Machlup, F. (1962). *The Production and Distribution of Knowledge in the United States*, Princeton, Princeton University Press.

Moran, T. P. (1981). The Command Language Grammar: A representation for the user interface of interactive computer systems. *International Journal of Man-Machine Studies*, 15, 3–50.

Moran, T. (1983). Getting into a system: External-internal task mapping analysis. *Proceedings of the CHI'83 Human Factors in Computing Systems*, New York, ACM, pp. 45–49.

Newell, A., and Simon, H. A. (1972). *Human Problem Solving*, Englewood Cliffs, NJ, Prentice-Hall.

Price, H. E. (1985). The allocation of functions in systems. *Human Factors, 27*, 33–46.

Reisner, P. (1981). Formal grammar and human factors design of an interactive graphics system. *IEEE Transactions on Software Engineering*, SE-7, 229–240.

Reisner, P. (1984). Formal grammar as a tool for analyzing ease of use: Some fundamental concepts. In J. Thomas and M. Schneider (Eds.), *Human Factors in Computing Systems*, Norwood, NH, Ablex.

Sasso, W. (1985). A comparison of two potential bases for office analysis: Function and organization unit. Dissertation from the Graduate School of Business Administration, the University of Michigan.

Sasso, W., Olson, J. R., and Merten, A. (1985). A comparison of three methodologies for office analysis. Technical Report, Human-Computer Interaction Laboratory, University of Michigan.

Sirbu, M. A. Jr., Schoechet, S. R., Kunin, J. S., Hammer, M. M., Sutherland, J. B., and Zarmer, C. L. (1983). Office analysis: Methodology and Cases. Technical reports, MIT/LCS/TR-289.

11

Computer Support for Organizations: Toward an Organizational Science

Thomas W. Malone

Studies of human-computer interaction have, in the past, focused primarily on designing user interfaces to support individual problem solving. Much of the theoretical base for this work has grown out of cognitive science theories concerning the information processing involved when individual people solve problems, learn, and remember (e.g., see Card, Moran, and Newell, 1983, and the other chapters in this volume).

In this chapter, I shall suggest that it is becoming increasingly important to focus not just on isolated interactions between people and computers, but also on the interactions among groups of people that are mediated by computers. To provide a theoretical base for this new endeavor, I shall indicate how traditional cognitive and motivational perspectives can be extended to include groups of people and whole organizations. A critical component of this "organizational science" will be the analysis of the information processing necessary to coordinate the activities of separate agents. The computer systems that support group interactions will emphasize "organizational interfaces" as suggested by the following definitions:

1. *user interface*: the parts of a computer program that connect a human user to the capabilities provided by the computer;

2. *organizational interface*: the parts of a computer system that connect human users to each other and to the capabilities provided by computers.

Thus an organizational interface includes one or more user interfaces. Thinking of the problem in these new terms brings a number of additional

---

Portions of this paper have appeared previously in Malone (1985) and Malone and Smith (1984). The preparation of this chapter was supported in part by Citibank, N.A., and by the Center for Information Systems Research, Sloan School of Management, Massachusetts Institute of Technology. Many of the original ideas for the intelligent mail filter system arose in discussions with Michael Cohen. I would also like to thank John Carroll and Michael Rothkopf for helpful comments.

factors into focus. For example, in designing traditional programs for word processing, the user interface is designed to facilitate separate problem solving by isolated individuals. In designing programs for electronic mail, however, it is important to design an organizational interface that facilitates cooperative problem solving by groups of people. Even a very "easy to use" electronic mail system, for instance, that allows only explicitly named individual addressees will be much less useful in a large organization than one that includes centrally maintained distribution lists for identifying people who are interested in different topics.

1 Examples of Organizational Interfaces

In a sense, traditional data processing systems like accounting and order entry are examples of systems in which the organizational interface is important. In all these cases, the system does not simply support the work of single individuals but instead provides communication between people in many different parts of the organization. Just as traditional user interfaces were often extremely awkward and inflexible, however, the organizational interfaces embodied in traditional data processing systems were also often very rigid and inconvenient.

Now that computer capabilities are dramatically increasing and computer costs dramatically decreasing, many new and much less routine kinds of organizational interfaces are becoming feasible, and it is becoming increasingly important to make these interfaces more flexible and convenient. In this section, I shall briefly describe some examples of these new kinds of organizational interfaces. The examples are organized in three loosely-defined categories: *text sharing systems, project management systems,* and *collaborative authoring systems.*

- *Text sharing systems.* One important class of systems in which organizational interfaces are critical is what I shall call "text sharing systems." This class includes (1) electronic mail systems for transmitting messages to specific people (e.g., Uhlig, 1981), (2) computer conferencing systems in which it is easy for people to create new topics and subtopics and to add and delete themselves from topic interest lists (e.g., Hiltz and Turoff, 1978; see also Sarin and Greif, 1984), and (3) other structured systems that use links to represent the relationship between nodes of text stored in a common database (e.g., Trigg and Weiser, 1984; Lowe, 1984). For example, Lowe (1984) describes an information retrieval system in which the argumentation structure of a debate is explicitly represented (see also Brown, 1983). An argument about the desirability of introducing a new product, for instance, might include various claims, counterclaims, and pieces of evidence supporting different courses of action. Readers viewing the database of argumentation could see claims and their supporting evidence in order of importance (as determined by voting) or they could see various kinds of summaries (e.g., just the claims, not the evidence). Throughout this chapter, I shall use examples of text sharing systems to illustrate general points.

• *An intelligent mail filter.* One particular kind of text sharing system I shall use as an example is an "intelligent mail filter." It is a common experience in mature electronic mail communities for people either to (1) be overwhelmed with electronic "junk mail" or (2) to develop restrictive social norms about where to send messages, so that people sometimes fail to receive information they would have liked to see (e.g., Brotz, 1981). To help solve this problem, we are now designing an intelligent mail filter that will help people select the most useful pieces of electronic mail (or other semistructured information) from a large pool of less useful "junk mail" (see Malone et al., 1986; Brobst et al., 1985; Malone et al., in press). For previous discussions of the problem see Wilson et al. (1984) and Denning (1982).

Previous approaches to this problem have been limited primarily to (1) centrally maintained "distribution lists," (e.g., Brotz, 1981), (2) topic hierarchies in computer conferences (e.g., Hiltz and Turoff, 1978), and (3) simple keywords for selecting messages (e.g., Stallman, 1983). In later sections of this paper, I shall suggest how concepts from artificial intelligence, economics, and organization theory can be used to develop more sophisticated ways of filtering information in organizations.

• *Project management systems.* Another category of system used for organizational coordination includes project management systems. For instance, Sluizer and Cashman (1985) describe a "coordinator tool" that keeps track of activities and responsibilities so it can answer questions like the following:
On what task am I working now (in a specific role or in all my roles)?
What is Joe's long-term work load (in all his roles)?
Who is responsible for the next task in Project P?
Other project management systems automatically assign tasks to people (e.g., Kedzierski, 1982), construct schedules, and help allocate scarce resources, such as people, machines, and money (e.g., Fox et al., 1983).

• *Collaborative writing systems.* A different kind of system supports collaborative writing by two or more people (e.g., Goldstein and Bobrow, 1980; Engelbart, 1984). In the PIE system, for instance, successive versions of a document are constructed from overlays that contain each person's modifications of previous versions (Goldstein and Bobrow, 1980). For example, one author might construct a new version by accepting some of his collaborator's changes immediately, modifying others, and rejecting some altogether.

2 What Kinds of Theories Will Help in Designing Organizational Interfaces?

In order to design these new organizational interfaces well, we need some (explicit or implicit) theories about how computers can help organizations function. A natural place to look for such theories is in the growing literature concerned with the relationship between organizations and computers (e.g., see Keen and Scott Morton, 1978; Kling, 1980; Zuboff, 1982; Markus, 1983). This literature has been concerned almost exclusively with two main themes: (1) the *impacts* of computers on organizations, and (2) the *implementation* of computers in organizations. Unfortunately, neither of these bodies of literature provides much direct guidance for designing systems. In a few cases, the literature on impacts appears to recognize that the technology can have very different effects depending on how it is used (e.g., Walton and Vittori, 1983; Mohrman and Lawler, 1984), but all too often there seems to be an implicit assumption of technological determinism and an exclusive focus on computer technology as it has been used, not as it might be used. The literature on implementation of computers pays somewhat more attention to different ways of using computer technology by emphasizing, for example, the importance of "user involvement" in the selection and the design of computer systems (e.g., Mumford and Henshall, 1979). Here, too, however, the most common approach has been to take the technology as being mostly predetermined and to focus on what leads people to use it. To caricature the two bodies of literature, the impacts literature has often seemed to focus on "all the bad things that happen when you put in computers," and the implementation literature has seemed to focus on "how to get people to use computers, no matter how bad they are."

In contrast to both of these approaches, I suggest that we need to pay much more attention to how to design computer systems in the first place in such a way that they fit naturally into human organizations and have desirable impacts. In other words, I suggest that we need to focus much more on developing *design* theories, not just *explanatory or predictive* theories (e.g., see Simon, 1981). In addition to helping to design new computer systems, these theories may help design new organizational structures and processes, too.

Unlike explanatory theories ("Y because X") and predictive theories ("If X, then Y"), design theories emphasize how to achieve goals ("In order to achieve Y, do X"). Thus design theories may include, for example, (1) techniques for *clarifying goals* to be achieved by the systems (e.g., Sirbu, et al., 1984; Rockart, 1979), (2) *taxonomies of actions* that might help achieve goals, such as Malone's (1982a) taxonomy of user interface features that enhance enjoyableness, and (3) *guidelines for selecting actions* such as Norman's (1983) analysis of trade-offs in user interface design and Malone and Smith's (1984) analysis of trade-offs in organizational design.

3 Theoretical Perspectives on Organizations

There are a number of possible perspectives from which one can view organizations in order to develop design-oriented theories. Four of these perspectives appear repeatedly in the literature on organizations and computers (e.g., Kling, 1980; Keen and Scott Morton, 1978): *economic* (or "rational"), *structural* (or process-oriented), *human relations* (or "quality of work life"), and *political*. In this chapter, instead of adopting any of these perspectives directly, I shall suggest the outlines of what might be called a "cognitive science" or "organizational science" approach to many of the same issues.

Cognitive science and artificial intelligence appear to have made important progress in the last two decades by identifying a level of analysis that is common to both human minds and computers: that is, the information processing necessary to do things such as solve problems, learn, and remember (e.g., Norman, 1983).

I believe that similar progress is now possible by extending this approach to include the information processing that occurs when groups of agents perform these same tasks. As mentioned above, a critical component of this "organizational science" will be the analysis of the *information processing necessary to coordinate the activities of separate agents*, whether these agents are people or computers (see March and Simon, 1958; Malone, 1982b; Malone and Smith, 1984). Just as cognitive science shows the commonality in problems previously considered separately by disciplines such as psychology, computer science, and linguistics, this new point of view unifies problems previously considered separately in fields such as computer science, organization theory, and economics.

Since this new "organizational science" emphasizes information processing, and since it is precisely the dramatic changes in information processing technology that have led to our concern with organization interfaces in the first place, it seems quite likely that one of the most important application areas for this new intellectual approach will be in the design of organizational interfaces.

As I shall suggest below, however, the information processing perspective we shall need in order to understand properly how organizations function goes significantly beyond traditional cognitive analyses. For instance, while previous cognitive theories have included goals as a component of individual problem solving, in order to analyze organizational problem solving we shall often need to deal with conflicting goals held by different people.

There is another set of factors that, even though they are not easily analyzed in information processing terms and are not changing dramatically, are still of great importance in designing organizational interfaces. These are the factors that are emphasized in the human relations and "quality of work life" perspectives. Since these factors are primarily concerned with why people are motivated to pick the goals they do, I shall call this second perspective "motivational". The remainder of this section will be devoted to these two perspective on organizations: *information processing* and *motivational*.

Before discussing the two perspectives, however, one further word of clarification is in order. It is, unfortunately, all too common in the human sciences for people who find a particular perspective useful for some purposes to believe secretly (and sometimes claim openly) that the perspective is useful for all purposes. We might label this error the "nothing but" fallacy, as in "People are nothing but stimulus-response organisms" or "People are nothing but information processors." Sometimes, the "nothing but" error is incorrectly attributed to people who have not actually made it. For instance, it would be a mistake to assume that an airplane designer who modeled passengers as inert masses believed that the passengers never moved or had no feelings. Similarly, it would also be a mistake to assume that all information processing theorists believe people are "nothing but" information processors. In both cases, certain perspectives are useful for certain purposes, but not necessarily for others. To help prevent both forms of error here, I have explicitly included two widely used but complementary perspectives on organizations.

3.1 Information Processing Perspective

This perspective emphasizes the kinds of information used in an organization and how the information is communicated and processed. This point of view can be used to analyze many of the issues emphasized by the "structural" (e.g., Galbraith, 1973), economic (e.g., Hurwicz, 1973), political (e.g., Cyert and March, 1963), and "organizational communications" (e.g., Rice, 1980) perspectives. To illustrate this approach, I shall discuss some implications of research on multiagent problem solving for designing organizational interfaces.

The topic of problem solving has a long-standing and important place in the field of cognitive science (e.g., Newell and Simon, 1972; Newell, 1980), but with few exceptions (e.g., Smith and Davis, 1981; Kornfeld and Hewitt, 1981; Corkill and Lesser, 1983) this work has only analyzed the problem solving behavior of individual problem solvers. In order to extend this work to include multiple agent problem solving, we must begin to clarify what aspects of problem solving emerge only with multiple agents.

Newell (1980) summarizes the components of individual problem solving behavior in the following categories: (1) the *goals* the problem solver tries to achieve, (2) the *state-space* or set of possibilities that may be explored, (3) the *operators* or actions that the problem solver may take, (4) the *constraints* that must be satisfied by solutions, and (5) the *search control knowledge* that guides the problem solver in searching for solutions.

When multiple agents are involved in the problem solving (e.g., see Smith and Davis, 1981; Corkill and Lesser, 1983) at least two additional components emerge as being important: (6) *task assignment* or the ways subtasks are assigned to agents, and (7) *interagent communication*.[1] In the extended example at the end of this chapter, we shall examine the process of task assignment in greater detail. In this section, I shall discuss issues related to filtering interagent communication and dealing with goal conflicts between agents.

Filtering Interagent Communication

One of the problems that emerges with multiple agent problem solving is how to control the explosion of messages that may arise when each agent broadcasts all results to all other agents (e.g., Kornfeld, 1982). The beginnings of a solution to this problem are suggested by the Hearsay II problem solving architecture (Erman et al., 1980). This architecture contains a number of separate modules called "knowledge sources" (KSs) that communicate with each other through a global data structure called a "blackboard." Different KSs check the blackboard for situations to which they know how to respond and then post the results of their computations back on the blackboard for other KSs to use. To prevent all KSs from having to scan the entire blackboard, the Hearsay II blackboard was carefully structured so that different regions corresponded to different parts of the problem being solved.

We can think of text sharing systems in human organizations as a similar kind of "electronic blackboard." For the problem domain of the original Hearsay system (speech recognition), a fairly simple two-dimensional structure was used for the blackboard (time versus level of interpretation). For more complex problems in human organizations, we can use much more sophisticated structuring techniques, such as semantic networks and frame inheritance networks (e.g., Brachman and Schmolze, 1985).

For example, the users of our intelligent mail filtering system (Malone et al., 1986; Malone et al., in press) can conveniently compose messages using a network of different templates for different types of information (e.g., meeting announcements, bug reports). A meeting announcement template, for instance, has fields for "time," "place," "organizer," and "topic." Its subtype, seminar announcement, adds a field for "speaker." Then receivers of messages will be able to construct much more sophisticated filters than would be possible with simple keyword searches (e.g., "Show me all the announcements for seminars at MIT organized by people in my department except for seminars that occur on Tuesdays").

Different groups can develop detailed structures to represent the information of specific concern to them. For example, a product design team might have an elaborate network of message types describing different aspects of the product (e.g., market size estimates, response time specifications, alternative power supply vendors). Then, for instance, marketing specialists who believe that the critical factors determining potential market size for the product are cost and response time can devote most of their attention to the regions of the blackboard in which people discuss those two factors and ignore all the rest of the technical specifications for the product.

Goal Conflicts

Even though many organizational and economic models assume, for purposes of simplicity, that all members of an organization have the same goals, it is a fact of daily organizational life that conflicts of interest between people are frequent and often of great importance to how well an organization functions (e.g., see March and Simon, 1958; Cyert and March, 1963). Designers of organizational interfaces ignore this fact at their peril. Two ways that organizational interfaces can explicitly take goal conflicts into account involve *coalition formation* and *confidentiality*.

• *Coalition formation.* Information technology can clearly affect the formation of coalitions in organizations. For example, IBM's "Gripe Net" (Emmett, 1981) was an electronic mail system that allowed a group of geographically separated programmers who felt that their software product was being given too little attention in the company's product line to develop a slightly mutinous sense of camaraderie and power.

Whether this particular coalition was good or bad for IBM, many observers, of organizational behavior feel that the healthy formation of competing coalitions is an essential part of the functioning of organizations (e.g., Cyert and March, 1963; Mintzberg, 1983). Lowe's (1984) system for computer-mediated debate, which was described above, illustrates how a text sharing system might facilitate this process. In his system different people enter arguments, counterarguments, and evidence into a highly structured textual data base in such a way that constructive debate is facilitated and newcomers are able to see quickly the most important opposing points of view. Our perspective here suggests that a system like this might be even more useful in facilitating coalition formation if it includes the names (and electronic addresses) of the people who wrote and supported the views represented.

• *Confidentiality.* There are already a number of techniques for specifying and enforcing various kinds of access controls in computer systems (e.g., Saltzer and Schroeder, 1975; Fernandez, Summers, and Wood, 1981). The complexities of confidentiality in real organizations go far beyond the simple mechanisms proposed so far, however. Imagine, for instance, trying to decide whether to tell someone else in a company you work for about a serious problem in a product you are developing. You might consider factors like whether revealing the problem would hurt your reputation, how likely it is that the person could help you solve the problem, and what the consequences would be if you do not tell the person now and he finds out later. Though many of these factors would be quite difficult to represent, the more of them that can be automatically included in text sharing systems, the more useful the systems are likely to be.

3.2 Motivational Perspective

The information processing perspective in the previous section captures many important aspects of coordinating the activities of people in organizations, but it leaves out some of the most important factors about why people are there in the first place, how hard they work, and whether they find their activities satisfying or alienating (e.g., March and Simon, 1958).

Table 11.1
Motivational factors in organizations

I. Extrinsic motivations (pay, benefits, etc.)

II. Intrinsic motivations
A. Individual
1. Challenge
2. Curiousity
3. Task meaningfulness
4. Autonomy
B. Interpersonal
1. Cooperation
2. Competition
3. Recognition

This perspective is central to work in the "quality of work life" and "human relations" traditions (e.g., McGregor, 1960; Roethlisberger and Dickson, 1939; Likert, 1961; Argyris, 1973; Herzberg, 1968).

Table 11.1 shows a number of factors that affect motivation and satisfaction at work (adapted from Malone and Lepper, in press, and Hackman and Oldham, 1980). Some factors, such as pay, benefits, and working conditions, are primarily *extrinsic* to the tasks being performed. Herzberg (1968) hypothesizes that these "hygiene" factors may lead to dissatisfaction if they are below some acceptable level, but that they are not positive "motivators" for greater effort. In other words, these extrinsic factors may affect which goals people choose and whether they choose to participate in the organization at all (e.g., see March and Simon, 1958, chapter 4), but these factors alone would not usually lead to highly involving and satisfying jobs.

Other factors, however, are *intrinsic* to the tasks being performed, and they seem to be particularly important in determining the degree of involvement and satisfaction in an activity (e.g., see Herzberg, 1968). These factors are divided into two groups: (1) *individual motivations* that may be present in any activity and (2) *interpersonal motivations* that depend for their appeal on interactions between people.

- *Individual motivations.* Malone (1982a) discusses a number of suggestions for how individual motivational factors such as *challenge, fantasy,* and *curiosity* can be used to make user interfaces more interesting and enjoyable. For example, challenge can be enhanced by incorporating successive layers of complexity in an interface with each layer being mastered in turn as users become more skilled. When we expand our focus to include designing organizational interfaces, it becomes clear that computers make it possible and sometimes desirable to redesign whole jobs and organizations, as well as individual programs. For example, Hackman and Oldham's (1980) concept of "skill variety" in well-designed jobs can be seen as another way of increasing the challenge of a job.

There are two differences between the list of individual motivations presented here and that used by Malone (1982a). First, the category of "fantasy" was renamed (somewhat less evocatively) "task meaningfulness" in order to capture more directly Hackman and Oldham's notion that jobs are more satisfying when they involve the completion of a "whole" and identifiable piece of work ("task identity") that has a substantial impact on the lives of other people ("task significance"). In computer games and in some unavoidably dull jobs, it is possible to increase the meaningfulness of an activity by using fantasy (e.g., the task of controlling a factory process can be mapped into a fantasy display of piloting a space ship [Carroll and Thomas, 1980]). However, the implication of this new category name is that organizational interfaces should be designed to make the tasks themselves as meaningful as possible. For example, one of the reported benefits of a early office automation project was that bank clerks had their jobs restructured so that they no longer performed isolated clerical steps in a process they did not understand but instead handled all the steps in dealing with their assigned customers (Matteis, 1979; Lorsch, Gibson, and Seeger, 1975).

The second change is that Hackman and Oldham's category of "autonomy" was added to Malone's (1982a) list. The word "autonomy" was used here instead of "control" (as used by Malone and Lepper) to capture the sense that the freedom people have to determine how they work (and sometimes what work they do) is an important motivating factor even when they do not "control" anything else.

• *Interpersonal motivations.* When we are concerned with group interactions, three kinds of interpersonal motivations (*cooperation, competition,* and *recognition*) can be as important as individual motivations (see Malone and Lepper, in press). Organizational interfaces can be designed to engage these interpersonal motivations. For example, one of the problems that may arise in text sharing systems like those we have been discussing is how to motivate people to contribute information. In addition to the pricing schemes discussed in the example below, intrinsic motivations may be used for this purpose. For example, people's motivations for recognition by their peers might be engaged by a system in which rankings of the most widely read messages in different categories can be displayed along with their authors' names. This approach should be even more effective if messages that are rated by some readers as being very valuable are then automatically redistributed to a wider audience.

4 Example: Flexibility and Efficiency in Alternative Organizational Structures

So far in this chapter, we have discussed in general terms how an "organizational science" might be developed and how it could be applied to designing organizational interfaces. In the remainder of the chapter, I shall make a small part of these ideas more concrete by summarizing a specific model of organizational coordination that is presented in detail elsewhere (Malone and Smith, 1984; Malone, 1985). I shall show how the model can be used to help explain historical changes in American business structures and to suggest how to design new organizations that take advantage of the radically changing costs and capabilities of computer technology. To analyze different organizational structures, the model focuses explicitly on how tasks are assigned to people (or machines). This task assignment is, of course, only one of the important processes that occur in organizations, but as the applications below illustrate, the qualitative results based on this analysis appear to be widely applicable. In this sense, our models are similar in spirit to many mathematical models in which extremely simplified (and sometimes implausible) assumptions lead to powerful insights and qualitatively correct results.

To begin with, we can think of any organization as having (1) a set of goals to be achieved and (2) a set of processors that can perform the tasks (i.e., achieve the subgoals) necessary to reach these overall goals. For example, an automobile manufacturing company like General Motors can be thought of as having a set of goals (e.g., producing several different lines of automobiles—Chevrolet, Pontiac, Cadillac, etc.) and a set of processors to achieve those goals (e.g., the people and machines specialized for doing marketing, manufacturing, engineering, etc.) We shall be concerned here with the answers to two basic questions about how these goals and processors are organized:

1. Are the processors shared among goals or dedicated to single goals?
2. Is the decision making about which processors peform which tasks centralized or decentralized?

There are four possible combinations of answers to these two questions, and figure 11.1 shows the organizational structures that result from each

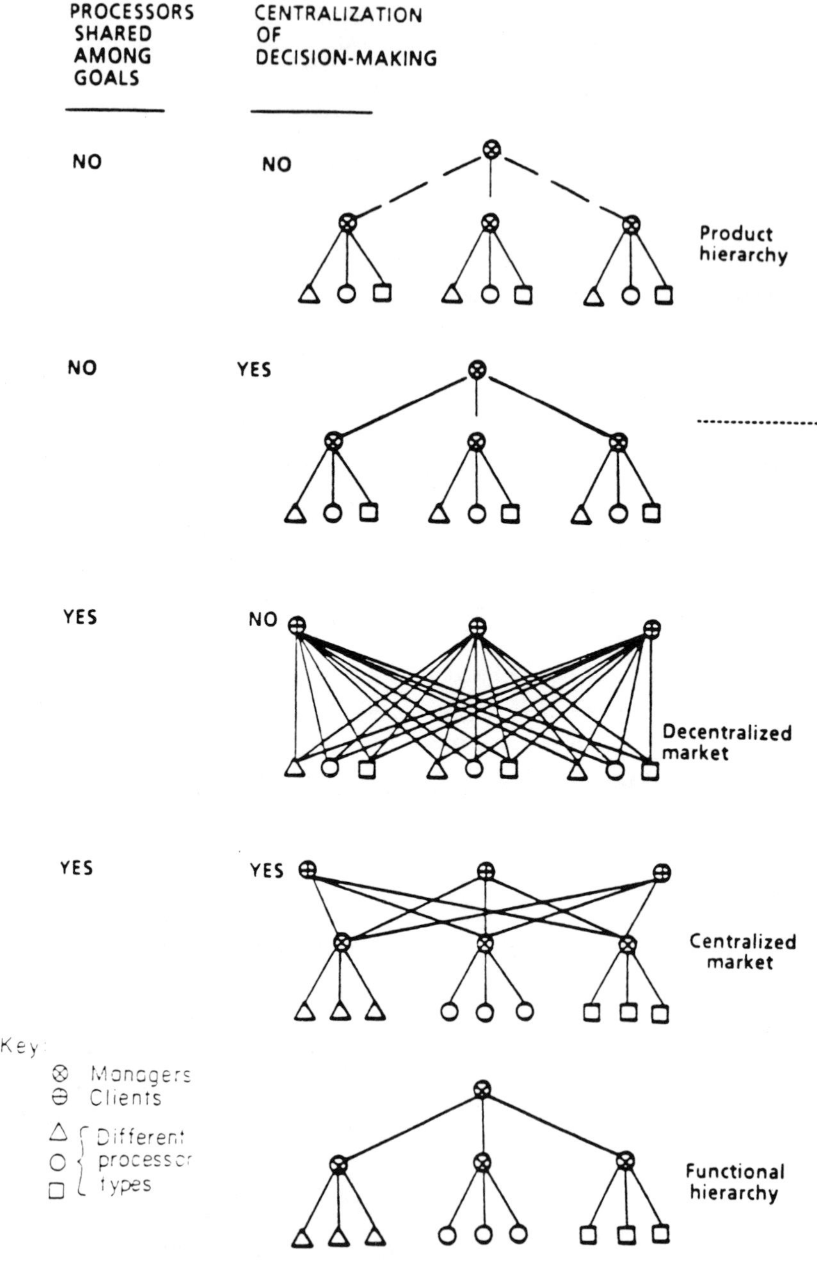

Figure 11.1
Alternative organizational forms.

combination. The structures are labeled with the terms used for describing human organizations, but analogous structures exist in computer systems as well. These generic organizational structures serve as the building blocks for much more complex organizations.

We shall compare the different organizational forms in terms of their *production costs,* their *coordination costs,* and their *vulnerability costs.* The assumptions we describe in this section and the appendix will allow us to measure these factors in the following terms: (1) production costs in terms of the delay in processing tasks, (2) coordination costs in terms of the minimum number of communication instances, or "messages," necessary to assign tasks to processors, and (3) vulnerability costs in terms of the costs of unexpected changes such as component failures.

• *Product hierarchy.* When processors are not shared among products and decision making is decentralized, the resulting organizational structure is a product hierarchy. In this structure there is a separate division for each product or major product line. (Sometimes the division is made along other "mission-oriented" lines such as geographical regions or market segments.). Each division has a "product manager" and its own separate departments for different functions such as marketing, manufacturing, and engineering. General Motors was one of the first major American corporations to adopt this form when it was reorganized from a structure with large centralized functional departments to one with separate divisions for Chevrolet, Pontiac, Cadillac, and other product lines (see Chandler, 1962).

In this form, the "executive office" may set long-range strategic directions, but it is not ordinarily involved in the operational coordination of tasks and processors. The lack of connection with the executive office for scheduling purposes is indicated by dashed lines in figure 11.1.

The solution to the task assignment problem that is implied by this form is simple: Whenever a task of a certain type needs to be done, the product manager assigns the task to the department that specializes in that type of task. In the "pure" form of a product hierarchy, there is only one department (or one processor) for each type of task, so the assignment decision is trivial.

When processors are not shared among products, but decision making about task assignment is centralized, the second structure shown in figure 11.1 results. The fact that the executive office performs all the operational coordination of tasks in all the divisions is indicated by the solid lines connecting the executive office to the divisions. This structure, which might be called an "overcentralized product hierarchy," is not labeled in the figure since it is inferior to the simple product hierarchy in terms of the factors we are considering. It requires more coordination than the simple product hierarchy (since there is an extra layer of management involved in all decisions), but it has no greater efficiency or flexibility than the simple product hierarchy.

• *Functional hierarchy.* In a functional hierarchy, as shown at the bottom of figure 11.1, processors of a similar type are pooled in functional departments and shared among products. This sharing reduces duplication of effort and allows processing loads to be balanced over all products. For example, having a single engineering department in a company instead of separate engineering departments in each division may reduce the need to duplicate expensive facilities and may allow a few people with specialized expertise to be shared among all products instead of having to hire separate specialists for each division. In an even simpler example, a company may need less manufacturing capacity if, instead of having to provide enough capacity in each division to meet peak demands, it can balance heavy demands for one product against ordinary demands for other products that share the same manufacturing facility.

In a purely functional hierarchy, the "executive office" must coordinate the operational processing for all products. The task assignment method implied by the "pure" form of this organizational structure is somewhat more complicated than for the product hierarchy, because an extra layer of management is involved: Whenever a task of a certain type needs to be done, the executive office delegates it to the functional manager of the appropriate type, who, in turn, assigns it to one of the processors in that department. In order to make this assignment intelligently, the functional manager needs to keep track of not only the priorities of the tasks but also the loads and capabilities of the processors in the department.

• *Decentralized market.* So far we have considered two hierarchical structures for coordinating task assignments. One of the important insights from the literature of organizational theory and economics (e.g., see Williamson, 1975) is that the same tasks can, in principle, be coordinated by either a market or a hierarchy. For example, General Motors does not need to make all the components that go into its finished products. Instead of manufacturing its own tires, for instance, it can purchase tires from other suppliers. When it does this, it is using a market to coordinate the same activities (i.e., tire production) that would otherwise have been coordinated by hierarchical management structures within General Motors.

We distinguish here between two kinds of markets: decentralized and centralized. In a decentralized market, processors are shared among goals, but the decision making about task assignment is decentralized. In the pure form, this means that all buyers are in contact with all possible sellers and they each make their own decisions about which transactions to accept. For instance, the real estate and apartment markets in many areas are examples of decentralized markets where buyers must communicate with many different possible sellers to find the product they select. We model this process as one in which buyers send some form of "request for bids" to sellers of the appropriate type and then select a seller from among the bids received. In this framework, advertising can be considered a special kind of implicitly requested "bid." In either case, a large number of "messages" must be exchanged in a decentralized market in order for buyers and sellers to select each other.

• *Centralized market.* In a centralized market, buyers do not need to contact all possible sellers because a broker is already in contact with the possible sellers. This centralization of decision making means that substantially fewer messages need to be exchanged compared to a decentralized market. For example, the stock market is a relatively centralized market. People who want to buy a particular stock do not need to contact all the people who own that stock; they only need to contact a broker who is also in contact with people who want to sell the stock.

From a task assignment point of view, a centralized market is identical to a functional hierarchy. Both have a single central scheduler for each type of task, both require the same number of messages for assignment, both have the same amount of load sharing among processors, and both have the same responses to component failures. Thus one of the insights provided by this analysis is that these two forms, which would often be considered very different, are identical in terms of the information processing variables we are considering here.

• *Other organizational forms.* As mentioned above, these four "pure" organizational forms serve as building blocks for the much more complex organizations we observe. For example, a "matrix" organization is a hybrid form in which a functional hierarchy is augmented by separate product managers for each product who have direct links to specialized processors in each functional division.

4.1 Trade-Offs among Organizational Structures

Now that we have distinguished among these generic organizational forms, one of the most important questions we can ask is what are the relative advantages of each. In particular, we are concerned with the trade-offs between efficiency and flexibility in the different structures.

• *Efficiency*. We shall view efficiency as being composed of two elements: *production costs* and *coordination costs*. Production costs are the costs of performing the basic tasks necessary to achieve the organization's goals—for example, the basic manufacturing, marketing, and engineering tasks necessary to produce automobiles. Coordination costs include all the "overhead" associated with deciding which tasks will be performed by which processors. In hierarchies, much of what managers do can be considered "coordination costs." In markets, the equivalent coordination costs include costs for the seller (e.g., advertising and sales) and the "search costs" for the buyer (e.g., the costs of talking to many different salespeople.)

• *Flexibility*. In addition to being part of efficiency, coordination costs are also a component of flexibility, since the amount of recoordination necessary to adapt to new situations helps determine how flexible a structure is. The other component of flexibility we shall consider is *vulnerability costs*, or the unavoidable costs of a changed situation that are incurred before the organization can adapt to the new situation. For example, when one of a company's major suppliers goes out of business, the company may have a number of costs associated with finding a new supplier, renegotiating a contract, and so forth. These costs are vulnerability costs.

• *Comparisons*. As shown in table 11.2, it is now possible to compare the different organizational structures on the dimensions of production costs, coordination costs, and vulnerability costs. All the evaluation criteria shown in the table are represented as costs, so in every column low is "good" and high is "bad."

Table 11.2
Trade-offs among alternative organizational forms[a]

	Evaluation criteria: efficiency, flexibility		
Organizational form	Production costs (average delay)	Coordination costs (message processing costs)	Vulnerability costs (average cost of component failure)
Product hierarchy	H	L	M
Decentralized market	M	H	L
Centralized market/functional hierarchy	M	M	M′

a. L = low costs ("good"); M = medium costs; H = high costs ("bad").

Some of the comparisons in the table can be justified on the basis of previous generalizations about organizational design (e.g., Galbraith, 1973; March and Simon, 1958; Gulick and Urwick, 1937). A formal approach by Malone and Smith (1984; see also Malone, 1985) shows how all the inequalities shown in the table can be derived mathematically from a fairly straightforward set of assumptions using queueing theory. The appendix of this paper summarizes these assumptions and gives intuitive explanations of the reasoning in the mathematical proofs.

4.2 Organizational Science Applications of the Model

Even though we have illustrated this analysis of organizational structures with examples from human organizations, it can be applied to organizations of computer processors as well. This subsection summarizes one application of the model to computer systems and one to human organizations.

Decentralized Scheduling for Computer Networks

There are several examples of computer systems organized as decentralized markets (Malone et al., 1986; Smith and Davis, 1981; Farber and Larson. 1972). For example, the Enterprise system (Malone et al., 1986) is a decentralized scheduler that allows personal computers connected by a network to share tasks in a way that assigns tasks to the "best" available processor at any time. Processors with tasks to be done are clients and other unused processors on the networks are contractors. Clients send out "requests for bids" for tasks to be done, and potential contractors respond with "bids" indicating their availability or cost for performing the tasks. The clients then select a bidder and send the task to the winning bidder.

It is easy to imagine an alternative implementation of this system as a centralized market with one processor on the network serving as a single centralized broker. Instead of broadcasting announcements of tasks to be done to all available contractors, client machines would simply send their requests to the scheduling node. The scheduling node would keep track of the availability of all the processors on the network and send the task to the best processor when it became available.

We are now in a position to evaluate some of the relative advantages and disadvantages of the centralized and decentralized systems.

As shown in table 11.2, the primary advantage of the decentralized system is its high reliability (low vulnerability costs), and its primary disadvantage is the number of messages that must be transmitted back and forth to construct schedules (high coordination costs). Which of these factors is most important in a given situation depends on the system load, the cost of sending bidding messages, the reliability of the machines involved, and the costs of scheduler failure.

In particular, Malone and Smith (1984) derive exact comparisons between the two systems, based on the formulas used in the proofs of the inequalities. Then using rough estimates of the parameters for the environment in which the prototype Enterprise system was implemented, they show that the decentralized market appears to have a slight advantage over the centralized market in this environment. The direction of this result was, in fact, counterintuitive for the developers of the system.

Historical Changes in American Business Structures

Figure 11.2 summarizes, in simplified form, the changes in the dominant organizational structures used by American businesses as described by Chandler (1962, 1977) and other business historians. From about 1850 to 1910, numerous small businesses coordinated by decentralized market began to be superseded by large-scale functionally organized hierarchies. These hierarchies continued to grow in size until, in the early and middle parts of this century, they were in turn replaced by the multidivisional product hierarchies that are prevalent today.

Malone and Smith (1984) show how these changes can be explained in terms of the factors we have been considering. The first change, from decentralized markets to functional hierarchies, can be explained by noting that as decentralized markets grow larger, their coordination costs increase much more rapidly than the coordination costs for the equivalent func-

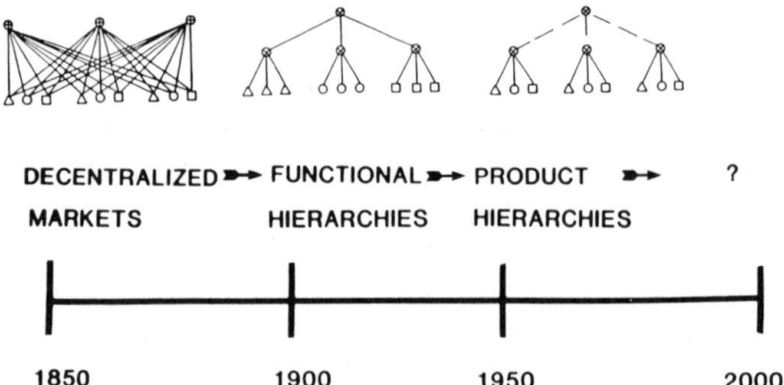

Figure 11.2
Changes of dominant organizational structures in American business.

tional hierarchies.[2] Thus, there will be situations where markets are preferred to functional hierarchies at one size, but where markets become less and less desirable as they grow. There is a pressure, then, for more and more of the activity that is coordinated by markets to be transferred into functional hierarchies in order to economize on coordination costs.

The second change, from functional hierarchies to product hierarchies, can be explained by observing how the relative importance of production costs and coordination costs was changing in the early part of this century. As table 11.2 shows, product hierarchies have lower coordination costs—but higher production costs—than functional hierarchies. During the period in question (roughly from 1920 to 1960), production processes became more and more efficient and constituted a smaller and smaller proportion of the total cost of products (e.g., see Jonscher, 1983). Meanwhile, there were fewer improvements in the efficiency of coordination processes, so coordination costs constituted an increasing proportion of the total costs of products. Thus product hierarchies, which economized on coordination costs instead of production costs, became increasingly attractive.

4.3 Implications for Designing Organizational Interfaces

This model gives us a systematic way of thinking about organizational coordination that can be useful in several ways in designing organizational interfaces. First, it helps predict what kinds of organizational structures will become more desirable with the widespread use of information technology. Second, it suggests specific ways of designing computer-based task assignment systems that support these new structures.

Effect of Widespread Use of Computers on Organizational Structure

In order to begin, we need to make some assumptions about which of the parameters in our model are directly affected by information technology. It seems plausible to hypothesize that the widespread use of computers in organizations may substantially decrease the "unit costs" of coordination—both the transmission and processing of information. This assumption is, of course, an empirically testable hypothesis, and there are at least some suggestive data that support it (e.g., Crawford, 1982). If coordination costs decrease, then coordination costs that would previously have been prohibitively high will, in some situations, become affordable.

According to our model, this could have at least two possible effects for companies presently organized as product hierarchies (see table 11.2). In some industries or firms, economizing on production costs is the most important strategic consideration. In these cases, our model suggests that product hierarchies should shift toward functional hierarchies in order to take advantage of the lower production costs in functional hierarchies. For example, some uses of computers (e.g., traditional "management information systems") might allow a greater efficiency and centralization of decision making by making it easier for top managers in large functional hierarchies to monitor and control their organizations (Galbraith, 1973; Walton and Vittori, 1983; Kling, 1980).

For many industries and companies, however, we believe that retaining maximum flexibility may be an even more important strategic consideration (e.g., see Piore and Sabel, 1984; Huber 1984). Our model suggests that these companies should shift toward being more like decentralized markets. The higher coordination requirements of these marketlike structures will now be more affordable, and markets provide the additional flexibility of being less vulnerable to sudden situational changes.

For example, information technology can lower the costs of marketlike transactions with innovations such as remote order entry terminals on customer premises, "electronic yellow pages," and on-line credit networks (see Ives and Learmonth, 1984, for examples of these and a number of related innovations already in use). Lowering these costs makes it easier for companies to use market mechanisms for rapidly adjusting to changes in supplies and demands.

There are two ways marketlike structures can be used for coordination. One way is with actual buying and selling between different companies. To make greater use of this mechanism for increasing flexibility, our economy will increasingly use products from numerous small firms whose activities are coordinated by decentralized markets rather than products from a few large hierarchies. The increasing importance of small entrepeneurial companies in many rapidly changing high-technology markets—particularly in the computers industry—provides an early indication of this trend (e.g., Rogers and Larsen, 1984).

Another, and perhaps more likely, possibility is that coordination mechanisms like those in a market will come to be used more and more inside large firms. For example, the widespread use of electronic mail, computer conferencing, and electronic markets (see below) can facilitate what some observers (e.g., Mintzberg, 1979; Toffler, 1970) have called "adhocracies," that is, rapidly changing organizations with many shifting project teams composed of people with different skills and knowledge. These organizations will rely heavily on networks of lateral relations at all levels of the organization rather than solely on the one-to-many hierarchical relations of traditional bureaucracies (e.g., Rogers, 1984; Naisbitt, 1982).

Computer-Based Internal Markets

Our model also suggests that any computer-aided task assignment system (e.g., Sluizer and Cashman, 1985; Kedzierski, 1982) should include not only descriptions of the tasks to be done and the capabilities of different people but also indications of the relative importance of different tasks. A market is a special kind of task assignment system in which importance is measured in money. It is easy to imagine similar kinds of project management systems that use a form of bidding with non-monetary "priority points" for task scheduling. To illustrate the point, I shall briefly describe a decentralized task assignment system that is exactly analogous to the system of priority points used for scheduling computer jobs by Malone et al. (1986).

In most projects there are tasks that can, in principle, be done by any of a number of project team members. The project manager does not always know enough about the skills, preferences, and availability of team members to do a good job of assigning these tasks to people. This is especially true when team members are working on several projects simultaneously. In these cases, a marketlike task assignment system can be of great value. Project managers can describe tasks and indicate their importance using priority points from a fixed budget of points they receive for the project. Then team members who are capable of doing the task can compare the importance of the task to their other tasks and decide whether they want to do the task and when they could complete it. Each team member who is interested submits a "bid" specifying an estimated completion time. The lowest bidder gets to do the job and accumulates the priority points associated with it. If no team member submits a satisfactory bid, the project manager may have to raise the priority points associated with the task. If team members finish a job substantially later than the completion time in their bid, they are penalized by losing priority points. The priority points accumulated by each team member can than be used in determining salaries, bonuses, or other forms of compensation.

A more elaborate version of this idea is suggested by the computer-mediated internal markets proposed by Turoff (1983). This system could help coordinate a range of activities from matching people and tasks to controlling information flows in a text sharing system. The basic premise is that there is an internal "free market" for information and services within an organization. Employees with desirable skills, for instance, can "contract out" some of their time to high bidders anywhere in the organization. In an extreme form of this system motivated and talented workers can "become their own boss" by fully paying off their own salary and devoting full time to being an information provider.

The market mechanism can also be used to help prevent unwanted information flows. For instance, the senders of unsolicited messages can be charged in proportion to the value of the time people will spend reading the messages, that is, more for long messages, more for messages sent to many people, and more for messages to highly paid recipients. In an even more extreme use of this idea, people who receive undesirable "junk mail" can indicate that fact and the sender will then be penalized by an additional surcharge (see Brobst et al., 1985, and Malone et al., in press, for an extended discussion).

5 Conclusion

Studies of people and computers have, in the past, fallen largely into two groups. On the one hand, there have been microlevel studies in the tradition of human factors and experimental psychology, which have focused on how to design individual user interfaces that were easy for people to learn and use. On the other hand, there have been macrolevel studies in the traditions of organization theory, economics, and other disciplines, which have largely taken computer technology as predetermined and focused on what effects it had or how to get people to use it.

In this chapter, I have tried to show how these two perspectives can be combined. I believe that we need to extend traditional cognitive points of view to include information processing and motivation of multiple agents in organizations. At the same time, we need to develop theoretical perspectives that do not view computer technology as a "black box" but instead have positive implications for designing computer systems that fit naturally into human organizations.

By extending the cognitive perspective to include not just individual information processing but also organizational information processing, this approach has several potential benefits for cognitive science. First, it seems likely that the transfer of insights back and forth between disciplines in this organizational science will be useful here, as it has been in other cognitive science endeavors. As computer system design comes to rely more and more on parallel processing architectures, lessons from human organizations, like the analysis of decentralized scheduling mechanisms described above, should become much more valuable. Even more intriguing for cognitive psychologists is the prospect of using lessons from human organizations and computer systems to develop better theories of how different processes within human brains are coordinated (e.g., Minsky, in press; Barnard, this volume). Finally, as Carroll remarks in the introduction to this volume, confronting the realities of designing computer systems that will be genuinely useful in human organizations provides a sobering test for the scope of our theories.

Appendix: Justifications for Organizational Form Comparisons

In this appendix, we give intuitive justifications of the qualitative comparisons in table 11.2. Formal proofs are included in Malone and Smith (1984) and Malone (1985).

Table 11.3 summarizes the assumptions made about different organizational structures. In addition, the following assumptions are made:

1. Productions costs are proportional to the average delay in processing tasks.
2. Tasks are randomly generated.
3. Processing each task takes a random amount of time.
4. Coordination costs are proportional to the number of messages sent between agents to assign tasks.
5 Vulnerability costs are proportional to the expected costs due to failures of processors or managers.
6. Both processors and scheduling managers sometimes fail (i.e., with probabilities greater than 0).
7. The cost of delaying a job in order to reassign it is less than the cost of disrupting an entire division or organization.
8. The cost of disrupting an entire organization is greater than the cost of disrupting a division.

Production Costs

The product hierarchy has the highest average delay in processing tasks because it uses slow processors that are not shared. The decentralized market, centralized market, and functional hierarchy all have a somewhat lower average delay time because they are able to take advantage of the "load leveling" that occurs when tasks are shared among a number of similar processors. For example, processors that would otherwise be idle can take on "overflow" tasks from busy processors, thus reducing the overall average delay.

Table 11.3
Assumptions about alternative organizational forms[a]

Organizational form	Production costs		Coordination costs		Vulnerability costs	
	Processors shared among products	Processor scale	Centralization of decision making	Minimum number of messages to assign task to best processor	Result of processor failure	Result of scheduler failure
Product hierarchy	No	Small	No	2	Division disrupted	—
Decentralized market	Yes	Small	No	$2m + 2$	Task reassigned	—
Centralized market/functional hierarchy	Yes	Small	Yes	4	Task reassigned	Entire organization disrupted

a. m = the number of processors in the market.

Coordination Costs

The product hierarchy requires the least number of messages for task assignment since each task is simply sent to the processor of the appropriate type in the division in which the task originates. The centralized market and functional hierarchy require more scheduling messages since tasks must be sent to a centralized manager (e.g., a functional manager or a broker) before being sent to the proper processor. The decentralized market requires the most messages of all since assigning each task requires sending "requests for bids" to a number of possible processors of the appropriate type and then receiving bids in return.

Vulnerability Costs

The decentralized market is the least vulnerable to component failure since if one processor fails, the task is only delayed until it can be transferred to another processor. The centralized market and functional hierarchy are somewhat more vulnerable since not only can tasks be delayed by the failure of individual processors, but also the entire system will fail if the centralized scheduling manager fails. The product hierarchy is also more vulnerable than the decentralized market because when a processor fails, tasks cannot be easily transferred to another similar processor.

Notes

1. A number of other factors, such as goal generation, problem decomposition, task prioritization, and result synthesis, are all important in multiagent problem solving, but they are present in single-agent problem solving as well.

2. The complete models used in Malone and Smith's explanations include two additional factors that were omitted here: (1) economies of sacle when large-scale processors are used instead of several small ones and (2) the effects of increasing the size of the economy as a whole.

References

Argyris, C. (1973). Some limits of rational man organizational theory. *Public Administration Review*, 253–267.

Barnard, P. (1987). Cognitive resources and the learning of human-computer dialogs.

Brachman, R. J., and Schmolze, J. G. (1985). An overview of the KL-ONE Knowledge Representation System. *Cognitive Science*, 9, 171–216.

Brobst, S. A., Malone, T. W., Grant, K. R., and Cohen, M. D. (1985). Toward intelligent message routing systems. *Proceedings of the Second International Symposium on Computer Message Systems*, Washington, DC. September.

Brotz, D. K. (1981). Laurel manual, Xerox Palo Alto Research Center Technical Report No. CSL-81-6, Palo Alto, CA, May.

Brown, J. S. (1983). Process versus product—a perspective on tools for communal and informal electronic learning. *Education in the Electronic Age*, Proceedings of a conference sponsored by Educational Broadcasting Corporation, WNET.

Card, S. K., Moran, T. P., and Newell, A. (1983). *The psychology of Human-Computer Interaction*, Hillsdale, NJ.

Carroll, J. M., and Thomas, J. C. (1980). Metaphor and the cognitive representation of computing systems. Yorktown Heights, NY: IBM Watson Research Center technical report no. RC 8302.

Chandler, A. D. (1962). *Strategy and Structure*, New York, Doubleday.

Chandler, A. D. (1977). *The Visible Hand: The Managerial Revolution in American Business*, Cambridge, MA, Belknap Press.

Corkill, D. D., and Lesser, V. R. (1983). The use of meta-level control for coordination in a distributed problem solving network. *Proceeding of the International Joint Conference on Artificial Intelligence.*

Crawford, A. B. (1982). Corporate electronic mail: A communication-intensive application of information technology, *MIS Quarterly*, September, 1–13.

Croft, W. B., and Lefkowitz, L. S. (1984). Task support in an office system. Technical report, Department of Computer and Information Science, University of Massachusetts, Amherst, MA.

Cyert, R. M., and March, J. G. (1963). *A Behavioral Theory of the Firm*, Englewood Cliffs, NJ, Prentice-Hall.

Denning, P. J. (1982). Electronic junk. *Communications of the ACM*, 25, 163–165.

Emmet, R. (1981). VNET or Gripenet? *Datamation*, 27, 48–58.

Engelbart, D. C. (1984). Collaboration support provisions in Augment. *Proceedings of the AFIPS 1984 Office AutoMation Conference*, Los Angeles, CA, February.

Erman, L. D., Hayes-Roth, F., Lesser, V. R., and Reddy, D. R. (1980). The Hearsay-II speech-understanding system: Integrating knowledge to resolve uncertainty. *Computing Surveys*, 12, 213–253.

Farber, D. J., and Larson, K. C. (1972). The structure of the distributed computing system—software. In J. Fox (Ed.), *Proceedings of the Symposium on Computer-Communications Networks and Teletraffic*, Brooklyn, NY, Polytechnic Press, pp. 539–545.

Fernandez, E., Summers, R., and Wood, C. (1981). *Database Security and Integrity*, Reading, MA, Addison-Wesley.

Fox, M., Greenberg, M., Sathi, A., Mattis, J., and Rychener, M. (1983). Callisto: An intelligent project Management system. Technical Report, Intelligent Systems Laboratory, Robotics Institute, Carnegie Mellon University, Pittsburgh, PA, November.

Galbraith, J. (1973). *Designing Complex Organizations*, Reading, MA, Addison-Wesley.

Goldstein, I. P., and Bobrow, D. (1980). Descriptions for a programming environment. *Proceedings of the 1st Annual National Conference on Artificial Intelligence*, Stanford, CA, August.

Gulick, I., and Urwick, L., Eds. (1937). *Papers on the Science of Administration*, New York, Institute of Public Administration, Columbia University.

Hackman, J. R., and Oldham, G. R. (1980). *Work Redesign*, Reading, MA, Addison-Wesley.

Herzberg, F. (1968). One more time: How do you motivate employees. *Harvard Business Review*, January/February, 53–62.

Hiltz, S. R., and Turoff, M. (1978). *The Network Nation: Human Communication via Computer*, Reading, MA, Addison-Wesley.

Huber, G. P. (1984). The nature and design of post-industrial organizations, *Management Science*, 30, 928–951.

Hurwicz, L. (1973). The design of resource allocation mechanisms. *American Economic Review Papers and Proceedings*, 58, 1–30.

Ives, B., and Learmonth, G. P. (1984). The information system as a competitive weapon. *Communications of the ACM*, 27, 1193–1201.

Jonscher, C. (1983). Information resources and productivity. *Information Economics and Policy*, 1, 13–35.

Kedzierski, B. (1982). Communication and management support in system development environments. *Proceedings of the Conference on Human Factors in Computer Systems*, Gaithersburg, MD, March.

Keen, P. G. W., and Scott Morton, M. S. (1978). *Decision Support Systems: An Organizational Perspective*, Reading, MA, Addison-Wesley.

Kling, R. (1980). Social analyses of computing: Theoretical perspectives in recent empirical research. *Computing Surveys*, 12, 61–110.

Kornfeld, W. A. (1982). Combinatorially implosive algorithms, *Communications of the ACM*, 25, 734–738.

Kornfeld, W. A., and Hewitt, C. (1981). The scientific community metaphor. *IEEE Transactions on Systems, Man, and Cybernetics*, SMC-11, 24–33.

Likert, R. (1961). *New Patterns of Management,* McGraw-Hill.

Lorsch, J. W., Gibson, C. F., and Seeger, J. A. (1975). First National City Bank Operating Group (A, A1, B, B1). Harvard Business School Case Nos. 9-474-165, 9-475-061, 9-474-166, and 9-475-062, Boston, MA, 1975.

Lowe, D. (1984). The Representation of Debate as a Basis for Information Storage and Retrieval. Unpublished Technical Report, Computer Science Dept., Stanford University, Stanford, CA January.

McGregor, D. (1960). *The Human Side of Enterprise,* New York; McGraw-Hill.

Malone, T. W. (1982a). Heuristics for designing enjoyable user interfaces: Lessons from computer games. *Proceedings of the CHI Conference on Human Factors in Computer Systems,* Gaithersburg, MD, March 15–17. (Reprinted in J. C. Thomas and M. L. Schneider, Eds., *Human Factors in Computer Systems,* Norwood, NJ, Ablex, 1984, 1–12.)

Malone, T. W. (1982b). Organizing information processing systems: Parallels between human organizations and computer systems. Xerox Palo Alto Research Center Working Paper, Palo Alto, CA, August.

Malone, T. W. (1985). Organizational structure and information technology: Elements of a formal theory. Massachusetts Institute of Technology, Center for Information Systems Research Working Paper #130, Sloan WP #1710-85, Management in the 1990's WP #85-011, August.

Malone, T. W., and Lepper, M. R. (in press). Making learning fun: A taxonomy of intrinsic motivations for learning. In R. E. Snow and M. J. Farr (Eds.), *Aptitude, Learning, and Instruction III: Conative and Affective Process Analyses,* Hillsdale, NJ, Erlbaum.

Malone, T. W., and Smith, S. A. (1984). Tradeoffs in designing organizations: Implications for new forms of human organizations and computer systems. Massachusetts Institute of Technology, Center for Information Systems Research Working Paper #112, Sloan WP #1541-84, March.

Malone, T. W., Grant, K. R., and Turbak, F. A. (1986). The information lens: An intelligent system for information sharing in organizations. To be published in *Proceedings of the CHI Conference on Human Factors in Computer Systems,* Boston, MA, April 13–17.

Malone, T. W., Fikes, R. E., Grant, K. R., and Howard, M. T. (1986). *Market-Like Task Scheduling in Distributed Computing Environments.* Massachusetts Institute of Technology, Center for Information Systems Research Working Paper #139, March.

Malone, T. W., Grant, K. R., Turbak, F. A., Brobst, S. A., and Cohen, M. D. (in press). Intelligent information sharing systems. *Communications of the ACM.*

March, J. G., and Simon, H. A. (1958). *Organizations,* New York, John Wiley.

Markus, L. (1983). Power, politics, and MIS implementation. *Communications of the ACM,* 430–444.

Marschak, J., and Radner, R. (1972). *Economic Theory of Teams.,* New Haven, Yale University Press.

Matteis, R. J. (1979). The new back office focuses on customer service. *Harvard Business Review,* 57, 146–159.

Minsky, M. (in press). *Society of Mind,* New York, Simon and Schuster.

Mintzberg, H. (1979). *The Structuring of Organizations,* Englewood Cliffs, NJ, Prentice-Hall.

Mintzberg, H. (1983). *Power in and around Organizations,* Englewood Cliffs, NJ, Prentice-Hall.

Mohrman, A. M., and Lawler, E. E. (1984). Information systems technology and organization: A review of theory and research. In W. F. McFarlan (Ed.), *The Information Systems Research Challenge,* Boston, Harvard Business School Press.

Mumford, E., and Henshall, D. (1979). *A Participative Approach to Computer Systems Design,* New York, John Wiley.

Naisbitt, J. (1982). *Megatrends,* New York, Warner.

Newell, A. (1980). Reasoning, problem solving, and decision processes: The problem space as a fundamental category. In R. Nickerson (Ed.), *Attention and Performance VIII,* Hillsdale, NJ, Erlbaum.

Newell, A., and Simon, H. A. (1972). *Human Problem Solving,* Englewood Cliffs, NJ, Prentice-Hall.

Norman, D. A. (1983). Design principles for human-computer interfaces. *Proceedings of the CHI'83 Conference on Human Factors in Computing Systems,* Boston, MA, December 12–15.

Pfeffer, J. (1981). *Power in Organizations,* Marshfield, MA, Pitman.

Piore, M. J., and Sabel, C. (1984). *The Second Industrial Divide,* New York, Basic Books.

Rice, R. E. (1980). Impacts of computer-mediated organizational and iterpersonal communication. In M. Williams (Ed.), *Annual Review of Information Science and Technology,* White Plains, NY, Knowledge Industry Publications.

Rockart, J. F. (1979). Chief executives define their own data needs. *Harvard Business Review.*

Roethlisberger, F. J., and Dickson, W. J. (1939). *Management and the Worker: An Account of a Research Program Conducted by the Western Electric Company, Hawthorne Works, Chicago,* Cambridge, MA, Harvard University Press.

Rogers, E. M. (1984). Information systems technology and organization: A sociological research perspective. In W. F. McFarlan (Ed.), *The Information Systems Research Challenge*. Boston, Harvard Business School Press.

Rogers, E. M., and Larsen, J. K. (1984). *Silicon Valley Fever: Growth of High Technology Culture*, New York, Basic Books.

Saltzer, J., and Schroeder, M. (1975). The protection of information in computer systems. *Proceedings of the IEEE*, 63, 1278–1308.

Sarin, S. K., and Greif, (1984). Software for interactive on-line conference. *Proceedings of the ACM-SIGOA Conference on Office Information Systems*, Toronto, Canada, June.

Simon, H. A. (1981). *The Sciences of the Artificial*, Cambridge, MA, MIT Press.

Sirbu, M., Schoichet, S., Kunin, J. S., Hammer, M., and Sutherland, J. (1984). OAM: An office analysis methodology. *Behaviour and Information Technology*, 3, 25–39.

Sluizer, S., and Cashman, P. (1985). XCP: An experimental tool for managing cooperative activity. *Proceedings of the ACM Computer Science Conference*, New Orleans, LA, March.

Smith R. G., and Davis, R. (1981). Frameworks for cooperation in distributed problem solving. *IEEE Transactions on Systems, Man, and Cybernetics*, SMC-11, 61–69.

Stallman, R. M. (1983). ZMail manual. MIT AI Lab Technical Report, Massachusetts Institute of Technology, Cambridge, MA, April.

Toffler, A. (1970). *Future Shock*, New York, Bantam Books.

Trigg, R. H., and Weiser, M. (1984). TEXTNET: A network-based approach to text handling. Unpublished Technical Report, Dept. of Computer Science, University of Maryland, College Park, MD.

Turoff, M. (1983). Information, value, and the internal marketplace. New Jersey Institute of Technology, Unpublished Manuscript, September.

Uhlig, R. P., Ed. (1981). *Computer Message Systems*, Amsterdam, North-Holland.

Walton, R. E., and Vittori, W. (1983). New information technology: Organizational problem or opportunity. *Office: Technology and People*, 1, 249–273.

Williamson, O. E. (1975). *Markets and Hierarchies*, New York, Free Press.

Wilson, P. A., Maude, T. I., Marshall, C. J., and Heaton, N. O. (1984). The active Mailbox—your on-line secretary. *Proceedings of the IFIP 6.5 Working Conference on Computer-based Message Services*, Nottingham, England, North-Holland.

Zuboff, S. (1982). New worlds of computer-mediated work. *Harvard Business Review*, 60, 142–152.

12 Cognitive Engineering–Cognitive Science

Donald A. Norman

There is an interesting interplay between theory and applications within a field. Although one thinks of an applied field as drawing from the knowledge, principles, facts, and theories of a science, in the cognitive sciences I find that application drives the science. The study of practical, applied problems reveals the deficiencies in the knowledge base of the science, providing important insights and data to the developing theoretical basis. This chapter focuses upon this last point: that the study of applications can add to the science.

Today, theory in cognitive science is unsettled, incomplete, and local: unsettled in that it is tentative, somewhat contradictory, and at best, only suggestive of the proper theory; incomplete in that it has major gaps and holes; local in that it concentrates upon the small at the expense of the whole. Now, for the purposes of applying knowledge, theories do not have to be perfect. All that matters is that they give sufficiently good approximations: they should produce results that are good enough for the application. Approximate theories will suffice. But we cannot have gaps.

Cognitive science, the theoretical science, can contribute to the applied field of human-computer interaction: examples of such contributions are presented in the other chapters of this book. But the contribution also goes the other way, from the applications to the science. In analyzing what goes on when people use computers, we enrich our understanding or what goes on in human performance in general and in what a theory of performance must cover.

The chapter was started at UCSD and completed while on sabbatical leave at the MRC Applied Psychology Unit, Cambridge, England. I thank the APU for the use of their facilities. The research at UCSD was partially supported by contract N0014-85-C-0133 NR 667-547 with the Personnel and Training Research Program of the Office of Naval Research and by a grant from the System Development Foundation.

1 Cognitive Engineering

Cognitive science is a fusion of many disciplines, all concerned with different aspects of cognition. It combines psychology, artificial intelligence, linguistics, sociology, anthropology, and philosophy. The combination seems essential, for each of the disciplines contributes an essential point of view and body of techniques, theories, and knowledge that is missed by the others. The scientific study of cognition requires the combined efforts of the various cognitive disciplines. The same story holds true for application. Indeed, I think that the case is even stronger for the need to combine disciplinary approaches. If the combination of the sciences yields cognitive science, then perhaps the combination of the applied areas of the disciplines should yield a cognitive engineering.

Why cognitive engineering? Why a new term? After all, there already exists several terms used to describe the applied side of psychology: ergonomics, human factors, and engineering psychology. I believe a new term is needed because a new approach is needed. More than just psychology is required. More than psychology coupled with engineering. We need all the disciplines of cognitive science, plus engineering. Moreover, the traditional fields have tended to restrict themselves, shunning this soft, mushy cognitive stuff in favor of behavioristic assessment, preferring empirical studies over theory, minimizing interdisciplinary approaches. The lack of theory in applications is particularly noteworthy. Until recently, there has been little or no appreciation of the importance of cognitive factors. I invented the term *cognitive engineering* to emphasize the cognitive aspects of human-machine interaction.[1] Actually, I encourage joining with ergonomics and human factors. Cognitive engineering is meant to combine with the applied disciplines, not to replace them. There is much good work in human factors. My argument is that it is essential to add cognition to the area. I would hope that such an argument would be unnecessary for the authors and readers of this book.

1.1 Is Cognitive Science a Subset of Cognitive Engineering?

To make a science of the design of human-machine interfaces will certainly require that we understand more of the human. But an interesting result occurs when we try to discover just what components of human behavior and thought are needed for the study of human-machine interaction. We soon discover that we need all of psychology—and more besides. We also need linguistics, sociology, some anthropology, and certainly a lot of computer science. In fact, for the applications of the science, the cognitive engineering needs so much from cognitive science that it is tempting to say that the science is a subset of the engineering, a statement somewhat at odds with conventional wisdom that suggests it is the other way around. But, actually, this will come as no surprise to any practitioner of a field: the breadth of knowledge required of a practitioner always exceeds that of the science. The scientist can afford to specialize, to restrict the area of enquiry to that which is manageable and productive. The sciences and their subareas have artificial boundaries, divisions erected for the convenience of the scientists. This is proper and appropriate for science. But the application of the science, the engineering side of things, cannot afford artificial boundaries. When we put a new machine into an office, the entire sociological structure of the office will change. And oftentimes the effect upon social structure will have more impact than the particulars of the hardware and the interface design (see the several chapters by Bannon 1986a, b, and Brown, 1986, in Norman and Draper, 1986). If the application is to be successful, the practitioner cannot ignore these aspects of the interaction. Social impact is just one of the unexpected interactions. In general, the impact of a system goes far beyond the area of any individual science. Those who would introduce these systems, including those who design and evaluate them, must therefore become knowledgeable about the whole range of cognitive sciences, or at least the range of applications of these sciences—and that is what a cognitive engineering should be about.

It is not hard to think of areas where general knowledge is required. For example, consider the "error messages" seemingly ever present in one's interaction with a computer system. Throughout the Norman and Draper book (1986) we argue that error messages should be part of the normal interactions of the system, part of the normal progression of a user toward the goal. The messages should therefore be considered a part of the dialog, not anything different or special. Both the computer system and the person must mutually attempt to work out a way of understanding and reaching the goal. This kind of approach to messages (and to instructional material in general, for error messages are really a part of instruction) requires understanding the nature of dialog, speech acts, and social conventions, as well as, of course, the person's knowledge structures and mental model of the system.

1.2 Application Pushing Theory: A Theory of Action

One major deficiency in our scientific understanding has forced itself upon me as a result of my studies of real interactions between people and computer systems. When I tried to analyze what was going on, I discovered that there were huge gaps. This, therefore, serves as a good example of how application can push theory.

Consider what happens when one wishes to do some real task. One starts with some goal in mind, although perhaps imprecisely specified—get the report finished, write a paper, finish the program, work on the budget. This goal defines the final state to be satisfied. Before it can lead to actions it must be transformed into more specific intentions, into specific action sequences that bridge the gap between what one would like to do (one's intentions) and the specific capabilities of the system (the allowable physical actions). Then the actions have to be physically performed, usually by typing or pointing. That is the output side. But there is still the critical evaluation side, the perception of the outcome, its interpretation and evaluation. Most goals are not satisfied with single actions. They require numerous sequences, with the who activity lasting hours or even days. There is a feedback loop, in which the results of one activity are used to direct further ones, in which goals lead to subgoals, intentions to subintentions—activities in which goals are forgotten, discarded, or reformulated. And if one then actually observes what really goes on in an office or home, one sees that the single activity is embedded in a continuing stream of other activities, competing for attention, being continually interrupted and resumed. How does one know where to resume an interrupted activity? What role do these interruptions play in the actual conduct of the task?

The set of problem areas is astounding. Yet psychology and cognitive science have remained remarkably silent about almost all of these areas. We do not know about how actions are initiated, how they are evaluated, or how they are reformulated. Some relevant understanding comes from the large literature on problem solving and the newer, smaller literature on planning. But these literatures turn out to focus on well-specified problems, on behavior that is not interrupted, on behavior that is easier to study and examine. What does happen in the world?

My attempts to understand this entire pattern of behavior have led me into uncharted waters. Some of the work starts off with relatively familiar topics, such as work in psychology and AI on problem solving and planning, and the GOMS model of Card, Moran, and Newell (1983: GOMS stands for Goals, Operators, Methods, and Selection). It soon encompasses social psychology and philosophy (for the theory of action). Sociology, especially ethnomethodology, has a lot to say about real work patterns and how people's behaviors deviate dramatically from their descriptions of their behaviors (and from their supervisor's descriptions). But nowhere is the story put together. No wonder: it is a most complex story.

My approach was to divide up the task into manageable components. One part of the example concerns the study of how people perform actions—a theory of action. This speaks of goals, intentions, and the internal specification of actions. The actual production of an action is only half the story, however. The other half involves the feedback loop: the perception, interpretation, and evaluation of the results of the action. This led me to postulate seven stages of action:

- forming the goal;
- forming the intention;
- specifying an action;
- executing the action;
- perceiving the system state;
- interpreting the system state;
- evaluating the outcome.

This is not an appropriate time to go into the details of the development (it is done in Norman, 1986). The point is simply that the need for such a theoretical analysis came about only through the needs of analyzing the interactions that went on between a person and a computer system. There is almost no psychological research on these issues. Yes, each of the seven stages corresponds to some subfield of psychology, but it is rare to see the total picture put together (the best example coming from 1960 in the work of Miller, Galanter, and Pribram).

But this analysis of stages of action still misses much of the complexity of real behavior. What about interruptions? What about social demands? Here again, there are problems badly in need of theory. I do not know the answers to these questions. The best I can do with the problem of task interruption is to discuss and analyze the situation, the first step being the two chapters by Cypher (1986) and by Miyata and Norman (1986). This is not satisfactory. Much more is required. But the first step is to specify the problem itself. Our research group used our book (Norman and Draper, 1986) as an opportunity to point out the issues, to discuss the complications of real interactions, and to cry out for more science in order to help the applications. It may not be fair to use my chapter in this book as a way of advertising what we did in that book, but the relevance to the point I am trying to make is clear. We called it "a book of questions, not answers."

Why? Because the demands of the application are pushing the theoretical side of the endeavor.

2 The Interface Experience

Now let us consider a different issue, how a full analysis of the interaction requires knowledge from across many disciplines. The example comes from the joint work that I have been doing with Ed Hutchins and Jim Hollan (again taken from that same book, Norman and Draper, 1986, this time the chapter by Hutchins, Hollan, and Norman, 1986). I describe the work briefly in the following sections, but it is useful first to review its origins. The work builds upon the analysis of the seven stages of action. We started with a basic question: Why are computers difficult to use? This led to an analysis of what Ben Shneiderman (1982, 1983) has called *direct manipulation* interfaces. In turn, this led us to ask what the notion of *directness* might mean. Brenda Laurel had been working on the subjective nature of the interface experience (Laurel, 1986), and her ideas proved to be critical. These were combined with a suggestion by Steve Draper (1986) about the relationship between the objects perceived as the output of the computer task and the objects upon which one acts. The result was that we realized that the term "direct" in the phrase "direct manipulation" was misleading. In fact, there are several different kinds of directness, each corresponding to a different aspect of the interface experience. Note the cast of characters who contributed to this analysis, for this is a clear case of interdisciplinary interaction: I come from psychology, Hutchins from anthropology, Hollan from both computer science and psychology, Shneiderman from computer science, Draper from artificial intelligence, and Laurel from drama (most of us also claim to be cognitive scientists).

2.1 Mapping Problems, Gulfs, and Bridges

Computers—and all complex machinery and system—can be difficult to learn, difficult to use. Many reasons for this are discussed throughout the chapters of this book, but one set of causes comes from an analysis of what must take place in order for a person to transform goals and intentions into a finished product. There are many things involved in the performance of a task. The person must transform mental goals and intentions into physical ones, thereby solving the mapping problem that relates psychological representations into physical actions. In order to interpret the outcomes, the person has to perceive the resulting system state, find the right mapping of the perceived state into physical variables, and then find the mapping from those physical variables into psychological ones. This analysis (summarized from Hutchins, Hollan, and Norman, 1986, and Norman, 1986) argues that there are two reasons why the use of a computer might add difficulties beyond that of the task itself:

1. The difficulties result from the *gulfs* that separate mental states from physical actions and states. There is a distinction between the *physical* variables that one manipulates and that provide information about the physical state of the system and the *psychological* variables that are of interest to the user. This is the essence of the mapping problem and the origin of the two gulfs that are to be bridged: The Gulf of Execution separates mental intentions from physical actions; The Gulf of Evaluation separates physical system state from the mental interpretation and evaluation of that state.

2. Computers can add to task difficulty when they stand between the person and the task, adding to the issues that must be dealt with to complete the task. When computers stand between, they act as an intermediary, requiring that the user be proficient in both the task domain and with the intermediary (the computer). Inasmuch as operations required of the intermediary are in addition to and orthogonal to the task, they can add to the overall complexity, even if that was not the intention of the designer.

To understand how we got to these conclusions requires an understanding of how we developed our theory. The theory had to combine a number of different things. First, it had to be built upon a theory of action, showing how one went from intentions to actions on the one hand and then from resulting system state to evaluation on the other. But this was not enough. The next step was to identify the relationship among these stages and the difficulties faced by users. This led us to the realization that there were two different kinds of problems, one the semantic mismatch between how a person would prefer to think about a task and the way in which the computer system required one to think—the semantic distance—and two, the physical (usually spatial) distance between the form of action or result desired and the form of action or display of the computer system—the articulatory distance.

Figure 12.1 summarizes the analysis. Here, the seven stages of action are arranged so as to show a cycle of activity that progresses from establishing the desired goal state through the execution of the physical action (this is the execution side of the cycle) and then from the perception of the

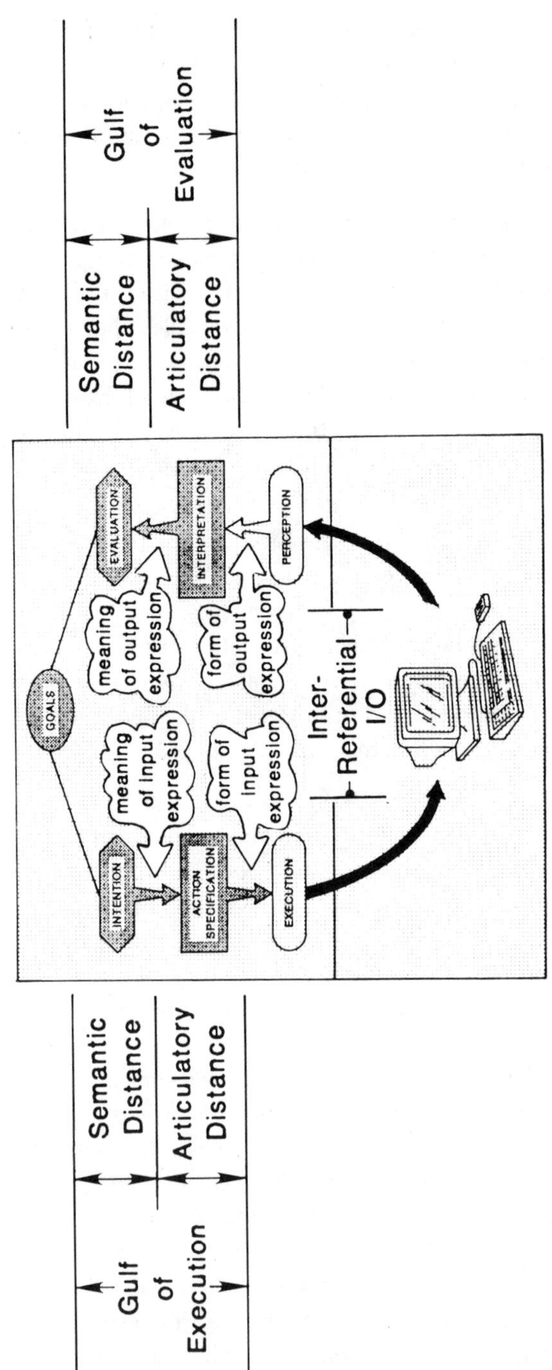

Figure 12.1
The seven stages of action and the Gulfs of Execution and Evaluation (from Hutchins, Hollan, and Norman, 1986).

physical state to its interpretation and evaluation (this is the evaluation side of the cycle). There are two kinds of gulfs: semantic and articulatory. The semantic gulf results from the difference between the language in which mental intentions and expectations are couched and the languages of allowable actions and resulting system states. The articulatory gulf reflects the mismatch between the intend actions and the physical implementation of them (on the action side) or between the expected relationship in the physical system and the manner in which these relationships are displayed to the user (on the evaluation side). Finally, the interreferential distance between input and output specifies the distinction between the objects upon which actions are performed and the objects upon which one perceives the output. In some systems these two are quite distinct, whereas in others the objects are identical.

This analysis finally allowed us to make sense of the subjective impressions of computer users. Some tasks always seemed more direct than others. In some systems—in particular, in some games and in high-quality aircraft simulators—there was a feeling of *direct engagement* with the objects of the task domain: one felt oneself as a part of the task, thinking in the language of the task, manipulating the objects of the domain directly, and getting feedback about the outcome directly. There did not appear to be a computer mediating between the user and the task.

The critical insight for understanding this subjective feeling came from the work of Laurel (1986), working from a background in drama, applying her analyses to computer games. Draper (1986) pointed out the critical relationship between the objects upon which one acts and the objects being perceived. Basically, when the objects of the action world differ from those of the perceptual world, there is apt to be an indirectness in the use of the system, the feeling that the computer acts as an intermediary standing between user and task. It is a master-servant relationship (the computer being the servant), not allowing the master to get directly involved. Laurel calls this a third person experience. On the other hand, when the objects of action and perception are the same, then there can be a feeling of direct engagement, of no intermediary between user and task. Laurel calls this a first-person experience.

2.2 Direct Manipulation Interfaces

These analyses now allow us to understand what is happening with the newer forms of interfaces, the kind that have come to be called "Direct Manipulation" (Shneiderman, 1982, 1983). This term has been overgeneralized and misused, but it refers to the kind of interface in which one directly moves the objects of interest on the computer screen. Thus, to initiate an action with such a system, one simply finds the object and performs the action upon it. For example, to move the location or change the size of a window on the display screen, in this form of interface, one physically moves a pointer to the desired location, or physically stretches the window to the desired size. This is direct manipulation in the best sense of the term: there is a direct relationship between the action desired (moving the window), the action required (moving the pointing device along the path one wishes the window to move), and the feedback about the outcome (the continual change in window position). In execution there is semantic directness (the desired actions map directly onto allowable actions) and there is articulatory directness (the hand motions mimic the window motions). In evaluation there is also both semantic and articulatory directness—the visual appearance directly reflects the state change and the movement of the window reflects intended movement. Finally, there is direct engagement with the object of the task domain: the object being acted upon is identical to the object the being perceived and evaluated. Thus, in moving the window in such a system, the user feels as if the world is under direct control.

These ideas are complex and this brief analysis does not explain them thoroughly. But even this brief treatment allows us to distinguish five different aspects of directness:

1. semantic directness in execution,
2. semantic directness in evaluation,
3. articulatory directness in execution,
4. articulatory directness in evaluation,
5. direct engagement—identity of the objects of execution and evaluation.

Note, however, that there seldom is such a thing as an interface that meets our standards for directness in a consistent way. So-called direct manipulation interfaces usually combine some direct mappings with a large number of arbitrary, abstract, and thereby indirect ones, Moreover, it is not always clear that directness (first-person experiences) is to be preferred: in some situations one wishes to have an intelligent intermediary, in which case the third-person, less direct situation would be superior. All in all, our main conclusion is that there exists a *space for interfaces*, a space created from the dimensions of directness we have identified, plus others. Each dimension in the space reflects one of the design considerations. No point in the space is superior to all others: each has its own set of virtues and limitations.

2.3 Implications for Cognitive Science and Engineering

This work suggests a new direction for both theory and practice. It suggests that what is important is the relationship between a person's psychological interpretation of the task and the way the system supports that interpretation. This is hardly news, but the distinction among the various aspects of the task is new: the distinctions between semantic and articulatory aspects of the actions and displays, the distinctions between execution and evaluation. And finally, the notion that the perception of the task changes when the relationship between the tasks acted upon and evaluated changes is quite new, a notion that has especially important consequences for theory as well as application.

The resulting design reflects the trade-offs among all the considerations. What is important is that the design space be known, that the space for interfaces be explicit, so that the design choices are made in an intelligent, informed way. This is one goal of cognitive engineering: to provide a set of design tools that allow for informed design.

The research that led us to this point is still at the early stages of its development. Much remains to be done, both on the theoretical side and on the engineering side. But the theoretical development would not have come about without two things: first, an interest in understanding just what went on when a person actually performed real tasks on real systems; second, the congruence of people with diverse academic backgrounds and training. This makes it a particularly good illustration of the close coupling that can exist between application and science. The result, I hope, is an advance both for the practice and the theory of human-computer interaction—a case of application driving theory and an illustration of the importance of integrating work across disciplines.

Note

1. In Europe, concern over a similar emphasis on cognition has resulted in the formation of an area—and an annual conference—called *cognitive ergonomics.*

References

Bannon, L. J. (1986a). Issues in design: Some notes. In D. A. Norman and S. W. Draper (Eds.), *User Centered System Design: New Perspectives on Human-Computer Interaction,* Hillsdale, NJ, Erlbaum Associates.

Bannon, L. J. (1986b). Helping users help each other. In D. A. Norman and S. W. Draper (Eds.), *User Centered System Design: New Perspectives on Human-Computer Interaction*, Hillsdale, NJ, Erlbaum Associates.

Brown, J. S. (1986). From cognitive to social ergonomics and beyond. In D. A. Norman and S. W. Draper (Eds.), *User Centered System Design: New Perspectives on Human-Computer Interaction*, Hillsdale, NJ, Erlbaum Associates.

Card, S., Moran, T., and Newell, A. (1983). *Applied Information-Processing Psychology*, Hillsdale, NJ, Erlbaum Associates.

Cypher, A. (1986). The structure of users' activities. In D. A. Norman and S. W. Draper (Eds.), *User Centered System Design: New Perspectives on Human-Computer Interaction*, Hillsdale, NJ, Erlbaum Associates.

Draper, S. W. (1986). Display managers as the basis for user-machine communication. In D. A. Norman and S. W. Draper (Eds.), *User Centered System Design: New Perspectives on Human-Computer Interaction*, Hillsdale, NJ, Erlbaum Associates.

Hutchins, E., Hollan, J. D., and Norman, D. A. (1986). Direct manipulation interfaces. In D. A. Norman and S. W. Draper (Eds.), *User Centered System Design: New Perspectives on Human-Computer Interaction*, Hillsdale, NJ, Erlbaum Associates.

Laurel, B. K. (1986). Interface as mimesis. In D. A. Norman and S. W. Draper (Eds.), *User Centered System Design: New Perspectives on Human-Computer Interaction*, Hillsdale, NJ, Erlbaum Associates.

Miller, G. A., Galanter, E., and Pribram, K. (1960). *Plans and the Structure of Behavior*, New York, Holt, Rinehart & Winston.

Miyata, Y., and Norman, D. A. (1986). Psychological issues in support of multiple activities. In D. A. Norman and S. W. Draper (Eds.), *User Centered System Design: New Perspectives on Human-Computer Interaction*, Hillsdale, NJ, Erlbaum Associates.

Norman, D. A. (1986). Cognitive engineering. In D. A. Norman and S. W. Draper (Eds.), *User Centered System Design: New Perspectives on Human-Computer Interaction*, Hillsdale, NJ, Erlbaum Associates.

Norman, D. A., and Draper, S. W. Eds. (1986). *User Centered System Design: New Perspectives on Human-Computer Interaction*, Hillsdale, NJ, Erlbaum Associates.

Shneiderman, B. (1982). The future of interactive systems and the emergence of direct manipulation. *Behavior and Information Technology*, 1, 237–256.

Shneiderman, B. (1983). Direct manipulation: A step beyond programming languages. *IEEE Computer*, 16 (8), 57–69.

Discussion: HCI, What Is It and What Research Is Needed?

Phyllis Reisner

Jack Carroll, in his preface, describes the interface as "computers as experienced and manipulated by human users." An interface, by definition, is a common boundary between two sides, the two "sides" in this case being the computer and the human. But there is a lack of symmetry around this interface. The two sides play very different roles. The principle object of study is the human. But the object of practical interest is the computer. In fact, the area of study in the field of human-computer interaction (HCI), as exemplified in this book, is not the *interaction* of humans and computers. The name is misleading. We already know what the computer will do. It will do whatever it has been programmed to do. The behavior of the human is our chief concern.

In the first part of this discussion chapter I have taken comments by various authors in the book as a point of departure. I am particularly concerned with trying to decide just what this field of HCI is, and isn't. Consensus about the nature of the field, even among those working in it, is decidely lacking. This first section is a statement of my own personal view of the field. My hope is that such personal statements, possibly leading to dialogue, will help us clarify this and other issues.

In the second section I have sketched some of the kinds of research and of practical work that are needed in HCI. Jack Carroll, in his preface, has issued a "call to arms" to cognitive scientists (and possibly others) for work in HCI. For those new to the field, in particular, this section is intended as a roadmap showing where to look for problems.

The third section discusses predictive modeling, an area that I consider one of the most important research areas at this time, and one that is well

---

Jack Carroll contributed much editing and some very good, pointed questions to this discussion chapter. John Whiteside and John Bennett both contributed some very useful comments. I acknowledge and thank them all.

represented in this book. In this third section, as in the second one, I have sketched some of the kinds of research that are needed.

1 What Is HCI?

What *is* the goal of this field of human-computer interaction? Quoting from the preface by Carroll again, "The principal goal is to provide an understanding of how human motivation, action, and experience place constraints on the usability of computer equipment." I agree in general with this formulation, but would like to relax the mildly negative emphasis on constraints. To me, the goal is simply to help create human interfaces that will in some sense be easy, pleasant, fruitful, or otherwise "good" for the person using them. To do so will require knowledge not only of human weaknesses but also of human abilities—and of human behavior—in using computers.

A major emphasis in this field is the focus on cognition as an important factor in the ease of use of the human-computer interface. Where earlier work on computer ease of use concentrated on physical factors, such as design of keyboards, and to some extent on perceptual factors, such as the size of letters on a display screen, current work is more concerned with such issues as understandability, memorability, and ease of learning how to use a system.

1.1 Is Human-Computer Interaction a Science?

Again in his preface, Jack Carroll speaks of an "applied science" of human-computer interaction. Can there be an applied science of human-computer interaction? In the strict sense of the word "science" as I understand it, the answer is no. A science is an attempt to understand the natural world (stars, people, materials, forces, . . .). Human-computer interaction is an attempt to learn how to build something—computer interfaces—with certain characteristics (e.g., ease of use). It is not an attempt to understand something in the natural world.

Even if we beg the question of "natural phenomena," and admit the study of human-computer interaction to the realm of potential scientific inquiry, the area still does not have the "flavor" of a science. The end goal in this area is very practical: help design better computer systems. It is important—and interesting—to study people in order to do so, but the end goal is a good interface design. The system designer will have practical questions in mind (e.g., is this interface easier to learn than that one). To answer such questions we may have to understand what people do when they use the systems, sometimes why they do it, and sometimes the why underneath the why. But there is a natural stopping point. When enough information is obtained to answer the practical questions, the inquiry stops.

This is not the case with a "real" science (such as cognitive psychology). In science (idealized, perhaps) answers to questions open up more questions. The best answer to a question is a better question. By analogy, the long-range goal in field such as human-computer interaction is to climb a hill to get to the top. The long-range goal of a science, on the other hand, is to climb a hill *in order to see the next hill or mountain*. This does not imply that HCI is static—far from it. There will probably always be new hills to climb, but they will not necessarily be the result of climbing present ones.

There is no serious harm in considering HCI a science. But communication is not helped by so doing. If I call a horse a hyena, no harm is done. I can still take a long and satisfying ride in the mountains. But I shall get some very strange looks when I talk about taking a ride on my hyena. There seems to be a tendency in our society to attempt to dignify many endeavors by the name "science." This attempt to dignify an endeavor in fact demeans it. By implication, it says that this is not a worthwhile activity in its own right. The usual quip, "Anything which calls itself science, isn't," is well-known.

1.2 HCI as Engineering

If HCI is not a science, what is it? As I see it, HCI is engineering: both practical, immediately applied engineering practice and more basic engineering research. The practice and the research sides of HCI are mutually dependent and complementary. The aim of the research is to make the practice better. And the practice is, and should be, a prime source of research problems.

As engineering *practice*, HCI attempts to help in the design of computer interfaces. The concerns are very pragmatic: increase market share, reduce catastrophic error, perhaps improve the "quality of life." It shares these pragmatic concerns with the field of human factors. In both its goals and its methodological approach to problems, HCI is, in fact, a subset of the field of human factors. It differs from some of the human factors work, if at all, only in the complexity of the problems and in the emphasis on cognition. But the motivation is the same: help design physical objects that people will use with pleasure and ease. Human factors in general, and HCI in particular, differ from what we usually think of as engineering only because humans, not materials, are the focus of study.

To say that this is engineering practice—a practical area—does not disparage it. While the goal is clear, how to achieve it is very far from obvious. The work we need to do is both challenging and exciting. Much of the practical work in this area requires both a research perspective and research skill. The discussion chapter in this book by John Whiteside and Dennis Wixon shows some challenges and approaches to achieving good interface design when trying to do so in a real situation.

HCI is also an engineering *research* area. In contrast to Whiteside and Wixon's emphasis on immediately practical HCI, most of the chapters in this book describe HCI research. The goal of HCI research, as I see it, is to develop knowledge, tools, and techniques that can then be used in HCI practice.

Both engineering research and scientific research have value. The same person can do both kinds of research, and they are typically interdependent. Galileo developing a telescope to look at the stars would be doing engineering research. Galileo describing the motions of the planets would be doing scientific research. Without the telescope, he would not have been able to see the planets. Without previous fundamental work on optics, there would have been no telescope. And without knowledge of the motion of planets, we would not have been able to travel to the moon.

Engineering research demands the same kinds of attitudes and skills as scientific research—and yields many of the same kinds of pleasures. But it has practical reality to circumscribe the choice of problems. This is an important benefit. For me, a serious problem in a "pure" or an academic field such as cognitive psychology (my original field) is that there are few if any a priori criteria for deciding which are the important research areas. Almost any question, depending on current tastes in the field, or possibly on research funding, is fair game. But in an applied area such as human-computer interaction there are specific, concrete questions that need to be answered.

1.3 Will the Application Drive the Science?

Norman says in his chapter, "The application drives the science." This is a memorable phrase. Chapters in this book show that applied questions lead to research that could eventually lead to "better" interfaces. This is not, however, what I would mean by an application driving a science. Improving interfaces would not be enough.

The key issues are (1) generality, and (2) actual use. For the application (human-computer interaction) truly to drive the science (cognitive science), results will have to generalize beyond HCI. If the end result of the research is a better human-computer interface, or even a set of better human-computer interfaces, or even a method of obtaining better human interfaces—this is not an application driving the science. For the application to drive the science, whatever comes out of the research must shed light on domains *other than* the design of computer interfaces. For this to happen, results must be potentially generalizable—I think some of the concepts such as Norman's seven stages in his action theory are potentially generalizable—and someone must actually *use* the concepts in some non-HCI area. Whether this will indeed happen is too early to tell.

2 What Research Is Needed

The amount of work that could be done is indeed staggering. Cognitive psychologists, with our training in empirical testing, concentration on cognitive issues, and ability to create behavioral definitions from vague concepts, are well equipped for it.

2.1 Concepts and Definitions

HCI is so new that clear, generally accepted definitions of some of the terms in it frequently do not exist. This applies to both the immediately practical work and to the research work that needs to be done. Developers want to design systems that are easy to use, natural, consistent, etc. Discussions can be very frustrating, and arguments interminable, because of the lack of definition of such terms. One of the real contributions to be made by cognitive psychologists is simply to decide on clear, behavioral definitions appropriate to the situation at hand—not always an easy task—and then to attempt to achieve a consensus by members of a design team. For example, by "easy to use," does one mean time to learn, time to perform after some criterion is reached, number or frequency of errors, severity of errors, subjective judgments of "easy," etc? "Natural" and "consistent" are harder. These are not well-defined concepts. Concepts such as these need to be formulated in ways that will permit experimentation and measurement.

The cognitive psychologist is particularly suited to this kind of very basic conceptual work. The part of the training of a cognitive scientist most important for this is so much a part of our thinking that we take it for granted. Cognitive psychologists (as any scientists) are trained to take imprecise notions and come up with behavioral definitions. It goes almost without saying that the cognitive psychologist has this training in areas dealing with cognition.

So, taking the notion of consistency, for example, can it be defined precisely—so that it can be measured? Can we measure the relationship of inconsistency to, e.g., learning or performance time? Can we do the same for "naturalness"? Are these even meaningful concepts? Once we have good definitions, we might be able to start making judgments about, for example, a trade-off between "consistency" and "naturalness." I am not assuming there will be just one answer. There may be different definitions and different trade-offs, in different situations. But without clear, behavioral definitions, it is almost impossible to proceed.

Much of the work in this book involves definition of concepts. Not all the concepts have yet reached the point of behavioral definition. However, even early verbal identification of concepts helps thinking and communication. Some examples in the book are: Malones's description of different kinds of organizational structures such as the decentralized network; Carroll and Rossson's notions of "production bias" and "assimilation bias;" Landauer's description of "highly available" command names (ones that are well-known, regularly spelled, etc.); Mayer's notion of the "microstructure" of a command language and his informal language for describing it, e.g., (CREATE, Prompt, Screen); Norman's elaboration of the concept of "direct manipulation" to include other kinds of "directness;" and numerous other examples.

2.2 Empirical Tests

Empirical testing is an obvious area for work by cognitive psychologists. There are variations on this theme. The first variation is testing of specific interfaces. Interfaces can be tested to identify flaws in design that would cause human error. The paper by Whiteside and Wixon gives examples of such human error. They can be tested to measure learning time, number of errors on some standard tasks, performance time, subjective "liking," or whatever is judged important. Such testing can be done on specific systems in isolation to obtain some figure of merit to be used by developers or marketing people. It can also be done for comparison against some criterion (e.g., 80% of typical users must be able to do these tasks in less than four hours). Or two or more interfaces can be tested to see which is better, again according to some criterion. Or specific, detailed design alternatives, such as which of two forms of a delete command in a text editor would be easier to learn or to use, can be compared.

Such testing may seem mundane and fairly straightforward. In fact, it can be extraordinarily challenging. The problem is one of size. To determine which of two expressions or words were the more difficult for people to learn or remember, one could clearly devise carefully controlled experiments. But how does one test a whole language, consisting of perhaps 30, 40, or more "words" and a potentially infinite number of sentences? Furthermore, how does one do it quickly, without the luxury of the caveats that abound in reporting of strictly scientific controlled experiments? To do such experimentation at all may not be difficult. To do it well can require a considerable amount of judgment. I think it requires the skills of both the researcher (e.g., to carefully control extraneous variables), and those of the engineer (e.g., to achieve results with limited resources). It also requires the temperament to live with less than perfect experimental control.

Experimental techniques that have been used in traditional cognitive science, or ones that are variations of such techniques, can sometimes solve problems in HCI research. An example in this book is the Robertson and Black work, cited in the chapter by Black, Kay, and Soloway. One problem with the kinds of modeling done by Polson, by Foss and DeRidder, by McKendree and Anderson (and by myself) is that analyses are essentially *guesses* at what a person's knowledge and goals are. Someone else, describing the same situation, might come up with a very different description. What is going on inside the user's head is not behaviorally observable. These descriptions about what is going on inside the user's head include guesses about both *what* a person is trying to do and about the *segmentation* of these intentions. Robertson and Black deal with the second problem—segmentation. Does a person try, for example, to locate a word to be deleted and start deleting it at the same time (using Black's example), or are these separate goals? The importance of the Robertson and Black work cited in Black's chapter is that a technique (location of pauses) used in psycholinguistic research is used to solve a problem in HCI research.

2.3 Research to Explain and Generalize Principles

At a somewhat more fundamental level, there is more experimentation to be done. In an earlier version of his preface, Jack Carroll pointed out that principles are beginning to emerge in this field: for example, that "direct pointing (via a mouse device or an electronic stylus) can be more efficient than pointing via directional keys...." Once the principles are firm, it would be useful to know *why* they are so. If the reason can be determined, then other principles might be inferred *without being first suggested by direct observation*. For example, one principle that is sometimes asserted is that in some circumstances menus are easier to use than command languages. An underlying psychological reason for this could be one we already know—recognition is easier than recall. Given this, what *other* HCI principles follow? Returning to the mouse versus stylus question, what is happening? Is the mouse easier because it is omnidirectional and there are consequently fewer human actions involved (move, check position of cursor, decide on next move, etc). If we can figure out what is happening, what other principles follow?

2.4 Data on Cognitive Processes

HCI needs data of the kind that cognitive psychologists are particularly qualified to obtain. There is a need for data to be used in the kinds of predictive modeling described in Olson's chapter and others. In particular, data are needed on times for certain human cognitive processes. There are some data in the landmark book by Card, Moran, and Newell, referenced frequently in this book by Polson and others. But this is the barest beginning. The data that are needed do not always exist or are not easy to find. For example, in some modeling I have been doing, I wanted information about the time to perform certain mental calculations. Data on mental arithmetic could be found in the literature, but not under the conditions I was dealing with, and not of the kinds of arithmetic involved.

2.5 Development and Testing of Guidelines

A particularly good source of ideas for research, particularly for experimental comparisons, is the guideline documents that have been compiled. These guidelines consist of suggestions such as where to position commands on a screen, preferable forms of abbreviation of commands, and when to use highlighting. Mayer's finding that users of BASIC made fewer errors when they knew the semantics (what happened inside the machine) as well as the syntax of BASIC could lead to a guideline: Teach semantics, as well as syntax, under the given conditions. (Other design alternatives, such as "Make the syntax more self-explanatory," would also be possible guidelines from his finding.) Some of the work described by Landauer could also lead to guidelines (e.g., "This is the best way to abbreviate," or "This is how to create command names").

Guidelines are, at this point, quite controversial. They serve a purpose if used with discretion. They can be useful as "memory prompts" for interface designers. They can also be useful in teaching interface design—if used carefully, to show the variety of issues to be considered. However, current guidelines have been compiled from a variety of sources; many if not most have not been experimentally verified; some may not even be correct—or not correct in certain contexts. Some are vague to the point of being useless. A clear, critical need is to clarify and test such guidelines. A good way to proceed would be simply to start reading, pick some guidelines that seem both wrong and important, and then test them against some reasonable alternative.

Another problem is that some of the guidelines are just *verbal* statements of what to do. There is often little or no measurement involved. So another need is measurement. How do these precepts relate to behavioral criteria of interest to designers (e.g., time to perform a task)?

Guidelines have also been criticized because they conflict. What should the designer do when one guideline conflicts with another? Which is more important? What are the trade-offs? There may not be general answers. But now, we have little or no experience on which even to base a judgment. Again, here is more opportunity for research.

2.6 Broader Coverage of the User Interface

In this book, most of the research is directed at teaching (learning) techniques and at input languages. Mayer's thesis that users of BASIC should be taught what happens inside the computer when they use BASIC, not just the language itself, is an example. Interestingly, what they are taught when using the high-level language BASIC resembles some of the lower-level, more detailed languages that BASIC was supposed to supplant for particular kinds of users. Other chapters also involve teaching/learning. McKendree and Anderson explore mechanisms that underlie skill acquisition. Clayton Lewis finds similarities between learning about computers and learning about mathematics. Carroll and Rosson want to mitigate "production bias"—an unwillingness to spend time learning instead of doing real work—quickly. To mitigate this bias, Carroll and Rosson have developed and tested, with good success, a "training wheels" version of a system—a subset of the functions of the system that can be learned quickly.

Other chapters deal with input. Landauer discusses selection of command names and also discusses menu structures. Norman's discussion of direct manipulation deals in part with input—I would consider direct manipulation a language in a very broad sense. Polson applies his modeling procedure to comparison of commands for a text editor. Foss and DeRidder's model also deals with transfer of training for an input language. Some of the models Olson describes in her survey have the same goal. Barnard's theoretical framework is also potentially applicable to input languages.

Other areas are virtually untouched: the area of output (what the computer shows the human), the area of documentation, and the area of specifying computer function (what the computer should do). There are a few examples in the book. In the area of output, Norman talks of direct manipulation in output (e.g., "The movement of the window reflects intended movement"). Carroll and Rosson mention a study by Rosson on organization of reference materials. Rosson suggests usage patterns be taken into account instead of the linear, alphabetical ordering she found. In the area of specifying function, Malone's paper is a good example. Malone extends the notion of human-computer interface to groups of people—suggesting some computer uses to facilitate human intercommunication. But the examples of work in these three areas are sparse. More work needs to be addressed in these other areas.

2.7 Development of a Research Framework

I said earlier that one advantage of this field is that reality can help circumscribe the choice of research problems. This is correct, but it is only part of the story. We have a criterion for selecting research problems—select those problems that will have the greatest effect on ease of use. But we still do not have a framework that will help us making these choices. We do not know which are the important problems. Landauer's discussion of the "contrived" experiments that were needed to demonstrate naming effects exemplifies this issue.

There is another problem, related to the lack of a research framework. At this point, the field of HCI is not *cumulative*. Solving one problem does not help with the next one. Empirical testing of specific interfaces, no matter how well done, does not advance the general state of the art. Testing one interface does not help with the next one—except in the skill and knowledge developed by the people doing the testing. Answering specific design questions is somewhat more general. But this is still not enough. Answering one question does not help with the next one. Deciding between different forms of a delete command does not help in choosing between menus and commands. There is no cohesion between the questions. Even developing one analysis technique does not lead to better analysis techniques. What this field needs is a framework to guide the research. I think this framework lies in the underlying cognitive processing being done. As of now, HCI is very far from having anything equivalent to the periodic table of chemical elements. Perhaps Barnard's model will be a step in this direction.

3 Modeling in HCI

One of the major advances we have seen recently in this field is the attempt to model human physical and cognitive performance in order to predict user performance. In my opinion, this is the most exciting area of HCI research at the present time. Foss and DeRidder, quoting Bryant Conant, say that "one of the signs of a mature science is a 'low degree of empiricism.'" That is, as the science matures, more and more answers can be derived from theory. Less experimentation is needed. Clearly, many, if not most, of the papers in this book involve some form of modeling.

Why model? First, of course, it economizes on effort. Behavioral tests are costly and time consuming. From a practical point of view, if the same answers can be obtained much faster from a model than from an empirical test, the economical thing to do is to model. There is another reason—related to the lack of a framework for selecting important research problems discussed earlier. We do not currently have a framework. I am hoping that we will, and betting that it will be based on underlying cognitive processing. But we may never have one. It may be that there are no really crucial very important problems—only myriad small ones. Many small problems, taken together, may result in unusable systems, but research on any particular problem may be disproportionate to the return expected. In such a situation what is needed is not solutions to specific problems at all. What is needed are *ways of analyzing problems as they arise.* In this sense, modeling techniques are extremely general. They can—if we develop them properly—be applied to problems that no one has yet encountered—at the time that answers are needed.

3.1 Some Goals of Modeling

In principle, it should be possible to develop models for any of the purposes that one does empirical testing: comparing designs, comparing systems, predicting parameters, such as learning or performance time. It might even be possible to develop models to locate some kinds of design flaws that lead to some kinds of human error. We are nowhere near such elaborate goals.

One goal of modeling is clear, explicit description. Such description, in itself, can lead to finding design flaws in a system. Many kinds of models consist of two parts—a descriptive part and an analysis based on the description. For example, listing the steps a user goes through would be a description, while counting the steps listed would be a simple form of analysis. Some models, in my experience, have already been of value in the real world—but simply because of the descriptive step. The simple act of describing, precisely, the steps a user is expected to go through in using a system can lead to the discovery of flaws in design that could lead to user error. The descriptive part of such models is really a form of task analysis. Thus, while few or none of the models developed so far have, as part of their analysis procedure, the *intent* to discover potential design flaws, simply writing down the preparatory, descriptive portion sometimes has this result. Whether or not such modeling will indeed discover flaws in design depends, however, on the person doing the modeling. This is why models need an explicit analysis procedure in addition to a description.

There is more value to models than simple task analysis, however. In some cases, the models give us a framework for thinking about problems. They tell us *how* to go about thinking through a design problem. In this, they really make explicit the kind of intuitive, possibly subconscious reasoning that the best designers have always done. With such knowledge explicit, the reasoning is available to those of us who may not have the best intuitions in all cases. I am very excited about this kind of modeling.

3.2 Stages in the Development of Models

There are various stages in the development of a model. Some of the chapters in this book are illustrative of the various stages. When we see a model in an early stage of development, this is an immediate opportunity to develop it further. The first stage in development of a model is simply the identification and labeling of relevant concepts. This is a very important stage. Without the concept of gravity, measurement of the acceleration due to gravity—the rate at which things fall—would not have been possible. Some of the work in this book is at this very important stage. Norman's concept of "semantic distance" is an example. The next stage in the development of a model is to define the concepts identified so that measurement is possible. One definition of semantic distance might involve, for example, the number of terms in common between a user and a designer of some input language. We might decide, for example, to define semantic distance as some function of the number of common terms divided by the number of terms for user and designer combined. A definition at this second stage might be a procedure, or even a language or code. Mayer's technique for describing the "microstructure" of BASIC statements is an example. He has given us a language or code (e.g., CREATE, Prompt, Screen) that would permit different analysts, in principle, to arrive at the same description of microstructure of a given BASIC statement. This second stage in the development of model basically gives us a way to be concrete about independent variables.

The third stage, of course, is to relate the independent to the dependent variables we are interested in. So if we had a precise definition of semantic distance, for example, we might then want to say that as semantic distance increases the number of errors also increases. We might even want to make a prediction about the mathematical form of the increase. Landauer's mathematical models involving menu depth and breadth are an example.

3.3 What to Model

One can choose to model many different kinds of things. Olson, for example, describes some models of a user's task—what he/she has to do to use an input language. The keystroke-level model referred to frequently in the book is an example. Such models can be models of the input language as it is supposed to be used. Another, very different kind of model—sometimes intended for the same kinds of predictions—attempts to model what is happening in the user's mind. The chapters by Polson, by Foss and DeRidder, and by McKendree and Anderson all describe such models of cognitive processing. Where the keystroke-level model might have one catchall factor ("mental processing is going on now") these models all describe that mental processing.

It is an open question whether modeling of mental processing is appropriate for making predictions in an engineering context. More precisely, it is still on open question for what kinds of predictions, or what kinds of problems, such detail is needed. This is an area in which research is needed. My personal suspicion is that such modeling may be more than is needed. Simpler models should suffice. I suspect that something more than "mental processing is going on," but less than modeling cognitive *processing* in detail, will be necessary and sufficient for a large number of problems. Until the Polson-like models are developed and tested, however, and until they are tested against simpler alternatives, we shall not be able to know how much modeling, for what payoff, is needed.

3.4 Can Models Replace Testing?

Polson suggests that his modeling technique might be used to replace or to complement fast prototyping. Can such modeling replace empirical testing? NO, NO, a thousand times NO. First of all, the Polson model describes *task complexity*—the difficulty of the task as it has been designed. It does not test *user perceived complexity*—difficulty of the task as the user perceives it. User perceived complexity can be greater than the task complexity itself because of some of the issues discussed elsewhere, such as inconsistency of commands or difficulty of learning names for commands. Only when all else is equal would task complexity be the same as user-perceived complexity. We rarely know, except in experimental situations, what "all else" consists of. It may be possible to extend this kind of model to include user-perceived complexity. This, too, is an open question. If so, however, there will still be a need for testing, for the following reason.

Most of the modeling procedures today are used to compare design alternatives. There are few, if any, that will systematically catch the flaws in design that will cause human error. I do not know how far we will be able to get in this area. Even if we develop tests to predict some kinds of errors, I seriously doubt that we will be able to predict all of them. Some behavioral testing will always be necessary—in new situations, at least. Whiteside and Wixon's example of a user trying to insert a diskette into a crack in the chassis is a fine example. I can image no kind of model that would have predicted this. The basic problem is the creativity of the human mind. Faced with something unknown, we try to make sense of it—and that sense is very likely not to be what the designer had in mind.

Behavioral tests and models are not in competition. They are complementary. Empirical tests are needed to determine whether the predictions of models are correct. Furthermore, when model and experiment do not agree, there is opportunity for further refinement or development of a model.

3.5 What Kinds of Research Are Needed on Modeling?

What limits use of models as tools now? Basically, they are not yet well developed. Many of the kinds of models needed do not yet even exist. Of the models developed, most have been used only in very limited laboratory tests—and usually by the developers themselves. Where data exist for parameter estimation, they have often been obtained from the data themselves or from fairly limited tests—not from a wide variety of circumstances. Most of the models, if not all, have not been tested *as engineering tools*. All of the above represent research opportunities.

What needs to be done? This is a wide open area. Many of the kinds of models needed do not yet exist. There has been little or no work to predict design flaws that would cause user error. The purpose of such models would be to predict *specific* user errors—what mistakes a user would make, and maybe even how frequently. Perhaps some of the kinds of errors described by Mayer or by Lewis would be a starting point for thinking about this. I suspect that AI or knowledge-based models will be needed to describe WHAT a person actually does know and can deduce, in order to compare this to what he/she should know. In addition, models that predict user performance or learning time usually or always assume error-free performance. So models are needed to predict—not only which errors, but the effect of errors on performance. Furthermore I can think of no modeling involving some of the components of the user interface: documentation and teaching, for example. I know of little or no work that attempts to model any of the guidelines discussed earlier. Such models might be based on description of physical or cognitive functioning. This, too, is wide open.

Another wide open area is empirical testing and development of the models that already exist, and of others that will come, *as design tools*. There are a number of facets to such testing and development. The first is the issue of replicability. When the models involve descriptions of cognitive processes, these are usually guesses. The specific productions written are assumptions about mental processes. We have not yet verified that these assumptions themselves are correct. This may not matter if the goal is to use the descriptions (productions) in testing a theory of the mechanism of skill acquisition, as do McKendree and Anderson. It does matter, however, if we want to use such models as engineering tools to predict ease of use. The problem is that we do not know whether different people would write the same productions to describe the same situation. Nor whether there would be different predictions if they did. If different people describe the same situation very differently—not just the words, but the concepts—and if the resultant predictions are also different, we would not have a stable measuring device. A ruler that changes its length with the person using it would not be too useful.

A second open area in the use of models as tools is the ease of use *of the tool*. I suspect that some of the tools will be difficult to use. (Writing a formal grammar, for example, can be tedious.) I suspect that writing a Polson-type model will also require training, and possibly even a particular type of background (cognitive psychology?). If we find tools that really do the job they are supposed to, but are not easy to use, then we may have to develop teaching techniques, computer aids, and documentation to help us use the tools effectively. And then we would have to *test* the teaching techniques, computer aids, and documentation for *their* ease of use. We may, in fact, have to do the same kinds of work, to make the modeling tools easy to use, that we have to do to make computer interfaces easy to use.

A third issue in the use of models as tools is that of benefit—and of cost/benefit. Do these models really tell us anything that we would not know without them? Some of the models require a great deal of work in order to choose the better of two designs (e.g., two ways of deleting text in a text editor). Would designers, without going through all this work, make the same, correct predictions? What percentage of them would do so? How about cognitive scientists; would they do better or worse? (My personal opinion, supported by informal tests run by a colleague (H. Dunsmore), is that some kinds of models do make correct predictions where some computer science students, at least, did not, but more work is clearly needed.) To find out the benefit of modeling, we would need to run experiments, with people using the various models, to test the models as tools. Another open question is comparison of the models. Some of the models make predictions about the same kinds of decisions. Are the decisions the same? Are some models easier to use than others? Are some of the notations easier to use than others? Are some models more accurate than others? Again, behavioral tests would be needed to find out.

4 Summary

HCI is a new and challenging area. There are good research problems, as well as practical ones, to be solved. Real needs exist to help in the selection of problems. There is work to be done in testing of specific interfaces, in explaining and generalizing principles, in obtaining data on cognitive processes, in development and testing of guidelines, and in extending almost all these kinds of work to components of the user interface that are virtually untouched. There is at present no framework to guide in the selection of problems. Any help along these lines, if possible, would be most useful. Development of models as engineering tools is a particularly exciting research area. Models need to be developed in areas where almost no work has been done. Both current and future models will need to be tested, and developed, as engineering tools. The amount of work that could be, and one hopes will be, done is truly staggering.

Discussion: Improving Human-Computer Interaction—a Quest for Cognitive Science

John Whiteside and Dennis Wixon

In his preface, Jack Carroll declares that an applied science of human-computer interaction grounded in the framework of cognitive science is at hand. This applied science, he promises, will both transform, for the better, the quality of human-computer interaction and also increase our theoretical knowledge about the workings of mind. This book is an attempt to share this vision with cognitive scientists generally, to communicate enthusiasm about this applied field with them, and to enlist their help. Its chapters constitute examples of early returns from this research effort.

Many of the authors state or imply that a great opportunity for cognitive science is at hand, an opportunity for a breakthrough in the understanding of mind and for a breakthrough in the design of systems that are truly used and enjoyed by people.

Opportunities for breakthrough have a double-edged characteristic; they generally involve putting at risk what one has—betting it, as it were, against the possibility of something better. Cognitive science is betting its paradigm, its world view, its methods, and its credibility. Industry is betting that cognitive scientists have something practical to offer. In this interaction, each camp will likely be called upon to reexamine some basic assumptions and ways of doing business.

We definitely share the excitement about the work. Below we share with the authors and readers some specific invitations to action, intended to hasten the breakthroughs we all seek.

The views expressed in this paper are those of the authors and do not reflect the views of Digital Equipment Corporation.

1 Could the Goals of This Effort Be Made Easier for Engineers to Understand?

The authors of these chapters have two broad goals. They want to increase our understanding about human cognitive functioning. They want to contribute to the design of systems that people can readily use and will enjoy. There is an underlying optimism that these goals are not in conflict and that progress along one front will lead to progress on the other. Throughout the papers there is a fusion of commitments—practical engineering commitments fused with theoretical science commitments. Carroll says that both can be served simultaneously. Reitman Olson speaks of studying cognition and developing easy-to-use systems in the same introductory sentence. Landauer hopes that the commitments of the fields are congruent. Don Norman sees strong contributions in both directions, and even makes the unusual suggestion that cognitive science may be a subset of cognitive engineering.

However, a number of authors sound cautionary notes. Phil Barnard says, "All too often specific cognitive theories are restricted in scope to a small class of simplified and well-delineated laboratory paradigms." Similarly, Tom Landauer writes, "Another and more fundamental reason for limited application of principles is that the way in which cognition has been studied in the psychology laboratory has promoted, by and large, an interest in variables of only theoretical importance, ones that can reveal something about the workings of the mind—but not necessarily ones having large and robust effects."

These cautionary notes suggest that if the cognitive scientists wish to influence the design of systems, they will need to be more specific and aggressive in their goals. We invite them to state clearly what they wish to achieve with respect to the design of working systems. An example would be to create a tutoring system for a computer language that would cut learning time in half and improve students' scores by 20%. The value of such a commitment is that it would focus research and, if successful, would provide a powerful example of what could be done. It would also lead the cognitive scientists to consider the complex problem of mapping from their core constructs to the complexities of an application environment.

Such examples may be critical in enlisting the engineers and corporations in the enterprise of using cognitive science to build systems. Clearly the support of engineers and corporations is critical since they are the ones who build and sell computer systems. A proven track record with real systems would be a powerful selling point. A successful experiment based on a limited system is considerably less convincing. Beyond selling some aspect of a particular method to a particular company, a working system based on a paradigm could profoundly increase the likelihood that cognitive science would succeed in influencing computer systems.

Another effect of trying to build a real system would be to acquaint cognitive scientists with what engineering is like. Engineering is very much a matter of making definite commitments about what is to be built and with what properties, at what cost, and by when. To speak effectively to the engineering world, cognitive scientists must develop more sympathy for the engineering perspective. Engineering is the business of actualizing, bringing to life, a workable, economic, whole solution to a known problem. This implies clearly identified goals to be attained, solutions that are picked over other solutions because of their relevance to and impact on the achievement of the goals, and implementation and iterative refinement of the solutions until a working system is built. This culture differs considerably from that of academic research. Goals, schedule, and resources simply do not play the same role in research as in engineering. If an experiment yields results that are not clear-cut, the researcher can suspend judgment till the next experiment. (The statistical decision procedures explicitly encourage such an approach.) In contrast, the product will get built anyway with or without the input from the human factors consultant. Thus, the goal is to give the best advice possible in a timely fashion.

What systems have already been affected by the work described here, and similar work that led up to it? In what time frame will the profound influence on interface design, predicted by McKendree and Anderson, be felt? We issue the following invitation to cognitive science researchers. Commit to building a system that will be used in the domain to which your current research project applies. Set definite goals for the usability of such a system in relation to the system that fulfills the same need today. Include in your planning a commitment to a schedule and a development cost. We can guarantee that whether the system developed succeeds or fails, you will come away with a greater appreciation for engineering in the real world and with a more robust model.

2 Could We Study Human-Computer Interaction in a Richer Context?

The problem of context is mentioned by many of the authors. There is a sense in which the preferred method of cognitive science is to remove things from their context for the purpose of understanding and analysis.

For example, McKendree and Anderson change the names of three of the four Lisp commands they use in their study. In all the cases where they make a change, they substitute a more mnemonic name. Similarly, Foss and DeRidder restricted the set of commands in various commercial editors in order to "minimize their similarity." This technique resulted in a more clear-cut test. But is generalization from these out-of-context circumstances to the larger and more realistic context really straightforward and assured? Barnard raises a similar concern when he points out that many of the experiments designed to test cognitive models require "that subjects construct special-purpose mental representations to cope with the particular conditions of the experiment."

By contrast, Landauer takes a contextualist position when he states, "There is no sense in which we can study cognition meaningfully divorced from the task contexts in which it finds itself in the world," and later in the same paragraph, "The science of mind is, I assert, not the science of what the mind can do in a laboratory situation artificially rigged to make it relevant to one of our theories, but what it does in a situation naturally or artificially rigged by itself and its culture."

On the other hand, Landauer's own experiment on editor command names, which he discusses in his chapter, used an editor with a command set at least an order of magnitude smaller than that in even the simplest commercial systems.

In our own product development work, we have found it fruitful to study the broadest and most realistic context possible. Whenever we constrain the situation, we miss something of value. As an example, we often do installation studies. In these, participants are asked to unpack equipment from the packing cartons and get it running. We do these studies in the laboratory, make notes and videotapes, and redesign the packaging materials and instructions on the basis of the difficulties that the participants have. What we completely missed by doing this in the lab, as opposed to at the customer site, was that customers were annoyed by and had difficulty disposing of the large amount of cardboard packaging material. In the lab, we simply removed it for them, in preparation for the next experiment; thus we were blind to the problem. As another example, although a mouse is in theory an optimal device (as Landauer points out), we have seen, in a "naturalistic" setting (an office), a user spill his coffee onto his papers and trousers by overly vigorous mouse movements. We have interviewed users who will not use a mouse for this and related reasons. They are not impressed by theoretical models that show it to be an optimal pointing device.

Now these examples, spilling coffee and getting rid of excess packaging material, may not be of concern to theoretical cognitive psychologists. However, they are absolutely vital to the building of computer systems that are genuinely used and enjoyed by people.

3 Why Not Tackle Real Systems?

Landauer suggests that research questions be motivated by practical interface problems. How much of the research described here was so motivated?

Polson describes an experiment involving the loading of a diskette into a drive and then performing some utility tasks. Careful reading reveals that the subjects did not actually load physical diskettes; rather the loading of diskettes was simulated. First the diskettes themselves were not real; instead, diagrams of diskettes and drives were presented on a computer terminal. Second, users never touched a physical diskette; instead, they pressed function keys. Thus, rather than performing physical actions, users traversed a series of menus. In addition, the feedback to users was controlled and artificial. For example, the system did not permit users to take correct actions that would have taken them off of Polson's predefined minimum path of actions for the task. User errors resulted in a presentation of the "user's goals" (the same ones postulated by the theory).

Contrast this experiment with observations we have seen of users actually trying to use diskettes. On one prototype, a pair of users successfully inserted a diskette, not into the drive, but into a seam in the plastic case that they mistook as the drive-slot. As a result of this experiment, the design of the case was modified. Notice that this practical consequence was a result of direct observation of real users working with real diskettes on a system prototype.

From this perspective, in trying to isolate the user's behavior from a broader context, Polson has for us lessened the practical value of observing the behavior.

Notice too that the tightly controlled, constrained nature of the experimental situation may blind the observer to aspects of the behavior that are unexpected and that might contribute to a breakthrough in understanding or design. We invite the authors to observe some people doing real work and to try to do this with as few theoretical preconceptions as possible, following a hermeneutic approach. We predict that they will find a rich set of observations and questions, which could serve as the basis for further modeling and theorizing.

4 Can We Learn from and Build on Systems That Exist Now?

Much of the work in this volume seems to take a radical or revolutionary approach to system design. It is critical of current human factors work as being limited in scope and too specific. Several of the authors see rapid prototyping and evaluation of working systems to be of limited value. But these criticisms raise larger issues. Why is rapid prototyping and empirical testing so widely advocated now? What makes these attractive? Why is it that currently available models do not enjoy comparable popularity? The fact is that there are strong reasons why rapid prototyping is popular. Such techniques may be popular precisely because they are limited in scope and specific. Prototyping appears to offer a way to test something that looks like the final interface including all the details. It offers a test of a specific system with conclusions limited to that system, which is exactly what the designer of that system needs.

The word rapid has been added to prototyping because its advocates are aware that they must have input early into the design cycle. While cognitive models may offer promise, their robustness and specificity are subjects of suspicion among engineers. We have heard engineers say, "When I see someone struggling with my interface, then I will fix it." Engineers tend to be a skeptical lot; they have little use for experiments or models laden with psychological assumptions. They tend to raise critical questions with respect to the assumptions inevitably involved in such research and models. Perhaps we should try for a rapprochement between the two techniques. Maybe cognitive science could provide a basis for the first prototype. Then the applicability of the generalizations from a formal model could be evaluated as part of a total system before they are integrated into a software design.

How people design interfaces is often thought to be a black art. However, certain generalizations seem true. One is that many, if not most, designers begin with an existing design and then seek to improve it; or they may take elements from a number of designs and combine them in unique and new ways. It is very rare in any engineering to start with the proverbial clean sheet. In our experience, empirical evaluation of existing interfaces has frequently had a profound impact on new designs. Frequently we have been able to uncover failures in existing products that would otherwise have been the basis of the next product; thus we avoided repeating the mistakes yet again. People advocating the use of formal models might adopt a similar approach. Can they be applied to existing interfaces to show problems? If not, can they be extended to do so? Such an application would be a powerful demonstration of the usefulness of such approaches.

5 Assume That Users Do Not Start with Goals

A number of the chapters claim that the best starting point for an analysis of user behavior is to assume that users have goals, and that these drive their behavior and determine what they will do. The GOMS model, discussed by Reitman Olson, has a "goal stack" in "short-term memory." Polson's production system assumes as its starting point (mentally?) representable goals that are manipulated and translated into action with the aid of various Pascal-like control structures. Likewise, Norman's theory of action assumes goals as a starting point. Black begins his chapter with the claim that "almost all of human behavior can be characterized in terms of goals and plans."

That is, the user's goals are assumed to precede behavior, to have clear conditions of satisfaction, to be interpretable outside of the larger context of the user's situation, to be organized in a strict hierarchy, and not to undergo radical, moment-to-moment transformation. There is also the supposition of independence of the goals from the methods by which they are to be achieved. Given such goals, users are then assumed (consciously?) to construct plans, select among methods, and then finally get around to doing something. Having done something, these users must now compare the results of their actions to the original goals and begin anew.

The discussion of goals and goal-oriented behavior presented in these chapters does not capture what we observe in the field or lab, in our studies and observations of users. In a tightly defined, carefully controlled laboratory situation, where the user has been given a set task, goals are perhaps identifiable. However, in a more representative situation, users are often unable to state unambiguous conditions of satisfaction, and are dependent on the context in which they are operating. To the extent that we can identify the users' goals at any time, they are not organized in any strict hierarchy and are radically transformed as events unfold. Further, users are constantly distracted from their goals, make up goals as a rationale after the fact, and state goals in general and often vague terms. In general, we see users acting first, thrown to the situation, and perhaps devising a goal, a posteriori, if asked to. In sum, we find that the notion of goals does not capture the phenomena of user-computer interaction in a compelling or practically useful way.

We invite the authors to ponder what the consequence might be for theoretical and practical work if one did not grant that almost all of human behavior can be characterized in terms of goals and plans. We suggest, as a possibility, an alternative assumption: Users do not start with goals at all; rather they are always already acting in a situation, thrown to it as it were, unreflectively and unanalytically. What would theories, models, and systems based on such assumptions look like?

6 Explore Alternatives to Studying People (Customers) as Objects to be Modeled

The folklore of interface design has it that really successful systems are ones designed by people who have an intimate, first-hand knowledge of the customers for whom the products are intended, and of what they do and what their needs are. We have trouble recognizing the human qualities in the "users" modeled in a number of the chapters: those by McKendree and Anderson, Reitman Olson, and Polson.

Instead of developing formal models of customers, would a feasible alternative for effective design be meeting with customers, perhaps working at their jobs to get a first-hand appreciation for the problems they face, and in general taking steps to develop a rich, empathetic awareness for their situation? Spreadsheets are said to have been developed by people with an intimate knowledge of accounting and the problems faced by accountants. The transaction-processing software for a major car-rental company is reputed to have been aided substantially by the fact that one of the designers of the interface worked behind the rental counter for several months.

Modeling has often focused on areas for which a formal description already exists, such as computer languages, physics, and mathematics. However, these only represent a small subset of the domain of human activity where we want to enlist the aid of computers. In addition, they are the easiest to model. The major challenge for formal modeling will be in application to areas that are not as well defined, like accounting the transactions involved at a car-rental agency, or, more generally, to office work itself.

A related issue concerns the origin of productions (to use Polson's term). Are these theoretical entities derived from the user or from a detached consideration of the system? Certainly there is a strong temptation to derive them from the system. After all, computer systems are readily considered in terms of production rules. However, do we then take the system as a standard and measure the user as departing from that? In some domains, such as the learning of computer languages, it may be desirable to take the language as a standard, but should we generalize that to any system?

7 Consider Interpretation a Viable Alternative to Explanation or Modeling

Some of the chapters—those by Polson; Reitman Olsen; McKendree and Anderson; Mayer; Black, Kay, and Soloway; and Barnard—are oriented toward providing models of human-computer interaction; that is, they attempt to provide us with a formal characterization. This characterization has elements that are assumed to have meaning independent of the context in which they occur. There are also formal rules that govern the interaction of the elements.

When Norman speaks of a subjective feeling of direct engagement, occasioned by a particular interface style, he is providing a very different type of account for us than a formal characterization. He is providing an interpretation, a sensible account that depends on our shared experience and concerns for its impact.

Formal modeling seeks explanation in terms of a supposed underlying true structure. Interpretation seeks a more relative truth, one that is sensible and appropriate to the situation at hand, but not absolute or timeless. Thus interpretation is much more contextually dependent than formal modeling. Practical design, however, is exactly the creation of things that will work well in a specific context.

Several of the chapters in this volume offer fresh interpretations. Malone analyzes the office in terms of the history of organizations and draws parallels between types of markets and possible internal structure. Lewis points to a number of the similarities and differences between computer skills and elementary mathematics. A less careful observer might see these two areas as monolithically the same or different, but the analysis here is much more subtle and illuminates new distinctions. Finally, Carroll and Rosson point to motivational and cognitive paradoxes involved in learning a computer system. This analysis suggests a horizon for understanding a fundamental question: Why is it that people do not use all the functionality available to them? From the perspective of a detached observer, the "mediocrity" of the typical user seems incomprehensible. By analyzing this problem in terms of fundamental paradoxes that are consistent with our own experience as users, Carroll and Rosson show that a headlong plunge to optimize the system or shape the user would be ill advised.

The interpretative framework offered in these chapters stands out for us and suggests the power gained from a more tentative, holistic, and contextualist framework.

8 Address the Political Realities of System Design

Suppose that a cognitive science of the user was well developed. Suppose we could look at a given domain and draw up a user interface design that reflected users' needs and system capabilities. In other words, suppose that our models and theories really worked.

Even if we knew the right way to build an interface, industry would not necessarily build products based on it. Every practicing human factors engineer can point to numerous instances where the correct design was obvious, yet was never implemented. A host of factors, far beyond the scope of cognitive psychology, determines what actually gets built. Even if an ideal system could be identified in theory, it would never actually be built. In the industrial setting, too many forces operate against this: time pressure, need for backward compatibility of systems, design by committee (everyone must have a say), ego involvement in design, economic constraints, marketing constraints, developers losing or not reading the design documents, and so forth. User interface design is at the mercy of strong emotions and powerful forces.

In sum, in industrial human factors, the technical and political aspects of the work are inseparable.

From our perspective in industry, system design suffers more from a lack of clarity in goals than a lack of knowledge. We actually know a great deal about building inconspicuous, unobtrusive, and nonobstinate systems. In practice, what we often lack is a clear, shared statement of what we are trying to accomplish in a given design.

An effective strategy for anyone interested in system design is to insist on clear operationally defined measures of usability. Currently, the terms such as easy to use, usable, user friendly, and so forth, have no shared meaning. This feeds into the emotion-laden, highly charged, political situation that interface design often is.

Models of users and the calculation of how users would perform can only be useful in the context of clearly defined product goals. Knowledge of what is right is only useful when there is a consensus about the goals or the purposes to which knowledge can be put. Perhaps models of users can help in design, but certainly like any other knowledge (empirical tests, guidelines, etc.), they can only make a contribution in a larger context of clear goals and commitments.

9 Make Specific Requests of Engineers and Managers

What exactly is cognitive science asking developers to do? What would be required for a developer to apply the knowledge gained from cognitive science? Are they required to be familiar with the academic work in this area and to determine for themselves how to apply it? Experience suggests that such application is not straightforward or simple. Generalizing from an experiment or from a model is not an easy undertaking. Guidelines are at least one attempt to concretize the results of experiments and models (and common sense) into easily followed recommendations. Yet designers and developers find guidelines hard to use and complain that they are too general or too specific, and do not apply to the particular system being developed.

A possible approach for cognitive scientists would be to offer clear statements of the conditions under which their models apply. One might say, for example, that such and such model can be used to develop tutorial systems for editors. Furthermore, cognitive scientists could offer a clear statement of a model's effectiveness; e.g., systems using this model have shown greater user acceptance and lower development costs than competitors. Thus, we ask that cognitive scientists state clearly where their models can be applied and what benefits industry can expect.

Finally, we must reiterate a suggestion we made in the first section. Build a working system based on the model you are developing, and evaluate the effectiveness and the cost of such a design effort. A working design tends simultaneously both to clarify those aspects that can be transferred to a new design and those that will require more original efforts.

10 Support the Act of Design

Is there a best design? Foss and DeRidder give a means of choosing between designs; this assumes a best design exists in theory. There is certainly no best house, or car, or work of art. In like fashion, there may be no best interface. We are struck by the diversity of preference for different interfaces. Text editors are a good example; there are literally hundreds of different ones in use in our own corporation. The merits and demerits of various editors are debated endlessly; people become quite emotional on the subject. Most users heavily customize their editors; many program their own. In our own immediate work group, no two individuals use exactly the same editor. Each individual insists that his or her interface is the best. In such a situation, Foss and DeRidder's goal to have a theoretical basis for choosing the best interface among alternatives just does not seem to fit. Is it possible that by insisting that there exists a best design, we are forcing choices instead of supporting diversity?

How are the research findings of the chapters in this book to be translated into design? Many of these chapters refer to such mental events as processes, operators, and systems. The use of hypothetical entities is a venerable and useful technique in science. But in order to be useful to system developers, these constructs must be linked to things that the designer can change. What could a designer do to encourage "control knowledge to find optimal methods"? How would software do this? A theory of mind without a link to behavior in a situation is not helpful to engineers building a system.

How do you create the design? Foss and DeRidder give a means of choosing between designs, not a means of creating a new one. Mayer suggests finding the user's mental models of graphics editors, and then instituting training to bring these mental models into conformance with a preexisting model of the system. Similarly, McKendree and Anderson suggest building an automated tutor that would monitor progress and select problems that need further practice. Clearly these approaches only suggest how to shape the user to respond appropriately to the system. They seem to be silent on how to design the system so that it fits the user's needs. As a practical matter, implementing these suggestions would have the effect of greatly increasing the cost of developing and maintaining products, and of asking customers to spend more time in training. Other approaches have different problems. For example, Reitman Olson argues that the designer will be limited until higher-level tools, such as OPS-5 and LOOPS, are widely available. Similarly, Barnard sees the need for an intelligent design tool, a computer program, which will tell developers how to apply the theoretical findings of cognitive science. He worries that such a tool may be far off. In the meantime, the designer can hope for compatible suggestions that come from focusing on single cognitive aspects.

So how do you create the design? Landauer says, in reference to activities like text editing and financial simulation, "Designing tools for this kind of activity is an intimately cognitive-psychological activity." Here he is clearly referring, not to the user's activity in using the tools, but to the designer's activity in creating the tools. But the remainder of the chapter is silent on design as a cognitive-psychological activity—indeed, on design at all.

All the methods discussed in the book seem to assume an already existing design, arrived at by an unspecified process. In this sense, formal modeling is not different than other design-support techniques, such as prototyping, use of guidelines, iterative testing, design reviews, and formal inspection. All are directed toward the refinement of an existing design. Where does the design come from initially?

11 Summary

We have offered a number of invitations to action to the authors and readership of this book. With Carroll, we see great promise for the future. We agree, with Landauer, that bringing theory into collision with the world-as-found should result in transformed theory (and a transformed world).

Index

Page numbers in italics refer to illustrations or tables.